THE ESSENTIAL SPINOZA

ETHICS AND RELATED WRITINGS

THE ESSENTIAL SPINOZA
ETHICS AND RELATED WRITINGS

Edited by Michael L. Morgan

With the Translations of Samuel Shirley

Hackett Publishing Company, Inc.
Indianapolis/Cambridge

12 11 10 09 08 07 06   1 2 3 4 5 6 7

For further information, please address:

Hackett Publishing Company, Inc.
P.O. Box 44937
Indianapolis, IN 46244–0937

www.hackettpublishing.com

Cover design by Abigail Coyle
Composition by Agnew's, Inc.
Printed at Edwards Brothers, Inc.

Library of Congress Cataloging-in-Publication Data
Spinoza, Benedictus de, 1632–1677.
    [Selections. English. 2006]
    The essential Spinoza : ethics and related writings / edited by
Michael L. Morgan ; with the translations of Samuel Shirley.
        p.   cm.
    Includes bibliographical references.
    ISBN 0-87220-804-4 — ISBN 0-87220-803-6 (pbk.)
    1. Philosophy—Early works to 1800.   2. Ethics—Early works to 1800.
I. Morgan, Michael L., 1944–   II. Title.
B3958.M67 2006
199′.492—dc22

                                              2005057432

CONTENTS

INTRODUCTION

THE SPIRIT OF THE MAN

In studying the works of Spinoza, the reader can be overwhelmed by the sense of abstract rigor and detachment. These characteristics may seem to some readers to be the product of an almost mechanical mental life. But this appearance notwithstanding, I am inclined to ascribe to Spinoza a romantic set of virtues. He is, among thinkers, extraordinarily creative and novel; his thinking is marked by a marvelous intensity and focus; and yet his deepest commitments are to the most embracing unity and sense of comprehensiveness that one can find in the tradition of Western philosophy. In short, Spinoza's writings and his thought are marked by a kind of heroism that is not only rare and beautiful: it is even breathtaking.

We are tempted to think that the notion of perspective, or point of view, so crucial to the world of art, was not of importance to philosophy until Kant and German Idealism made it so. Kant, it is said, taught us what metaphysics could and could not accomplish by his confining its investigations to the viewpoint of human experience; he then went on to distinguish between the detached point of view of the scientific inquirer and the engaged point of view of the moral agent. From those beginnings, German Idealism and its twentieth-century legacy made the notion of perspective, or point of view, central to philosophical accounts of human existence and human experience, from Fichte, Schelling, and Kant to Schopenhauer and Nietzsche, to Husserl, Heidegger, and beyond. And with this legacy came a series of struggles—between the natural and the human sciences, between existentialism and scientific philosophy, and between relativism and objectivism.

But perspective was at the center of Spinoza's system. His thinking reveals a passion for unity and totality, which is coupled with a scrupulous fidelity to the integrity of the individual particular. There is no parochialism in Spinoza. His commitment to the progress of scientific inquiry into the natural world belied any such limitation in behalf of his cognitive goals. In every way, in every dimension of our lives, Spinoza saw the common; likewise, he saw unity and wholeness. But at the same time, his allegiance to the universality of the ethical life and of its virtues did not annul the personal perspective of human experience. For him, life was always our human struggle against our finite limitations of perspective and particularity. Life was not life without such limitations, but neither could life be what it might be if we were satisfied with them. The world, of necessity, was filled with particular objects, but they existed within a single order. We are among those objects, and our goal is to do what we can, in knowledge and conduct, to live with our particularity and yet to transcend it. Spinoza was fully aware of both the necessity and the complexity of human perspective; he knew what that perspective meant to the hopes for scientific knowledge; for the burdens of religious, moral, and political conflict; and for the possibility of a truly blessed life. In a certain sense, perspective is the fulcrum on which all of Spinoza's thinking turns.

Spinoza lived in a world distant from our own. No amount of historical detail and reconstruction can adequately place us in the complex world of Western Europe in the seventeenth century. So much was new, yet so much was old. And Spinoza was immersed in all that complexity, in a world that was, by virtue of its economic and geographical situation, at a crossroads. Spinoza knew about religious orthodoxies and religious reform; about traditional culture and novelties; about old texts and new thinking; and about the tensions between conservative political practice and liberal hopes and aspirations. And he knew about the risks. To him, reason in humans was akin to reason in nature; one order permeated everything and enabled us, as rational beings, to understand ourselves and the whole, and so to live peacefully and calmly within that whole. This one order was the key to science, ethics, and religion. In fact, it was the key to all of life. It was Spinoza's goal to show it, clarify it, explain it, and teach it, to the benefit of all humankind.

But if the key that unlocked the secrets of possibility for us as human beings was unity and totality—the wholeness and order of all things—the reality that grounded the aspiration to this unity and order was the fact that each of us, as natural objects and human beings, was located precisely in that unity and order, which was determined in every way and thereby endowed with a very particular point of view on the whole. In a letter to Henry Oldenburg of November 1665 (Ep32), as Spinoza attempts to clarify the nature of parts and wholes, he provides us with a famous image of this fact. He tells us that each of us is like a little worm in the blood. Nature is like the entire circulatory system or the entire organism; each of us lives within that system or organism, interacting with only a small part of it and experiencing only a very limited region. Even if we grasp the fact that there is a total system and even if we understand its principles to some degree, our experience is so circumscribed and narrow that we are bound to make mistakes about our understanding of the system and our place in it. Myopia confines our understanding, no matter how we seek to overcome it. Yet we do: we aspire to experience every detail, every event, and every item as part of the whole, to see it from the perspective of the whole rather than from our own narrow point of view. Our success is limited, however. We can free ourselves from prejudices and blindness, but only to a degree. Also, we can see ourselves and act in terms of the whole, but only within limits. Our goal is to free ourselves from the distortions and corruptions of our finitude—to become free, active, and rational. These goals are all the same, to become like the whole, which is what tradition dignifies with the title "God" or "divine" or "the Highest Good."

I do not believe that Spinoza saw this challenge and sort of life as an escape from the world. History was riddled not only with strife and conflict but also with prejudice and persecution. Life certainly could be better—it could be in harmony with nature rather than in a struggle with it. Religious and political institutions could be renovated to serve human purposes, and human life could be refashioned as well. The ancient Stoics had understood that life in harmony with nature was the best human life and that in order to achieve such harmony, one had to understand nature. Natural philosophy or science was both the highest achievement of human rationality and the key to living the best human life. Spinoza, I believe, fully sympathized with the broad strokes of this program. Like the Stoics, he revered reason and our rational capacities. And also like the Stoics, he saw the reason in us and the reason in nature as intimately linked. Finally, he saw natural philosophy as the key to opening the door of the highest good and the way through that door as leading to tranquility of spirit, harmony with nature, and peace. To be sure, Spinoza was a modern. Natural philosophy included the developments and achievements of the new science, which was conducted in the spirit of Descartes and others, and which was grounded in mathematics and a priori reasoning about natural events and causal relations. But if the science was modern and mathematical and if the metaphysics was constructed as a foundation for that science, the overall role for it and its goals were very similar to those of the ancient Stoics: union with the whole of nature through knowledge of the natural order.

Moreover, Spinoza would call the goal of this human project "blessedness." He did not shy away from using the religious terminology that was the vocabulary of the Judaism and Christianity with which he was so familiar. Indeed, it is a remarkable feature of his temperament that his thinking never totally rejected religious themes, beliefs, and vocabulary as much as it sought to refine and refashion them. One might make this comment about virtually all the great seventeenth-century philosophers, that they did not decisively reject the religious world out of which they emerged and in which they lived. Rather, they sought to retool that world, to come to a new understanding of religious life, and to revise religious concepts and terminology. Even those, such as Hobbes and Spinoza, who were censored and vilified as atheists, did not reject religion. In fact, from our perspective, we can appreciate their philosophical goals as being epistemological, ethical, and religious, all at once. Spinoza, in these terms, was a religious visionary, moral innovator, and philosopher–scientist. His passion for unity and wholeness made any fragmentation of this conglomerate undesirable; but the reality was that in his day, given the way that these and other domains of life were lived and experienced, any such fragmentation was quite impossible.

Hence, Spinoza's scientific philosophy and ethics aimed at tranquillity in a conflicted and turbulent world; his vision did not seek escape from that world but rather sought a renovation of it. His was a worldview for life, not for an escape from life. It recommended changes in one's behavior, beliefs, practices, and institutions. His worldview was, as he put it in the *Ethics*, a meditation on life and not on death.

We could seek the perspective of eternity in order to redeem the unavoidable perspective of finitude; but as living and natural beings, we could not escape the latter, and as human beings, we should not avoid the former. This is the gist of Spinoza's philosophy, ethics, and religion. And the key to grasping this picture of our hopes and realities is reason, which is the ability within us that enables us to understand and make sense of our world and ourselves.

THE PHILOSOPHY

Spinoza presents us with the totality of his system in one work, the *Ethics*. He also has left us with a preliminary version of that work, a couple of introductions to his philosophy, and examples of applications of it—to politics and religion. Yet all of this does not make it easy to grasp his philosophical system.

To me, Spinoza is remarkable for his creativity. He was an heir of a philosophical terminology that came down to the seventeenth century from antiquity, the recovery of ancient philosophies and texts, and its presence in the medieval philosophical tradition. He did not invent terms like "substance," "attribute," "mode," "affect," "essence," "necessity," and "eternity." Rather, he was taught the terms, the way they were used, what they meant, and more. And he was taught how they figured in the thinking of Descartes, who was, for Spinoza, the bridge between the philosophical tradition and the new philosophy and new science. What Spinoza did was to take the philosophical tradition, Descartes' accomplishment, and his own passionate commitments, and to blend them into a new whole, a new worldview. At one level, that worldview is an extension and a modification of Cartesian metaphysics; at another, it has its own character, and it demands a view of the natural order that is very different from that of Descartes.

Spinoza has a relentless mind. His commitment to reason involves a commitment to consistency and rigor. This is not to say that he does not allow his reason to leap to conclusions that seem strange and even recalcitrant, and it is not to say that he never makes mistakes. What I mean is that he can be understood as starting with certain concepts whose meanings are clear and correct to him, and then pushing the consequences of accepting those concepts. He can also be understood as observing what Descartes had achieved and yet as believing that Descartes had failed to follow reason to its relentless conclusions because of prejudices, that is, biases to which Descartes had clung and that Spinoza saw as distortions. In the case of the concept of substance, for example, Spinoza thought that he and Descartes largely agreed about what substance means, but Spinoza also thought that if so, there was no justification for treating minds and bodies as substances. Moreover, if the principle of sufficient reason was foundational for scientific inquiry and if the natural world and even eternal truths were created by God, then a deep contingency would lie at the heart of nature and human knowledge. And even if one were to treat the physical world as a collection of bodies that causally interact and that are capable of being understood by scientific inquiry, why exclude the mind and mental occurrences from similar understanding? Is it not only a prejudice grounded in traditional theological commitments to isolate the mind or the soul and to allow it special privileges and to grant it special features? Is it not more consistent with our understanding of nature, science, and the human good to treat the mind and mental phenomena just as one would treat physical ones, and yet to do so in a nonreductivist way, that is, without simply treating mental events as identical in some sense to physiological ones?

Although it may be a bit of a caricature, it is helpful to see Spinoza as seeking a middle ground regarding the treatment of mind, soul, and mental phenomena in a world where the physical sciences are beginning to take shape in new and exciting ways. On the one hand, the Cartesian strategy could be seen as having isolated the mind in order to save the integrity of certain theological commitments, such as the belief in free will and in the immortality of the soul. Science could not study the mind and mental phenomena in the same way that it could study the physical world, using mathematical reasoning and applying it to causality, motion, and so forth. The strategy of materialists like Hobbes, on the other hand, could be seen as assimilating the mind and mental phenomena to physical ones, that is, basically to motions of various kinds, and as defining mental processes and experiences in terms of motions of physical bodies. What Spinoza achieves—its problems notwithstanding—is a middle road. He constructs a view of nature as a whole in which physical events and mental ones are both understandable, in which they are related but separate, and in which the sciences of both the physical world and the mental world are related but distinct. While it may be that Kant, Dilthey, and Neo-Kantian developments and later debates about the distinction between the natural sciences and the human sciences look as though they are built on Cartesian foundations, there is also a sense in which they build on Spinozist ones as well. To the degree that the social sciences and psychology are conceived as requiring a scientific treatment of mental phenomena, these sciences are Spinoza's heirs, whether or not that scientific treatment is conceived of as similar to or different from the methodology of the natural sciences. Indeed, one can even treat the post-Kantian developments of Wilfrid Sellars, John McDowell, and others to distinguish the domain of the mental and the "space of reasons" as distinct from the physical or the "space of causes" as a development of Spinoza and of his commitment to demystifying the mind as well as the body and to making both accessible to rational understanding, and thereby, in a sense, to human control.

There are two keys to this Spinozist achievement. The first key is to conceive of the totality of the natural world both as the sum of all facts, that is, all things in all of their determinations, and as the ordering force that determines all those facts to be just the ways they are. To conceive of nature both as God and as substance gives the natural world the unity and orderliness that Spinoza believes science aspires to understand, and makes it the case that everything we do and are finds its rational place within the totality of nature. The second key to Spinoza's system concerns the "channels" whereby the single ordering force, or principle—"God" as the single active causal determining force of all there is—actually determines things and their states in the world. At the highest level, where these "channels" are virtually identical to God or the one and only substance but that are nonetheless wholly distinct from each other, Spinoza calls these "attributes" of substance; and although he thinks that in principle the one and only substance has all the attributes that there are, there are but two that determine the world in which we live—thought and extension. In short, all the modes—things and their states—that make up the natural world are modes of thought and extension; and even though scholars have debated exactly how the distinction between these attributes should be understood, I take it that what Spinoza means is that we understand the single array of facts in the world by using both the physical sciences and the psychological sciences. In the famous Proposition 7 of Part II of the *Ethics* and in the scholium to that proposition, Spinoza indicates just this, that the order and connection of ideas or mental phenomena are one and the same as the order and connection of physical ones; it is a proposition with countless important implications throughout the remainder of the *Ethics* and Spinoza's system.

As far as our attempts to understand the world go, then, for Spinoza these attempts are self-contained and comprehensive. All worldly facts should be examined and studied in the same way; there is a uniformity to all of nature. Mental modes interact causally with mental modes, and physical modes interact causally with physical modes. But since, strictly speaking, there is just one set of facts in nature, this perception means that these two types of scientific understanding are self-contained. We do not use physical causes to help us understand mental phenomena, nor do we use mental causes to help us understand physical phenomena. Moreover, since the sciences of both physical and mental phenomena apply to all things in the world, Spinoza must show in what sense even inanimate things have mental or ideational correlates and what distinguishes animals and most preeminently human beings among worldly things, that is, what we mean when we say that animals and humans have minds or souls.

I do not mean to suggest that on all these matters, Spinoza was clear and lucid throughout his career and that he never changed his mind. A careful study of the early *Treatise on the Emendation of the Intellect* and the *Short Treatise*, for example, shows how his thinking developed into the shape we find in the *Ethics*, and we are helped to some degree in understanding how Spinoza's ideas developed by some of the letters in his correspondence. But the basic character of his thinking, I believe, did not change from the time around his excommunication in 1656 until his death in 1677. Throughout his life Spinoza was always committed to finding a way to unite science, ethics, and religion, and to articulate a metaphysical system that would make the whole of nature, human life, and religious themes comprehensible. His system was an attempt to work out what made nature unified and an ordered whole, and then to see what that picture implied.

THE TEXTS

The book you have before you is an edited selection from the comprehensive collection of Spinoza's works that was published a short time ago, *Spinoza: Complete Works* (Hackett Publishing Company, 2002). I have focused on the *Ethics* and included as well the most important other works of Spinoza that deal with themes introduced in that central work.

The reader who wants to go on and read further in Spinoza's works, especially those on political and religious issues, should consult the complete collection that includes the totality of Spinoza's writings, all that scholars now have come to think that he left us.

The corpus of Spinoza's works contain a fascinating diversity. There is at its center, of course, the presentation of his system, the *Ethics*. Begun in the early 1660s, this work was probably completed about 1674. It is his lifework, the centerpiece of what came to be known as Spinozism, and is one of the great accomplishments of world philosophy and Western intellectual culture.

In addition to the *Ethics* and his philosophical system, Spinoza has left us what we might call four different introductions to that work and that system. The first is *Principles of Cartesian Philosophy*, his handbook on Cartesian philosophy, originally composed as a guide to tutoring a student in Descartes' *Principles of*

Philosophy and useful for what it shows us about Spinoza's early appreciation of Descartes. The second is his youthful, unfinished work, the *Treatise on the Emendation of the Intellect*. Largely a work on method and definition, this short essay places Spinoza's project within an ethical context. The third introduction is the unfinished *Short Treatise on God, Man, and His Well-Being*, which is a preliminary attempt to begin the system and which Spinoza set aside when he decided to turn to the early parts of the *Ethics*. And finally, we can treat the anonymous treatise on biblical interpretation and politics, the *Theological-Political Treatise*, as an introductory work, insofar as it seeks to persuade those with an affinity for philosophy and science to read Scripture; understand its central ethical teaching; revise traditional interpretations of notions such as prophecy, law, and miracles; and appreciate the relation between church and state. What we have, then, is a mansion with four entrances, any one of which can enable us to enter the vast complex of Spinoza's world. In this collection, we include the whole of the *Ethics* and of the *Treatise on the Emendation of the Intellect*, and selections from the *Principles of Cartesian Philosophy* and the *Short Treatise*.

Furthermore, Spinoza has given us, in the *Theological-Political Treatise* and in the unfinished *Political Treatise*, two examples of how his system might be applied more fully to areas dealt with in only a cursory way in the *Ethics*—in these cases, religion and politics. To be sure, in both cases, there are already indications in the *Ethics* about how Spinoza thinks that we should understand religious concepts and institutions, and also political life. Especially in various scholia and in the appendix to Part I, he notes how traditional ideas such as creation, miracles, teleology, and free will must be either revised or jettisoned altogether. And in Part IV of the *Ethics*, Spinoza sets out the rudiments of his contract theory and of his views on the foundations and purposes of the state. And finally, in Part V, in the famous final propositions of the work, Spinoza defends and reinterprets what he takes to be the eternity of the mind and the goal of the ethical life, an "intellectual love of God" that is blessedness itself—a goal, he says, that is as difficult as it is rare.

Lastly, among the writings of Spinoza that we possess are a sampling of his correspondence—letters to him and many by him. Here not only are we helped to understand better his philosophical and religious views, but also we are given valuable information about the chronology of his works, about his friends and associates, and about his life. Included in the current collection are nearly half of Spinoza's correspondence, with special attention to those letters that shed light on the *Ethics* and his philosophical system.

Michael L. Morgan

EDITORIAL NOTES
AND ABBREVIATIONS

A NOTE ON THE TRANSLATIONS

Of the translations included here, all but those from the *Short Treatise* are by Samuel Shirley. For the selection from the *Short Treatise* we have used the translation of A. Wolf, first published in 1910; it has been carefully examined by Bieneke Heitjama and Inge Van Der Cruysse and is edited by the editor; Wolf used the older A manuscript of the *Short Treatise* and presented alternative readings from the B manuscript in notes. We follow his decisions except in a few cases and provide Spinoza's notes as well as, on some occasions, when important for the reader, alternative versions. An explanation of the system of annotation appears before the first footnote of each work. The Chronology of Spinoza's life and times is based on the chronology prepared by Lee Rice for *The Letters*.

For translations of the works of Spinoza that are not included in this volume or that not included in their entirety, please see *Spinoza: Complete Works*, edited by Michael L. Morgan, containing the translations of Samuel Shirley, published by Hackett Publishing Company in 2002. That volume includes a complete index to the Spinoza corpus. A number of Spinoza's works are also available from Hackett in single editions, all in the translations of Samuel Shirley. Of special interest are the introductions and notes of Steven Barbone and Lee Rice to *The Letters*, to *Political Treatise*, and to *Principles of Cartesian Philosophy, with Metaphysical Thoughts*. Also of special interest are Seymour Feldman's introductions and notes to the *Ethics* and to the *Theological-Political Treatise*. The best and most comprehensive biography of Spinoza is that of Steven Nadler, *Spinoza: A Life* (Cambridge: Cambridge University Press, 1999).

A complete list of the translations used for this volume is as follows:

Treatise on the Emendation of the Intellect and Ethics   Spinoza, Baruch. *Ethics, Treatise on the Emendation of the Intellect*, and *Selected Letters*. Translated by Samuel Shirley. Edited and introduced by Seymour Feldman. Indianapolis: Hackett Publishing Company, 1992.

Short Treatise   Spinoza, Baruch. *Spinoza's Short Treatise on God, Man, and His Well-Being*. Translated and edited, with an introduction and commentary, by A. Wolf. London: Adam and Charles Black, 1910.

Principles of Cartesian Philosophy   Spinoza, Baruch. *Principles of Cartesian Philosophy* with *Metaphysical Thoughts* and *Lodewijk Meyer's Inaugural Dissertation*. Translated by Samuel Shirley with introduction and notes by Steven Barbone and Lee Rice. Indianapolis: Hackett Publishing Company, 1998.

The Letters   Spinoza, Baruch. *The Letters*. Translated by Samuel Shirley. Introduction and notes by Steven Barbone, Lee Rice, and Jacob Adler. Indianapolis: Hackett Publishing Company, 1995.

ABBREVIATIONS

Works of Spinoza

CM   *Metaphysical Thoughts (Cogitata Metaphysica)* (CM1/2 is Part 1, Chapter 2)

E   *Ethics (Ethica)* (followed by arabic numeral for part and internal references)

Ep   *Letters (Epistolae)* (followed by arabic numeral)

KV   *Short Treatise (Korte Verhandeling)* (KV1/2/3 is Part 1, Chapter 2, Paragraph 3)

PPC   *Principles of Cartesian Philosophy (Principia Philosophiae Cartesianae)* (followed by arabic numeral for part and internal references)

TIE   *Treatise on the Emendation of the Intellect (Tractatus de Intellectus Emendatione)* (followed by arabic numeral for paragraph)

TP   *Political Treatise (Tractatus Politicus)* (TP1/2 is Chapter 1, Paragraph 2)

TTP   *Theological-Political Treatise (Tractatus Theologico-Politicus)* (followed by chapter and page number)

Parts of Spinoza's Works

App   Appendix
Art   Article
Ax   Axiom
Cor   Corollary
Def   Definition
Dem   Demonstration
Exp   Explication
GenSchol   General Scholium
Lem   Lemma
P   Proposition
Post   Postulate
Pref   Preface
Prol   Prologue
Schol   Scholium

Works of Descartes

Med	*Meditations* (followed by arabic numeral)
PPH	*Principles of Philosophy*
Rep	*Replies to Objections*

Page numbers, where given for Descartes' *Meditations*, are from Descartes, *Meditations on First Philosophy*, third edition, translated by Donald Cress (Indianapolis: Hackett, 1993) and the Adam-Tannery (AT) edition: Descartes, *Oeuvres de Descartes*, 11 volumes, revised edition, edited by Charles Adam and Paul Tannery (Paris: Vrin 1964–1976: reprinted 1996).

CHRONOLOGY

1536   Calvin publishes the *Institution of the Christian Religion.*

1565   Beginning of the war of independence of the Spanish-Dutch region against Spain.

1579   The "Union of Utrecht" establishes the United Provinces.

1594   Publication of Socinus' *De Christo Servatore.*

1600? The Espinosa family emigrates from Portugal to Nantes and thence to Amsterdam.

1603   Arminius and Gomar debate at Leiden on the questions of tolerance and freedom of the will.

1610   Uytenbogaert, a disciple of Arminius and teacher of Oldenbarneveldt, publishes the *Remonstrant Manifesto.*

1618   The Thirty Years War begins.

1619   The Synod of Dordrecht condemns Arminianism and puts Oldenbarnevelt to death. The Collegiant sect is formed. Descartes is a soldier in the army of Maurice of Nassau.

1628   Descartes is living in Holland.

1629   **18 October:** Lodewijk Meyer is baptized at the Old Church in Amsterdam.

1630   **4 November:** Johan Bouwmeester is born in Amsterdam.

1632   **24 November:** Birth of Baruch d'Espinosa at Amsterdam.

1633   Papal condemnation of Galileo, who is placed under house arrest. Descartes decides not to publish *Le Monde.*

1638   The founding of the great Portuguese Synagogue of Amsterdam. Spinoza is registered as a student in the Hebrew school.

1640   Beginning of the English civil war.

1641   Descartes' *Meditationes de Prima Philosophia* is published.

1642   Hobbes publishes *De Cive.*

1644   Descartes publishes *Principia Philosophiae.*

1647   Descartes' *Méditations Metaphysiques* is published in French translation.

1648   The Peace of Munster. Definitive establishment of the United Provinces.

1649   Charles I of England is executed.

1650   **11 February:** Death of Descartes.   **6 November:** A failed coup d'état by William II of Orange. Jan de Witt becomes the Grand Pensioner of the Netherlands.

1651   Beginning of the Anglo-Dutch War. Hobbes publishes *Leviathan.* **30 March:** Bouwmeester is enrolled in philosophy courses at the University of Leiden.

1653   A decree by the States General prohibits the publication and diffusion of Socinian works and ideas.

1654   End of the Anglo-Dutch War. Spinoza begins to meet with a group of "churchless Christians" (Pieter Balling, Jarig Jelles, Jan Rieuwertsz, Franciscus Van den Enden) in Amsterdam.   **19 September:** Meyer is enrolled as a student in philosophy at the University of Leiden.

1656   **27 July:** Spinoza is banished from the Jewish community in Amsterdam. He begins the study of humanities, Latin, philosophy, and theater at the school of the ex-Jesuit Van den Enden.   **6 October:** Decree of the States of Holland and of Frisia prohibiting the teaching of Cartesianism.

1657   The play *Philedonius* of Van den Enden is produced in Amsterdam. Spinoza is still studying with Van den Enden and may also be enrolled at the University of Leiden.

1658   **27 May:** Bouwmeester receives a doctorate in medicine from the University of Leiden.   **25 September:** Meyer is enrolled in courses in medicine at Leiden. Spinoza begins work on the *Treatise on the Emendation of the Intellect* (unfinished).

1659   Adriaan Koerbagh receives a doctorate in medicine from the University of Leiden.

1660   Restoration of the Stuarts in England. Spinoza leaves Amsterdam and moves to Rijnsburg, where he is a familiar visitor among Collegiant circles. He begins work on the *Short Treatise on God, Man, and His Well-Being.*   **19 March:** Meyer receives a doctorate in philosophy from the University of Leiden.   **20 March:** Meyer receives a doctorate in medicine.

1662   Founding of the Royal Society. Oldenburg is its joint secretary, and Boyle and Newton are charter members. Spinoza completes the first part of the (tripartite) *Ethics.* He begins work on the *Principles of Cartesian Philosophy* and *Metaphysical Thoughts.*

1663   Simon de Vries meets with Spinoza at a meeting of the "Spinozistic Circle" in Amsterdam (Ep8). Letters 12 and 12a from Spinoza to Meyer, the latter concerning the publication of the *Principles of Cartesian*

Philosophy. Spinoza is installed at Voorburg. He there publishes the *Principles of Cartesian Philosophy* with *Metaphysical Thoughts* as appendix. **31 July:** Spinoza writes to Oldenburg and introduces Petrus Serrarius. **3 August:** Spinoza writes to Meyer concerning Meyer's editorship and preface to the *Principles of Cartesian Philosophy,* which is published several months later.

1664   Beginning of the (second) Anglo-Dutch War.

1665   **28 January:** Spinoza's Letter 21 to Blyenbergh on the interpretation of Scripture.   Spinoza makes several visits to Amsterdam, where he probably visits with Meyer during March and April.   **26 May:** The new Amsterdam Theater opens with Meyer as its director.   **June:** Having completed the first drafts of Parts II and III of the (tripartite) *Ethics,* Spinoza writes to Bouwmeester (Ep28).

1666   **10 June:** Spinoza's Letter 37 to Bouwmeester.

1667   End of the (second) Anglo-Dutch War. Spinoza's Letter 40 to Jelles mentions Isaac Vossius as a friend.

1668   Adriaan Koerbagh's *Een Bloemhof* is published. The author is condemned by ecclesiastical authorities, and imprisoned on 19 July.

1669   **15 October:** Adriaan Koerbagh dies in prison.

1670   Spinoza publishes (anonymously and in Latin) the *Theological-Political Treatise:* ecclesiastical condemnations follow. Posthumous publication of the *Pensées* of Pascal.

1671   Spinoza is installed at The Hague, where he prevents (possibly at the suggestion of Jan de Witt) the appearance of the vernacular edition of the *Theological-Political Treatise* (Ep44).

1672   Louis XIV invades Holland. The French army occupies Utrecht (May). William II of Orange becomes *stadtholder* (July).   **20 August:** Jan de Witt and his brother are massacred by a mob probably inspired by Calvinist clergy.

1673   Spinoza declines the chair of philosophy at Heidelberg (Ep47, Ep48). Spinoza visits the military camp of the Prince de Condé.   **13 November:** The French occupation of Utrecht ends.   **19 July:** The States of Holland publish a formal condemnation of the *Theological-Political Treatise* and "other heretical and atheistic writings," including the works of Hobbes and the Socinians.   Malebranche publishes the *Recherche de la Vérité,* which is accused of being of Spinozist inspiration.

1675   Spinoza completes and circulates the *Ethics* but declines to publish it. He begins work on the *Political Treatise.* Spinoza writes to G. H. Schuller (Ep72) expressing his distrust of Leibniz.

1676   **16 January:** The curator of the University of Leiden issues a new promulgation against Cartesianism.   The Synod of The Hague orders an inquiry into the authorship of the *Theological-Political Treatise.*

1677   **21 February:** Death of Spinoza. His friends edit and publish the *Opera Posthuma* and *Nagelate Schriften,* all of whose contents are condemned by the political authorities and Calvinists the following year.

1680   **22 October:** Death of Bouwmeester.

1687   Newton publishes the first edition of the *Mathematical Principles of Natural Philosophy.*

1688   The "Glorious Revolution": William III becomes King of England.

1689   Locke publishes his *Letter on Tolerance* and his *Essay on Civil Government.*

1697   In his *Dictionnaire Historique et Critique,* Bayle characterizes Spinoza as *"un athée de système, étrangement vertueux."*

1710   Leibniz publishes his *Theodicy.*

ETHICS

Spinoza prepared to publish the Ethics, the comprehensive account of his philosophical system, in 1674. The work and its five parts had been completed after over a decade's labor, and after the turmoil of the years since the Short Treatise and the publication of the Principles of Cartesian Philosophy. The time had come but at the advice of friends, Spinoza felt the danger and the risks too deeply. As he reported to Henry Oldenburg in the fall of 1675, he was attacked both by theologians and by Cartesians and felt compelled to halt publication (Ep68; see Jonathan Israel, Radical Enlightenment, 286–7). Indeed, the work—one of the classics of Western philosophy—was only finally published in 1677 after Spinoza's death, in the Opera Posthuma, edited by his friends and published by Jan Rieuwertsz. Within a year, on 25 June 1678, it was censored by the States of Holland and West-Friesland as a "profane, atheistic, and blasphemous book."

Some scholars believe that the appendix to the Short Treatise, probably composed in 1661 or early 1662, including seven axioms about substance, its attributes, and causality, together with four demonstrations about substance, was already an early version of the mathematically, geometrically organized content of the first book of the Ethics. By late 1662 or early 1663, with Spinoza in Rijnsburg, his Amsterdam friends had a copy of an early chapter of Part I "On God." Pieter Balling had delivered it to Simon de Vries, and it soon became the topic of meetings in Amsterdam where it was read and discussed. On and off, then, from 1661 to 1674, Spinoza worked on the Ethics, his magnum opus, paying the promissory note made in the TIE and setting out the details of his philosophical account of nature, mind, and the good life.

By June 1665, Spinoza seems to have had a complete draft in hand, a work of three parts, most likely following the design of the Short Treatise—"on God, man, and his well-being." Eventually, by 1675, of course, the Ethics had been revised and expanded, taking on its now famous five-part structure—on God, humankind and human epistemology, the passions, human bondage to the passions, and rational freedom. A June 1665 letter to Johan Bouwmeester, an Amsterdam friend and associate of Lodewijk Meyer, suggests that the original Part III was nearly complete and ready to be translated from Latin into Dutch, perhaps by Bouwmeester himself (Ep28). This third part contained much of what is found in Parts IV and V of the version we now have. Hence, by the time Spinoza turned, that autumn of 1665, to the Theological-Political Treatise, his system was complete.

A remarkable work it was. The Ethics's five parts famously lay out a system in the style of Euclid's geometry—starting from definitions and axioms and working through theorems or propositions with corollaries, notes or scholia, appendices, and more. The axiomatic style mirrors the system's rationality and exemplifies the way knowledge should be grasped. As the system proceeds from metaphysics through its account of human nature, knowledge, and emotion, to its

1

understanding of human flaws and aspirations, and finally to the ethical goal of human life (a life of freedom and understanding), the work both grounds itself and motivates its readers to conduct their lives according to the best conception of what human life can and should be. In short, Spinoza's magnum opus earns its title.

The book's contents are, in broad terms, well known. Spinoza's is an early modern naturalism, a set of principles underlying a rational, scientific view of religion, nature, psychology, and ethics. In Part I he defines crucial terms such as substance, attribute, mode, eternity, and God. He demonstrates that only one substance, with infinite attributes, exists; it does so necessarily, and every mode that follows from it occurs with precise and necessary determination. This one eternal, necessary, determinate substance is God, and hence nature or the natural world is either identical to it or to certain ways of understanding it. Modes of substance are not properties of substance, as in classical philosophy, but rather things in the world existing in precise states or ways. Modes are manifestations of substance and its attributes, which might be thought of as regulative natural forces.

In Part II, Spinoza introduces the two attributes by which we understand substance and in terms of which substance is manifest to our experience—thought and extension—and builds an account of the mental and physical dimensions of nature. This account leads to a set of propositions about human experience and cognition and, in Part III, of human emotions, feelings, and more, all as the psychological correlates of physical states of the human body. The causal structure of physical bodies, determined by their proportion of motion and rest, and influenced by the lawful interactions of bodies, is correlated with mental states, some cognitive, others affective, in all of nature and in particular in the minds of human beings. Spinoza's psychology is grounded in his physics and in the conception of conatus, the striving of each being to persevere and to manifest its essence; here is the dynamic element in Spinoza's vitalistic conception of nature. In human beings, the conatus takes on certain predictable psychological features. Ultimately, people seek to satisfy desires, feel joy and pleasure, and enhance their well-being, and these goals require increasing harmonious activity within nature and the diminishing of the passions, which mark a person's subordination to beings external to it and failure to satisfy its own preservation. This goal requires as complete and perfect a knowledge of nature as one can attain, a knowledge that corresponds in the mind to the maximizing of life-enhancing physical states on the body's part. Later in the Ethics, Spinoza calls this cognitive goal the "intellectual love of God" or "blessedness," and, in the notorious concluding section of Part V, he associates it with the mind's eternity and thereby with the traditional notion of the immortality of the soul.

Within the confines of this naturalistic system, Spinoza installs some claims that, even in his own day, became famous and even notorious. He also took some steps that have remained perplexing, if not confusing. Spinoza's natural world, for example, is not created, nor does it permit contingency or the existence of miracles. Furthermore, insofar as extension is an attribute of substance, Spinoza's God is physically extended; Spinoza could be and was charged with a kind of atheistic materialism. His natural world is also wholly determined and without goals or purposes. While Spinoza's God is material, human beings—unities of the physical and psychological—are as necessary and determined as God or nature. For this reason, Spinoza denies the existence of free will but not the existence of freedom, which he regards as a feature of actions that are active and rational, performed with a minimum of constraint and external coercion. In this sense, moreover, God is the only perfect being and human life an effort of imitatio dei. People are free, to the degree that they love God, understand God, and indeed emulate God, but for Spinoza these activities and aspirations are no different from seeking to understand nature and to live in harmony with natural law.

There are many obvious outcomes of this ethic of rational self-discipline and peace of mind. One is a life of democratic republicanism in which all citizens equally collaborate in a lawful society aimed at enhancing the well-being of all rational citizens and restraining harmful self-interest in behalf of this goal. In his last years Spinoza would turn, out of a sense of urgency, to an elaboration of these political implications.

M.L.M.

CONTENTS

PART I
CONCERNING GOD

Definitions

1. By that which is self-caused I mean that whose essence involves existence; or that whose nature can be conceived only as existing.

2. A thing is said to be finite in its own kind [*in suo genere finita*] when it can be limited by another thing of the same nature. For example, a body is said to be finite because we can always conceive of another body greater than it. So, too, a thought is limited by another thought. But body is not limited by thought, nor thought by body.

3. By substance I mean that which is in itself and is conceived through itself; that is, that the conception of which does not require the conception of another thing from which it has to be formed.

4. By attribute I mean that which the intellect perceives of substance as constituting its essence.

5. By mode I mean the affections of substance, that is, that which is in something else and is conceived through something else.

6. By God I mean an absolutely infinite being, that is, substance consisting of infinite attributes, each of which expresses eternal and infinite essence.

Exp   I say "absolutely infinite," not "infinite in its kind." For if a thing is only infinite in its kind, one may deny that it has infinite attributes. But if a thing is absolutely infinite, whatever expresses essence and does not involve any negation belongs to its essence.

7. That thing is said to be free [*liber*] which exists solely from the necessity of its own nature, and is determined to action by itself alone. A thing is said to be necessary [*necessarius*] or rather, constrained [*coactus*], if it is determined by another thing to exist and to act in a definite and determinate way.

8. By eternity I mean existence itself insofar as it is conceived as necessarily following solely from the definition of an eternal thing.

Exp   For such existence is conceived as an eternal truth, just as is the essence of the thing, and therefore cannot be explicated through duration or time, even if duration be conceived as without beginning and end.

Axioms

1. All things that are, are either in themselves or in something else.

2. That which cannot be conceived through another thing must be conceived through itself.

3. From a given determinate cause there necessarily follows an effect; on the other hand, if there be no determinate cause, it is impossible that an effect should follow.

4. The knowledge of an effect depends on, and involves, the knowledge of the cause.

5. Things which have nothing in common with each other cannot be understood through each other; that is, the conception of the one does not involve the conception of the other.

6. A true idea must agree with that of which it is the idea [*ideatum*].

7. If a thing can be conceived as not existing, its essence does not involve existence.

P1   *Substance is by nature prior to its affections.*

Proof   This is evident from Defs. 3 and 5.

P2   *Two substances having different attributes have nothing in common.*

Proof   This too is evident from Def. 3; for each substance must be in itself and be conceived through itself; that is, the conception of the one does not involve the conception of the other.

P3   *When things have nothing in common, one cannot be the cause of the other.*

Proof   If things have nothing in common, then (Ax. 5) they cannot be understood through one another, and so (Ax. 4) one cannot be the cause of the other.

P4   *Two or more distinct things are distinguished from one another either by the difference of the attributes of the substances or by the difference of the affections of the substances.*

Proof   All things that are, are either in themselves or in something else (Ax. 1); that is (Defs. 3 and 5), nothing exists external to the intellect except substances and their affections. Therefore, there can be nothing external to the intellect through which several things can be distinguished from one another except substances or (which is the same thing) (Def. 4) the attributes and the affections of substances.

P5   *In the universe there cannot be two or more substances of the same nature or attribute.*

Proof   If there were several such distinct substances, they would have to be distinguished from one another either by a difference of attributes or by a difference of affections (Pr. 4). If they are distinguished only by a difference of attributes, then it will be granted that there cannot be more than one substance of the same attribute. But if they are distinguished by a difference of affections, then, since substance is by nature prior to its affections (Pr. 1), disregarding therefore its affections and considering substance in itself, that is (Def. 3 and Ax. 6), considering it truly, it cannot be conceived as distinguishable from another substance. That is (Pr. 4), there cannot be several such substances but only one.

P6   *One substance cannot be produced by another substance.*

Proof   In the universe there cannot be two substances of the same attribute (Pr. 5), that is (Pr. 2), two substances having something in common. And so (Pr. 3) one cannot be the cause of the other; that is, one cannot be produced by the other.

Cor   Hence it follows that substance cannot be produced by anything else. For in the universe there exists nothing but substances and their affections, as is evident from Ax. 1 and Defs. 3 and 5. But, by Pr. 6, it cannot be produced by another substance. Therefore, substance cannot be produced by anything else whatsoever.

Another Proof   This can be proved even more readily by the absurdity of the contradictory. For if substance could be produced by something else, the knowledge of substance would have to depend on the knowledge of its cause (Ax. 4), and so (Def. 3) it would not be substance.

P7   *Existence belongs to the nature of substance.*

Proof   Substance cannot be produced by anything else (Cor. Pr. 6) and is there-fore self-caused [*causa sui*]; that is (Def. 1), its essence necessarily involves exis-tence; that is, existence belongs to its nature.

P8   *Every substance is necessarily infinite.*

Proof   There cannot be more than one substance having the same attribute (Pr. 5), and existence belongs to the nature of substance (Pr. 7). It must therefore exist either as finite or as infinite. But it cannot exist as finite, for (Def. 2) it would have to be limited by another substance of the same nature, and that substance also would have to exist (Pr. 7). And so there would exist two substances of the same attribute, which is absurd (Pr. 5). Therefore, it exists as infinite.

Schol 1   Since in fact to be finite is in part a negation and to be infinite is the unqualified affirmation of the existence of some nature, it follows from Proposi-tion 7 alone that every substance must be infinite.

Schol 2   I do not doubt that for those who judge things confusedly and are not accustomed to know things through their primary causes it is difficult to grasp the proof of Proposition 7. Surely, this is because they neither distinguish between the modification of substances and substances themselves, nor do they know how things are produced. And so it comes about that they ascribe to substances a be-ginning which they see natural things as having; for those who do not know the true causes of things confuse everything. Without any hesitation they imagine trees as well as men talking and stones as well as men being formed from seeds; indeed, any forms whatsoever are imagined to change into any other forms. So too, those who confuse the divine nature with human nature easily ascribe to God human emotions, especially so long as they are ignorant of how the latter are pro-duced in the mind. But if men were to attend to the nature of substance, they would not doubt at all the truth of Proposition 7; indeed, this Proposition would be an axiom to all and would be ranked among universally accepted truisms. For by substance they would understand that which is in itself and is conceived through itself; that is, that the knowledge of which does not require the knowl-edge of any other thing. By modifications they would understand that which is in another thing, and whose conception is formed from the thing in which they are. Therefore, in the case of nonexistent modifications we can have true ideas of them since their essence is included in something else, with the result that they can be conceived through that something else, although they do not exist in actuality ex-ternally to the intellect. However, in the case of substances, because they are con-ceived only through themselves, their truth external to the intellect is only in themselves. So if someone were to say that he has a clear and distinct—that is, a true—idea of substance and that he nevertheless doubts whether such a substance exists, this would surely be just the same as if he were to declare that he has a true idea but nevertheless suspects that it may be false (as is obvious to anyone who gives his mind to it). Or if anyone asserts that substance is created, he at the same time asserts that a false idea has become true, than which nothing more absurd can be conceived. So it must necessarily be admitted that the existence of substance is as much an eternal truth as is its essence.

From here we can derive in another way that there cannot be but one [substance] of the same nature, and I think it worthwhile to set out the proof here. Now to do this in an orderly fashion I ask you to note:

1. The true definition of each thing involves and expresses nothing beyond the nature of the thing defined. Hence it follows that—

2. No definition involves or expresses a fixed number of individuals, since it expresses nothing but the nature of the thing defined. For example, the definition of a triangle expresses nothing other than simply the nature of a triangle, and not a fixed number of triangles.

3. For each individual existent thing there must necessarily be a definite cause for its existence.

4. The cause for the existence of a thing must either be contained in the very nature and definition of the existent thing (in effect, existence belongs to its nature) or must have its being independently of the thing itself.

From these premises it follows that if a fixed number of individuals exist in Nature, there must necessarily be a cause why those individuals and not more or fewer exist. If, for example, in Nature twenty men were to exist (for the sake of greater clarity I suppose that they exist simultaneously and that no others existed in Nature before them), in order to account for the existence of these twenty men, it will not be enough for us to demonstrate the cause of human nature in general; it will furthermore be necessary to demonstrate the cause why not more or fewer than twenty men exist, since (Note 3) there must necessarily be a cause for the existence of each one. But this cause (Notes 2 and 3) cannot be contained in the nature of man, since the true definition of man does not involve the number twenty. So (Note 4) the cause of the existence of these twenty men, and consequently of each one, must necessarily be external to each one, and therefore we can reach the unqualified conclusion that whenever several individuals of a kind exist, there must necessarily be an external cause for their existence. Now since existence belongs to the nature of substance (as has already been shown in this Scholium) the definition of substance must involve necessary existence, and consequently the existence of substance must be concluded solely from its definition. But the existence of several substances cannot follow from the definition of substance (as I have already shown in Notes 2 and 3). Therefore, from the definition of substance it follows necessarily that there exists only one substance of the same nature, as was proposed.

P9   *The more reality or being a thing has, the more attributes it has.*

Proof   This is evident from Definition 4.

P10   *Each attribute of one substance must be conceived through itself.*

Proof   For an attribute is that which intellect perceives of substance as constituting its essence (Def. 4), and so (Def. 3) it must be conceived through itself.

Schol   From this it is clear that although two attributes be conceived as really distinct, that is, one without the help of the other, still we cannot deduce therefrom that they constitute two entities, or two different substances. For it is in the nature of substance that each of its attributes be conceived through itself, since all the attributes it possesses have always been in it simultaneously, and one could not have been produced by another; but each expresses the reality or being of substance. So it is by no means absurd to ascribe more than one attribute to one substance. Indeed, nothing in Nature is clearer than that each entity must be conceived under some attribute, and the more reality or being it has, the more are its attributes which express necessity, or eternity, and infinity. Consequently, nothing can be clearer than this, too, that an absolutely infinite entity must necessarily be defined (Def. 6) as an entity consisting of infinite attributes, each of which expresses a definite essence, eternal and infinite. Now if anyone asks by what mark can we distinguish between different substances, let him read the following Propositions, which show that in Nature there exists only one substance, absolutely infinite. So this distinguishing mark would be sought in vain.

P11   *God, or substance consisting of infinite attributes, each of which expresses eternal and infinite essence, necessarily exists.*

Proof   If you deny this, conceive, if you can, that God does not exist. Therefore (Ax. 7), his essence does not involve existence. But this is absurd (Pr. 7). Therefore, God necessarily exists.

Second Proof   For every thing a cause or reason must be assigned either for its existence or for its nonexistence. For example, if a triangle exists, there must be a reason, or cause, for its existence. If it does not exist, there must be a reason or cause which prevents it from existing, or which annuls its existence. Now this reason or cause must either be contained in the nature of the thing or be external to it. For example, the reason why a square circle does not exist is indicated by its very nature, in that it involves a contradiction. On the other hand, the reason for the existence of substance also follows from its nature alone, in that it involves existence (Pr. 7). But the reason for the existence or nonexistence of a circle or a triangle does not follow from their nature, but from the order of universal corporeal Nature. For it is from this latter that it necessarily follows that either the triangle necessarily exists at this moment or that its present existence is impossible. This is self-evident, and therefrom it follows that a thing necessarily exists if there is no reason or cause which prevents its existence. Therefore, if there can be no reason or cause which prevents God from existing or which annuls his existence, we are bound to conclude that he necessarily exists. But if there were such a reason or cause, it would have to be either within God's nature or external to it; that is, it would have to be in another substance of another nature. For if it were of the same nature, by that very fact it would be granted that God exists. But a substance of another nature would have nothing in common with God (Pr. 2), and so could neither posit nor annul his existence. Since, therefore, there cannot be external to God's nature a reason or cause that would annul God's existence, then if indeed he does not exist, the reason or cause must necessarily be in God's nature, which would therefore involve a contradiction. But to affirm this of a Being absolutely infinite and in the highest degree perfect is absurd. Therefore, neither in God nor external to God is there any cause or reason which would annul his existence. Therefore, God necessarily exists.

A Third Proof   To be able to not exist is weakness; on the other hand, to be able to exist is power, as is self-evident. So if what now necessarily exists is nothing but finite entities, then finite entities are more potent than an absolutely infinite Entity—which is absurd. Therefore, either nothing exists, or an absolutely infinite Entity necessarily exists, too. But we do exist, either in ourselves or in something else which necessarily exists (Ax. 1 and Pr. 7). Therefore, an absolutely infinite Entity—that is (Def. 6), God—necessarily exists.

Schol   In this last proof I decided to prove God's existence a posteriori so that the proof may be more easily perceived, and not because God's existence does not follow a priori from this same basis. For since the ability to exist is power, it follows that the greater the degree of reality that belongs to the nature of a thing, the greater amount of energy it has for existence. So an absolutely infinite Entity or God will have from himself absolutely infinite power to exist, and therefore exists absolutely.

But perhaps many will not readily find this proof convincing because they are used to considering only such things as derive from external causes. Of these things they observe that those which come quickly into being—that is, which readily exist—likewise readily perish, while things which they conceive as more complex they regard as more difficult to bring into being—that is, not so ready to exist. However, to free them from these misconceptions I do not need at this point to show what measure of truth there is in the saying, "Quickly come, quickly go," neither need I raise the question whether or not everything is equally easy in respect of Nature as a whole. It is enough to note simply this, that I am not here speaking of things that come into being through external causes, but only of substances, which (Pr. 6) cannot be produced by any external cause. For whether they consist of many parts or few, things that are brought about by external causes owe whatever degree of perfection or reality they possess entirely to the power of the external cause, and so their existence has its origin solely in the perfection of the external cause, and not in their own perfection. On the other hand, whatever perfection substance possesses is due to no external cause; therefore its existence, too, must follow solely from its own nature, and is therefore nothing else but its essence. So perfection does not annul a thing's existence: on the contrary, it posits it; whereas imperfection annuls a thing's existence. So there is nothing of which we can be more certain than the existence of an absolutely infinite or perfect Entity; that is, God. For since his essence excludes all imperfection and involves absolute perfection, it thereby removes all reason for doubting his existence and affords the utmost certainty of it. This, I think, must be quite clear to all who give a modicum of attention to the matter.

P12 *No attribute of substance can be truly conceived from which it would follow that substance can be divided.*

Proof The parts into which substance thus conceived would be divided will either retain the nature of substance or they will not. In the first case each part will have to be infinite (Pr. 8) and self-caused (Pr. 6) and consist of a different attribute (Pr. 5); and so several substances could be formed from one substance, which is absurd (Pr. 6). Furthermore, the parts would have nothing in common with the whole (Pr. 2), and the whole could exist and be conceived without its parts (Def. 4 and Pr. 10), the absurdity of which none can doubt. But in the latter case in which the parts will not retain the nature of substance—then when the whole substance would have been divided into equal parts it would lose the nature of substance and would cease to be. This is absurd (Pr. 7).

P13 *Absolutely infinite substance is indivisible.*

Proof If it were divisible, the parts into which it would be divided will either retain the nature of absolutely infinite substance, or not. In the first case, there would therefore be several substances of the same nature, which is absurd (Pr. 5). In the second case, absolutely infinite substance can cease to be, which is also absurd (Pr. 11).

Cor From this it follows that no substance, and consequently no corporeal substance, insofar as it is substance, is divisible.

Schol The indivisibility of substance can be more easily understood merely from the fact that the nature of substance can be conceived only as infinite, and that a part of substance can mean only finite substance, which involves an obvious contradiction (Pr. 8).

P14 *There can be, or be conceived, no other substance but God.*

Proof Since God is an absolutely infinite being of whom no attribute expressing the essence of substance can be denied (Def. 6), and since he necessarily exists (Pr. 11), if there were any other substance but God, it would have to be explicated through some attribute of God, and so there would exist two substances with the same attribute, which is absurd (Pr. 5). So there can be no substance external to God, and consequently no such substance can be conceived. For if it could be conceived, it would have to be conceived necessarily as existing; but this is absurd (by the first part of this proof). Therefore, no substance can be or be conceived external to God.

Cor 1 Hence it follows quite clearly that God is one: that is (Def. 6), in the universe there is only one substance, and this is absolutely infinite, as I have already indicated in Schol. Pr. 10.

Cor 2 It follows that the thing extended and the thing thinking are either attributes of God or (Ax. 1) affections of the attributes of God.

P15 *Whatever is, is in God, and nothing can be or be conceived without God.*

Proof   Apart from God no substance can be or be conceived (Pr. 14), that is (Def. 3), something which is in itself and is conceived through itself. Now modes (Def. 5) cannot be or be conceived without substance; therefore, they can be only in the divine nature and can be conceived only through the divine nature. But nothing exists except substance and modes (Ax. 1). Therefore, nothing can be or be conceived without God.

Schol   Some imagine God in the likeness of man, consisting of mind and body, and subject to passions. But it is clear from what has already been proved how far they stray from the true knowledge of God. These I dismiss, for all who have given any consideration to the divine nature deny that God is corporeal. They find convincing proof of this in the fact that by body we understand some quantity having length, breadth, and depth, bounded by a definite shape; and nothing more absurd than this can be attributed to God, a being absolutely infinite.

At the same time, however, by other arguments which they try to prove their point, they show clearly that in their thinking corporeal or extended substance is set completely apart from the divine nature, and they assert that it is created by God. But they have no idea from what divine power it could have been created, which clearly shows that they don't know what they are saying. Now I have clearly proved—at any rate, in my judgment (Cor. Pr. 6 and Schol. 2 Pr. 8)—that no substance can be produced or created by anything else. Furthermore, in Proposition 14 we showed that apart from God no substance can be or be conceived, and hence we deduced that extended substance is one of God's infinite attributes.

However, for a fuller explanation I will refute my opponents' arguments, which all seem to come down to this. Firstly, they think that corporeal substance, insofar as it is substance, is made up of parts, and so they deny that it can be infinite, and consequently that it can pertain to God. This they illustrate with many examples, of which I will take one or two. They say that if corporeal substance is infinite, suppose it to be divided into two parts. Each of these parts will be either finite or infinite. If the former, then the infinite is made up of two finite parts, which is absurd. If the latter, then there is an infinite which is twice as great as another infinite, which is also absurd.

Again, if an infinite length is measured in feet, it will have to consist of an infinite number of feet; and if it is measured in inches, it will consist of an infinite number of inches. So one infinite number will be twelve times greater than another infinite number.

Lastly, if from one point in an infinite quantity two lines, AB and AC, be drawn of fixed and determinate length, and thereafter be produced to infinity, it is clear that the distance between B and C continues to increase and finally changes from a determinate distance to an indeterminate distance.

As these absurdities follow, they think, from supposing quantity to be infinite, they conclude that corporeal substance must be finite and consequently cannot pertain to God's essence.

The second argument is also drawn from God's consummate perfection. Since

God, they say, is a supremely perfect being, he cannot be that which is acted upon. But corporeal substance, being divisible, can be acted upon. It therefore follows that corporeal substance does not pertain to God's essence.

These are the arguments I find put forward by writers who thereby seek to prove that corporeal substance is unworthy of the divine essence and cannot pertain to it. However, the student who looks carefully into these arguments will find that I have already replied to them, since they are all founded on the same supposition that material substance is composed of parts, and this I have already shown to be absurd (Pr. 12 and Cor. Pr. 13). Again, careful reflection will show that all those alleged absurdities (if indeed they are absurdities, which is not now under discussion) from which they seek to prove that extended substance is finite do not at all follow from the supposition that quantity is infinite, but that infinite quantity is measurable and is made up of finite parts. Therefore, from the resultant absurdities no other conclusion can be reached but that infinite quantity is not measurable and cannot be made up of finite parts. And this is exactly what we have already proved (Pr. 12). So the weapon they aimed at us is in fact turned against themselves. If therefore from this "reductio ad absurdum" argument of theirs they still seek to deduce that extended substance must be finite, they are surely just like one who, having made the supposition that a circle has the properties of a square, deduces therefrom that a circle does not have a center from which all lines drawn to the circumference are equal. For corporeal substance, which can be conceived only as infinite, one, and indivisible (Prs. 8, 5, and 12) they conceive as made up of finite parts, multiplex, and divisible, so as to deduce that it is finite. In the same way others, too, having supposed that a line is composed of points, can find many arguments to prove that a line cannot be infinitely divided. Indeed, it is just as absurd to assert that corporeal substance is composed of bodies or parts as that a body is composed of surfaces, surfaces of lines, and lines of points. This must be admitted by all who know clear reason to be infallible, and particularly those who say that a vacuum cannot exist. For if corporeal substance could be so divided that its parts were distinct in reality, why could one part not be annihilated while the others remain joined together as before? And why should all the parts be so fitted together as to leave no vacuum? Surely, in the case of things which are in reality distinct from one another, one can exist without the other and remain in its original state. Since therefore there is no vacuum in Nature (of which [more] elsewhere[1]) and all its parts must so harmonize that there is no vacuum, it also follows that the parts cannot be distinct in reality; that is, corporeal substance, insofar as it is substance, cannot be divided.

If I am now asked why we have this natural inclination to divide quantity, I reply that we conceive quantity in two ways, to wit, abstractly, or superficially—in other words, as represented in the imagination—or as substance, which we do

---

Notes without brackets are Spinoza's. Bracketed notes are those of Seymour Feldman (main annotator for this work), translator Samuel Shirley, and Michael L. Morgan.

[1] [If this refers to anything in Spinoza's extant works, it must be to his early *Descartes's Principles of Philosophy* II.2–3.—S.F.]

only through the intellect. If therefore we consider quantity insofar as we represent it in the imagination—and this is what we more frequently and readily do—we find it to be finite, divisible, and made up of parts. But if we consider it intellectually and conceive it insofar as it is substance—and this is very difficult—then it will be found to be infinite, one, and indivisible, as we have already sufficiently proved. This will be quite clear to those who can distinguish between the imagination and the intellect, especially if this point also is stressed, that matter is everywhere the same, and there are no distinct parts in it except insofar as we conceive matter as modified in various ways. Then its parts are distinct, not really but only modally. For example, we conceive water to be divisible and to have separate parts insofar as it is water, but not insofar as it is material substance. In this latter respect it is not capable of separation or division. Furthermore, water, qua water, comes into existence and goes out of existence; but qua substance it does not come into existence nor go out of existence [*corrumpitur*].

I consider that in the above I have also replied to the second argument, since this too is based on the supposition that matter, insofar as it is substance, is divisible and made up of parts. And even though this were not so, I do not know why matter should be unworthy of the divine nature, since (Pr. 14) there can be no substance external to God by which it can be acted upon. All things, I repeat, are in God, and all things that come to pass do so only through the laws of God's infinite nature and follow through the necessity of his essence (as I shall later show). Therefore, by no manner of reasoning can it be said that God is acted upon by anything else or that extended substance is unworthy of the divine nature, even though it be supposed divisible, as long as it is granted to be eternal and infinite.

But enough of this subject for the present.

P16 *From the necessity of the divine nature there must follow infinite things in infinite ways [modis] (that is, everything that can come within the scope of infinite intellect).*

Proof This proposition should be obvious to everyone who will but consider this point, that from the given definition of any one thing the intellect infers a number of properties which necessarily follow in fact from the definition (that is, from the very essence of the thing), and the more reality the definition of the thing expresses (that is, the more reality the essence of the thing defined involves), the greater the number of its properties. Now since divine nature possesses absolutely infinite attributes (Def. 6), of which each one also expresses infinite essence in its own kind, then there must necessarily follow from the necessity of the divine nature an infinity of things in infinite ways (that is, everything that can come within the scope of the infinite intellect).

Cor 1 Hence it follows that God is the efficient cause of all things that can come within the scope of the infinite intellect.

Cor 2 Secondly, it follows that God is the cause through himself, not *per accidens*.

Cor 3   Thirdly, it follows that God is absolutely the first cause.

P17   *God acts solely from the laws of his own nature, constrained by none.*

Proof   We have just shown that an infinity of things follow, absolutely, solely from the necessity of divine nature, or—which is the same thing—solely from the laws of that same nature (Pr. 16); and we have proved (Pr. 15) that nothing can be or be conceived without God, but that everything is in God. Therefore, there can be nothing external to God by which he can be determined or constrained to act. Thus, God acts solely from the laws of his own nature and is constrained by none.

Cor 1   Hence it follows, firstly, that there is no cause, except the perfection of his nature, which either extrinsically or intrinsically moves God to act.

Cor 2   It follows, secondly, that God alone is a free cause. For God alone exists solely from the necessity of his own nature (Pr. 11 and Cor. 1 Pr. 14) and acts solely from the necessity of his own nature (Pr. 17). So he alone is a free cause (Def. 7).

Schol   Others take the view that God is a free cause because—so they think— he can bring it about that those things which we have said follow from his nature—that is, which are within his power—should not come about; that is, they should not be produced by him. But this is as much as to say that God can bring it about that it should not follow from the nature of a triangle that its three angles are equal to two right angles, or that from a given cause the effect should not follow, which is absurd.

Furthermore, I shall show later on without the help of this proposition that neither intellect nor will pertain to the nature of God. I know indeed that there are many who think they can prove that intellect in the highest degree and free will belong to the nature of God; for they say they know of nothing more perfect which they may attribute to God than that which is the highest perfection in us. Again, although they conceive of God as having in actuality intellect in the highest degree, they yet do not believe he can bring about the existence of everything which in actuality he understands, for they think they would thereby be nullifying God's power. If, they say, he had created everything that is within his intellect, then he would not have been able to create anything more; and this they regard as inconsistent with God's omnipotence. So they have preferred to regard God as indifferent to everything and as creating nothing but what he has decided, by some absolute exercise of will, to create. However, I think I have shown quite clearly (Pr. 16) that from God's supreme power or infinite nature an infinity of things in infinite ways—that is, everything—has necessarily flowed or is always following from that same necessity, just as from the nature of a triangle it follows from eternity to eternity that its three angles are equal to two right angles. Therefore, God's omnipotence has from eternity been actual and will remain for eternity in the same actuality. In this way, I submit, God's omnipotence is established as being far more perfect. Indeed my opponents—let us speak frankly—seem to be denying God's omnipotence. For they are obliged to admit that God understands an infinite number of creatable things which nevertheless he can never create. If this were not so, that is, if he were to create all the things that he understands, he would exhaust his omnipotence, according to them, and render himself imperfect. Thus, to affirm God as perfect they are reduced to having to affirm at the same time that he cannot bring about everything that is within the bounds of his power. I cannot imagine anything more absurd than this, or more inconsistent with God's omnipotence.

Furthermore, I have something here to say about the intellect and will that is usually attributed to God. If intellect and will do indeed pertain to the eternal essence of God, one must understand in the case of both these attributes something very different from the meaning widely entertained. For the intellect and will that would constitute the essence of God would have to be vastly different from human intellect and will, and would have no point of agreement except the name. They could be no more alike than the celestial constellation of the Dog and the dog that barks. This I will prove as follows. If intellect does pertain to the divine nature, it cannot, like man's intellect, be posterior to (as most thinkers hold) or simultaneous with the objects of understanding, since God is prior in causality to all things (Cor. 1 Pr. 16). On the contrary, the truth and formal essence of things is what it is because it exists as such in the intellect of God as an object of thought. Therefore, God's intellect, insofar as it is conceived as constituting God's essence, is in actual fact the cause of things, in respect both of their essence and their existence. This seems to have been recognized also by those who have asserted that God's intellect, will, and power are one and the same. Since therefore God's intellect is the one and only cause of things, both of their essence and their existence, as we have shown, it must necessarily be different from them both in respect of essence and existence. For that which is caused differs from its cause precisely in what it has from its cause. For example, a man is the cause of the existence of another man, but not of the other's essence; for the essence is an eternal truth. So with regard to their essence the two men can be in full agreement, but they must differ with regard to existence; and for that reason if the existence of the one should cease, the existence of the other would not thereby cease. But if the essence of the one could be destroyed and rendered false, so too would the essence of the other. Therefore, a thing which is the cause of the essence and existence of some effect must differ from that effect both in respect of essence and existence. But God's intellect is the cause of the essence and existence of man's intellect. Therefore, God's intellect, insofar as it is conceived as constituting the divine essence, differs from man's intellect both in respect of essence and existence, and cannot agree with it in any respect other than name—which is what I sought to prove. In the matter of will, the proof is the same, as anyone can readily see.

P18   *God is the immanent, not the transitive, cause of all things.*

Proof   All things that are, are in God, and must be conceived through God (Pr. 15), and so (Cor. 1 Pr. 16) God is the cause of the things that are in him, which is the first point. Further, there can be no substance external to God (Pr. 14); that is (Def. 3), a thing which is in itself external to God—which is the second point. Therefore, God is the immanent, not the transitive, cause of all things.

P19   *God [is eternal], that is, all the attributes of God are eternal.*

Proof   God is substance (Def. 6) which necessarily exists (Pr. 11); that is (Pr. 7), a thing to whose nature it pertains to exist, or—and this is the same thing—a thing from whose definition existence follows; and so (Def. 8) God is eternal. Further, by the attributes of God must be understood that which expresses the essence of the Divine substance (Def. 4), that is, that which pertains to substance. It is this, I say, which the attributes themselves must involve. But eternity pertains to the nature of substance (as I have shown in Pr. 7). Therefore, each of the attributes must involve eternity, and so they are all eternal.

Schol   This proposition is also perfectly clear from the manner in which I proved the existence of God (Pr. 11). From this proof, I repeat, it is obvious that God's existence is, like his essence, an eternal truth. Again, I have also proved God's eternity in another way in Proposition 19 of my *Descartes's Principles of Philosophy*, and there is no need here to go over that ground again.

P20   *God's existence and his essence are one and the same.*

Proof   God and all his attributes are eternal (Pr. 19); that is, each one of his attributes expresses existence (Def. 8). Therefore, the same attributes of God that explicate his eternal essence (Def. 4) at the same time explicate his eternal existence; that is, that which constitutes the essence of God at the same time constitutes his existence, and so his existence and his essence are one and the same.

Cor 1   From this it follows, firstly, that God's existence, like his essence, is an eternal truth.

Cor 2   It follows, secondly, that God is immutable; that is, all the attributes of God are immutable. For if they were to change in respect of existence, they would also have to change in respect of essence (Pr. 10); that is—and this is self-evident—they would have to become false instead of true, which is absurd.

P21   *All things that follow from the absolute nature of any attribute of God must have existed always, and as infinite; that is, through the said attribute they are eternal and infinite.*

Proof   Suppose this proposition be denied and conceive, if you can, that something in some attribute of God, following from its absolute nature, is finite and has a determinate existence or duration; for example, the idea of God in Thought. Now Thought, being assumed to be an attribute of God, is necessarily infinite by its own nature (Pr. 11). However, insofar as it has the idea of God, it is being supposed as finite. Now (Def. 2) it cannot be conceived as finite unless it is determined through Thought itself. But it cannot be determined through Thought itself insofar as Thought constitutes the idea of God, for it is in that respect that

Thought is supposed to be finite. Therefore, it is determined through Thought insofar as Thought does not constitute the idea of God, which Thought must nevertheless necessarily exist (Pr. 11). Therefore, there must be Thought which does not constitute the idea of God, and so the idea of God does not follow necessarily from its nature insofar as it is absolute Thought. (For it is conceived as constituting and as not constituting the idea of God.) This is contrary to our hypothesis. Therefore, if the idea of God in Thought, or anything in some attribute of God (it does not matter what is selected, since the proof is universal), follows from the necessity of the absolute nature of the attribute, it must necessarily be infinite. That was our first point.

Furthermore, that which thus follows from the necessity of the nature of some attribute cannot have a determinate existence, or duration. If this be denied, suppose that there is in some attribute of God a thing following from the necessity of the nature of the attribute, for example, the idea of God in Thought, and suppose that this thing either did not exist at some time, or will cease to exist in the future. Now since Thought is assumed as an attribute of God, it must necessarily exist, and as immutable (Pr. 11 and Cor. 2 Pr. 20). Therefore, outside the bounds of the duration of the idea of God (for this idea is supposed at some time not to have existed, or will at some point cease to exist), Thought will have to exist without the idea of God. But this is contrary to the hypothesis, for it is supposed that when Thought is granted the idea of God necessarily follows. Therefore, the idea of God in Thought, or anything that necessarily follows from the absolute nature of some attribute of God, cannot have a determinate existence, but is eternal through that same attribute. That was our second point. Note that the same holds for anything in an attribute of God which necessarily follows from the absolute nature of God.

P22 *Whatever follows from some attribute of God, insofar as the attribute is modified by a modification that exists necessarily and as infinite through that same attribute, must also exist both necessarily and as infinite.*

Proof This proposition is proved in the same way as the preceding one.

P23 *Every mode which exists necessarily and as infinite must have necessarily followed either from the absolute nature of some attribute of God or from some attribute modified by a modification which exists necessarily and as infinite.*

Proof A mode is in something else through which it must be conceived (Def. 5); that is (Pr. 15), it is in God alone and can be conceived only through God. Therefore, if a mode is conceived to exist necessarily and to be infinite, both these characteristics must necessarily be inferred or perceived through some attribute of God insofar as that attribute is conceived to express infinity and necessity of existence, or (and by Def. 8 this is the same) eternity; that is (Def. 6 and Pr. 19), insofar as it is considered absolutely. Therefore, a mode which exists necessarily and as infinite must have followed from the absolute nature of some attribute of God, either directly (Pr. 21) or through the mediation of some modification which follows from the absolute nature of the attribute; that is (Pr. 22), which exists necessarily and as infinite.

P24   *The essence of things produced by God does not involve existence.*

Proof   This is evident from Def. 1. For only that whose nature (considered in itself) involves existence is self-caused and exists solely from the necessity of its own nature.

Cor   Hence it follows that God is the cause not only of the coming into existence of things but also of their continuing in existence, or, to use a scholastic term, God is the cause of the being of things [*essendi rerum*]. For whether things exist or do not exist, in reflecting on their essence we realize that this essence involves neither existence nor duration. So it is not their essence which can be the cause of either their existence or their duration, but only God, to whose nature alone existence pertains (Cor. 1 Pr. 14).

P25   *God is the efficient cause not only of the existence of things but also of their essence.*

Proof   If this is denied, then God is not the cause of the essence of things, and so (Ax. 4) the essence of things can be conceived without God. But this is absurd (Pr. 15). Therefore, God is also the cause of the essence of things.

Schol   This proposition follows more clearly from Pr. 16; for from that proposition it follows that from the given divine nature both the essence and the existence of things must be inferred. In a word, in the same sense that God is said to be self-caused he must also be said to be the cause of all things. This will be even clearer from the following Corollary.

Cor   Particular things are nothing but affections of the attributes of God, that is, modes wherein the attributes of God find expression in a definite and determinate way. The proof is obvious from Pr. 15 and Def. 5.

P26   *A thing which has been determined to act in a particular way has necessarily been so determined by God; and a thing which has not been determined by God cannot determine itself to act.*

Proof   That by which things are said to be determined to act in a particular way must necessarily be something positive (as is obvious). So God, from the necessity of his nature, is the efficient cause both of its essence and its existence (Prs. 25 and 16)—which was the first point. From this the second point quite clearly follows as well. For if a thing which has not been determined by God could determine itself, the first part of this proposition would be false, which, as I have shown, is absurd.

P27   *A thing which has been determined by God to act in a particular way cannot render itself undetermined.*

Proof   This proposition is evident from Axiom 3.

P28   *Every individual thing, i.e., anything whatever which is finite and has a determinate existence, cannot exist or be determined to act unless it be determined to* *exist and to act by another cause which is also finite and has a determinate existence, and this cause again cannot exist or be determined to act unless it be determined to exist and to act by another cause which is also finite and has a determinate existence, and so ad infinitum.*

Proof Whatever is determined to exist and to act has been so determined by God (Pr. 26 and Cor. Pr. 24). But that which is finite and has a determinate existence cannot have been produced by the absolute nature of one of God's attributes, for whatever follows from the absolute nature of one of God's attributes is infinite and eternal (Pr. 21). It must therefore have followed from God or one of his attributes insofar as that is considered as affected by some mode; for nothing exists but substance and its modes (Ax. 1 and Defs. 3 and 5), and modes (Cor. Pr. 25) are nothing but affections of God's attributes. But neither could a finite and determined thing have followed from God or one of his attributes insofar as that is affected by a modification which is eternal and infinite (Pr. 22). Therefore, it must have followed, or been determined to exist and to act, by God or one of his attributes insofar as it was modified by a modification which is finite and has a determinate existence. That was the first point. Then again this cause or this mode (the reasoning is the same as in the first part of this proof) must also have been determined by another cause, which is also finite and has a determinate existence, and again this last (the reasoning is the same) by another, and so ad infinitum.

Schol Since some things must have been produced directly by God (those things, in fact, which necessarily follow from his absolute nature) and others through the medium of these primary things (which other things nevertheless cannot be or be conceived without God), it follows, firstly, that God is absolutely the proximate cause of things directly produced by him. I say "absolutely" [*absolute*], and not "within their own kind" [*suo genere*], as some say. For the effects of God can neither be nor be conceived without their cause (Pr. 15 and Cor. Pr. 24). It follows, secondly, that God cannot properly be said to be the remote cause of individual things, unless perchance for the purpose of distinguishing these things from things which he has produced directly, or rather, things which follow from his absolute nature. For by "remote cause" we understand a cause which is in no way conjoined with its effect. But all things that are, are in God, and depend on God in such a way that they can neither be nor be conceived without him.

P29 *Nothing in nature is contingent, but all things are from the necessity of the divine nature determined to exist and to act in a definite way.*

Proof Whatever is, is in God (Pr. 15). But God cannot be termed a contingent thing, for (Pr. 11) he exists necessarily, not contingently. Again, the modes of the divine nature have also followed from it necessarily, not contingently (Pr. 16), and that, too, whether insofar as the divine nature is considered absolutely (Pr. 21) or insofar as it is considered as determined to act in a definite way

(Pr. 27). Furthermore, God is the cause of these modes not only insofar as they simply exist (Cor. Pr. 26), but also insofar as they are considered as determined to a particular action (Pr. 26). Now if they are not determined by God (Pr. 26), it is an impossibility, not a contingency, that they should determine themselves. On the other hand (Pr. 27), if they are determined by God, it is an impossibility, not a contingency, that they should render themselves undetermined. Therefore, all things are determined from the necessity of the divine nature not only to exist but also to exist and to act in a definite way. Thus, there is no contingency.

Schol   Before I go any further, I wish to explain at this point what we must understand by "*Natura naturans*" and "*Natura naturata.*" I should perhaps say not "explain," but "remind the reader," for I consider that it is already clear from what has gone before that by "*Natura naturans*" we must understand that which is in itself and is conceived through itself; that is, the attributes of substance that express eternal and infinite essence; or (Cor. 1 Pr. 14 and Cor. 2 Pr. 17), God insofar as he is considered a free cause. By "*Natura naturata*" I understand all that follows from the necessity of God's nature, that is, from the necessity of each one of God's attributes; or all the modes of God's attributes insofar as they are considered as things which are in God and can neither be nor be conceived without God.

P30   *The finite intellect in act or the infinite intellect in act must comprehend the attributes of God and the affections of God, and nothing else.*

Proof   A true idea must agree with its object [*ideatum*] (Ax. 6); that is (as is self-evident), that which is contained in the intellect as an object of thought must necessarily exist in Nature. But in Nature (Cor. 1 Pr. 14) there is but one substance — God — and no other affections (Pr. 15) than those which are in God and that can neither be nor be conceived (Pr. 15) without God. Therefore, the finite intellect in act or the infinite intellect in act must comprehend the attributes of God and the affections of God, and nothing else.

P31   *The intellect in act, whether it be finite or infinite, as also will, desire, love, etc., must be related to* Natura naturata, *not to* Natura naturans.

Proof   By intellect (as is self-evident) we do not understand absolute thought, but only a definite mode of thinking which differs from other modes such as desire, love, etc., and so (Def. 5) must be conceived through absolute thought — that is (Pr. 15 and Def. 6), an attribute of God which expresses the eternal and infinite essence of thought — in such a way that without this attribute it can neither be nor be conceived; and therefore (Schol. Pr. 29) it must be related to *Natura naturata*, not to *Natura naturans*, just like the other modes of thinking.

Schol   The reason for my here speaking of the intellect in act is not that I grant there can be any intellect in potentiality, but that, wishing to avoid any confusion, I want to confine myself to what we perceive with the utmost clarity, to wit, the very act of understanding, than which nothing is more clearly apprehended by us. For we can understand nothing that does not lead to a more perfect cognition of the understanding.

P32   *Will cannot be called a free cause, but only a necessary cause.*

Proof   Will, like intellect, is only a definite mode of thinking, and so (Pr. 28) no single volition can exist or be determined to act unless it is determined by another cause, and this cause again by another, and so ad infinitum. Now if will be supposed infinite, it must also be determined to exist and to act by God, not insofar as he is absolutely infinite substance, but insofar as he possesses an attribute which expresses the infinite and eternal essence of Thought (Pr. 23). Therefore, in whatever way will is conceived, whether finite or infinite, it requires a cause by which it is determined to exist and to act; and so (Def. 7) it cannot be said to be a free cause, but only a necessary or constrained cause.

Cor 1   Hence it follows, firstly, that God does not act from freedom of will.

Cor 2   It follows, secondly, that will and intellect bear the same relationship to God's nature as motion-and-rest and, absolutely, as all natural phenomena that must be determined by God (Pr. 29) to exist and to act in a definite way. For will, like all the rest, stands in need of a cause by which it may be determined to exist and to act in a definite manner. And although from a given will or intellect infinite things may follow, God cannot on that account be said to act from freedom of will any more than he can be said to act from freedom of motion-and-rest because of what follows from motion-and-rest (for from this, too, infinite things follow). Therefore, will pertains to God's nature no more than do other natural phenomena. It bears the same relationship to God's nature as does motion-and-rest and everything else that we have shown to follow from the necessity of the divine nature and to be determined by that divine nature to exist and to act in a definite way.

P33   *Things could not have been produced by God in any other way or in any other order than is the case.*

Proof   All things have necessarily followed from the nature of God (Pr. 16) and have been determined to exist and to act in a definite way from the necessity of God's nature (Pr. 29). Therefore, if things could have been of a different nature or been determined to act in a different way so that the order of Nature would have been different, then God's nature, too, could have been other than it now is, and therefore (Pr. 11) this different nature, too, would have had to exist, and consequently there would have been two or more Gods, which (Cor. 1 Pr. 14) is absurd. Therefore, things could not have been produced by God in any other way or in any other order than is the case.

Schol 1   Since I have here shown more clearly than the midday sun that in things there is absolutely nothing by virtue of which they can be said to be "contingent," I now wish to explain briefly what we should understand by "contingent"; but I must first deal with "necessary" and "impossible." A thing is termed "necessary" either by reason of its essence or by reason of its cause. For a thing's existence necessarily follows either from its essence and definition or from a given efficient cause. Again, it is for these same reasons that a thing is termed "impossible"—that is, either because its essence or definition involves a contradiction or because there is no external cause determined to bring it into existence. But a thing is termed "contingent" for no other reason than the deficiency of our knowledge. For if we do not know whether the essence of a thing involves a contradiction, or if, knowing full well that its essence does not involve a contradiction, we still cannot make any certain judgment as to its existence because the chain of causes is hidden from us, then that thing cannot appear to us either as necessary or as impossible. So we term it either "contingent" or "possible."

Schol 2   It clearly follows from the above that things have been brought into being by God with supreme perfection, since they have necessarily followed from a most perfect nature. Nor does this imply any imperfection in God, for it is his perfection that has constrained us to make this affirmation. Indeed, from its contrary it would clearly follow (as I have just shown) that God is not supremely perfect, because if things had been brought into being in a different way by God, we should have to attribute to God another nature different from that which consideration of a most perfect Being has made us attribute to him.

However, I doubt not that many will ridicule this view as absurd and will not give their minds to its examination, and for this reason alone, that they are in the habit of attributing to God another kind of freedom very different from that which we (Def. 7) have assigned to him, that is, an absolute will. Yet I do not doubt that if they were willing to think the matter over and carefully reflect on our chain of proofs they would in the end reject the kind of freedom which they now attribute to God not only as nonsensical but as a serious obstacle to science. It is needless for me here to repeat what was said in the Scholium to Proposition 17. Yet for their sake I shall proceed to show that, even if it were to be granted that will pertains to the essence of God, it would nevertheless follow from his perfection that things could not have been created by God in any other way or in any other order. This will readily be shown if we first consider—as they themselves grant—that on God's decree and will alone does it depend that each thing is what it is. For otherwise God would not be the cause of all things. Further, there is the fact that all God's decrees have been sanctioned by God from eternity, for otherwise he could be accused of imperfection and inconstancy. But since the eternal does not admit of "when" or "before" or "after," it follows merely from God's perfection that God can never decree otherwise nor ever could have decreed otherwise; in other words, God could not have been prior to his decrees nor can he be without them. "But," they will say, "granted the supposition that God had made a different universe, or that from eternity he had made a different decree concerning Nature and her order, no imperfection in God would follow therefrom." But if they say this, they will be granting at the same time that God can change his decrees. For if God's decrees had been different from what in fact he has decreed regarding Nature and her order—that is, if he had willed and conceived differently concerning Nature—he would necessarily have had a different intellect and a different will from that which he now has. And if it is permissible to attribute to God a different intellect and a different will without any change in his essence and perfection, why should he not now be able to change his decrees concerning created things, and nevertheless remain equally perfect? For his intellect and will regarding created things and their order have the same relation to his essence and perfection, in whatever manner it be conceived.

Then again, all philosophers whom I have read grant that in God there is no intellect in potentiality but only intellect in act. Now since all of them also grant that his intellect and will are not distinct from his essence, it therefore follows from this, too, that if God had had a different intellect in act and a different will, his essence too would necessarily have been different. Therefore—as I deduced from the beginning—if things had been brought into being by God so as to be different from what they now are, God's intellect and will—that is (as is granted), God's essence—must have been different, which is absurd. Therefore, since things could not have been brought into being by God in any other way or order—and it follows from God's supreme perfection that this is true—surely we can have no sound reason for believing that God did not wish to create all the things that are in his intellect through that very same perfection whereby he understands them.

"But," they will say, "there is in things no perfection or imperfection; that which is in them whereby they are perfect or imperfect, and are called good or bad, depends only on the will of God. Accordingly, if God had so willed it he could have brought it about that that which is now perfection should be utmost imperfection, and vice versa." But what else is this but an open assertion that God, who necessarily understands that which he wills, can by his will bring it about that he should understand things in a way different from the way he understands them—and this, as I have just shown, is utterly absurd. So I can turn their own argument against them, as follows. All things depend on the power of God. For things to be able to be otherwise than as they are, God's will, too, would necessarily have to be different. But God's will cannot be different (as we have just shown most clearly from the consideration of God's perfection). Therefore, neither can things be different.

I admit that this view which subjects everything to some kind of indifferent will of God and asserts that everything depends on his pleasure diverges less from the truth than the view of those who hold that God does everything with the good in mind. For these people seem to posit something external to God that does not depend upon him, to which in acting God looks as if it were a model, or to which he aims, as if it were a fixed target. This is surely to subject God to fate; and no more absurd assertion can be made about God, whom we have shown to be the first and the only free cause of both the essence and the existence of things. So I need not spend any more time in refuting this absurdity.

P34   *God's power is his very essence.*

Proof   From the sole necessity of God's essence it follows that God is self-caused (Pr. 11) and the cause of all things (Pr. 16 and Cor.). Therefore, God's power, whereby he and all things are and act, is his very essence.

P35   *Whatever we conceive to be within God's power necessarily exists.*

Proof   Whatever is within God's power must be so comprehended in his essence (Pr. 34) that it follows necessarily from it, and thus necessarily exists.

P36   *Nothing exists from whose nature an effect does not follow.*

Proof   Whatever exists expresses God's nature or essence in a definite and determinate way (Cor. Pr. 25); that is (Pr. 34), whatever exists expresses God's power, which is the cause of all things, in a definite and determinate way, and so (Pr. 16) some effect must follow from it.

APPENDIX

I have now explained the nature and properties of God: that he necessarily exists, that he is one alone, that he is and acts solely from the necessity of his own nature, that he is the free cause of all things and how so, that all things are in God and are so dependent on him that they can neither be nor be conceived without him, and lastly, that all things have been predetermined by God, not from his free will or absolute pleasure, but from the absolute nature of God, his infinite power. Furthermore, whenever the opportunity arose I have striven to remove prejudices that might hinder the apprehension of my proofs. But since there still remain a considerable number of prejudices, which have been, and still are, an obstacle— indeed, a very great obstacle—to the acceptance of the concatenation of things in the manner which I have expounded, I have thought it proper at this point to bring these prejudices before the bar of reason.

Now all the prejudices which I intend to mention here turn on this one point, the widespread belief among men that all things in Nature are like themselves in acting with an end in view. Indeed, they hold it as certain that God himself directs everything to a fixed end; for they say that God has made everything for man's sake and has made man so that he should worship God. So this is the first point I shall consider, seeking the reason why most people are victims of this prejudice and why all are so naturally disposed to accept it. Secondly, I shall demonstrate its falsity; and lastly I shall show how it has been the source of misconceptions about good and bad, right and wrong, praise and blame, order and confusion, beauty and ugliness, and the like.

However, it is not appropriate here to demonstrate the origin of these misconceptions from the nature of the human mind. It will suffice at this point if I take as my basis what must be universally admitted, that all men are born ignorant of the causes of things, that they all have a desire to seek their own advantage, a desire of which they are conscious. From this it follows, firstly, that men believe that they are free, precisely because they are conscious of their volitions and desires; yet concerning the causes that have determined them to desire and will they do not think, not even dream about, because they are ignorant of them. Secondly, men act always with an end in view, to wit, the advantage that they seek. Hence it happens that they are always looking only for the final causes of things done, and are satisfied when they find them, having, of course, no reason for further doubt. But if they fail to discover them from some external source, they have no recourse but to turn to themselves, and to reflect on what ends would normally determine them to similar actions, and so they necessarily judge other minds by their own. Further, since they find within themselves and outside themselves a considerable number of means very convenient for the pursuit of their own advantage — as, for instance, eyes for seeing, teeth for chewing, cereals and living creatures for food, the sun for giving light, the sea for breeding fish — the result is that they look on all the things of Nature as means to their own advantage. And realizing that these were found, not produced by them, they come to believe that there is someone else who produced these means for their use. For looking on things as means, they could not believe them to be self-created, but on the analogy of the means which they are accustomed to produce for themselves, they were bound to conclude that there was some governor or governors of Nature, endowed with human freedom, who have attended to all their needs and made everything for their use. And having no information on the subject, they also had to estimate the character of these rulers by their own, and so they asserted that the gods direct everything for man's use so that they may bind men to them and be held in the highest honor by them. So it came about that every individual devised different methods of worshipping God as he thought fit in order that God should love him beyond others and direct the whole of Nature so as to serve his blind cupidity and insatiable greed. Thus it was that this misconception developed into superstition and became deep-rooted in the minds of men, and it was for this reason that every man strove most earnestly to understand and to explain the final causes of all things. But in seeking to show that Nature does nothing in vain — that is, nothing that is not to man's advantage — they seem to have shown only this, that Nature and the gods are as crazy as mankind.

Consider, I pray, what has been the upshot. Among so many of Nature's blessings they were bound to discover quite a number of disasters, such as storms, earthquakes, diseases and so forth, and they maintained that these occurred because the gods were angry at the wrongs done to them by men, or the faults committed in the course of their worship. And although daily experience cried out against this and showed by any number of examples that blessings and disasters befall the godly and the ungodly alike without discrimination, they did not on that account abandon their ingrained prejudice. For they found it easier to regard this fact as one among other mysteries they could not understand and thus maintain their innate condition of ignorance rather than to demolish in its entirety the theory they had constructed and devise a new one. Hence they made it axiomatic that the

judgment of the gods is far beyond man's understanding. Indeed, it is for this reason, and this reason only, that truth might have evaded mankind forever had not
Mathematics, which is concerned not with ends but only with the essences and
properties of figures, revealed to men a different standard of truth. And there are
other causes too—there is no need to mention them here—which could have
made men aware of these widespread misconceptions and brought them to a true
knowledge of things.

I have thus sufficiently dealt with my first point. There is no need to spend time
in going on to show that Nature has no fixed goal and that all final causes are but
figments of the human imagination. For I think that this is now quite evident, both
from the basic causes from which I have traced the origin of this misconception
and from Proposition 16 and the Corollaries to Proposition 32, and in addition
from the whole set or proofs I have adduced to show that all things in Nature proceed from all eternal necessity and with supreme perfection. But I will make this
additional point, that this doctrine of Final Causes turns Nature completely up-
side down, for it regards as an effect that which is in fact a cause, and vice versa.
Again, it makes that which is by nature first to be last; and finally, that which is
highest and most perfect is held to be the most imperfect. Omitting the first two
points as self-evident, Propositions 21, 22, and 23 make it clear that that effect is
most perfect which is directly produced by God, and an effect is the less perfect
in proportion to the number of intermediary causes required for its production.
But if the things produced directly by God were brought about to enable him to
attain an end, then of necessity the last things for the sake of which the earlier
things were brought about would excel all others. Again, this doctrine negates
God's perfection; for if God acts with an end in view, he must necessarily be seeking something that he lacks. And although theologians and metaphysicians may
draw a distinction between a purpose arising from want and an assimilative purpose,[2] they still admit that God has acted in all things for the sake of himself, and
not for the sake of the things to be created. For prior to creation they are not able
to point to anything but God as a purpose for God's action. Thus they have to admit that God lacked and desired those things for the procurement of which he
willed to create the means—as is self-evident.

I must not fail to mention here that the advocates of this doctrine, eager to display their talent in assigning purpose to things, have introduced a new style of
argument to prove their doctrine, i.e., a reduction, not to the impossible, but to

---

[2] [Spinoza alludes here to a late scholastic distinction between two kinds of purposes, or goals: (1) a
purpose that satisfies some internal need or lack (*fines indigentiae*); and (2) a purpose that aims
to share what one already has with others who lack it (*fines assimilationis*). In the present case, this
distinction implies that when God does something purposively, he acts not to fulfill a need he has,
but to benefit creatures. In their commentaries on the *Ethics*, both Lewis Robinson and Harry Wolfson refer to the seventeenth-century Dutch theologian A. Heereboord as Spinoza's source for this
distinction (L. Robinson, *Kommentar zu Spinoza's Ethik* [Leipzig, 1928], pp. 234–235; H. Wolfson,
The Philosophy of Spinoza [New York, 1969], vol. 1, p. 432).
    The theologians derided by Spinoza hoped to avoid by means of this distinction the suggestion
that if God acts purposively, he does so because of a need on his part.]

ignorance, thus revealing the lack of any other argument in its favor. For example, if a stone falls from the roof on somebody's head and kills him, by this method of arguing they will prove that the stone fell in order to kill the man; for if it had not fallen for this purpose by the will of God, how could so many circumstances (and there are often many coinciding circumstances) have chanced to concur? Perhaps you will reply that the event occurred because the wind was blowing and the man was walking that way. But they will persist in asking why the wind blew at that time and why the man was walking that way at that very time. If you again reply that the wind sprang up at that time because on the previous day the sea had begun to toss after a period of calm and that the man had been invited by a friend, they will again persist—for there is no end to questions—"But why did the sea toss, and why was the man invited for that time?" And so they will go on and on asking the causes of causes, until you take refuge in the will of God—that is, the sanctuary of ignorance. Similarly, when they consider the structure of the human body, they are astonished, and being ignorant of the causes of such skillful work they conclude that it is fashioned not by mechanical art but by divine or supernatural art, and is so arranged that no one part shall injure another.

As a result, he who seeks the true causes of miracles and is eager to understand the works of Nature as a scholar, and not just to gape at them like a fool, is universally considered an impious heretic and denounced by those to whom the common people bow down as interpreters of Nature and the gods. For these people know that the dispelling of ignorance would entail the disappearance of that astonishment, which is the one and only support for their argument and for safeguarding their authority. But I will leave this subject and proceed to the third point that I proposed to deal with.

When men become convinced that everything that is created is created on their behalf, they were bound to consider as the most important quality in every individual thing that which was most useful to them, and to regard as of the highest excellence all those things by which they were most benefited. Hence they came to form these abstract notions to explain the natures of things: Good, Bad, Order, Confusion, Hot, Cold, Beauty, Ugliness; and since they believed that they are free, the following abstract notions came into being: Praise, Blame, Right, Wrong. The latter I shall deal with later on after I have treated of human nature; at this point I shall briefly explain the former.

All that conduces to well-being and to the worship of God they call Good, and the contrary, Bad. And since those who do not understand the nature of things, but only imagine things, make no affirmative judgments about things themselves and mistake their imagination for intellect, they are firmly convinced that there is order in things, ignorant as they are of things and of their own nature. For when things are in such arrangement that, being presented to us through our senses, we can readily picture them and thus readily remember them, we say that they are well arranged; if the contrary, we say that they are ill arranged, or confused. And since those things we can readily picture we find pleasing compared with other things, men prefer order to confusion, as though order were something in Nature other than what is relative to our imagination. And they say that God has created all things in an orderly way, without realizing that they are thus attributing human imagination to God—unless perchance they mean that God, out of consideration for the human imagination, arranged all things in the way that men could most easily imagine. And perhaps they will find no obstacle in the fact that there are any number of things that far surpass our imagination, and a considerable number that confuse the imagination because of its weakness.

But I have devoted enough time to this. Other notions, too, are nothing but modes of imagining whereby the imagination is affected in various ways, and yet the ignorant consider them as important attributes of things because they believe—as I have said—that all things were made on their behalf, and they call a thing's nature good or bad, healthy or rotten and corrupt, according to its effect on them. For instance, if the motion communicated to our nervous system by objects presented through our eyes is conducive to our feeling of well-being, the objects which are its cause are said to be beautiful, while the objects which provoke a contrary motion are called ugly. Those things that we sense through the nose are called fragrant or fetid; through the tongue, sweet or bitter, tasty or tasteless; those that we sense by touch are called hard or soft, rough or smooth, and so on. Finally, those that we sense through our ears are said to give forth noise, sound, or harmony, the last of which has driven men to such madness that they used to believe that even God delights in harmony. There are philosophers who have convinced themselves that the motions of the heavens give rise to harmony. All this goes to show that everyone's judgment is a function of the disposition of his brain, or rather, that he mistakes for reality the way his imagination is affected. Hence it is no wonder—as we should note in passing—that we find so many controversies arising among men, resulting finally in skepticism. For although human bodies agree in many respects, there are very many differences, and so one man thinks good what another thinks bad; what to one man is well ordered, to another is confused; what to one is pleasing, to another is displeasing, and so forth. I say no more here because this is not the place to treat at length of this subject, and also because all are well acquainted with it from experience. Everybody knows those sayings: "So many heads, so many opinions," "everyone is wise in his own sight," "brains differ as much as palates," all of which show clearly that men's judgment is a function of the disposition of the brain, and they are guided by imagination rather than intellect. For if men understood things, all that I have put forward would be found, if not attractive, at any rate convincing, as Mathematics attests.

We see therefore that all the notions whereby the common people are wont to explain Nature are merely modes of imagining, and denote not the nature of anything but only the constitution of the imagination. And because these notions have names as if they were the names of entities existing independently of the imagination I call them "entities of imagination" [*entia imaginationis*] rather than "entities of reason" [*entia rationis*]. So all arguments drawn from such notions against me can be easily refuted. For many are wont to argue on the following lines: If everything has followed from the necessity of God's most perfect nature, why does Nature display so many imperfections, such as rottenness to the point of putridity, nauseating ugliness, confusion, evil, sin, and so on? But, as I have just pointed out, they are easily refuted. For the perfection of things should be measured solely from their own nature and power; nor are things more or less perfect to the extent that they please or offend human senses, serve or oppose human interests. As to those who ask why God did not create men in such a way that they should be governed solely by reason, I make only this reply, that he lacked not material for creating all things from the highest to the lowest degree of perfection; or, to speak more accurately, the laws of his nature were so comprehensive as to suffice for the production of everything that can be conceived by an infinite intellect, as I proved in Proposition 16.

These are the misconceptions which I undertook to deal with at this point. Any other misconception of this kind can be corrected by everyone with a little reflection.

PART II
OF THE NATURE AND ORIGIN OF THE MIND

I now pass on to the explication of those things that must necessarily have followed from the essence of God, the eternal and infinite Being; not indeed all of them — for we proved in Proposition 16, Part I that from his essence there must follow infinite things in infinite ways — but only those things that can lead us as it were by the hand to the knowledge of the human mind and its utmost blessedness.

Definitions

1. By "body" I understand a mode that expresses in a definite and determinate way God's essence insofar as he is considered as an extended thing. (See Cor. Pr. 25, I.)

2. I say that there pertains to the essence of a thing that which, when granted, the thing is necessarily posited, and by the annulling of which the thing is necessarily annulled; or that without which the thing can neither be nor be conceived, and, vice versa, that which cannot be or be conceived without the thing.

3. By idea I understand a conception of the Mind which the Mind forms because it is a thinking thing.

Exp   I say "conception" rather than "perception" because the term perception seems to indicate that the Mind is passive to its object whereas conception seems to express an activity of the Mind.

4. By an adequate idea I mean an idea which, insofar as it is considered in itself without relation to its object, has all the properties, that is, intrinsic characteristics, of a true idea [*ideatum*].

Exp   I say "intrinsic" so as to exclude the extrinsic characteristic — to wit the agreement of the idea with that of which it is an idea.

5. Duration is the indefinite continuance of existing.

Exp I say "indefinite" because it can in no wise be determined through the nature of the existing thing, nor again by the thing's efficient cause which necessarily posits, but does not annul, the existence of the thing.

6. By reality and perfection I mean the same thing.

7. By individual things [*res singulares*] I mean things that are finite and have a determinate existence. If several individual things concur in one act in such a way as to be all together the simultaneous cause of one effect, I consider them all, in that respect, as one individual.

Axioms

1. The essence of man does not involve necessary existence; that is, from the order of Nature it is equally possible that a certain man exists or does not exist.

2. Man thinks.

3. Modes of thinking such as love, desire, or whatever emotions are designated by name, do not occur unless there is in the same individual the idea of the thing loved, desired, etc. But the idea can be without any other mode of thinking.

4. We feel a certain body to be affected in many ways.

5. We do not feel or perceive any individual things except bodies and modes of thinking. [N.B.: For Postulates, see after Proposition 13.]

P1 *Thought is an attribute of God; i.e., God is a thinking thing.*

Proof Individual thoughts, or this and that thought, are modes expressing the nature of God in a definite and determinate way (Cor. Pr. 25, I). Therefore, there belongs to God (Def. 5, I) an attribute the conception of which is involved in all individual thoughts, and through which they are conceived. Thought, therefore, is one of God's infinite attributes, expressing the eternal and infinite essence of God (Def. 6, I); that is, God is a thinking thing.

Schol This Proposition is also evident from the fact that we can conceive of an infinite thinking being. For the more things a thinking being can think, the more reality or perfection we conceive it to have. Therefore, a being that can think infinite things in infinite ways is by virtue of its thinking necessarily infinite. Since therefore by merely considering Thought we conceive an infinite being, Thought is necessarily one of the infinite attributes of God (Defs. 4 and 6, I), as we set out to prove.

P2 *Extension is an attribute of God; i.e., God is an extended thing.*

Proof This Proposition is proved in the same way as the preceding proposition.

P3 *In God there is necessarily the idea both of his essence and of everything that necessarily follows from his essence.*

Proof For God can (Pr. 1, II) think infinite things in infinite ways, or (what is the same thing, by Pr. 16, I) can form the idea of his own essence and of everything that necessarily follows from it. But all that is in God's power necessarily exists (Pr. 35, I). Therefore, such an idea necessarily exists, and only in God (Pr. 15, I).

Schol By God's power the common people understand free will and God's right over all things that are, which things are therefore commonly considered as contingent. They say that God has power to destroy everything and bring it to nothing. Furthermore, they frequently compare God's power with that of kings. But this doctrine we have refuted in Cors. 1 and 2, Pr. 32, I; and in Pr. 16, I, we proved that God acts by the same necessity whereby he understands himself; that is, just as it follows from the necessity of the divine Nature (as is universally agreed) that God understands himself, by that same necessity it also follows that God acts infinitely in infinite ways. Again, we showed in Pr. 34, I that God's power is nothing but God's essence in action, and so it is as impossible for us to conceive that God does not act as that God does not exist. Furthermore if one wished to pursue the matter, I could easily show here that the power that common people assign to God is not only a human power (which shows that they conceive God as a man or like a man) but also involves negation of power. But I am reluctant to hold forth so often on the same subject. I merely request the reader most earnestly to reflect again and again on what we said on this subject in Part I from Proposition 16 to the end. For nobody will rightly apprehend what I am trying to say unless he takes great care not to confuse God's power with a king's human power or right.

P4 *The idea of God, from which infinite things follow in infinite ways, must be one, and one only.*

Proof Infinite intellect comprehends nothing but the attributes of God and his affections (Pr. 30, I). But God is one, and one only (Cor. 1, Pr. 14, I). Therefore, the idea of God, from which infinite things follow in infinite ways, must be one, and one only.

P5 *The formal being[1] of ideas recognizes God as its cause only insofar as he is considered as a thinking thing, and not insofar as he is explicated by any other attribute; that is, the ideas both of God's attributes and of individual things recognize as their efficient cause not the things of which they are ideas, that is, the things perceived, but God himself insofar as he is a thinking thing.*

Proof This is evident from Pr. 3, II. For there our conclusion that God can form the idea of his own essence and of everything that necessarily follows therefrom was inferred solely from God's being a thinking thing, and not from his being the object of his own idea. Therefore, the formal being of ideas recognizes God as its cause insofar as he is a thinking thing. But there is another proof, as follows. The formal being of ideas is a mode of thinking (as is self-evident); that is (Cor. Pr. 25, I), a mode which expresses in a definite manner the nature of God insofar as he is a thinking thing, and so does not involve (Pr. 10, I) the conception of any other attribute of God. Consequently (Ax. 4, I), it is the effect of no other attribute but thought; and so the formal being of ideas recognizes God as its cause only insofar as he is considered as a thinking thing.

---

[1] [I.e., their existence as ideas.—M.L.M.]

P6   *The modes of any attribute have God for their cause only insofar as he is considered under that attribute, and not insofar as he is considered under any other attribute.*

Proof   Each attribute is conceived through itself independently of any other (Pr. 10, I). Therefore, the modes of any attribute involve the conception of their own attribute, and not that of any other. Therefore, they have God for their cause only insofar as he is considered under the attribute of which they are modes, and not insofar as he is considered under any other attribute (Ax. 4, I).

Cor   Hence it follows that the formal being of things that are not modes of thinking does not follow from the nature of God by reason of his first having known them; rather, the objects of ideas follow and are inferred from their own attributes in the same way and by the same necessity as we have shown ideas to follow from the attribute of Thought.

P7   *The order and connection of ideas is the same as the order and connection of things.*

Proof   This is evident from Ax. 4, I; for the idea of what is caused depends on the knowledge of the cause of which it is the effect.

Cor   Hence it follows that God's power of thinking is on par with his power of acting. That is, whatever follows formally from the infinite nature of God, all this follows from the idea of God as an object of thought in God according to the same order and connection.

Schol   At this point, before proceeding further, we should recall to mind what I have demonstrated above—that whatever can be perceived by infinite intellect as constituting the essence of substance pertains entirely to the one sole substance. Consequently, thinking substance and extended substance are one and the same substance, comprehended now under this attribute, now under that. So, too, a mode of Extension and the idea of that mode are one and the same thing, expressed in two ways. This truth seems to have been glimpsed by some of the Hebrews,[2] who hold that God, God's intellect, and the things understood by God are one and the same. For example, a circle existing in Nature and the idea of the existing circle—which is also in God—are one and the same thing, explicated through different attributes. And so, whether we conceive Nature under the attribute of Extension or under the attribute of Thought or under any other attribute, we find one and the same order, or one and the same connection of causes—that is, the same things following one another. When I said that God is the cause, e.g., of the idea of a circle only insofar as he is a thinking thing, and of a circle only insofar as he is an extended thing, my reason was simply this, that the formal being of the idea of a circle can be perceived only through another mode of thinking as its proximate

---

[2] [The reference is most likely to Moses Maimonides, *The Guide of the Perplexed*, Part 1, Chapter 68.—S.F.]

cause, and that mode through another, and so ad infinitum, with the result that as long as things are considered as modes of thought, we must explicate the order of the whole of Nature, or the connection of causes, through the attribute of Thought alone; and insofar as things are considered as modes of Extension, again the order of the whole of Nature must be explicated through the attribute of Extension only. The same applies to other attributes. Therefore God, insofar as he consists of infinite attributes, is in fact the cause of things as they are in themselves. For the present, I cannot give a clearer explanation.

P8   *The ideas of nonexisting individual things or modes must be comprehended in the infinite idea of God in the same way as the formal essences of individual things or modes are contained in the attributes of God.*

Proof   This proposition is obvious from the preceding one, but may be understood more clearly from the preceding Scholium.

Cor   Hence it follows that as long as individual things do not exist except insofar as they are comprehended in the attributes of God, their being as objects of thought—that is, their ideas—do not exist except insofar as the infinite idea of God exists; and when individual things are said to exist not only insofar as they are comprehended in the attributes of God but also insofar as they are said to have duration, their ideas also will involve the existence through which they are said to have duration.

Schol   Should anyone want an example for a clearer understanding of this matter, I can think of none at all that would adequately explicate the point with which I am here dealing, for it has no parallel. Still, I shall try to illustrate it as best I can. The nature of a circle is such that the rectangles formed from the segments of its intersecting chords are equal. Hence an infinite number of equal rectangles are contained in a circle, but none of them can be said to exist except insofar as the circle exists, nor again can the idea of any one of these rectangles be said to exist except insofar as it is comprehended in the idea of the 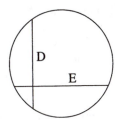 circle. Now of this infinite number of intersecting chords let two, E and D, exist. Now indeed their ideas also exist not only insofar as they are merely comprehended in the idea of the circle but also insofar as they involve the existence of those rectangles, with the result that they are distinguished from the other ideas of the other rectangles.

P9   *The idea of an individual thing existing in actuality has God for its cause not insofar as he is infinite but insofar as he is considered as affected by another idea of a thing existing in actuality, of which God is the cause insofar as he is affected by a third idea, and so ad infinitum.*

Proof   The idea of an individual actually existing thing is an individual mode of thinking distinct from other modes (Cor. and Schol. Pr. 8, II), and so (Pr. 6, II) it has God as its cause only insofar as he is a thinking thing. But not (Pr. 28, I) insofar as he is a thinking thing absolutely, but insofar as he is considered as affected by another definite mode of thinking. And of this latter God is also the cause insofar as he is affected by another definite mode of thinking, and so ad infinitum. But the order and connection of ideas is the same as the order and connection of causes (Pr. 7, II). Therefore, an individual idea is caused by another idea; i.e., God insofar as he is considered as affected by another idea. And this last idea is caused by God, insofar as he is affected by yet another idea, and so ad infinitum.

Cor   Whatsoever happens in the individual object of any idea, knowledge of it is in God only insofar as he has the idea of that object.

Proof   Whatsoever happens in the object of any idea, the idea of it is in God (Pr. 3, II) not insofar as he is infinite, but insofar as he is considered as affected by another idea of an individual thing (preceding Pr.). But the order and connection of ideas is the same as the order and connection of things (Pr. 7, II). Therefore, the knowledge of what happens in an individual object is in God only insofar as he has the idea of that object.

P10   *The being of substance does not pertain to the essence of man; i.e., substance does not constitute the form [forma] of man.*

Proof   The being of substance involves necessary existence (Pr. 7, I). So if the being of substance pertained to the essence of man, man would necessarily be granted together with the granting of substance (Def. 2, II) and consequently man would necessarily exist, which is absurd (Ax. 1, II). Therefore . . . etc.

Schol   This Proposition is also proved from Pr. 5, I, which states that there cannot be two substances of the same nature. Now since many men can exist, that which constitutes the form of man is not the being of substance. This Proposition is furthermore evident from the other properties of substance—that substance is by its own nature infinite, immutable, indivisible, etc., as everyone can easily see.

Cor   Hence it follows that the essence of man is constituted by definite modifications of the attributes of God.

Proof   For the being of substance does not pertain to the essence of man (preceding Pr.), which must therefore be something that is in God, and which can neither be nor be conceived without God; i.e., an affection or mode (Cor. Pr. 25, I) which expresses the nature of God in a definite and determinate way.

Schol   All must surely admit that nothing can be or be conceived without God. For all are agreed that God is the sole cause of all things, both of their essence and of their existence; that is, God is the cause of things not only in respect of their coming into being [*secundum fieri*], as they say, but also in respect of their being. But at the same time many assert that that without which a thing can neither be nor be conceived pertains to the essence of the thing, and so they believe that either the nature of God pertains to the essence of created things or that created things can either be or be conceived without God; or else, more probably, they hold no consistent opinion. I think that the reason for this is their failure to observe the proper order of philosophical inquiry. For the divine nature, which they should have considered before all else—it being prior both in cognition and in Nature—they have taken to be last in the order of cognition, and the things that are called objects of sense they have taken as prior to everything. Hence it has come about that in considering natural phenomena, they have completely disregarded the divine nature. And when thereafter they turned to the contemplation of the divine nature, they could find no place in their thinking for those fictions on which they had built their natural science, since these fictions were of no avail in attaining knowledge of the divine nature. So it is little wonder that they have contradicted themselves on all sides.

But I pass over these points, for my present purpose is restricted to explaining why I have not said that that without which a thing can neither be nor be perceived pertains to the essence of the thing. My reason is that individual things can neither be nor be conceived without God, and yet God does not pertain to their essence. But I did say that that necessarily constitutes the essence of a thing which, when posited, posits the thing, and by the annulling of which the thing is annulled; i.e., that without which the thing can neither be nor be conceived, and vice versa, that which can neither be nor be conceived without the thing.

P11 *That which constitutes the actual being of the human mind is basically nothing else but the idea of an individual actually existing thing.*

Proof The essence of man (Cor. Pr. 10, II) is constituted by definite modes of the attributes of God, to wit (Ax. 2, II), modes of thinking. Of all these modes the idea is prior in nature (Ax. 3, II), and when the idea is granted, the other modes— modes to which the idea is prior by nature—must be in the same individual (Ax. 3, II). And so the idea is that which basically constitutes the being of the human mind. But not the idea of a nonexisting thing; for then (Cor. Pr. 8, II) the idea itself could not be said to exist. Therefore, it is the idea of an actually existing thing. But not the idea of an infinite thing, for an infinite thing (Prs. 21 and 22, I) must always necessarily exist, and this is absurd (Ax. 1, II). Therefore, that which first constitutes the actual being of the human mind is the idea of an individual actually existing thing.

Cor Hence it follows that the human mind is part of the infinite intellect of God; and therefore when we say that the human mind perceives this or that, we are saying nothing else but this: that God—not insofar as he is infinite but insofar as he is explicated through the nature of the human mind, that is, insofar as he constitutes the essence of the human mind—has this or that idea. And when we say that God has this or that idea not only insofar as he constitutes the essence of the human mind but also insofar as he has the idea of another thing simultaneously with the human mind, then we are saying that the human mind perceives a thing partially or inadequately.

Schol   At this point our readers will no doubt find themselves in some difficulty and will think of many things that will give them pause. So I ask them to proceed slowly step by step with me, and to postpone judgment until they have read to the end.

P12   *Whatever happens in the object of the idea constituting the human mind is bound to be perceived by the human mind; i.e., the idea of that thing will neces-sarily be in the human mind. That is to say, if the object of the idea constituting the human mind is a body, nothing can happen in that body without its being perceived by the mind.*

Proof   Whatever happens in the object of any idea, knowledge thereof is neces-sarily in God (Cor. Pr. 9, II) insofar as he is considered as affected by the idea of that object; that is (Pr. 11, II), insofar as he constitutes the mind of something. So whatever happens in the object of the idea constituting the human mind, knowl-edge thereof is necessarily in God insofar as he constitutes the nature of the hu-man mind; that is (Cor. Pr. 11, II), knowledge of that thing is necessarily in the mind; i.e., the mind perceives it.

Schol   This Proposition is also obvious, and is more clearly understood from Schol. Pr. 7, II, above.

P13   *The object of the idea constituting the human mind is the body—i.e., a def-inite mode of extension actually existing, and nothing else.*

Proof   If the body were not the object of the human mind, the ideas of the af-fections of the body would not be in God (Cor. Pr. 9, II) insofar as he constitutes our mind, but insofar as he constitutes the mind of another thing; that is (Cor. Pr. 11, II), the ideas of the affections of the body would not be in our mind. But (Ax. 4, II) we do have ideas of the affections of a body. Therefore, the object of the idea constituting the human mind is a body, a body actually existing (Pr. 11, II). Again, if there were another object of the mind apart from the body, since nothing exists from which some effect does not follow (Pr. 36, I), there would necessarily have to be in our mind the idea of some effect of it (Pr. 12, II). But (Ax. 5, II) there is no such idea. Therefore, the object of our mind is an existing body, and nothing else.

Cor   Hence it follows that man consists of mind and body, and the human body exists according as we sense it.

Schol   From the above we understand not only that the human Mind is united to the Body but also what is to be understood by the union of Mind and Body. But nobody can understand this union adequately or distinctly unless he first gains ad-equate knowledge of the nature of our body. For what we have so far demonstrated is of quite general application, and applies to men no more than to other indi-viduals, which are all animate, albeit in different degrees. For there is necessarily in God an idea of each thing whatever, of which idea God is the cause in the same way as he is the cause of the idea of the human body. And so whatever we have asserted of the idea of the human body must necessarily be asserted of the idea of each thing. Yet we cannot deny, too, that ideas differ among themselves as do their objects, and that one is more excellent and contains more reality than another, just as the object of one idea is more excellent than that of another and contains more reality. Therefore, in order to determine the difference between the human mind and others and in what way it surpasses them, we have to know the nature of its object (as we have said), that is, the nature of the human body. Now I cannot here explain this nature, nor is it essential for the points that I intend to demonstrate. But I will make this general assertion, that in proportion as a body is more apt than other bodies to act or be acted upon simultaneously in many ways, so is its mind more apt than other minds to perceive many things simultaneously; and in proportion as the actions of one body depend on itself alone and the less that other bodies concur with it in its actions, the more apt is its mind to understand distinctly. From this we can realize the superiority of one mind over others, and we can furthermore see why we have only a very confused knowledge of our body, and many other facts which I shall deduce from this basis in what follows. Therefore, I have thought it worthwhile to explicate and demonstrate these things more carefully. To this end there must be a brief preface concerning the nature of bodies.

Axiom 1   All bodies are either in motion or at rest.

Axiom 2   Each single body can move at varying speeds.

Lemma 1   Bodies are distinguished from one another in respect of motion-and-rest, quickness and slowness, and not in respect of substance.

Proof   The first part of this Lemma I take to be self-evident. As to bodies not being distinguished in respect of substance, this is evident from both Pr. 5 and Pr. 8, Part I, and still more clearly from Schol. Pr. 15, Part I.

Lemma 2   All bodies agree in certain respects.

Proof   All bodies agree in this, that they involve the conception of one and the same attribute (Def. 1, II), and also in that they may move at varying speeds, and may be absolutely in motion or absolutely at rest.

Lemma 3   A body in motion or at rest must have been determined to motion or rest by another body, which likewise has been determined to motion or rest by another body, and that body by another, and so ad infinitum.

Proof   Bodies are individual things (Def. 1, II) which are distinguished from one another in respect of motion-and-rest (Lemma 1), and so (Pr. 28, I) each body must have been determined to motion or rest by another individual thing, namely, another body (Pr. 6, II), which is also in motion or at rest (Ax. 1). But this body again—by the same reasoning—could not have been in motion or at rest unless it had been determined to motion or rest by another body, and this body again—by the same reasoning—by another body, and so on, ad infinitum.

Cor   Hence it follows that a body in motion will continue to move until it is determined to rest by another body, and a body at rest continues to be at rest until it is determined to move by another body. This, too, is self-evident; for when I suppose, for example, that a body A is at rest and I give no consideration to other moving bodies, I can assert nothing about body A but that it is at rest. Now if it should thereafter happen that body A is in motion, this surely could not have resulted from the fact that it was at rest; for from that fact nothing else could have followed than that body A should be at rest. If on the other hand A were supposed to be in motion, as long as we consider only A, we can affirm nothing of it but that it is in motion. If it should thereafter happen that A should be at rest, this surely could not have resulted from its previous motion; for from its motion nothing else could have followed but that A was in motion. So this comes about from a thing that was not in A, namely, an external cause by which the moving body A was determined to rest.

Axiom 1   All the ways in which a body is affected by another body follow from the nature of the affected body together with the nature of the body affecting it, so that one and the same body may move in various ways in accordance with the various natures of the bodies causing its motion; and, on the other hand, different bodies may be caused to move in different ways by one and the same body.

Axiom 2   When a moving body collides with a body at rest and is unable to cause it to move, it is reflected so as to continue its motion, and the angle between the

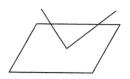

line of motion of the reflection and the plane of the body at rest with which it has collided is equal to the angle between the line of incidence of motion and the said plane.

So far we have been discussing the simplest bodies, those which are distinguished from one another solely by motion-and-rest, quickness and slowness. Now let us advance to composite bodies.

Definition   When a number of bodies of the same or different magnitude form close contact with one another through the pressure of other bodies upon them, or if they are moving at the same or different rates of speed so as to preserve an unvarying relation of movement among themselves, these bodies are said to be united with one another and all together to form one body or individual thing, which is distinguished from other things through this union of bodies.

Axiom 3   The degree of difficulty with which the parts of an individual thing or composite body can be made to change their position and consequently the degree of difficulty with which the individual takes on different shapes is proportional to the extent of the surface areas along which they are in close contact. Hence bodies whose parts maintain close contact along large areas of their surfaces I term hard; those whose parts maintain contact along small surface areas I term soft; while those whose parts are in a state of motion among themselves I term liquid.

Lemma 4   If from a body, or an individual thing composed of a number of bodies, certain bodies are separated, and at the same time a like number of other bodies of the same nature take their place, the individual thing will retain its nature as before, without any change in its form [*forma*].

Proof   Bodies are not distinguished in respect of substance (Lemma 1). That which constitutes the form of the individual thing consists in a union of bodies (preceding definition). But this union, by hypothesis, is retained in spite of the continuous change of component bodies. Therefore, the individual thing will retain its own nature as before, both in respect of substance and of mode.

Lemma 5   If the parts of an individual thing become greater or smaller, but so proportionately that they all preserve the same mutual relation of motion-and-rest as before, the individual thing will likewise retain its own nature as before without any change in its form.

Proof   The reasoning is the same as in the preceding Lemma.

Lemma 6   If certain bodies composing an individual thing are made to change the existing direction of their motion, but in such a way that they can continue their motion and keep the same mutual relation as before, the individual thing will likewise preserve its own nature without any change of form.

Proof   This is evident; for, by hypothesis, the individual thing retains all that we, in defining it, asserted as constituting its form.

Lemma 7   Furthermore, the individual thing so composed retains its own nature, whether as a whole it is moving or at rest, and in whatever direction it moves, provided that each constituent part retains its own motion and continues to communicate this motion to the other parts.

Proof   This is evident from its definition, which you will find preceding Lemma 4.

Schol   We thus see how a composite individual can be affected in many ways and yet preserve its nature. Now previously we have conceived an individual thing composed solely of bodies distinguished from one another only by motion-and-rest and speed of movement; that is, an individual thing composed of the simplest bodies. If we now conceive another individual thing composed of several individual things of different natures, we shall find that this can be affected in many other ways while still preserving its nature. For since each one of its parts is composed of several bodies, each single part can therefore (preceding Lemma), without any change in its nature, move with varying degrees of speed and consequently communicate its own motion to other parts with varying degrees of speed. Now if we go on to conceive a third kind of individual thing composed of this second kind, we shall find that it can be affected in many other ways without any change in its form. If we thus continue to infinity, we shall readily conceive the whole of Nature as one individual whose parts—that is, all the constituent bodies—vary in infinite ways without any change in the individual as a whole.

If my intention had been to write a full treatise on body, I should have had to expand my explications and demonstrations. But I have already declared a different intention, and the only reason for my dealing with this subject is that I may readily deduce therefrom what I have set out to prove.

Postulates

1. The human body is composed of very many individual parts of different natures, each of which is extremely complex.
2. Of the individual components of the human body, some are liquid, some are soft, and some are hard.
3. The individual components of the human body, and consequently the human body itself, are affected by external bodies in a great many ways.
4. The human body needs for its preservation a great many other bodies, by which, as it were [*quasi*], it is continually regenerated.
5. When a liquid part of the human body is determined by an external body to impinge frequently on another part which is soft, it changes the surface of that part and impresses on it certain traces of the external body acting upon it.
6. The human body can move external bodies and dispose them in a great many ways.

P14   *The human mind is capable of perceiving a great many things, and this capacity will vary in proportion to the variety of states which its body can assume.*

Proof   The human body (Posts. 3 and 6) is affected by external bodies in a great many ways and is so structured that it can affect external bodies in a great many ways. But the human mind must perceive all that happens in the human body (Pr. 12, II). Therefore, the human mind is capable of perceiving very many things, and . . . etc.

P15   *The idea which constitutes the formal being of the human mind is not simple, but composed of very many ideas.*

Proof   The idea which constitutes the formal being of the human mind is the idea of the body (Pr. 13, II), which is composed of a great number of very composite individual parts (Postulate 1). But in God there is necessarily the idea of every individual component part (Cor. Pr. 8, II). Therefore (Pr. 7, II), the idea of the human body is composed of these many ideas of the component parts.

P16   *The idea of any mode wherein the human body is affected by external bodies must involve the nature of the human body together with the nature of the external body.*

Proof   All the modes wherein a body is affected follow from the nature of the body affected together with the nature of the affecting body (Ax. 1 after Cor. Lemma 3). Therefore, the idea of these modes will necessarily involve the nature of both bodies (Ax. 4, I). So the idea of any mode wherein the human body is affected by an external body involves the nature of the human body and the external body.

Cor 1   Hence it follows that the human mind perceives the nature of very many bodies along with the nature of its own body.

Cor 2   Secondly, the ideas that we have of external bodies indicate the constitution of our own body more than the nature of external bodies. This I have explained with many examples in Appendix, Part I.

P17   *If the human body is affected in a way [modo] that involves the nature of some external body, the human mind will regard that same external body as actually existing, or as present to itself, until the human body undergoes a further modification which excludes the existence or presence of the said body.*

Proof   This is evident; for as long as the human body is thus affected, so long will the human mind (Pr. 12, II) regard this affection of the body; that is (by the preceding Proposition), so long will it have the idea of a mode existing in actuality, an idea involving the nature of an external body; that is, an idea which does not exclude but posits the existence or presence of the nature of the external body. So the mind (Cor. 1 of the preceding proposition) will regard the external body as actually existing, or as present, until . . . etc.

Cor   The mind is able to regard as present external bodies by which the human body has been once affected, even if they do not exist and are not present.

Proof   When external bodies so determine the fluid parts of the human body that these frequently impinge on the softer parts, they change the surfaces of these softer parts (Post. 5). Hence it comes about (Ax. 2 after Cor. Lemma 3) that the fluid parts are reflected therefrom in a manner different from what was previously the case; and thereafter, again coming into contact with the said changed surfaces in the course of their own spontaneous motion, they are reflected in the same way as when they were impelled toward those surfaces by external bodies. Consequently, in continuing this reflected motion they affect the human body in the same manner, which manner will again be the object of thought in the mind (Pr. 12, II); that is (Pr. 17, II), the mind will again regard the external body as present. This will be repeated whenever the fluid parts of the human body come into contact with those same surfaces in the course of their own spontaneous motion. Therefore, although the external bodies by which the human body has once been affected may no longer exist, the mind will regard them as present whenever this activity of the body is repeated.

Schol   So we see how it comes about that we regard as present things which are not so, as often happens. Now it is possible that there are other causes for this fact, but it is enough for me at this point to have indicated one cause through which I can explicate the matter just as if I had demonstrated it through its true cause. Yet I do not think that I am far from the truth, since all the postulates that I have assumed contain scarcely anything inconsistent with experience; and after demonstrating that the human body exists just as we sense it (Cor. Pr. 13, II), we may not doubt experience.

    In addition (preceding Cor. and Cor. 2 Pr. 16, II), this gives a clear understanding of the difference between the idea, e.g., of Peter which constitutes the essence of Peter's mind, and on the other hand the idea of Peter which is in another man, say Paul. The former directly explicates the essence of Peter's body, and does not involve existence except as long as Peter exists. The latter indicates the constitution of Paul's body rather than the nature of Peter; and so, while that constitution of Paul's body continues to be, Paul's mind will regard Peter as present to him although Peter may not be in existence. Further, to retain the usual terminology, we will assign the word "images" [*imagines*] to those affections of the human body the ideas of which set forth external bodies as if they were present to us, although they do not represent shapes. And when the mind regards bodies in this way, we shall say that it "imagines" [*imaginari*].

At this point, to begin my analysis of error, I should like you to note that the imaginations of the mind, looked at in themselves, contain no error; i.e., the mind does not err from the fact that it imagines, but only insofar as it is considered to lack the idea which excludes the existence of those things which it imagines to be present to itself. For if the mind, in imagining nonexisting things to be present to it, knew at the same time that those things did not exist in fact, it would surely impute this power of imagining not to the defect but to the strength of its own nature, especially if this faculty of imagining were to depend solely on its own nature; that is (Def. 7, I), if this faculty of imagining were free.

P18   *If the human body has once been affected by two or more bodies at the same time, when the mind afterward imagines one of them, it will straightway remember the others too.*

Proof   The mind imagines (preceding Cor.) any given body for the following reason, that the human body is affected and conditioned by the impressions of an external body in the same way as it was affected when certain of its parts were acted upon by the external body. But, by hypothesis, the human mind was at that time conditioned in such a way that the mind imagined two bodies at the same time. Therefore, it will now also imagine two bodies at the same time, and the mind, in imagining one of them, will straightway remember the other as well.

Schol   Hence we clearly understand what memory is. It is simply a linking of ideas involving the nature of things outside the human body, a linking which occurs in the mind parallel to the order and linking of the affections of the human body. I say, firstly, that it is only the linking of those ideas that involve the nature of things outside the human body, not of those ideas that explicate the nature of the said things. For they are in fact (Pr. 16, II) ideas of the affections of the human body which involve the nature both of the human body and of external bodies. Secondly, my purpose in saying that this linking occurs in accordance with the order and linking of the affections of the human body is to distinguish it from the linking of ideas in accordance with the order of the intellect whereby the mind perceives things through their first causes, and which is the same in all men.

Furthermore, from this we clearly understand why the mind, from thinking of one thing, should straightway pass on to thinking of another thing which has no likeness to the first. For example, from thinking of the word "pomum" [apple] a Roman will straightway fall to thinking of the fruit, which has no likeness to that articulated sound nor anything in common with it other than that the man's body has often been affected by them both; that is, the man has often heard the word "pomum" while seeing the fruit. So everyone will pass on from one thought to another according as habit in each case has arranged the images in his body. A soldier, for example, seeing the tracks of a horse in the sand will straightway pass on from thinking of the horse to thinking of the rider, and then thinking of war, and so on. But a peasant, from thinking of a horse, will pass on to thinking of a plough, and of a field, and so on. So every person will pass on from thinking of one thing to thinking of another according as he is in the habit of joining together and linking the images of things in various ways.

P19 *The human mind has no knowledge of the body, nor does it know it to exist, except through ideas of the affections by which the body is affected.*

Proof   The human mind is the very idea or knowledge of the human body (Pr. 13, II), and this idea is in God (Pr. 9, II) insofar as he is considered as affected by another idea of a particular thing; or, since (Post. 4) the human body needs very many other bodies by which it is continually regenerated, and the order and connection of ideas is the same (Pr. 7, II) as the order and connection of causes, this idea is in God insofar as he is considered as affected by the ideas of numerous particular things. Therefore, God has the idea of the human body, or knows the human body, insofar as he is affected by numerous other ideas, and not insofar as he constitutes the nature of the human mind; that is (Cor. Pr. 11, II), the human mind does not know the human body. But the ideas of the affections of the body are in God insofar as he does constitute the nature of human mind; i.e., the human mind perceives these affections (Pr. 12, II) and consequently perceives the human body (Pr. 16, II), and perceives it as actually existing (Pr. 17, II). Therefore, it is only to that extent that the human mind perceives the human body.

P20 *There is also in God the idea or knowledge of the human mind, and this follows in God and is related to God in the same way as the idea or knowledge of the human body.*

Proof   Thought is an attribute of God (Pr. 1, II), and so (Pr. 3, II) the idea of both Thought and its affections—and consequently of the human mind as well—must necessarily be in God. Now this idea or knowledge of the mind does not follow in God insofar as he is infinite, but insofar as he is affected by another idea of a particular thing (Pr. 9, II). But the order and connection of ideas is the same as the order and connection of causes (Pr. 7, II). Therefore, the idea or knowledge of the mind follows in God and is related to God in the same way as the idea or knowledge of the body.

P21 *This idea of the mind is united to the mind in the same way as the mind is united to the body.*

Proof   That the mind is united to the body we have shown from the fact that the body is the object of the mind (Prs. 12 and 13, II), and so by the same reasoning the idea of the mind must be united to its object—that is, to the mind itself—in the same way as the mind is united to the body.

Schol This proposition is understood far more clearly from Schol. Pr. 7, II. There we showed that the idea of the body and the body itself—that is (Pr. 13, II), mind and body—are one and the same individual thing, conceived now under the attribute of Thought and now under the attribute of Extension. Therefore, the idea of the mind and the mind itself are one and the same thing, conceived under one and the same attribute, namely, Thought. The idea of the mind, I repeat, and the mind itself follow in God by the same necessity and from the same power of thought. For in fact the idea of the mind—that is, the idea of an idea—is nothing other than the form [*forma*] of the idea insofar as the idea is considered as a mode of thinking without relation to its object. For as soon as anyone knows something, by that very fact he knows that he knows, and at the same time he knows that he knows that he knows, and so on ad infinitum. But I will deal with this subject later.

P22 *The human mind perceives not only the affections of the body but also the ideas of these affections.*

Proof The ideas of ideas of affections follow in God and are related to God in the same way as ideas of affections, which can be proved in the same manner as Pr. 20, II. But the ideas of affections of the body are in the human mind (Pr. 12, II); that is (Cor. Pr. 11, II), in God insofar as he constitutes the essence of the human mind. Therefore, the ideas of these ideas will be in God insofar as he has knowledge or the idea of the human mind; that is (Pr. 21, II), they will be in the human mind itself, which therefore perceives not only the affections of the body but also the ideas of these affections.

P23 *The mind does not know itself except insofar as it perceives ideas of affections of the body.*

Proof The idea or knowledge of the mind (Pr. 20, II) follows in God and is related to God in the same way as the idea or knowledge of the body. But since (Pr. 19, II) the human mind does not know the human body—that is (Cor. Pr. 11, II), since the knowledge of the human body is not related to God insofar as he constitutes the nature of the human mind—therefore, neither is knowledge of the mind related to God insofar as he constitutes the essence of the human mind. And so (Cor. Pr. 11, II) the human mind to that extent does not know itself. Again, the ideas of the affections by which the body is affected involve the nature of the human body (Pr. 16, II); that is (Pr. 13, II), they are in agreement [*conveniunt*] with the nature of the mind. Therefore, the knowledge of these ideas will necessarily involve knowledge of the mind. But (preceding Pr.) the knowledge of these ideas is in the human mind. Therefore, the human mind knows itself but only to that extent.

P24 *The human mind does not involve an adequate knowledge of the component parts of the human body.*

Proof   The component parts of the human body do not pertain to the essence of the body itself save insofar as they preserve an unvarying relation of motion with one another (Def. after Cor. Lemma 3), and not insofar as they can be considered as individual things apart from their relation to the human body. For the parts of the human body (Post. 1) are very composite individual things, whose parts can be separated from the human body (Lemma 4) without impairing in any way its nature and specific reality [*forma*], and can establish a quite different relation of motion with other bodies (Ax. 1 after Lemma 3). Therefore (Pr. 3, II), the idea or knowledge of any component part will be in God, and will be so (Pr. 9, II) insofar as he is considered as affected by another idea of a particular thing, a particular thing which is prior in Nature's order to the part itself (Pr. 7, II). Further, the same holds good of any part of an individual component part of the human body, and so of any component part of the human body there is knowledge in God insofar as he is affected by very many ideas of things, and not insofar as he has the idea only of the human body, that is (Pr. 13, II), the idea that constitutes the nature of the human mind. So (Cor. Pr. 11, II) the human mind does not involve adequate knowledge of the component parts of the human body.

P25   *The idea of any affection of the human body does not involve an adequate knowledge of an external body.*

Proof   We have shown that the idea of an affection of the human body involves the nature of an external body insofar as the external body determines the human body in some definite way (Pr. 16, II). But insofar as the external body is an individual thing that is not related to the human body, the idea or knowledge of it is in God (Pr. 9, II) insofar as God is considered as affected by the idea of another thing which is (Pr. 7, II) prior in nature to the said external body. Therefore, an adequate knowledge of the external body is not in God insofar as he has the idea of an affection of the human body; i.e., the idea of an affection of the human body does not involve an adequate knowledge of an external body.

P26   *The human mind does not perceive any external body as actually existing except through the ideas of affections of its own body.*

Proof   If the human body is not affected in any way by an external body, then (Pr. 7, II) neither is the idea of the human body—that is (Pr. 13, II), the human mind—affected in any way by the idea of the existence of that body; i.e., it does not in any way perceive the existence of that external body. But insofar as the human body is affected in some way by an external body, to that extent it perceives the external body (Pr. 16, II, with Cor. 1).

Cor   Insofar as the human mind imagines [*imaginatur*] an external body, to that extent it does not have an adequate knowledge of it.

Proof   When the human mind regards external bodies through the ideas of affections of its own body, we say that it imagines [*imaginatur*] (see Schol. Pr. 17, II), and in no other way can the mind imagine external bodies as actually existing (preceding Pr.). Therefore, insofar as the mind imagines external bodies (Pr. 25, II), it does not have adequate knowledge of them.

P27   *The idea of any affection of the human body does not involve adequate knowledge of the human body.*

Proof   Any idea whatsoever of any affection of the human body involves the nature of the human body only to the extent that the human body is considered to be affected in some definite way (Pr. 16, II). But insofar as the human body is an individual thing that can be affected in many other ways, the idea . . . etc. (see Proof Pr. 25, II).

P28   *The ideas of the affections of the human body, insofar as they are related only to the human mind, are not clear and distinct, but confused.*

Proof   The ideas of the affections of the human body involve the nature both of external bodies and of the human body itself (Pr. 16, II), and must involve the nature not only of the human body but also of its parts. For affections are modes in which parts of the human body (Post. 3), and consequently the body as a whole, are affected. But (Prs. 24 and 25, II) an adequate knowledge of external bodies, as also of the component parts of the human body, is not in God insofar as he is considered as affected by the human mind, but insofar as he is considered as affected by other ideas. Therefore, these ideas of affections, insofar as they are related only to the human mind, are like conclusions without premises; that is, as is self-evident, confused ideas.

Schol   The idea that constitutes the nature of the human mind is likewise shown, when considered solely in itself, not to be clear and distinct, as is also the idea of the human mind and the ideas of affections of the human body insofar as they are related only to the human mind, as everyone can easily see.

P29   *The idea of the idea of any affection of the human body does not involve adequate knowledge of the human mind.*

Proof   The idea of an affection of the human body (Pr. 27, II) does not involve adequate knowledge of the body itself; in other words, it does not adequately express the nature of the body; that is (Pr. 13, II), it does not adequately agree [*convenit*] with the nature of the mind. So (Ax. 6, I) the idea of this idea does not adequately express the nature of the human mind; i.e., it does not involve an adequate knowledge of it.

Cor   Hence it follows that whenever the human mind perceives things after the common order of nature, it does not have an adequate knowledge of itself, nor of its body, nor of external bodies, but only a confused and fragmentary knowledge. For the mind does not know itself save insofar as it perceives ideas of the affections of the body (Pr. 23, II). Now it does not perceive its own body (Pr. 19, II) except through ideas of affections of the body, and also it is only through these affections that it perceives external bodies (Pr. 26, II). So insofar as it has these ideas, it has adequate knowledge neither of itself (Pr. 29, II) nor of its own body (Pr. 27, II) nor of external bodies (Pr. 25, II), but only a fragmentary [*mutilatam*] and confused knowledge (Pr. 28, II and Schol.).

Schol   I say expressly that the mind does not have an adequate knowledge, but only a confused and fragmentary knowledge, of itself, its own body, and external bodies whenever it perceives things from the common order of nature, that is, whenever it is determined externally—namely, by the fortuitous run of circumstance—to regard this or that, and not when it is determined internally, through its regarding several things at the same time, to understand their agreement, their differences, and their opposition. For whenever it is conditioned internally in this or in another way, then it sees things clearly and distinctly, as I shall later show.

P30   *We can have only a very inadequate knowledge of the duration of our body.*

Proof   The duration of our body does not depend on its essence (Ax. 1, II), nor again on the absolute nature of God (Pr. 21, I), but (Pr. 28, I) it is determined to exist and to act by causes which are also determined by other causes to exist and to act in a definite and determinate way, and these again by other causes, and so ad infinitum. Therefore, the duration of our body depends on the common order of nature and the structure of the universe. Now there is in God adequate knowledge of the structure of the universe insofar as he has ideas of all the things in the universe, and not insofar as he has only the idea of the human body (Cor. Pr. 9, II). Therefore, knowledge of the duration of our body is very inadequate in God insofar as he is considered only to constitute the nature of the human mind. That is (Cor. Pr. 11, II), this knowledge is very inadequate in the human mind.

P31   *We can have only a very inadequate knowledge of the duration of particular things external to us.*

Proof   Each particular thing, just like the human body, must be determined by another particular thing to exist and to act in a definite and determinate way, and this latter thing again by another, and so on ad infinitum (Pr. 28, I). Now since we have shown in the preceding Proposition that from this common property of particular things we can have only a very inadequate knowledge of the duration of the human body, in the case of the duration of particular things we have to come to the same conclusion: that we can have only a very inadequate knowledge thereof.

Cor   Hence it follows that all particular things are contingent and perishable. For we can have no adequate knowledge of their duration (preceding Pr.), and that is what is to be understood by contingency and perishability (Schol. 1, Pr. 33, I). For apart from this there is no other kind of contingency (Pr. 29, I).

P32   *All ideas are true insofar as they are related to God.*

Proof   All ideas, which are in God, agree completely with the objects of which they are ideas (Cor. Pr. 7, II), and so they are all true (Ax. 6, I).

P33   *There is nothing positive in ideas whereby they can be said to be false.*

Proof   If this be denied, conceive, if possible, a positive mode of thinking which constitutes the form [*forma*] of error or falsity. This mode of thinking cannot be in God (preceding Pr.), but neither can it be or be conceived externally to God (Pr. 15, I). Thus there can be nothing positive in ideas whereby they can be called false.

P34   *Every idea which in us is absolute, that is, adequate and perfect, is true.*

Proof   When we say that there is in us an adequate and perfect idea, we are saying only this (Cor. Pr. 11, II), that there is adequate and perfect idea in God insofar as he constitutes the essence of our mind. Consequently, we are saying only this, that such an idea is true (Pr. 32, II).

P35   *Falsity consists in the privation of knowledge which inadequate ideas, that is, fragmentary and confused ideas, involve.*

Proof   There is nothing positive in ideas which constitutes the form [*forma*] of falsity (Pr. 33, II). But falsity cannot consist in absolute privation (for minds, not bodies, are said to err and be deceived), nor again in absolute ignorance, for to be ignorant and to err are different. Therefore, it consists in that privation of knowledge which inadequate knowledge, that is, inadequate and confused ideas, involves.

Schol   In Schol. Pr. 17, II I explained how error consists in the privation of knowledge, but I will give an example to enlarge on this explanation. Men are deceived in thinking themselves free, a belief that consists only in this, that they are conscious of their actions and ignorant of the causes by which they are determined. Therefore, the idea of their freedom is simply the ignorance of the cause of their actions. As to their saying that human actions depend on the will, these are mere words without any corresponding idea. For none of them knows what the will is and how it moves the body, and those who boast otherwise and make up stories of dwelling places and habitations of the soul provoke either ridicule or disgust.

As another example, when we gaze at the sun, we see it as some two hundred feet distant from us. The error does not consist in simply seeing the sun in this way but in the fact that while we do so we are not aware of the true distance and the cause of our seeing it so. For although we may later become aware that the sun is more than six hundred times the diameter of the earth distant from us, we shall nevertheless continue to see it as close at hand. For it is not our ignorance of its true distance that causes us to see the sun to be so near; it is that the affection of our body involves the essence of the sun only to the extent that the body is affected by it.

P36   *Inadequate and confused ideas follow by the same necessity as adequate, or clear and distinct, ideas.*

Proof   All ideas are in God (Pr. 15, I), and insofar as they are related to God, they are true (Pr. 32, II) and adequate (Cor. Pr. 7, II). So there are no inadequate or confused ideas except insofar as they are related to the particular mind of some-one (see Prs. 24 and 28, II). So all ideas, both adequate and inadequate, follow by the same necessity (Cor. Pr. 6, II).

P37   *That which is common to all things (see Lemma 2 above) and is equally in the part as in the whole does not constitute the essence of any one particular thing.*

Proof   If this is denied, conceive, if possible, that it does constitute the essence of one particular thing, B. Therefore, it can neither be nor be conceived without B (Def. 2, II). But this is contrary to our hypothesis. Therefore, it does not pertain to B's essence, nor does it constitute the essence of any other particular thing.

P38   *Those things that are common to all things and are equally in the part as in the whole can be conceived only adequately.*

Proof   Let A be something common to all bodies, and equally in the part of any body as in the whole. I say that A can be conceived only adequately. For its idea (Cor. Pr. 7, II) will necessarily be in God both insofar as he has the idea of the human body and insofar as he has the ideas of affections of the human body, af-fections which partly involve the natures of both the human body and external bodies (Prs. 16, 25, and 27, II). That is (Prs. 12 and 13, II), this idea will neces-sarily be adequate in God insofar as he constitutes the human mind; that is, in-sofar as he has the ideas which are in the human mind. Therefore, the mind (Cor. Pr. 11, II) necessarily perceives A adequately, and does so both insofar as it per-ceives itself and insofar as it perceives its own body or any external body; nor can A be perceived in any other way.

Cor   Hence it follows that there are certain ideas or notions common to all men. For (by Lemma 2) all bodies agree in certain respects, which must be (preceding Pr.) conceived by all adequately, or clearly and distinctly.

P39   *Of that which is common and proper to the human body and to any exter-nal bodies by which the human body is customarily affected, and which is equally in the part as well as in the whole of any of these bodies, the idea also in the mind will be adequate.*

Proof   Let A be that which is common and proper to the human body and to any external bodies and which is equally in the human body as in those same ex-ternal bodies, and which is finally equally in the part of any external body as in the whole. There will be in God an adequate idea of A (Cor. Pr. 7, II) both inso-far as he has the idea of the human body and insofar as he has ideas of those posited external bodies. Let it now be supposed that the human body is affected by an ex-ternal body through that which is common to them both, that is, A. The idea of this affection will involve the property A (Pr. 16, II), and so (Cor. Pr. 7, II) the idea of this affection, insofar as it involves the property A, will be adequate in God in-sofar as he is affected by the idea of the human body; that is (Pr. 13, II), insofar as he constitutes the nature of the human mind. So this idea will also be adequate in the human mind (Cor. Pr. 11, II).

Cor   Hence it follows that the mind is more capable of perceiving more things adequately in proportion as its body has more things in common with other bodies.

P40   *Whatever ideas follow in the mind from ideas that are adequate in it are also adequate.*

Proof   This is evident. For when we say that an idea follows in the human mind from ideas that are adequate in it, we are saying no more than that there is in the divine intellect an idea of which God is the cause, not insofar as he is infinite nor insofar as he is affected by ideas of numerous particular things, but only insofar as he constitutes the essence of the human mind.

Schol 1   I have here set forth the causes of those notions that are called "common," and which are the basis of our reasoning processes. Now certain axioms or notions have other causes which it would be relevant to set forth by this method of ours; for thus we could establish which notions are useful compared with others, and which are of scarcely any value. And again, we could establish which notions are common to all, which ones are clear and distinct only to those not laboring under prejudices [*praejudiciis*] and which ones are ill-founded. Furthermore, this would clarify the origin of those notions called "secondary"—and consequently the axioms which are based on them—as well as other related questions to which I have for some time given thought. But I have decided not to embark on these questions at this point because I have set them aside for another treatise,[3] and also to avoid wearying the reader with too lengthy a discussion of this subject. Nevertheless, to omit nothing that it is essential to know, I shall briefly deal with the question of the origin of the so-called "transcendental terms," such as "entity," "thing," "something" [*ens, res, aliquid*].

These terms originate in the following way. The human body, being limited, is capable of forming simultaneously in itself only a certain number of distinct images. (I have explained in Schol. Pr. 17, II what an image is.) If this number be exceeded, these images begin to be confused, and if the number of distinct images which the body is capable of forming simultaneously in itself be far exceeded, all the images will be utterly confused with one another. This being so, it is evident from Cor. Pr. 17 and Pr. 18, II that the human mind is able to imagine simultaneously and distinctly as many bodies as there are images that can be formed simultaneously in its body. But when the images in the body are utterly confused, the mind will also imagine all the bodies confusedly without any distinction, and will comprehend them, as it were, under one attribute, namely, that of entity, thing, etc. This conclusion can also be reached from the fact that images are not always equally vivid, and also from other causes analogous to these, which I need not here explicate. For it all comes down to this, that these terms signify ideas confused in the highest degree.

Again, from similar causes have arisen those notions called "universal," such as "man," "horse," "dog," etc.; that is to say, so many images are formed in the

---

[3] [This is Spinoza's incomplete essay, *On the Improvement of the Understanding.*]

human body simultaneously (e.g., of man) that our capacity to imagine them is surpassed, not indeed completely, but to the extent that the mind is unable to imagine the unimportant differences of individuals (such as the complexion and stature of each, and their exact number) and imagines distinctly only their common characteristic insofar as the body is affected by them. For it was by this that the body was affected most repeatedly, by each single individual. The mind expresses this by the word "man," and predicates this word of an infinite number of individuals. For, as we said, it is unable to imagine the determinate number of individuals.

But it should be noted that not all men form these notions in the same way; in the case of each person the notions vary according as that thing varies whereby the body has more frequently been affected, and which the mind more readily imagines or calls to mind. For example, those who have more often regarded with admiration the stature of men will understand by the word "man" an animal of upright stature, while those who are wont to regard a different aspect will form a different common image of man, such as that man is a laughing animal, a featherless biped, or a rational animal. Similarly, with regard to other aspects, each will form universal images according to the conditioning of his body. Therefore, it is not surprising that so many controversies have arisen among philosophers who have sought to explain natural phenomena through merely the images of these phenomena.

Schol 2   From all that has already been said it is quite clear that we perceive many things and form universal notions:

1. From individual objects presented to us through the senses in a fragmentary [*mutilate*] and confused manner without any intellectual order (see Cor. Pr. 29, II); and therefore I call such perceptions "knowledge from casual experience."

2. From symbols. For example, from having heard or read certain words we call things to mind and we form certain ideas of them similar to those through which we imagine things (Schol. Pr. 18, II).

Both these ways of regarding things I shall in future refer to as "knowledge of the first kind," "opinion," or "imagination."

3. From the fact that we have common notions and adequate ideas of the properties of things (see Cor. Pr. 38 and 39 with its Cor., and Pr. 40, II). I shall refer to this as "reason" and "knowledge of the second kind."

Apart from these two kinds of knowledge there is, as I shall later show, a third kind of knowledge, which I shall refer to as "intuition." This kind of knowledge proceeds from an adequate idea of the formal essence of certain attributes of God to an adequate knowledge of the essence of things. I shall illustrate all these kinds of knowledge by one single example. Three numbers are given; it is required to find a fourth which is related to the third as the second to the first. Tradesmen have no hesitation in multiplying the second by the third and dividing the product by the first, either because they have not yet forgotten the rule they learned without proof from their teachers, or because they have in fact found this correct in the case of very simple numbers, or else from the force of the proof of Proposition 19 of the

Seventh Book of Euclid, to wit, the common property of proportionals. But in the case of very simple numbers, none of this is necessary. For example, in the case of the given numbers 1, 2, 3, everybody can see that the fourth proportional is 6, and all the more clearly because we infer in one single intuition the fourth number from the ratio we see the first number bears to the second.

P41   *Knowledge of the first kind is the only cause of falsity; knowledge of the second and third kind is necessarily true.*

Proof   In the preceding Scholium we asserted that all those ideas which are inadequate and confused belong to the first kind of knowledge; and thus (Pr. 35, II) this knowledge is the only cause of falsity. Further, we asserted that to knowledge of the second and third kind there belong those ideas which are adequate. Therefore (Pr. 34, II), this knowledge is necessarily true.

P42   *Knowledge of the second and third kind, and not knowledge of the first kind, teaches us to distinguish true from false.*

Proof   This Proposition is self-evident. For he who can distinguish the true from the false must have an adequate idea of the true and the false; that is (Schol. 2 Pr. 40, II), he must know the true and the false by the second or third kind of knowledge.

P43   *He who has a true idea knows at the same time that he has a true idea, and cannot doubt its truth.*

Proof   A true idea in us is one which is adequate in God insofar as he is explicated through the nature of the human mind (Cor. Pr. 11, II). Let us suppose, then, that there is in God, insofar as he is explicated through the nature of the human mind, an adequate idea, A. The idea of this idea must also necessarily be in God, and is related to God in the same way as the idea A (Pr. 20, II, the proof being of general application). But by our supposition the idea A is related to God insofar as he is explicated through the nature of the human mind. Therefore, the idea of the idea A must be related to God in the same way; that is (Cor. Pr. 11, II), this adequate idea of the idea A will be in the mind which has the adequate idea A. So he who has an adequate idea, that is, he who knows a thing truly (Pr. 34, II), must at the same time have an adequate idea, that is, a true knowledge of his knowledge; that is (as is self-evident), he is bound at the same time to be certain.

Schol   I have explained in the Scholium to Pr. 21, II what is an idea of an idea; but it should be noted that the preceding proposition is sufficiently self-evident. For nobody who has a true idea is unaware that a true idea involves absolute certainty. To have a true idea means only to know a thing perfectly, that is, to the utmost degree. Indeed, nobody can doubt this, unless he thinks that an idea is some dumb thing like a picture on a tablet, and not a mode of thinking, to wit, the very act of understanding. And who, pray, can know that he understands some thing unless he first understands it? That is, who can know that he is certain of something unless he is first certain of it? Again, what standard of truth can there be that is clearer and more certain than a true idea? Indeed, just as light makes manifest both itself and darkness, so truth is the standard both of itself and falsity.

I think I have thus given an answer to those questions which can be stated as follows: If a true idea is distinguished from a false one only inasmuch as it is said to correspond with that of which it is an idea, then a true idea has no more reality or perfection than a false one (since they are distinguished only by an extrinsic characteristic) and consequently neither is a man who has true ideas superior to one who has only false ideas. Secondly, how do we come to have false ideas? And finally, how can one know for certain that one has ideas which correspond with that of which they are ideas? I have now given an answer, I repeat, to these problems. As regards the difference between a true and a false idea, it is clear from Pr. 35, II that the former is to the latter as being to non-being. The causes of falsity I have quite clearly shown from Propositions 19 to 35 with the latter's Scholium, from which it is likewise obvious what is the difference between a man who has true ideas and one who has only false ideas. As to the last question, how can a man know that he has an idea which corresponds to that of which it is an idea, I have just shown, with abundant clarity, that this arises from the fact that he does have an idea that corresponds to that of which it is an idea; that is, truth is its own standard. Furthermore, the human mind, insofar as it perceives things truly, is part of the infinite intellect of God (Cor. Pr. 11, II), and thus it is as inevitable that the clear and distinct ideas of the mind are true as that God's ideas are true.

P44   *It is not in the nature of reason to regard things as contingent, but as necessary.*

Proof   It is in the nature of reason to perceive things truly (Pr. 41, II), to wit (Ax. 6, I), as they are in themselves; that is (Pr. 29, I), not as contingent, but as necessary.

Cor 1   Hence it follows that it solely results from imagination [*imaginatio*] that we regard things, both in respect of the past and of the future, as contingent.

Schol   I shall explain briefly how this comes about. We have shown above (Pr. 17, II and Cor.) that although things may not exist, the mind nevertheless always imagines them as present unless causes arise which exclude their present existence. Further, we have shown (Pr. 18, II) that if the human body has once been affected by two external bodies at the same time, when the mind later imagines one of them, it will straightway call the other to mind as well; that is, it will regard both as present to it unless other causes arise which exclude their present existence. Furthermore, nobody doubts that time, too, is a product of the imagination, and arises from the fact that we see some bodies move more slowly than others, or more quickly, or with equal speed. Let us therefore suppose that yesterday a boy saw Peter first of all in the morning, Paul at noon, and Simon in the evening, and that today he again sees Peter in the morning. From Pr. 18, II it is clear that as soon as he sees the morning light, forthwith he will imagine the sun as traversing the same tract of sky as on the previous day, that is, he will imagine a whole day, and he will imagine Peter together with morning, Paul with midday, and Simon with evening; that is, he will imagine the existence of Paul and Simon with reference to future time. On the other hand, on seeing Simon in the evening he will refer Paul and Peter to time past by imagining them along with time past. This train of events will be the more consistent the more frequently he sees them in that order. If it should at some time occur that on another evening he sees James instead of Simon, then the following morning he will imagine along with evening now Simon, now James, but not both together. For we are supposing that he has seen only one of them in the evening, not both at the same time. Therefore, his imagination will waver, and he will imagine, along with a future evening, now one, now the other; that is, he will regard neither of them as going to be there for certain, but both of them contingently. This wavering of the imagination occurs in the same way if the imagination be of things which we regard with relation to past or present time, and consequently we shall imagine things, as related both to present and past or future time, as contingent.

Cor 2 It is in the nature of reason to perceive things in the light of eternity [*sub quadam specie aeternitatis*].

Proof It is in the nature of reason to regard things as necessary, not as contingent (previous Pr.). Now it perceives this necessity truly (Pr. 41, II); that is, as it is in itself (Ax. 6, I). But (Pr. 16, I) this necessity is the very necessity of God's eternal nature. Therefore, it is in the nature of reason to regard things in this light of eternity. Furthermore, the basic principles of reason are those notions (Pr. 38, II) which explicate what is common to all things, and do not explicate (Pr. 37, II) the essence of any particular thing, and therefore must be conceived without any relation to time, but in the light of eternity.

P45 *Every idea of any body or particular thing existing in actuality necessarily involves the eternal and infinite essence of God.*

Proof The idea of a particular thing actually existing necessarily involves both the essence and the existence of the thing (Cor. Pr. 8, II). But particular things cannot be conceived without God (Pr. 15, I). Now since they have God for their cause (Pr. 6, II) insofar as he is considered under that attribute of which the things themselves are modes, their ideas (Ax. 4, I) must necessarily involve the conception of their attribute; that is (Def. 6, I), the eternal and infinite essence of God.

Schol Here by existence I do not mean duration, that is, existence insofar as it is considered in the abstract as a kind of quantity. I am speaking of the very nature of existence, which is attributed to particular things because they follow in infinite numbers in infinite ways from the eternal necessity of God's nature (Pr. 16, I). I am speaking, I repeat, of the very existence of particular things insofar as they are in God. For although each particular thing is determined by another particular thing to exist in a certain manner, the force by which each perseveres in existing follows from the eternal necessity of God's nature. See Cor. Pr. 24, I.

P46   *The knowledge of the eternal and infinite essence of God which each idea involves is adequate and perfect.*

Proof   The proof of the preceding proposition is universally valid, and whether a thing be considered as a part or a whole, its idea, whether of whole or part, involves the eternal and infinite essence of God (preceding Pr.). Therefore, that which gives knowledge of the eternal and infinite essence of God is common to all things, and equally in the part as in the whole. And so this knowledge will be adequate (Pr. 38, II).

P47   *The human mind has an adequate knowledge of the eternal and infinite essence of God.*

Proof   The human mind has ideas (Pr. 22, II) from which (Pr. 23, II) it perceives itself, its own body (Pr. 19, II), and external bodies (Cor. 1, Pr. 16 and Pr. 17, II) as actually existing, and so it has an adequate knowledge of the eternal and infinite essence of God (Prs. 45 and 46, II).

Schol   Hence we see that God's infinite essence and his eternity are known to all. Now since all things are in God and are conceived through God, it follows that from this knowledge we can deduce a great many things so as to know them adequately and thus to form that third kind of knowledge I mentioned in Schol. 2 Pr. 40, II, of the superiority and usefulness of which we shall have occasion to speak in Part V. That men do not have as clear a knowledge of God as they do of common notions arises from the fact that they are unable to imagine God as they do bodies, and that they have connected the word "God" with the images of things which they commonly see; and this they can scarcely avoid, being affected continually by external bodies. Indeed, most errors result solely from the incorrect application of words to things. When somebody says that the lines joining the center of a circle to its circumference are unequal, he surely understands by circle, at least at that time, something different from what mathematicians understand. Likewise, when men make mistakes in arithmetic, they have different figures in mind from those on paper. So if you look only to their minds, they indeed are not mistaken; but they seem to be wrong because we think that they have in mind the figures on the page. If this were not the case, we would not think them to be wrong, just as I did not think that person to be wrong whom I recently heard shouting that his hall had flown into his neighbor's hen, for I could see clearly what he had in mind. Most controversies arise from this, that men do not correctly express what is in their mind, or they misunderstand another's mind. For, in reality, while they are hotly contradicting one another, they are either in agreement or have different things in mind, so that the apparent errors and absurdities of their opponents are not really so.

P48   *In the mind there is no absolute, or free, will. The mind is determined to this or that volition by a cause, which is likewise determined by another cause, and this again by another, and so ad infinitum.*

Proof   The mind is a definite and determinate mode of thinking (Pr. 11, II), and thus (Cor. 2, Pr. 17, I) it cannot be the free cause of its actions: that is, it cannot possess an absolute faculty of willing and nonwilling. It must be determined to will this or that (Pr. 28, I) by a cause, which likewise is determined by another cause, and this again by another, etc.

Schol   In the same way it is proved that in the mind there is no absolute faculty of understanding, desiring, loving, etc. Hence it follows that these and similar faculties are either entirely fictitious or nothing more than metaphysical entities or universals which we are wont to form from particulars. So intellect and will bear the same relation to this or that idea, this or that volition, as stoniness to this or that stone, or man to Peter and Paul. As to the reason why men think they are free, we explained that in the Appendix to Part I.

But before proceeding further, it should here be noted that by the will I mean the faculty of affirming and denying, and not desire. I mean, I repeat, the faculty whereby the mind affirms or denies what is true or what is false, not the desire whereby the mind seeks things or shuns them. But now that we have proved that these faculties are universal notions which are not distinct from the particulars from which we form them, we must inquire whether volitions themselves are anything more than ideas of things. We must inquire, I say, whether there is in the mind any other affirmation and denial apart from that which the idea, insofar as it is an idea, involves. On this subject see the following proposition and also Def. 3, II, lest thought becomes confused with pictures. For by ideas I do not mean images such as are formed at the back of the eye—or if you like, in the middle of the brain—but conceptions of thought.

P49   *There is in the mind no volition, that is, affirmation and negation, except that which an idea, insofar as it is an idea, involves.*

Proof   There is in the mind (preceding Pr.) no absolute faculty of willing and nonwilling, but only particular volitions, namely, this or that affirmation, and this or that negation. Let us therefore conceive a particular volition, namely, a mode of thinking whereby the mind affirms that the three angles of a triangle are equal to two right angles. This affirmation involves the conception, or idea, of a triangle; that is, it cannot be conceived without the idea of a triangle. For to say that A must involve the conception of B is the same as to say that A cannot be conceived without B. Again, this affirmation (Ax. 3, II) cannot even be without the idea of a triangle. Therefore, this idea can neither be nor be conceived without the idea of a triangle. Furthermore, this idea of a triangle must involve this same affirmation, namely, that its three angles are equal to two right angles. Therefore, vice versa, this idea of a triangle can neither be nor be conceived without this affirmation, and so (Def. 2, II) this affirmation belongs to the essence of the idea of a triangle, and is nothing more than the essence itself. And what I have said of this volition (for it was arbitrarily selected) must also be said of every volition, namely, that it is nothing but an idea.

Cor   Will and intellect are one and the same thing.

Proof   Will and intellect are nothing but the particular volitions and ideas (Pr. 48, II and Schol.). But a particular volition and idea are one and the same thing (preceding Pr.). Therefore, will and intellect are one and the same thing.

Schol   By this means we have removed the cause to which error is commonly attributed. We have previously shown that falsity consists only in the privation that fragmentary and confused ideas involve. Therefore, a false idea, insofar as it is false, does not involve certainty. So when we say that a man acquiesces in what is false and has no doubt thereof, we are not thereby saying that he is certain, but only that he does not doubt, or that he acquiesces in what is false because there is nothing to cause his imagination to waver. On this point see Schol. Pr. 44, II. So however much we suppose a man to adhere to what is false, we shall never say that he is certain. For by certainty we mean something positive (Pr. 43, II and Schol.), not privation of doubt. But by privation of certainty we mean falsity.

But for a fuller explanation of the preceding proposition some things remain to be said. Then, again, there is the further task of replying to objections that may be raised against this doctrine of ours. Finally, to remove every shred of doubt, I have thought it worthwhile to point out certain advantages of this doctrine. I say certain advantages, for the most important of them will be better understood from what we have to say in Part V.

I begin, then, with the first point, and I urge my readers to make a careful distinction between an idea—i.e., a conception of the mind—and the images of things that we imagine. Again, it is essential to distinguish between ideas and the words we use to signify things. For since these three—images, words, and ideas—have been utterly confused by many, or else they fail to distinguish between them through lack of accuracy, or, finally, through lack of caution, our doctrine of the will, which it is essential to know both for theory and for the wise ordering of life, has never entered their minds. For those who think that ideas consist in images formed in us from the contact of external bodies are convinced that those ideas of things whereof we can form no like image are not ideas, but mere fictions fashioned arbitrarily at will. So they look on ideas as dumb pictures on a tablet, and misled by this preconception they fail to see that an idea, insofar as it is an idea, involves affirmation or negation. Again, those who confuse words with idea, or with the affirmation which an idea involves, think that when they affirm or deny something merely by words contrary to what they feel, they are able to will contrary to what they feel. Now one can easily dispel these misconceptions if one attends to the nature of thought, which is quite removed from the concept of extension. Then one will clearly understand that an idea, being a mode of thinking, consists neither in the image of a thing nor in words. For the essence of words and images is constituted solely by corporeal motions far removed from the concept of thought. With these few words of warning, I turn to the aforementioned objections.

The first of these rests on the confident claim that the will extends more widely than the intellect, and therefore is different from it. The reason for their belief that the will extends more widely than the intellect is that they find—so they say—that they do not need a greater faculty of assent, that is, of affirming and denying, than they already possess, in order to assent to an infinite number of other things that we do not perceive, but that we do need an increased faculty of understanding. Therefore, will is distinct from intellect, the latter being finite and the former infinite.

Second, it may be objected against us that experience appears to tell us most indisputably that we are able to suspend judgment so as not to assent to things that we perceive, and this is also confirmed by the fact that nobody is said to be deceived insofar as he perceives something, but only insofar as he assents or dissents. For instance, he who imagines a winged horse does not thereby grant that there is a winged horse; that is, he is not thereby deceived unless at the same time he grants that there is a winged horse. So experience appears to tell us most indisputably that the will, that is, the faculty of assenting, is free, and different from the faculty of understanding.

Third, it may be objected that one affirmation does not seem to contain more reality than another; that is, we do not seem to need greater power in order to affirm that what is true is true than to affirm that what is false is true. On the other hand, we do perceive that one idea has more reality or perfection than another. For some ideas are more perfect than others in proportion as some objects are superior to others. This, again, is a clear indication that there is a difference between will and intellect.

Fourth, it may be objected that if man does not act from freedom of will, what would happen if he should be in a state of equilibrium like Buridan's ass? Will he perish of hunger and thirst? If I were to grant this, I would appear to be thinking of an ass or a statue, not of a man. If I deny it, then the man will be determining himself, and consequently will possess the faculty of going and doing whatever he wants.

Besides these objections there may possibly be others. But since I am not obliged to quash every objection that can be dreamed up, I shall make it my task to reply to these objections only, and as briefly as possible.

To the first objection I reply that, if by the intellect is meant clear and distinct ideas only, I grant that the will extends more widely than the intellect, but I deny that the will extends more widely than perceptions, that is, the faculty of conceiving. Nor indeed do I see why the faculty of willing should be termed infinite any more than the faculty of sensing. For just as by the same faculty of willing we can affirm an infinite number of things (but in succession, for we cannot affirm an infinite number of things simultaneously), so also we can sense or perceive an infinite number of bodies (in succession) by the same faculty of sensing. If my objectors should say that there are an infinite number of things that we cannot sense, I retort that we cannot grasp them by any amount of thought, and consequently by any amount of willing. But, they say, if God wanted to bring it about that we should perceive these too, he would have had to give us a greater faculty of perceiving, but not a greater faculty of willing than he has already given us. This is the same as saying that if God wishes to bring it about that we should understand an infinite number of other entities, he would have to give us a greater intellect than he already has, so as to encompass these same infinite entities, but not a more universal idea of entity. For we have shown that the will is a universal entity, or the idea whereby we explicate all particular volitions; that is, that which is common to all particular volitions. So if they believe that this common or universal idea of volitions is a faculty, it is not at all surprising that they declare this faculty to extend beyond the limits of the intellect to infinity. For the term "universal" is applied equally to one, to many, and to an infinite number of individuals.

To the second objection I reply by denying that we have free power to suspend judgment. For when we say that someone suspends judgment, we are saying only that he sees that he is not adequately perceiving the thing. So suspension of judgment is really a perception, not free will. To understand this more clearly, let us conceive a boy imagining a winged horse and having no other perception. Since this imagining involves the existence of a horse (Cor. Pr. 17, II), and the boy perceives nothing to annul the existence of the horse, he will regard the horse as present and he will not be able to doubt its existence, although he is not certain of it. We experience this quite commonly in dreams, nor do I believe there is anyone who thinks that while dreaming he has free power to suspend judgment regarding the contents of his dream, and of bringing it about that he should not dream what he dreams that he sees. Nevertheless, it does happen that even in dreams we suspend judgment, to wit, when we dream that we are dreaming. Furthermore, I grant that nobody is deceived insofar as he has a perception; that is, I grant that the imaginings of the mind, considered in themselves, involve no error (see Schol. Pr. 17, II). But I deny that a man makes no affirmation insofar as he has a perception. For what else is perceiving a winged horse than affirming wings of a horse? For if the mind should perceive nothing apart from the winged horse, it would regard the horse as present to it, and would have no cause to doubt its existence nor any faculty of dissenting, unless the imagining of the winged horse were to be connected to an idea which annuls the existence of the said horse, or he perceives that the idea which he has of the winged horse is inadequate. Then he will either necessarily deny the existence of the horse or he will necessarily doubt it.

In the above I think I have also answered the third objection by my assertion that the will is a universal term predicated of all ideas and signifying only what is common to all ideas, namely, affirmation, the adequate essence of which, insofar as it is thus conceived as an abstract term, must be in every single idea, and the same in all in this respect only. But not insofar as it is considered as constituting the essence of the idea, for in that respect particular affirmations differ among themselves as much as do ideas. For example, the affirmation which the idea of a circle involves differs from the affirmation which the idea of a triangle involves as much as the idea of a circle differs from the idea of a triangle. Again, I absolutely deny that we need an equal power of thinking to affirm that what is true is true as to affirm that what is false is true. For these two affirmations, if you look to their meaning and not to the words alone, are related to one another as being to non-being. For there is nothing in ideas that constitutes the form of falsity (see Pr. 35, II with Schol. and Schol. Pr. 47, II). Therefore, it is important to note here how easily we are deceived when we confuse universals with particulars, and mental constructs [*entia rationis*] and abstract terms with the real.

As to the fourth objection, I readily grant that a man placed in such a state of equilibrium (namely, where he feels nothing else but hunger and thirst and perceives nothing but such-and-such food and drink at equal distances from him) will die of hunger and thirst. If they ask me whether such a man is not to be reckoned an ass rather than a man, I reply that I do not know, just as I do not know how one should reckon a man who hangs himself, or how one should reckon babies, fools, and madmen.

My final task is to show what practical advantages accrue from knowledge of this doctrine, and this we shall readily gather from the following points:

1. It teaches that we act only by God's will, and that we share in the divine nature, and all the more as our actions become more perfect and as we understand God more and more. Therefore, this doctrine, apart from giving us complete tranquillity of mind, has the further advantage of teaching us wherein lies our greatest happiness or blessedness, namely, in the knowledge of God alone, as a result of which we are induced only to such actions as are urged on us by love and piety. Hence we clearly understand how far astray from the true estimation of virtue are those who, failing to understand that virtue itself and the service of God are happiness itself and utmost freedom, expect God to bestow on them the highest rewards in return for their virtue and meritorious actions as if in return for the basest slavery.

2. It teaches us what attitude we should adopt regarding fortune, or the things that are not in our power, that is, the things that do not follow from our nature; namely, to expect and to endure with patience both faces of fortune. For all things follow from God's eternal decree by the same necessity as it follows from the essence of a triangle that its three angles are equal to two right angles.

3. This doctrine assists us in our social relations, in that it teaches us to hate no one, despise no one, ridicule no one, be angry with no one, envy no one. Then again, it teaches us that each should be content with what he has and should help his neighbor, not from womanish pity, or favor, or superstition, but from the guidance of reason as occasion and circumstance require. This I shall demonstrate in Part IV.

4. Finally, this doctrine is also of no small advantage to the commonwealth, in that it teaches the manner in which citizens should be governed and led; namely, not so as to be slaves, but so as to do freely what is best.

And thus I have completed the task I undertook in this Scholium, and thereby I bring to an end Part II, in which I think I have explained the nature of the human mind and its properties at sufficient length and as clearly as the difficult subject matter permits, and that from my account can be drawn many excellent lessons, most useful and necessary to know, as will partly be disclosed in what is to follow.

PART III
Concerning the Origin and Nature of the Emotions

Preface

Most of those who have written about the emotions [*affectibus*] and human conduct seem to be dealing not with natural phenomena that follow the common laws of Nature but with phenomena outside Nature. They appear to go so far as to conceive man in Nature as a kingdom within a kingdom. They believe that he disturbs rather than follows Nature's order, and has absolute power over his actions, and is determined by no other source than himself. Again, they assign the cause of human weakness and frailty not to the power of Nature in general, but to some defect in human nature, which they therefore bemoan, ridicule, despise, or, as is most frequently the case, abuse. He who can criticize the weakness of the human mind more eloquently or more shrilly is regarded as almost divinely inspired. Yet there have not been lacking outstanding figures who have written much that is excellent regarding the right conduct of life and have given to mankind very sage counsel; and we confess we owe much to their toil and industry. However, as far as I know, no one has defined the nature and strength of the emotions, and the power of the mind in controlling them. I know, indeed, that the renowned Descartes, though he too believed that the mind has absolute power over its actions, does explain human emotions through their first causes, and has also zealously striven to show how the mind can have absolute control over the emotions. But in my opinion he has shown nothing else but the brilliance of his own genius, as I shall demonstrate in due course; for I want now to return to those who prefer to abuse or deride the emotions and actions of men rather than to understand them. They will doubtless find it surprising that I should attempt to treat of the faults and follies of mankind in the geometric manner, and that I should propose to bring logical reasoning to bear on what they proclaim is opposed to reason, and is vain, absurd, and horrifying. But my argument is this: in Nature nothing happens which can be attributed to its defectiveness, for Nature is always the same, and its force and power of acting is everywhere one and the same; that is, the laws and rules of Nature according to which all things happen and change from one form to another are everywhere and always the same. So our approach to the understanding of the nature of things of every kind should likewise be one and the same; namely, through the universal laws and rules of Nature. Therefore the emotions of hatred, anger, envy, etc., considered in themselves, follow from the same necessity and force of Nature as all other particular things. So these emotions are assignable to definite causes through which they can be understood, and have definite properties, equally deserving of our investigation as the properties of any other thing, whose mere contemplation affords us pleasure. I shall, then, treat of the nature and strength of the emotions, and the mind's power over them, by the same method as I have used in treating of God and the mind, and I shall consider human actions and appetites just as if it were an investigation into lines, planes, or bodies.

Definitions

1. I call that an adequate cause whose effect can be clearly and distinctly perceived through the said cause. I call that an inadequate or partial cause whose effect cannot be understood through the said cause alone.

2. I say that we are active when something takes place, in us or externally to us, of which we are the adequate cause; that is, (by preceding Def.), when from our nature there follows in us or externally to us something which can be clearly and distinctly understood through our nature alone. On the other hand, I say that we are passive when something takes place in us, or follows from our nature, of which we are only the partial cause.

3. By emotion [*affectus*] I understand the affections of the body by which the body's power of activity is increased or diminished, assisted or checked, together with the ideas of these affections.

Thus, if we can be the adequate cause of one of these affections, then by emotion I understand activity, otherwise passivity.

Postulates

1. The human body can be affected in many ways by which its power of activity is increased or diminished; and also in many other ways which neither increase nor diminish its power of activity.

This postulate or axiom rests on Postulate 1 and Lemmata 5 and 7, following Pr. 13, II.

2. The human body can undergo many changes and nevertheless retain impressions or traces of objects (see Post. 5, II) and consequently the same images of things for the definition of which see Schol. Pr. 17, II.

P1   *Our mind is in some instances active and in other instances passive. Insofar as it has adequate ideas, it is necessarily active; and insofar as it has inadequate ideas, it is necessarily passive.*

Proof   In every human mind, some of its ideas are adequate, others are fragmentary and confused (Schol. Pr. 40, II). Now ideas that are adequate in someone's mind are adequate in God insofar as he constitutes the essence of that mind (Cor. Pr. 11, II); and furthermore those ideas that are inadequate in the mind are also adequate in God (same Cor.), not insofar as he contains in himself the essence of that mind only, but insofar as he contains the minds of other things as well. Again, from any given idea some effect must necessarily follow (Pr. 36, I), of which God is the adequate cause (Def. 1, III) not insofar as he is infinite but insofar as he is considered as affected by the given idea (Pr. 9, II). But in the case of an effect of which God is the cause insofar as he is affected by an idea which is adequate in someone's mind, that same mind is its adequate cause (Cor. Pr. 11, II). Therefore our mind (Def. 2, III), insofar as it has adequate ideas, is necessarily active—which is the first point. Again, whatever necessarily follows from an idea that is adequate in God not insofar as he has in himself the mind of one man only, but insofar as he has the minds of other things simultaneously with the mind of the said man, the mind of that man is not the adequate cause of it, but the partial cause (Cor. Pr. 11, II), and therefore (Def. 2, III) insofar as the mind has inadequate ideas, it is necessarily passive—which was the second point. Therefore our mind etc.

Cor   Hence it follows that the more the mind has inadequate ideas, the more it is subject to passive states [*passionibus*]; and, on the other hand, it is the more active in proportion as it has a greater number of adequate ideas.

P2   *The body cannot determine the mind to think, nor can the mind determine the body to motion or rest, or to anything else (if there is anything else).*

Proof   All modes of thinking have God for their cause insofar as he is a thinking thing, and not insofar as he is explicated by any other attribute (Pr. 6, II). So that which determines the mind to think is a mode of Thinking, and not of Extension; that is (Def. 1, II), it is not the body. That was our first point. Now the motion-and-rest of a body must arise from another body, which again has been determined to motion or rest by another body, and without exception whatever arises in a body must have arisen from God insofar as he is considered as affected by a mode of Extension, and not insofar as he is considered as affected by a mode of Thinking (Pr. 6, II); that is, it cannot arise from mind, which (Pr. 11, II) is a mode of Thinking. That was our second point. Therefore the body cannot . . . etc.

Schol   This is more clearly understood from Schol. Pr. 7, II, which tells us that mind and body are one and the same thing, conceived now under the attribute of Thought, now under the attribute of Extension. Hence it comes about that the order or linking of things is one, whether Nature be conceived under this or that attribute, and consequently the order of the active and passive states of our body is simultaneous in Nature with the order of active and passive states of the mind. This is also evident from the manner of our proof of Pr. 12, II.

Yet, although the matter admits of no shadow of doubt, I can scarcely believe, without the confirmation of experience, that men can be induced to examine this view without prejudice, so strongly are they convinced that at the mere bidding of the mind the body can now be set in motion, now be brought to rest, and can perform any number of actions which depend solely on the will of the mind and the exercise of thought. However, nobody as yet has determined the limits of the body's capabilities: that is, nobody as yet has learned from experience what the body can and cannot do, without being determined by mind, solely from the laws of its nature insofar as it is considered as corporeal. For nobody as yet knows the structure of the body so accurately as to explain all its functions, not to mention that in the animal world we find much that far surpasses human sagacity, and that sleepwalkers do many things in their sleep that they would not dare when awake— clear evidence that the body, solely from the laws of its own nature, can do many things at which its mind is amazed.

Again, no one knows in what way and by what means mind can move body, or how many degrees of motion it can impart to body and with what speed it can cause it to move. Hence it follows that when men say that this or that action of the body arises from the mind which has command over the body, they do not know what they are saying, and are merely admitting, under a plausible cover of words, that they are ignorant of the true cause of that action and are not concerned to discover it.

"But," they will say, "whether or not we know by what means the mind moves the body, experience tells us that unless the mind is in a fit state to exercise thought, the body remains inert. And again, experience tells us that it is solely within the power of the mind both to speak and to keep silent, and to do many other things which we therefore believe to depend on mental decision." Now as to the first point, I ask, does not experience also tell them that if, on the other hand, the body is inert, the mind likewise is not capable of thinking? When the body is at rest in sleep, the mind remains asleep with it and does not have that power of entertaining thoughts which it has when awake. Again, I think that all have experienced the fact that the mind is not always equally apt for concentrating on the same object; the mind is more apt to regard this or that object according as the body is more apt to have arising in it the image of this or that object.

"But," they will say, "it is impossible that the causes of buildings, pictures, and other things of this kind, which are made by human skill alone, should be deduced solely from the laws of Nature considered only as corporeal, nor is the human body capable of building a temple unless it be determined and guided by mind." However, I have already pointed out that they do not know what the body can do, or what can be deduced solely from a consideration of its nature, and that experience abundantly shows that solely from the laws of its nature many things occur which they would never have believed possible except from the direction of mind—for instance, the actions of sleepwalkers, which they wonder at when they are awake. A further consideration is the very structure of the human body, which far surpasses in ingenuity all the constructions of human skill; not to mention the point I made earlier, that from Nature, considered under any attribute whatsoever, infinite things follow.

As to the second point, the human condition would indeed be far happier if it were equally in the power of men to keep silent as to talk. But experience teaches us with abundant examples that nothing is less within men's power than to hold their tongues or control their appetites. From this derives the commonly held view that we act freely only in cases where our desires are moderate, because our appetites can then be easily held in check by the remembrance of another thing that frequently comes to mind; but when we seek something with a strong emotion that cannot be allayed by the remembrance of some other thing, we cannot check our desires. But indeed, had they not found by experience that we do many things of which we later repent, and that frequently, when we are at the mercy of conflicting emotions, we "see the better and do the worse," there would be nothing to prevent them from believing that all our actions are free. A baby thinks that it freely seeks milk, an angry child that it freely seeks revenge, and a timid man that he freely seeks flight. Again, the drunken man believes that it is from the free decision of the mind that he says what he later, when sober, wishes he had not said. So, too, the delirious man, the gossiping woman, the child, and many more of this sort think that they speak from free mental decision, when in fact they are unable to restrain their torrent of words. So experience tells us no less clearly than reason that it is on this account only that men believe themselves to be free, that they are conscious of their actions and ignorant of the causes by which they are determined; and it tells us too that mental decisions are nothing more than the appetites themselves, varying therefore according to the varying disposition of the body. For each man's actions are shaped by his emotion; and those who furthermore are a prey to conflicting emotions know not what they want, while those who are free from emotion are driven on to this or that course by a slight impulse.

   Now surely all these considerations go to show clearly that mental decision on the one hand, and the appetite and physical state of the body on the other hand, are simultaneous in nature; or rather, they are one and the same thing which, when considered under the attribute of Thought and explicated through Thought, we call decision, and when considered under the attribute of Extension and deduced from the laws of motion-and-rest, we call a physical state. This will become clearer from later discussion, for there is now another point which I should like you to note as very important. We can take no action from mental decision unless the memory comes into play; for example, we cannot utter a word unless we call the word to mind. Now it is not within the free power of the mind to remember or to forget anything. Hence comes the belief that the power of the mind whereby we can keep silent or speak solely from mental decision is restricted to the case of a remembered thing. However, when we dream that we are speaking, we think that we do so from free mental decision; yet we are not speaking, or if we are, it is the result of spontaneous movement of the body. Again, we dream that we are keeping something secret, and that we are doing so by the same mental decision that comes into play in our waking hours when we keep silent about what we know. Finally, we dream that from a mental decision we act as we dare not act when awake. So I would very much like to know whether in the mind there are two sorts of decisions, dreamland decisions and free decisions. If we don't want to carry madness so far, we must necessarily grant that the mental decision that is believed to be free is not distinct from imagination and memory, and is nothing but the affirmation which an idea, insofar as it is an idea, necessarily involves (Pr. 49, II). So these mental decisions arise in the mind from the same necessity as the ideas of things existing in actuality, and those who believe that they speak, or keep silent, or do anything from free mental decision are dreaming with their eyes open.

P3   *The active states [actiones] of the mind arise only from adequate ideas; its passive states depend solely on inadequate ideas.*

Proof   The first thing that constitutes the essence of the mind is nothing else but the idea of a body actually existing (Prs. 11 and 13, II), which idea is composed of many other ideas (Pr. 15, II), of which some are adequate (Cor. Pr. 38, II) while others are inadequate (Cor. Pr. 29, II). Therefore, whatever follows from the nature of the mind and must be understood through the mind as its proximate cause must necessarily follow from an adequate idea or an inadequate idea. But insofar as the mind has inadequate ideas, it is necessarily passive (Prop. 1, III). Therefore, the active states of mind follow solely from adequate ideas, and thus the mind is passive only by reason of having inadequate ideas.

Schol   We therefore see that passive states are related to the mind only insofar as the mind has something involving negation: that is, insofar as the mind is considered as part of Nature, which cannot be clearly and distinctly perceived through itself independently of other parts. By the same reasoning I could demonstrate that passive states are a characteristic of particular things just as they are of the mind, and cannot be perceived in any other way; but my purpose is to deal only with the human mind.

P4   *No thing can be destroyed except by an external cause.*

Proof   This proposition is self-evident, for the definition of anything affirms, and does not negate, the thing's essence: that is, it posits, and does not annul, the thing's essence. So as long as we are attending only to the thing itself, and not to external causes, we can find nothing in it which can destroy it.

P5   *Things are of a contrary nature, that is, unable to subsist in the same subject, to the extent that one can destroy the other.*

Proof   If they were able to be in agreement with one other, or to coexist in the same subject, there could be something in the said subject which could destroy it, which is absurd (preceding Pr.). Therefore . . . etc.

P6   *Each thing, insofar as it is in itself, endeavors to persist in its own being.*

Proof   Particular things are modes whereby the attributes of God are expressed in a definite and determinate way (Cor. Pr. 25, I), that is (Pr. 34, I), they are things which express in a definite and determinate way the power of God whereby he is and acts, and no thing can have in itself anything by which it can be destroyed, that is, which can annul its existence (Pr. 4, III). On the contrary, it opposes everything that can annul its existence (preceding Pr.); and thus, as far as it can and as far as it is in itself, it endeavors to persist in its own being.

P7   *The conatus[1] with which each thing endeavors to persist in its own being is nothing but the actual essence of the thing itself.*

---

[1] [The term "conatus" plays an important role in Spinoza's psychology. It expresses Spinoza's view that each thing exemplifies an inherent tendency toward self-preservation and activity. This term has a long history, going back to Cicero, who used it to express Aristotle's and the Stoics' notion of

Proof   From the given essence of a thing certain things necessarily follow (Pr. 36, I), nor do things effect anything other than that which necessarily follows from their determinate nature (Pr. 29, I). Therefore, the power of any thing, or the conatus with which it acts or endeavors to act, alone or in conjunction with other things, that is (Pr. 6, III), the power or conatus by which it endeavors to persist in its own being, is nothing but the given, or actual, essence of the thing.

P8   *The conatus with which each single thing endeavors to persist in its own being does not involve finite time, but indefinite time.*

Proof   If it involved a limited period of time which would determine the duration of the thing, then solely from the power by which the thing exists it would follow that it could not exist after that limited period of time, but is bound to be destroyed. But (Pr. 4, III), this is absurd. Therefore, the conatus with which a thing exists does not involve any definite period of time. On the contrary (by the same Pr. 4, III), if it is not destroyed by an external cause, it will always continue to exist by that same power by which it now exists. Therefore, this conatus involves an indefinite time.

P9   *The mind, both insofar as it has clear and distinct ideas and insofar as it has confused ideas, endeavors to persist in its own being over an indefinite period of time, and is conscious of this conatus.*

Proof   The essence of the mind is constituted by adequate and inadequate ideas (as we showed in Pr. 3, III), and so (Pr. 7, III) it endeavors to persist in its own being insofar as it has both these kinds of ideas, and does so (Pr. 8, III) over an indefinite period of time. Now since the mind (Pr. 23, II) is necessarily conscious of itself through the ideas of the affections of the body, therefore the mind is conscious of its conatus (Pr. 7, III).

Schol   When this conatus is related to the mind alone, it is called Will [*voluntas*]; when it is related to mind and body together, it is called Appetite [*appetitus*], which is therefore nothing else but man's essence, from the nature of which there necessarily follow those things that tend to his preservation, and which man is thus determined to perform. Further, there is no difference between appetite and Desire [*cupiditas*] except that desire is usually related to men insofar as they are conscious of their appetite. Therefore, it can be defined as follows: desire is "appetite accompanied by the consciousness thereof."

It is clear from the above considerations that we do not endeavor, will, seek after or desire because we judge a thing to be good. On the contrary, we judge a thing to be good because we endeavor, will, seek after and desire it.

P10   *An idea that excludes the existence of our body cannot be in our mind, but is contrary to it.*

---

impulse (*horme*). It was later used by medieval and early modern philosophers, such as Hobbes, to connote the natural tendency of an organism to preserve itself.]

Proof   Whatsoever can destroy our body cannot be therein (Pr. 5, III), and so neither can its idea be in God insofar as he has the idea of our body (Cor. Pr. 9, II); that is (Prs. 11 and 13, II), the idea of such a thing cannot be in our mind. On the contrary, since (Prs. 11 and 13, II) the first thing that constitutes the essence of the mind is the idea of an actually existing body, the basic and most important element of our mind is the conatus (Pr. 7, III) to affirm the existence of our body. Therefore, the idea that negates the existence of our body is contrary to our mind.

P11   *Whatsoever increases or diminishes, assists or checks, the power of activity of our body, the idea of the said thing increases or diminishes, assists or checks the power of thought of our mind.*

Proof   This proposition is evident from Pr. 7, II, or again from Pr. 14, II.

Schol   We see then that the mind can undergo considerable changes, and can pass now to a state of greater perfection, now to one of less perfection, and it is these passive transitions [*passiones*] that explicate for us the emotions of Pleasure [*laetitia*] and Pain [*tristitia*]. So in what follows I shall understand by pleasure "the passive transition of the mind to a state of greater perfection," and by pain "the passive transition of the mind to state of less perfection." The emotion of pleasure when it is simultaneously related to mind and body I call Titillation [*titillatio*] or Cheerfulness [*hilaritas*]; the emotion of pain when it is similarly related I call Anguish [*dolor*] or Melancholy [*melancholia*]. But be it noted that titillation and anguish are related to man when one part of him is affected more than others, cheerfulness and melancholy when all parts are equally affected. As to Desire [*cupiditas*], I have explained what it is in Schol. Pr. 9, III, and I acknowledge no primary emotion other than these three [i.e., pleasure, pain, and desire]; for I shall subsequently show that the others arise from these three. But before going further, I should like to explain Pr. 10, III at greater length, so that there may be a clearer understanding of the way in which an idea may be contrary to an idea.

In Schol. Pr. 17, II we demonstrated that the idea which constitutes the essence of the mind involves the existence of the body for as long as the body exists. Then from what we proved in Cor. Pr. 8, II and its Schol., it follows that the present existence of our mind depends solely on this, that the mind involves the actual existence of the body. Finally we proved that the power of the mind whereby it imagines [*imaginatur*] and remembers things depends also on this (Prs. 17 and 18, II, and Schol.), that it involves the actual existence of the body. From this it follows that the present existence of the mind and its capacity to perceive through the senses are annulled as soon as the mind ceases to affirm the present existence of the body. But the cause of the mind's ceasing to affirm this existence of the body cannot be the mind itself (Pr. 4, III), nor again that the body ceases to be. For (Pr. 6, II) the cause of the mind's affirming the existence of the body is not that the body began to exist; therefore, by the same reasoning, it does not cease to affirm the existence of the body on account of the body's ceasing to be. This results from another idea, which excludes the present existence of our body and consequently that of our mind, and which is therefore contrary to the idea that constitutes the essence of our mind (Pr. 8, II).

P12   *The mind, as far as it can, endeavors to think of those things that increase or assist the body's power of activity.*

Proof   As long as the human body is affected in a manner that involves the nature of an external body, so long will the human mind regard that latter body as present (Pr. 17, II). Consequently (Pr. 7, II), as long as the human mind regards some external body as present, that is (Schol. Pr. 17, II), thinks of it, so long is the human body affected in a manner that involves the nature of that external body. Accordingly, as long as the mind thinks of those things that increase or assist our body's power of activity, so long is the body affected in ways that increase or assist its power of activity (Post. 1, III); and, consequently, so long is the mind's power of thinking increased or assisted (Pr. 11, III). Therefore (Pr. 6 or 9, III), the mind, as far as it can, endeavors to think of those things.

P13   *When the mind thinks of those things that diminish or check the body's power of activity, it endeavors, as far as it can, to call to mind those things that exclude the existence of the former.*

Proof   As long as the mind thinks of something of this kind, so long is the power of mind and body diminished or checked (as we have proved in the preceding proposition). Nevertheless the mind will continue to think of it until it thinks of another thing that excludes the present existence of the former (Pr. 17, II); that is, (as we have just demonstrated), the power of mind and body is diminished or checked until the mind thinks of something else that excludes the thing's existence, something which the mind therefore (Pr. 9, III) endeavors, as far as it can, to think of or call to mind.

Cor   Hence it follows that the mind is averse to thinking of things that diminish or check its power and the body's power.

Schol   From what has been said we clearly understand what are Love [*amor*] and Hatred [*odium*]. Love is merely "pleasure accompanied by the idea of an external cause," and hatred is merely "pain accompanied by the idea of an external cause." Again, we see that he who loves necessarily endeavors to have present and to preserve the thing that he loves; on the other hand, he who hates endeavors to remove and destroy the thing that he hates. But we shall deal with these matters more fully in due course.

P14   *If the mind has once been affected by two emotions at the same time, when it is later affected by the one it will also be affected by the other.*

Proof   If the human body has once been affected by two bodies at the same time, when the mind later thinks of the one it will straightway recall the other too (Pr. 18, II). Now the images formed by the mind reflect the affective states of our body more than the nature of external bodies (Cor. 2, Pr. 16, II). Therefore if the body, and consequently the mind (Def. 3, III), has once been affected by two emotions, when it is later affected by the one, it will also be affected by the other.

P15   *Anything can indirectly [per accidens] be the cause of Pleasure, Pain, or Desire.*

Proof   Let it be supposed that the mind is affected by two emotions simultaneously, of which one neither increases nor diminishes its power of activity, and the other either increases it or diminishes it (Post. 1, III). From the preceding proposition it is clear that when the mind is later affected by the former as its true cause—which, by hypothesis, of itself neither increases nor diminishes the mind's power of thinking—it will straightway be affected by the other, which does increase or diminish its power of thinking; that is (Schol. Pr. 11, III), it will be affected by pleasure or pain. So the former will be the cause of pleasure or pain, not through itself, but indirectly. In this same way it can readily be demonstrated that the former thing can indirectly be the cause of desire.

Cor   From the mere fact that we have regarded a thing with the emotion of pleasure or pain of which it is not itself the efficient cause, we may love or hate that thing.

Proof   From this mere fact it comes about (Pr. 14, III) that the mind, when later thinking of this thing, is affected by the emotion of pleasure or pain; that is (Schol. Pr. 11, III), the power of the mind and body is increased or diminished, etc. Consequently (Pr. 12, III), the mind desires to think of the said thing, or is averse to it (Cor. Pr. 13, III); that is (Schol. Pr. 13, III), it loves or hates the said thing.

Schol   Hence we understand how it can come about that we love or hate some things without any cause known to us, but merely from Sympathy and Antipathy, as they are called. We should also classify in this category those objects that affect us with pleasure or pain from the mere fact that they have some resemblance to objects that are wont to affect us with the same emotions, as I shall demonstrate in the next Proposition.

I realize that the writers who first introduced the terms "sympathy" and "antipathy" intended them to mean certain occult qualities. Nevertheless, I think it is permissible for us to denote by them qualities that are also familiar or manifest.

P16   *From the mere fact that we imagine a thing to have something similar to an object that is wont to affect the mind with pleasure or pain, we shall love it or hate it, although the point of similarity is not the efficient cause of these emotions.*

Proof   By hypothesis, the point of similarity has been regarded by us in the object with the emotion of pleasure or pain; and so (Pr. 14, III) when the mind is affected by its image, it will also straightway be affected by the one or other emotion. Consequently, the thing which we perceive to have this said point of similarity will indirectly be the cause of pleasure or pain (Pr. 15, III); and thus (preceding Corollary), we shall love or hate the thing even though the point of similarity is not the efficient cause of these emotions.

P17   *If we imagine that a thing which is wont to affect us with an emotion of pain has something similar to another thing which is wont to affect us with an equally great emotion of pleasure, we shall hate it and love it at the same time.*

Proof   By hypothesis, this thing is in itself a cause of pain, and (Schol. Pr. 13, III) insofar as we imagine it with this emotion, we hate it. But, in addition, insofar as we imagine it to have something similar to another thing which is wont to affect us with an equally great emotion of pleasure, we shall love it with an equally strong emotion of pleasure (preceding Pr.). So we shall hate it and love it at the same time.

Schol   This condition of the mind arising from two conflicting emotions is called "vacillation," which is therefore related to emotion as doubt is related to imagination (Schol. Pr. 44, II), and there is no difference between vacillation and doubt except in respect of intensity. But it should be observed that in the preceding Proposition I deduced these vacillations from causes which are, in the case of one emotion, a direct cause, and in the case of the other an indirect cause. This I did because they could in this way be more readily deduced from what had preceded, and not because I deny that vacillations generally arise from an object which is the efficient cause of both emotions. For the human body is composed (Post. 1, II) of very many individual bodies of different nature, and so (Ax. 1 after Lemma 3, q.v. after Pr. 13, II) it can be affected by one and the same body in many different ways; on the other hand, since one and the same thing can be affected in many ways, it can likewise affect one and the same part of the body in different ways. From this we can readily conceive that one and the same object can be the cause of many conflicting emotions.

P18   *From the image of things past or future man is affected by the same emotion of pleasure or pain as from the image of a thing present.*

Proof   As long as a man is affected by the image of a thing, he will regard the thing as present even though it may not exist (Pr. 17, II and Cor.), and he does not think of it as past or future except insofar as its image is joined to the image of past or future time (Schol. Pr. 44, II). Therefore the image of a thing, considered solely in itself, is the same whether it be related to future, past, or present; that is (Cor. 2, Pr. 16, II), the state of the body, or the emotion, is the same whether the image be of a thing past or future or present. So the emotion of pleasure, and of pain, is the same whether the image be of a thing past or future or present.

Schol 1   Here I call a thing past or future insofar as we have been, or shall be, affected by it; for example, insofar as we have seen or shall see it, it has refreshed or will refresh us, it has injured or will injure us, etc. For insofar as we imagine it in this way, to that extent we affirm its existence; that is, the body is not affected by any emotion that excludes the existence of the thing, and so (Pr. 17, II) the body is affected by the image of the thing in the same way as if the thing itself were present. However, since it is generally the case that those who have had much experience vacillate when they are regarding a thing as future or past and are generally in doubt as to its outcome (Schol. Pr. 44, II), the result is that emotions that arise from similar images of things are not so constant, but are generally disturbed by images of other things until men become more assured of the outcome.

Schol 2   From what has just been said we understand what is Hope [*spes*], Fear [*metus*], Confidence [*securitas*], Despair [*desperatio*], Joy [*gaudium*], and Disappointment [*conscientiae morsus*]. Hope is "inconstant pleasure, arising from the image of a thing future or past, of whose outcome we are in doubt." Fear is "inconstant pain, likewise arising from the image of a thing in doubt." Now if the element of doubt be removed from these emotions, hope becomes confidence and fear becomes despair, that is "pleasure or pain arising from a thing which we have feared or have hoped." Joy is "pleasure arising from the image of a past thing of whose outcome we have been in doubt." Finally, disappointment is "the pain opposite to joy."

P19   *He who imagines that what he loves is being destroyed will feel pain. If, however, he imagines that it is being preserved, he will feel pleasure.*

Proof   The mind, as far as it can, endeavors to imagine whatever increases or assists the body's power of activity (Pr. 12, III), that is (Schol. Pr. 13, III), those things it loves. But the imagination is assisted by whatever posits the existence of the thing, and, on the other hand, is checked by whatever excludes the existence of the thing (Pr. 17, II). Therefore, the images of things that posit the existence of the loved object assist the mind's conatus wherewith it endeavors to imagine the loved object, that is (Schol. Pr. 11, III), they affect the mind with pleasure. On the other hand, those things that exclude the existence of the loved object check that same conatus of the mind, that is (by the same Scholium), they affect the mind with pain. Therefore, he who imagines that what he loves is being destroyed will feel pain, . . . etc.

P20   *He who imagines that a thing that he hates is being destroyed will feel pleasure.*

Proof   The mind (Pr. 13, III) endeavors to imagine whatever excludes the existence of things whereby the body's power of activity is diminished or checked; that is (Schol. Pr. 13, III), it endeavors to imagine whatever excludes the existence of things that it hates. So the image of a thing that excludes the existence of what the mind hates assists this conatus of the mind; that is (Schol. Pr. 11, III), it affects the mind with pleasure. Therefore, he who thinks that that which he hates is being destroyed will feel pleasure.

P21   *He who imagines that what he loves is affected with pleasure or pain will likewise be affected with pleasure or pain, the intensity of which will vary with the intensity of the emotion in the object loved.*

Proof   As we have shown in Proposition 19, III, the images of things which posit the existence of the object loved assist the mind's conatus whereby it endeavors to think of the object loved. But pleasure posits the existence of that which feels pleasure, and the more so as the emotion of pleasure is stronger; for pleasure (Schol. Pr. 11, III) is a transition to a state of greater perfection. Therefore the image, which is in the lover, of the pleasure of the object loved, assists his mind's conatus; that is (Schol. Pr. 11, III), it affects the lover with pleasure, and all the more to the extent that this emotion is in the object loved. That was the first point. Again, insofar as a thing is affected with some pain, to that extent it is being destroyed, and the more so according to the extent to which it is affected with pain (same Schol. Pr. 11, III). Thus (Pr. 19, III), he who imagines that what he loves is affected with pain will likewise be affected with pain, the intensity of which will vary with the intensity of this emotion in the object loved.

P22   *If we imagine that someone is affecting with pleasure the object of our love, we shall be affected with love toward him. If on the other hand we think that he is affecting with pain the object of our love, we shall likewise be affected with hatred toward him.*

Proof   He who affects with pleasure or pain the object of our love affects us also with pleasure or pain, assuming that we think of the object of our love as affected with that pleasure or pain (preceding Pr.). But it is supposed that this pleasure or pain is in us accompanied by the idea of an external cause. Therefore (Schol. Pr. 13, III), if we think that someone is affecting with pleasure or pain the object of our love, we shall be affected with love or hatred toward him.

Schol   Proposition 21 explains to us what is Pity [*commiseratio*], which we may define as "pain arising from another's hurt." As for pleasure arising from another's good, I know not what to call it. Furthermore, love toward one who has benefited another we shall call Approval [*favor*], and on the other hand hatred toward one who has injured another we shall call Indignation [*indignatio*]. Finally, it should be observed that we pity not only the thing which we have loved (as we have demonstrated in Pr. 21), but also a thing for which we have previously felt no emotion, provided that we judge it similar to ourselves (as I shall show in due course). Likewise, we approve of one who has benefited someone like ourselves; and on the other hand, we are indignant with one who has injured someone like ourselves.

P23   *He who imagines that what he hates is affected with pain will feel pleasure; if, on the other hand, he thinks of it as affected with pleasure, he will feel pain. Both of these emotions will vary in intensity inversely with the variation of the contrary emotion in that which he hates.*

Proof   Insofar as the thing hated is affected with pain, it is being destroyed, and the more so according to the degree of pain (Schol. Pr. 11, III). So (Pr. 20, III) he who imagines the object hated to be affected with pain will, on the contrary, be affected with pleasure, and the more so as he imagines the object hated to be affected with more pain. That was the first point. Again, pleasure posits the existence of that which feels pleasure (same Schol. Pr. 11, III), and the more so as the pleasure is conceived to be greater. If anyone imagines him whom he hates to be affected with pleasure, this thought will check his conatus (Pr. 13, III): that is (Schol. Pr. 11, III), he who hates will be affected with pain, etc.

Schol   This pleasure can scarcely be unalloyed and devoid of conflict of feeling. For (as I shall forthwith demonstrate in Proposition 27) insofar as he imagines a thing similar to himself to be affected with an emotion of pain, to that extent he is bound to feel pain, and contrariwise if he imagines it to be affected with pleasure. But here it is only his hate that we are considering.

P24   *If we imagine someone to be affecting with pleasure a thing that we hate, we shall be affected with hate toward him too. If on the other hand we think of him as affecting with pain the said thing, we shall be affected with love toward him.*

Proof   The proof follows the same lines as Pr. 22, III.

Schol   These and similar emotions of hatred are related to Envy [*invidia*], which can therefore be defined as "hatred insofar as it is considered to dispose a man to rejoice in another's hurt and to feel pain at another's good."

P25   *We endeavor to affirm of ourselves and of an object loved whatever we imagine affects us or the loved object with pleasure, and, on the other hand, to negate whatever we imagine affects us or the loved object with pain.*

Proof   What we imagine affects the object loved with pleasure or pain affects us with pleasure or pain (Pr. 21, III). Now the mind (Pr. 12, III) endeavors, as far as it can, to think of things that affect us with pleasure; that is (Pr. 17, II and Cor.), to regard them as present; and, on the other hand (Pr. 13, III), to exclude the existence of things that affect us with pain. Therefore, we endeavor to affirm of ourselves and the loved object whatever we imagine affects us or the object loved with pleasure, and vice versa.

P26   *We endeavor to affirm of that which we hate whatever we imagine affects it with pain, and on the other hand to deny what we imagine affects it with pleasure.*

Proof   This proposition follows from Proposition 23, III, as does the preceding proposition from Proposition 21, III.

Schol   Thus we see that it easily happens that a man may have too high an opinion of himself and of the object loved, and on the other hand too mean an opinion of the object of his hatred. This way of thinking, when it concerns the man who has too high an opinion of himself, is called Pride [*superbia*], and is a kind of madness, in that a man dreams with his eyes open that he can do all those things that his imagination encompasses, which he therefore regards as real, exulting in them, as long as he is incapable of thinking of those things that exclude their existence and limit his power of activity. Therefore, pride is "pleasure arising from the fact that a man has too high an opinion of himself." Again, "pleasure that arises from the fact that a man has too high an opinion of another" is called Overesteem [*existimatio*]. Finally, "pleasure arising from the fact that a man has too mean an opinion of another" is called Disparagement [*despectus*].

P27   *From the fact that we imagine a thing like ourselves, toward which we have felt no emotion, to be affected by an emotion, we are thereby affected by a similar emotion.*

Proof   Images of things are affections of the human body, the ideas of which set before us external bodies as present (Schol. Pr. 17, II); that is (Pr. 16, II), the ideas of these affections involve the nature of our own body and simultaneously the nature of the external body as present. If therefore the nature of the external body is similar to the nature of our own body, then the idea of the external body in our thinking will involve an affection of our own body similar to the affection of the external body. Consequently, if we imagine someone like ourselves to be affected by an emotion, this thought will express an affection of our own body similar to that emotion. So from the fact that we imagine a thing like ourselves to be affected by an emotion, we are affected by a similar emotion along with it. But if we hate a thing similar to ourselves, to that extent (Pr. 23, III) we shall be affected by a contrary, not similar, emotion along with it.

Schol   This imitation of emotions, when it is related to pain, is called Pity (see Schol. Pr. 22, III), but when it is related to desire it is called Emulation [*aemulatio*], which is therefore "nothing else but the desire of some thing which has been engendered in us from the belief that others similar to ourselves have this same desire."

Cor 1   If we believe that someone, for whom we have felt no emotion, affects with pleasure a thing similar to ourselves, we shall be affected by love toward him. If, on the other hand, we believe that he affects the said object with pain, we shall be affected with hatred toward him.

Proof   This is proved from the preceding Proposition in the same way as Proposition 22 from Proposition 21, III.

Cor 2   The fact that its distress affects us with pain cannot cause us to hate a thing that we pity.

Proof   If we could hate it on that account, then (Pr. 23, III) we should be pleased at its pain, which is contrary to our hypothesis.

Cor 3   As far as we can, we endeavor to free from distress the thing that we pity.

Proof   That which affects with pain a thing that we pity affects us too with similar pain (preceding Pr.), and so we shall endeavor to devise whatever annuls the existence of the former or destroys it (Pr. 13, III): that is (Schol. Pr. 9, III), we shall seek to destroy it; i.e., we shall be determined to destroy it. So we shall endeavor to free from its distress the thing we pity.

Schol   This will or appetite to do good which arises from our pitying the thing to which we wish to do good is called Benevolence [*benevolentia*], which is therefore "nothing else but desire arising from pity." As to love and hatred toward one who has done good or ill to a thing that we think to be like ourselves, see Schol. Pr. 22, III.

P28   *We endeavor to bring about whatever we imagine to be conducive to pleasure; but we endeavor to remove or destroy whatever we imagine to be opposed to pleasure and conducive to pain.*

Proof   As far as we can, we endeavor to imagine whatever we think to be conducive to pleasure (Pr. 12, III): that is (Pr. 17, II), we endeavor, as far as we can, to regard it as present, that is, existing in actuality. But the conatus of the mind, that is, its power to think, is equal to and simultaneous in nature with the conatus of the body, that is, its power to act (as clearly follows from Cor. Pr. 7 and Cor. Pr. 11, II). Therefore in an absolute sense we endeavor, that is, we seek and purpose (which is the same thing by Schol. Pr. 9, III), to bring about its existence. That was our first point. Further, if we imagine that which we believe to be the cause of pain, that is (Schol. Pr. 13, III), that which we hate, as being destroyed, we shall feel pleasure (Pr. 20, III), and so (by the first part of this proposition) we shall endeavor to destroy it, or (Pr. 13, III) to remove it from us so as not to regard it as present. That was our second point. Therefore we endeavor to bring about . . . etc.

P29   *We also endeavor to do whatever we imagine men[2] to regard with pleasure, and on the other hand we shun doing whatever we imagine men to regard with aversion.*

Proof   From the fact that we imagine men love or hate something, we shall love or hate the same thing (Pr. 27, III); that is (Schol. Pr. 13, III), from that very fact we shall feel pleasure or pain at the presence of the thing. So (preceding Pr.) we shall endeavor to do whatever we imagine men love or regard with pleasure . . . etc.

Schol   This conatus to do, and also to avoid doing, something simply in order to please men is called Ambition [*ambitio*], especially when we endeavor so earnestly to please the multitude that we do, or avoid doing, things to our own hurt or another's hurt; otherwise, it is called Kindliness [*humanitas*]. Again, the pleasure with which we think of another's action whereby he has endeavored to please us I call Praise [*laus*], and the pain with which, on the other hand, we dislike his action I call Blame [*vituperium*].

P30   *If anyone has done something which he imagines affects others with pleasure, he will be affected with pleasure accompanied by the idea of himself as cause; that is, he will regard himself with pleasure. If, on the other hand, he imagines he has done something which affects others with pain, he will regard himself with pain.*

Proof   He who imagines he affects others with pleasure or pain will by that very fact be affected with pleasure or pain (Pr. 27, III). Now since man (Prs. 19 and 23, II) is conscious of himself through the affections by which he is determined to act, he who has done something which he thinks affects others with pleasure will be affected with pleasure along with the consciousness of himself as cause; that is, he will regard himself with pleasure. The contrary likewise follows.

---

[2] Here, and in what follows, by "men" I understand men for whom we have felt no emotion.

Schol   Since love (Schol. Pr. 13, III) is pleasure accompanied by the idea of an external cause, and hate is pain also accompanied by the idea of an external cause, this pleasure and this pain are species of love and hatred. But as love and hatred have reference to external objects, we shall assign different names to these emotions. The pleasure that is accompanied by an external cause we shall call Honor [*gloria*], and the pain that is its opposite we shall call Shame [*pudor*]; but be it understood that this is when the pleasure or pain arises from a man's belief that he is praised or blamed. Otherwise, the pleasure that is accompanied by the idea of an internal cause I shall call Self-contentment [*Acquiescentia in se ipso*], and the pain that is its opposite I shall call Repentance [*paenitentia*]. Again, since it is possible (Cor. Pr. 17, II) that the pleasure with which a man imagines he affects others is only imaginary, and (Pr. 25, III) everyone endeavors to imagine of himself whatever he thinks affects himself with pleasure, it can easily happen that a vain man may be proud and imagine that he is popular with everybody, when he in fact is obnoxious.

P31   *If we think that someone loves, desires, or hates something that we love, desire, or hate, that very fact will cause us to love, desire, or hate the thing more steadfastly. But if we think he dislikes what we love, or vice versa, then our feelings will fluctuate.*

Proof   From the mere fact that we imagine someone loves something, we shall love that same thing (Pr. 27, III). But even apart from this consideration we are supposing that we love that same thing. Therefore, to the existing love there is added a further cause whereby it is nurtured, and by that very fact we shall love more steadfastly the object of our love. Again, from the fact that we think someone dislikes something, we shall dislike the same thing (by the same proposition). But if we suppose that at the same time we love the thing, we shall therefore at the same time love and dislike that thing; that is (see Schol. Pr. 17, III), our feelings will fluctuate.

Cor   From this and from Pr. 28, III it follows that everyone endeavors, as far as he can, that what he loves should be loved by everyone, and what he hates should be hated by everyone. Hence that saying of the poet:

> As lovers, let our hopes and fears be alike,
> Insensitive is he who loves what another leaves.[3]

Schol   This conatus to bring it about that everyone should approve of one's loves and hates is in reality ambition (see Schol. Pr. 29, III). So we see that it is in everyone's nature to strive to bring it about that others should adopt his attitude to life; and while all strive equally to this end they equally hinder one another, and in all seeking the praise or love of all, they provoke mutual dislike.

P32   *If we think that someone enjoys something that only one person can possess, we shall endeavor to bring it about that he should not possess that thing.*

---

3 [Ovid, *Amores*, 11, 19.—S.S.]

Proof   From the mere fact that we imagine somebody to enjoy something (Pr. 27, III and Cor. 1) we shall love that thing and desire to enjoy it. But by hypothesis we think that this pleasure is impeded by the fact that that person is enjoying the thing in question. Therefore (Pr. 28, III), we shall endeavor to bring it about that he should not possess it.

Schol   We therefore see that human nature is in general so constituted that men pity the unfortunate and envy the fortunate, in the latter case with a hatred proportionate to their love of what they think another possesses (by the preceding Proposition). Furthermore, we see that from the same property of human nature from which it follows that men are compassionate, it likewise follows that they are prone to envy and ambition. Finally, we shall find that common experience confirms all these points, especially if we turn our attention to childhood. For we find that children, their bodies being, as it were, continually in a state of equilibrium, laugh or weep merely from seeing others laugh or weep, and whatever else they see others do they immediately want to imitate. In short, they want for themselves whatever they see others take pleasure in because, as we have said, the images of things are the very affections of the human body, that is, the ways in which the human body is affected by external causes and disposed to this or that action.

P33   *If we love something similar to ourselves, we endeavor, as far as we can, to bring it about that it should love us in return.*

Proof   We endeavor, as far as we can, to think of something we love in preference to other things (Pr. 12, III). So if the thing be like ourselves, we shall endeavor to affect it with pleasure in preference to other things (Pr. 29, III); that is, we shall endeavor, as far as we can, to bring it about that the object of our love should be affected with pleasure accompanied by the idea of ourselves, that is (Schol. Pr. 13, III), that it should love us in return.

P34   *The greater the emotion with which we imagine the object of our love is affected toward us, the greater will be our vanity.*

Proof   By the preceding proposition, we endeavor to bring it about, as far as we can, that the object of our love should love us in return; that is (Schol. Pr. 13, III), that the object of our love should be affected with pleasure accompanied by the idea of ourselves. So the greater the pleasure with which we think that the object of our love is affected because of us, the more is this endeavor assisted; that is (Pr. 11, III and Schol.), the greater the pleasure with which we are affected. Now since our pleasure is due to our having affected with pleasure another person like ourselves, we regard ourselves with pleasure (Pr. 30, III). Therefore, the greater the emotion with which we think the object loved is affected toward us, with that much greater pleasure shall we regard ourselves; that is (Schol. Pr. 30, III), the greater will be our vanity.

P35   *If anyone thinks that there is between the object of his love and another person the same or a more intimate bond of friendship than there was between them* *when he alone used to possess the object loved, he will be affected with hatred toward the object loved and will envy his rival.*

Proof   The greater the love wherewith one thinks the object of his love is affected toward him, the greater will be his vanity (by the preceding proposition); that is (Schol. Pr. 30, III), the more he will be pleased. So (Pr. 28, III) he will endeavor, as far as he can, to imagine the object loved as bound to him as intimately as possible, and this conatus, or appetite, is fostered if he imagines someone else desires the same thing for himself (Pr. 31, III). But we are supposing that this conatus, or appetite, is checked by the image of the object loved accompanied by the image of him with whom the object loved is associating. Therefore (Schol. Pr. 11, III), this will cause him to be affected with pain accompanied by the idea of the object loved as cause and simultaneously by the image of his rival; that is (Schol. Pr. 13, III), he will be affected with hatred toward the object loved and at the same time toward his rival (Cor. Pr. 15, III), whom he will envy because (Pr. 23, III) he enjoys the object loved.

Schol   This hatred toward the object of one's love, joined with envy, is called Jealousy [*zelotypia*], which is therefore nothing else but "vacillation arising from simultaneous love and hatred accompanied by the idea of a rival who is envied." Furthermore, this hatred toward the object of his love will be greater in proportion to the pleasure wherewith the jealous man was wont to be affected as a result of the returning of his love by the object of his love, and also in proportion to the emotion wherewith he was affected toward him whom he thinks of as being intimately associated with the object of his love. For if he used to hate him, that very fact will make him hate the object of his love (Pr. 24, III) because he thinks of it as affecting with pleasure that which he hates, and also (Cor. Pr. 15, III) because he is compelled to associate the image of the object of his love with the image of one whom he hates. This is generally the case with love toward a woman; for he who thinks of a woman whom he loves as giving herself to another will not only feel pain by reason of his own appetite being checked but also, being compelled to associate the image of the object of his love with the sexual parts of his rival, he feels disgust for her. Then there is in addition the fact that the jealous man will not receive the same warm welcome as he was wont to receive from the object of his love, and this is a further reason for the lover's pain, as I shall now demonstrate.

P36   *He who recalls a thing which once afforded him pleasure desires to possess the same thing in the same circumstances as when he first took pleasure therein.*

Proof   Whatever a man has seen together with the object that has afforded him pleasure will be indirectly a cause of pleasure (Pr. 15, III), and so (Pr. 28, III) he will desire to possess all this together with the object that afforded him pleasure, that is, he will desire to possess the object along with all the same attendant circumstances as when he first took pleasure in the object.

Cor   If therefore he finds one of those attendant circumstances missing, the lover will feel pain.

Proof Insofar as he finds some attendant circumstance missing, to that extent he imagines something that excludes its existence. Now since he desires that thing or circumstance (preceding proposition) by reason of his love, then (Pr. 19, III) insofar as he thinks it to be lacking he will feel pain.

Schol This pain, insofar as it regards the absence of that which we love, is called Longing [*desiderium*].

P37 *The desire arising from pain or pleasure, hatred or love, is proportionately greater as the emotion is greater.*

Proof Pain diminishes or checks man's power of activity (Schol. Pr. 11, III), that is (Pr. 7, III), it diminishes or checks the conatus wherewith a man endeavors to persist in his own being; and therefore it is contrary to this conatus (Pr. 5, III), and the conatus of a man affected by pain is entirely directed to removing the pain. But, by the definition of pain, the greater the pain, the greater the extent to which it must be opposed to man's power of activity. Therefore the greater the pain, with that much greater power of activity will a man endeavor to remove the pain; that is (Schol. Pr. 9, III), with that much greater desire, or appetite, will he endeavor to remove the pain. Again, since pleasure (Schol. Pr. 11, III) increases or assists man's power of activity, it can readily be demonstrated in the same way that a man affected with pleasure desires nothing other than to preserve it, and with all the greater desire as the pleasure is greater. Finally, since hatred and love are emotions of pain or pleasure, it follows in the same way that the conatus, appetite, or desire arising through hatred or love is greater in proportion to the hatred and love.

P38 *If anyone has begun to hate the object of his love to the extent that his love is completely extinguished, he will, other things being equal, bear greater hatred toward it than if he had never loved it, and his hatred will be proportionate to the strength of his former love.*

Proof If anyone begins to hate the object of his love, more of his appetites are checked than if he had never loved it. For love is pleasure (Schol. Pr. 13, III), which a man endeavors to preserve as far as he can (Pr. 28, III), and this he does (same Schol.) by regarding the object loved as present and affecting it with pleasure (Pr. 21, III), as far as he can. This conatus (preceding Pr.) is the greater as the love is greater, as also is the conatus that the object loved should return his love (Pr. 33, III). But these conatus are checked by hatred toward the object loved (Cor. Pr. 13 and Pr. 23, III). Therefore, for this reason, too, the lover will be affected with pain (Schol. Pr. 11, III) which will be proportionate to his previous love; that is, in addition to the pain that was the cause of his hatred, a further pain arises from the fact that he has loved the object. Consequently, he will regard the loved object with a greater emotion of pain, that is (Schol. Pr. 13, III), he will bear greater hatred toward it than if he had not loved it, and his hatred will be proportionate to the strength of his former love.

P39 *He who hates someone will endeavor to injure him unless he fears that he will suffer a greater injury in return. On the other hand, he who loves someone will by that same law endeavor to benefit him.*

Proof To hate someone is (Schol. Pr. 13, III) to imagine someone to be the cause of one's pain. So (Pr. 28, III) he who hates someone will endeavor to remove or destroy him. But if he fears from him something more painful, or (which is the same thing), a greater injury, which he thinks he can avoid by not inflicting the harm he was intending on him whom he hates, he will desire to refrain from so doing (same Pr. 28, III), and this conatus (Pr. 37, III) will be greater than that which was directed toward inflicting harm. This latter conatus will therefore prevail, as we have said. The second part of this proof proceeds on the same lines. Therefore, he who hates someone . . . etc.

Schol By "good" I understand here every kind of pleasure and furthermore whatever is conducive thereto, and especially whatever satisfies a longing of any sort. By "bad" I understand every kind of pain, and especially that which frustrates a longing. For I have demonstrated above (Schol. Pr. 9, III) that we do not desire a thing because we judge it to be good; on the contrary, we call the object of our desire good, and consequently the object of our aversion bad. Therefore, it is according to his emotion that everyone judges or deems what is good, bad, better, worse, best, or worst. Thus the miser judges wealth the best thing, and its lack the worst thing. The ambitious man desires nothing so much as public acclaim, and dreads nothing so much as disgrace. To the envious man nothing is more pleasant than another's unhappiness, and nothing more obnoxious than another's happiness. Thus, every man judges a thing good or bad, advantageous or disadvantageous, according to his own emotion.

Now the emotion whereby a man is so disposed as to refrain from what he wants to do or to choose to do what he does not want is called Timidity [*timor*], which is merely fear insofar as a man is thereby disposed to avoid by a lesser evil what he judges to be a future evil (see Pr. 28, III). But if the evil that he fears is disgrace, then timidity is called Bashfulness [*verecundia*]. Finally, if the desire to avoid a future evil is checked by the apprehension of another evil, so that he does not know what preference to make, then fear is called Consternation [*consternatio*], especially if both the feared evils are of the greatest.

P40 *He who imagines he is hated by someone to whom he believes he has given no cause for hatred will hate him in return.*

Proof He who imagines someone to be affected with hatred will by that very fact himself be affected with hatred (Pr. 27, III), that is (Schol. Pr. 13, III), pain accompanied by the idea of an external cause. But, by hypothesis, he himself thinks that there is no other cause of this pain than he who hates him. Therefore, from the fact that he imagines that he is hated by someone, he will be affected by pain accompanied by the idea of him who hates him; that is (by the same Schol.), he will hate that person.

Schol   But if he thinks that he has provided just cause for hatred, then (Pr. 30, III and Schol.) he will be affected with shame. But this (Pr. 25, III) is rarely the case. Furthermore, this reciprocation of hatred can also arise from the fact that hatred is followed by a conatus to injure him who is hated (Pr. 39, III). So he who imagines he is hated by someone will imagine him to be the cause of some evil or pain, and so he will be affected with pain, or fear, accompanied by the idea of him who hates him as being the cause; that is, he will be affected with hatred in return, as we said above.

Cor 1   He who imagines that one he loves is affected with hatred toward him, will suffer the conflicting emotions of hatred and love. For insofar as he imagines he is hated by him, he is determined to hate him in return (preceding Pr.). But, by hypothesis, he nevertheless loves him. Therefore, he will suffer the conflicting emotions of hatred and love.

Cor 2   If anyone imagines that he has suffered some injury through hatred at the hands of one toward whom he has previously felt no emotion, he will immediately endeavor to return the said injury.

Proof   He who imagines that someone is affected with hatred toward him will hate him in return (preceding Pr.), and he will endeavor to devise anything that can affect that person with pain (Pr. 26, III), and will seek to inflict it on him (Pr. 39, III). But, by hypothesis, the first thing of that kind that comes to his mind is the injury that has been inflicted on himself. Therefore, he will immediately endeavor to inflict that same injury on that person.

Schol   The conatus to inflict injury on one whom we hate is called Anger [*ira*]. The conatus to return an injury which we have suffered is called Revenge [*vindicta*].

P41   *If anyone thinks that he is loved by someone and believes that he has given no cause for this (which is possible through Cor. Pr. 15 and Pr. 16, III), he will love him in return.*

Proof   This is proved in the same way as the preceding proposition. See also its Scholium.

Schol   If he believes that he has given just cause for this love, he will exult in it (Pr. 30, III and Schol.), which is more often the case (Pr. 25, III); and we have said that the contrary occurs when someone thinks that he is hated by someone (see Schol. preceding Pr.). Now this reciprocal love, and consequently (Pr. 39, III) the conatus to benefit one who loves us and who (same Pr. 39, III) endeavors to benefit us, is called Gratitude [*gratia seu gratitudo*]. So it is evident that men are far more inclined to revenge than to repay a benefit.

Cor   He who imagines that he is loved by one whom he hates will feel conflicting emotions of hate and love. This is proved in the same way as the first corollary of the preceding proposition.

Schol   If hatred prevails, he will endeavor to injure him by whom he is loved, and this emotion is called Cruelty [*crudelitas*], especially if it is believed that he who loves has not given any cause for hatred between them.

P42   *He who, moved by love or hope of honor, has conferred a benefit on someone, will feel pain if he sees that the benefit is ungratefully received.*

Proof   He who loves a thing similar to himself endeavors, as far as he can, to bring it about that he is loved in return (Pr. 33, III). So he who through love confers a benefit upon someone does so through his longing to be loved in return; that is (Pr. 34, III), through hope of honor, or (Schol. Pr. 30, III) pleasure. Thus (Pr. 12, III), he will endeavor as far as he can to imagine this cause of honor, i.e., to regard it as actually existing. But, by hypothesis, he thinks of something else that excludes the existence of the said cause. Therefore (Pr. 19, III), by that very fact he will feel pain.

P43   *Hatred is increased by reciprocal hatred, and may on the other hand be destroyed by love.*

Proof   If someone thinks that one whom he hates is affected with hatred toward him, a new source of hatred thereby arises (Pr. 40, III), while the old hatred, by hypothesis, still continues. But if, on the other hand, he thinks that the said person is affected with love toward him, insofar as he thinks this, he regards himself with pleasure (Pr. 30, III), and to that extent (Pr. 29, III) he will endeavor to please him; that is (Pr. 41, III), to that extent he endeavors not to hate him nor affect him with any pain. This conatus (Pr. 37, III) will vary proportionately to the strength of the emotion from which it arises, and so if it should be greater than the emotion which arises from hatred whereby he endeavors to affect the object of his hatred with pain (Pr. 26, III), it will prevail over it and will eradicate the feeling of hatred.

P44   *Hatred that is fully overcome by love passes into love, and the love will therefore be greater than if it had not been preceded by hatred.*

Proof   The proof proceeds along the same lines as that of Pr. 38, III. For he who begins to love the object that he hated, that is, used to regard with pain, will feel pleasure by the very fact that he loves, and to this pleasure which love involves (see its Def. in Schol. Pr. 13, III) is added the further pleasure arising from the fact that the conatus to remove the pain which hatred involves (as we demonstrated in Pr. 37, III) is very much assisted, accompanied by the idea of the one whom he hated as being the cause.

Schol   Although this is so, nobody will endeavor to hate an object or be affected with pain in order to enjoy this greater feeling of pleasure; that is, nobody will desire to suffer hurt in the hope of recovering his health. For everyone will endeavor always to preserve his own being and to remove pain, as far as he can. If it were possible to conceive the contrary, that a man should want to hate someone so that he might later feel greater love for him, he will always want to be hating him. For the greater was the hatred, the greater will be the love; so he will always want his hatred to go on growing. And for the same reason a man will endeavor to be more and more ill so as later to enjoy greater pleasure from the restoration of health. So he will always endeavor to be ill, which is absurd (Pr. 6, III).

P45   *If anyone imagines that someone similar to himself is affected with hatred toward a thing similar to himself, which he loves, he will hate him.*

Proof   The object loved returns the hatred of him who hates it (Pr. 40, III), and so the lover who thinks that someone hates the object loved is thereby made to think of the object of his love as affected by hatred, that is (Schol. Pr. 13, III), as affected by pain. Consequently he feels pain (Pr. 21, III), a pain that is accompanied by the idea of him who hates the object of his love as being the cause; that is (Schol. Pr. 13, III), he will hate him.

P46   *If anyone is affected with pleasure or pain by someone of a class or nation different from his own and the pleasure or pain is accompanied by the idea of that person as its cause, under the general category of that class or nation, he will love or hate not only him but all of that same class or nation.*

Proof   This is evident from Pr. 16, III.

P47   *The pleasure that arises from our imagining that the object of our hatred is being destroyed or is suffering some other harm is not devoid of some feeling of pain.*

Proof   This is evident from Pr. 27, III. For insofar as we imagine a thing similar to ourselves to be affected with pain, to that extent we feel pain.

Schol   This Proposition can also be proved from Cor. Pr. 17, II. For whenever we call a thing to mind, although it may not actually exist, we regard it as present, and the body is affected in the same way. Therefore insofar as his remembrance of the thing is strong, to that extent the man is determined to regard it with pain. And whereas this determination, the image of the thing still persisting, is checked by the remembrance of those things that exclude its existence, it is not completely annulled, and so the man feels pleasure only insofar as this determination is checked. Hence it comes about that the pleasure that arises from the harm suffered by the object of our hatred is revived whenever we call to mind the said thing. For, as we have said, when the image of the said thing is activated, since it involves the existence of the thing it determines one to regard the thing with the same pain as when one was wont to regard it when it did exist. But since one has associated with the image of the said thing other images which exclude its existence, this determination to pain is immediately checked, and one feels a renewed pleasure, and this is so whenever the series of events is repeated.

It is this same cause that makes men feel pleasure whenever they recall some past ill and makes them enjoy talking about perils from which they have been saved. For when they imagine some peril they regard it as though it were still to come and are determined to fear it, a determination which is again checked by the idea of their escape which they associated with the idea of this peril when they did in fact escape it. This idea makes them feel safe once more, and so their pleasure is renewed.

P48   *Love and hatred toward, say, Peter are destroyed if the pain involved in the latter and the pleasure involved in the former are associated with the idea of a different cause; and both emotions are diminished to the extent that we think Peter not to have been the only cause of either emotion.*

Proof   This is evident merely from the definitions of love and hatred, for which see Schol. Pr. 13, III. For pleasure is called love for Peter, and pain, hatred for Peter, for this reason alone, that Peter is considered the cause of the one or other emotion. When this consideration is completely or partly removed, the emotion toward Peter disappears or is diminished.

P49   *Love and hatred toward a thing that we think of as free must both be greater, other conditions being equal, than toward a thing subject to necessity.*

Proof   A thing that we think of as free has to be perceived through itself independently of other things (Def. 7, I). If therefore we think it to be the cause of pleasure or pain, by that very fact we shall love or hate it (Schol. Pr. 13, III), and with the utmost love or hatred that can arise from the postulated emotion (preceding Pr.). But if we think of the thing which is the cause of the said emotion as subject to necessity, then we shall think of it not as the sole cause of the said emotion but together with other causes (same Def. 7, I), and so (preceding Pr.) love and hatred toward it will be less.

Schol   Hence it follows that, deeming themselves to be free, men feel more love and hatred toward one another than toward other things. Then there is the additional factor of imitation of emotions, for which see Prs. 27, 34, 40, and 43, III.

P50   *Anything can be the indirect cause of hope or fear.*

Proof   This proposition is proved in the same way as Pr. 15, III, q.v., together with Schol. 2, Pr. 18, III.

Schol   Things that are indirectly causes of hope or fear are called good or bad omens. Again, insofar as these same omens are the cause of hope or fear, to that extent they are the cause of pleasure or pain (by Defs. of hope and fear, q.v., Schol. 2, Pr. 18, III), and consequently (Cor. Pr. 15, III) to that extent we love or hate them and (Pr. 28, III) we endeavor to procure them as means to fulfil our hopes or to remove them as obstacles or causes of fear. Furthermore, it follows from Pr. 25, III that we are so constituted by nature that we are ready to believe what we hope and reluctant to believe what we fear, and that we overestimate and underestimate in such cases. This is the origin of Superstition [*superstitiones*], to which men are everywhere a prey.

I do not think it worthwhile to demonstrate here the vacillations that arise from hope and fear, since it follows merely from the definition of these emotions that there is no hope without fear and no fear without hope (as I shall explain at greater length in due course). Furthermore, insofar as we hope or fear something, to that extent we love or hate it, and so everyone can easily apply to hope and fear what we have said concerning love and hatred.

P51   *Different men can be affected in different ways by one and the same object, and one and the same man can be affected by one and the same object in different ways at different times.*

Proof   The human body (Post. 3, II) is affected by external bodies in a great many ways. So two men may be affected at the same time in different ways, and so (Ax. 1 after Lemma 3, q.v., after Pr. 13, II) they can be affected by one and the same object in different ways. Again (same Post.), the human body can be affected now in one way, now in another, and consequently (same Ax.) it can be affected in different ways at different times by one and the same object.

Schol   We therefore see that it is possible that what one man loves, another hates, what one man fears, another fears not, and that one and the same man may now love what he previously hated and may now dare what he previously feared, and so on. Again, since everyone according to his emotions judges what is good, what is bad, what is better and what is worse (Schol. Pr. 39, III), it follows that men vary as much in judgment as in emotion.[4] So it comes about that in comparing different men we distinguish between them solely by difference of emotion, and call some fearless, others timid, and others by other epithets. For example, I shall call fearless one who despises an evil that I am wont to fear, and if furthermore I have regard to the fact that his desire to inflict injury on one he hates and to benefit one whom he loves is not checked by apprehension of an evil which is wont to restrain me, I shall call him daring. Again, he who fears an evil which I am wont to despise will appear to me timid, and if furthermore I have regard to the fact that his desire is checked by apprehension of an evil which cannot restrain me, I shall say he is cowardly. And this is how everyone judges. Finally, as a result of this characteristic of man and the variability of his judgment—such as the fact that man's judgment is often governed solely by emotion, and that things which he believes to make for pleasure or pain and which he therefore (Pr. 28, III) endeavors to promote or remove are often merely imaginary, not to mention other points mentioned in Part II concerning the uncertainty of things—we readily conceive that a man may often be responsible for the pain and pleasure that he feels; that is, for being affected both with pain and pleasure, accompanied by the idea of himself as its cause. Thus, we readily understand what repentance [*paenitentia*] and self-contentment are. Repentance is pain accompanied by the idea of oneself as its

---

[4] We have shown in Schol. Pr. 13, II that this can be so although the human mind is part of the divine intellect.

cause, and self-contentment is pleasure accompanied by the idea of oneself as its cause, and these emotions are extremely intense since men believe themselves to be free (see Pr. 49, III).

P52   *To an object that we have previously seen in conjunction with others or that we imagine to have nothing but what is common to many other objects, we shall not give as much regard as to that which we imagine to have something singular.*

Proof   As soon as we think of an object that we have seen in conjunction with others, we immediately recall the others as well (Pr. 18, II and Schol.) and thus from regarding the one we immediately pass on to regarding another. The same holds good of an object which we think to have nothing but what is common to many others. For by that very fact we suppose that we are regarding in it nothing that we have not previously seen in other objects. But in supposing that we perceive in some object something special that we have never seen before we are saying only this, that the mind, while regarding that object, contains nothing in itself to the contemplation of which it can pass on from contemplation of that object. Therefore, the mind is determined to regard only that object. Therefore . . . etc.

Schol   This affection of the mind, or thought of a special thing, insofar as it alone engages the mind is called Wonder [*admiratio*], which, if evoked by an object that we fear, is called Consternation, because wonder at an evil keeps a man so paralyzed in regarding it alone that he is incapable of thinking of other things whereby he might avoid the evil. But if that which we wonder at be a man's prudence, industry, or something of that sort, since by that very fact we regard the man as far surpassing us, then wonder is called Veneration [*veneratio*]; otherwise, if we are wondering at a man's anger, envy, and so on, we call it Horror [*horror*]. Again, if we wonder at the prudence, industry, etc. of a person we love, our love will thereby be the greater (Pr. 12, III), and this love joined with wonder or veneration we call Devotion [*devotio*]. We may also in the same manner conceive hatred, hope, confidence, and other emotions as joined with wonder, and thus we can deduce more emotions than can be signified by accepted terms. Hence it is clear that the names for emotions have been taken from common usage rather than from detailed knowledge of them.

The opposite of wonder is Contempt [*contemptus*], whose cause, however, is generally as follows. From seeing someone wondering at loving, fearing, etc. something, or because something at first sight seems similar to things that we wonder at, love, fear, etc. (by Pr. 15 and Cor. and Pr. 27, III), we are determined to wonder at, love, fear, etc. the same thing. But if from the presence of the thing or from closer contemplation we are compelled to deny of it all that can be the cause of wonder, love, fear, etc., then the mind from the very presence of the thing remains determined to reflect on what is lacking in the object rather than what is in it, whereas from the presence of an object it is customary for the mind to reflect especially on what is in the object. Further, just as devotion arises from wonder at a thing that we love, so does Derision [*irrisio*] from contempt for a thing we hate or have feared, and Scorn [*dedignatio*] from contempt of folly, just as veneration from wonder at prudence. Finally, we can conceive of love, hope, honor, and other emotions as joined with contempt, and therefrom we can deduce yet other emotions, which again we are not wont to distinguish from others by special names.

P53   *When the mind regards its own self and its power of activity, it feels pleasure, and the more so the more distinctly it imagines itself and its power of activity.*

Proof   Man knows himself only through the affections of his body and their ideas (Prs. 19 and 23, II). When therefore it happens that the mind can regard its own self, by that very fact it is assumed to pass to a state of greater perfection, that is (Schol. Pr. 11, III), to be affected with pleasure, and the more so the more distinctly it is able to imagine itself and its power of activity.

Cor   The more a man imagines he is praised by others, the more this pleasure is fostered. For the more he thinks he is praised by others, the more he thinks that others are affected with pleasure by him, and this accompanied by the idea of himself (Schol. Pr. 29, III). So (Pr. 27, III) he is affected with greater pleasure, accompanied by the idea of himself.

P54   *The mind endeavors to think only of the things that affirm its power of activity.*

Proof   The mind's conatus, or power, is the very essence of the mind (Pr. 7, III). But the essence of the mind affirms only what the mind is and can do (as is self-evident), and not what the mind is not and cannot do. So the mind endeavors to think only of what affirms, or posits, its power of activity.

P55   *When the mind thinks of its own impotence, by that very fact it feels pain.*

Proof   The essence of the mind affirms only what the mind is and can do; that is, it is of the nature of the mind to think only of those things that affirm its power of activity (preceding Pr.). Therefore, when we say that the mind, in regarding itself, thinks of its own impotence, we are simply saying that while the mind is endeavoring to think of something that affirms its power of activity, this conatus is checked; that is, it feels pain (Schol. Pr. 11, III).

Cor   This pain is fostered all the more if one thinks he is blamed by others. The proof is on the same lines as Cor. Pr. 53, III.

Schol   This pain, accompanied by the idea of our own impotence, is called Humility [*humilitas*]. The pleasure that arises from regarding ourselves is called Self-love [*philautia*] or Self-contentment [*acquiescentia in se ipso*]. And since this pleasure is repeated whenever a man regards his own capabilities, that is, his power of activity, the result is again that everyone is eager to tell of his exploits and to boast of his strength both of body and mind, and for this reason men bore one another. From this it again follows that men are by nature envious (see Schol. Pr. 24, and Schol. Pr. 32, III), that is, they rejoice at the weakness of their fellows and are pained at their accomplishments. For whenever a man imagines his own actions he is affected with pleasure (Pr. 53, III), and the more so as his actions express greater perfection and he imagines them more distinctly; that is (by what was said in Schol. 1, Pr. 40, II), the more he can distinguish them from the actions of others and regard them as something special. Therefore, everybody will most enjoy regarding himself when he regards in himself something that he denies of others. But if what he affirms of himself belongs to the universal idea of man or animal, he will derive no such great joy therefrom, and he will on the other hand feel pain if he thinks of his actions as inferior, compared with the actions of others. This pain (Pr. 28, III) he will endeavor to remove by wrongly interpreting the actions of his fellows or by embellishing his own as much as he can. It is therefore clear that men are prone to hatred and envy, and this is accentuated by their upbringing. For parents are wont to incite their children to excellence solely by the spur of honor and envy. But perhaps there remains a shadow of doubt on the grounds that we not infrequently admire the virtues of men and venerate them. To remove this shadow of doubt I shall add the following Corollary.

Cor   Nobody envies another's virtue unless he is his peer.

Proof   Envy is hatred itself (Schol. Pr. 24, III) or pain (Schol. Pr. 13, III); that is (Schol. Pr. 11, III), an affection whereby a man's power of activity, that is, his conatus, is checked. Now man (Schol. Pr. 9, III) endeavors or desires to do nothing save what can follow from his given nature. Therefore, a man will not desire to be attributed to himself any power of activity, or (which is the same thing) virtue, which is proper to the nature of another and foreign to his own. So his desire cannot be checked, that is (Schol. Pr. 11, III), he cannot be pained, by reason of his regarding some virtue in somebody unlike himself; consequently he cannot envy him. But he would envy his peer, who is assumed to be of the same nature as himself.

Schol   So when we said in Schol. Pr. 52, III that we venerate a man as a result of wondering at his prudence, strength of mind, and so on, this comes about (as is obvious from the proposition) because we think these virtues are special to him and not common to our nature, and so we do not envy him them any more than we envy trees their height, lions their strength, etc.

P56   *There are as many kinds of pleasure, pain, desire and consequently of every emotion that is compounded of these (such as vacillation) or of every emotion that is derived from these (love, hatred, hope, fear, etc.), as there are kinds of objects by which we are affected.*

Proof   Pleasure, pain, and consequently the emotions that are compounded of these or derived from them are passive emotions (Schol. Pr. 11, III). Now we are necessarily passive (Pr. 1, III) insofar as we have inadequate ideas, and only insofar as we have inadequate ideas are we passive (Pr. 3, III). That is to say (Schol. Pr. 40, II), we are necessarily passive only to the extent that we form mental images [*imaginamur*], i.e. (Pr. 17, II and Schol.), to the extent that we are affected in a way that involves both the nature of our own body and the nature of an external body. Therefore the explication of the nature of every passive emotion must necessarily include an expression of the nature of the object by which we are affected. The pleasure arising from object A involves the nature of object A and the pleasure arising from object B involves the nature of object B, and so these two emotions of pleasure are different in nature because they arise from causes of different natures. So too the emotion of pain that arises from one object is different in nature from the pain that arises from a different cause, and this must also be understood of love, hatred, hope, fear, and vacillation. Therefore, there are necessarily as many kinds of pleasure, pain, love, hatred, etc. as there are kinds of objects by which we are affected. Now desire is the very essence, or nature, of each individual insofar as that is conceived as determined by some given state of its constitution to do something (Schol. Pr. 9, III). Therefore, according as each individual is affected from external causes with various kinds of pleasure, pain, love, hate, etc., that is, according as his nature is conditioned in various ways, so must his desire be of different kinds; and the nature of one desire must differ from the nature of another to the same extent as the emotions, from which each single desire arises, differ amongst themselves. Therefore, there are as many kinds of desire as there are kinds of pleasure, pain, love, etc., and consequently (by what has been proved) as there are kinds of objects by which we are affected.

Schol   Among the kinds of emotional states which (by the preceding proposition) must be very numerous, most noteworthy are Dissipation [*luxuria*], Drunkenness [*ebrietas*], Lust [*libido*], Avarice [*avaritia*], and Ambition [*ambitio*], which are only concepts springing from love or desire, and which explicate the nature of both these emotions through the objects to which they are related. For by dissipation, drunkenness, lust, avarice, and ambition we mean quite simply uncontrolled love or desire for feasting, drinking, sex, riches, and popular acclaim. Furthermore, these emotions have no opposites insofar as we distinguish them from other emotions solely through the objects to which they are related. For Self-control [*temperantia*], Sobriety [*sobrietas*], and Chastity [*castitas*], which we are wont to oppose to dissipation, drunkenness, and lust, are not emotions or passive states, but indicate the power of the mind that controls these emotions.

However, I cannot here give an account of the remaining kinds of emotion, for they are as many as there are kinds of objects; nor, if I could, is it necessary. For it suffices for our purpose, which is to determine the strength of the emotions and the power of the mind over them, to have a general definition of all the individual emotions. It is sufficient, I repeat, to understand the common properties of the emotions and the mind so as to determine the nature and the extent of the mind's power in controlling and checking the emotions. So although there is a great difference between this and that emotion of love, hatred, or desire, e.g. between the love toward one's children and love toward one's wife, there is no need for us to investigate these differences and to trace any further the nature and origin of the emotions.

P57   *Any emotion of one individual differs from the emotion of another to the extent that the essence of the one individual differs from the essence of the other.*

Proof This proposition is obvious from Ax. 1, q.v., after Lemma 3 Schol. Pr. 13, II. But we shall nevertheless prove it from the definitions of the three primary emotions.

All emotions are related to desire, pleasure or pain, as is made clear by the definitions we have given of them. Now desire is the very nature or essence of every single individual (see its definition in Schol. Pr. 9, III). Therefore, the desire of each individual differs from the desire of another to the extent that the nature or essence of the one differs from the essence of the other. Again, pleasure and pain are passive emotions whereby each individual's power, that is, his conatus to persist in his own being, is increased or diminished, assisted or checked (Pr. 11, III and Schol.). But by the conatus to persist in one's own being, insofar as it is related to mind and body together, we understand appetite and desire (Schol. Pr. 9, III). Therefore, pleasure and pain is desire or appetite, insofar as it is increased or diminished, assisted or checked, by external causes; that is, (by the same Schol.), it is each individual's very nature. So each individual's pleasure or pain differs from the pleasure or pain of another to the extent that the nature or essence of the one also differs from that of the other. Consequently, any emotion . . . etc.

Schol Hence it follows that the emotions of animals that are called irrational (for now that we know the origin of mind we can by no means doubt that beasts have feelings) differ from the emotions of men as much as their nature differs from human nature. Horse and man are indeed carried away by lust to procreate, but the former by equine lust, the latter by human lust. So too the lusts and appetites of insects, fishes, and birds are bound to be of various different kinds. So although each individual lives content with the nature wherewith he is endowed and rejoices in it, that life wherewith each is content and that joy are nothing other than the idea or soul [*anima*] of the said individual, and so the joy of the one differs from the joy of another as much as the essence of the one differs from the essence of the other. Finally, it follows from the preceding proposition that there is also no small difference between the joy which guides the drunkard and the joy possessed by the philosopher, a point to which I wish to draw attention in passing.

So much for emotions that are related to man insofar as he is passive. It remains for me to add a few words concerning emotions that are related to man insofar as he is active.

P58 *Besides the pleasure and desire that are passive emotions, there are other emotions of pleasure and desire that are related to us insofar as we are active.*

Proof When the mind conceives itself and its power to act, it feels pleasure (Pr. 53, III). Now the mind necessarily regards itself when it conceives a true, that is, adequate, idea (Pr. 43, II). But the mind does conceive adequate ideas (Schol. 2, Pr. 40, II). Therefore it feels pleasure, too, insofar as it conceives adequate ideas, that is (Pr. 1, III), insofar as it is active. Again, it is both insofar as it has clear and distinct ideas and insofar as it has confused ideas that the mind endeavors to persist in its own being (Pr. 9, III). But by conatus we understand desire (Schol.

Pr. 9, III). Therefore, desire is also related to us insofar as we understand, i.e., insofar as we act (Pr. 1, III).

P59   *Among all the emotions that are related to the mind insofar as it is active, there are none that are not related to pleasure or desire.*

Proof   All emotions are related to desire, pleasure or pain, as is shown by the definitions we have given of them. Now by pain we understand that which diminishes or checks the mind's power of thinking (Pr. 11, III, and Schol.). So insofar as the mind feels pain, to that extent its power of understanding, that is, its power of activity, is diminished or checked (Pr. 1, III). So no emotions of pain can be related to the mind insofar as it is active, but only emotions of pleasure and desire, which (preceding Pr.) are to that extent also related to the mind.

Schol   All the activities which follow from emotions that are related to the mind insofar as it exercises understanding I refer to Strength of mind [*fortitudo*], which I subdivide into Courage [*animositas*] and Nobility [*generositas*]. By courage I understand "the desire whereby every individual endeavors to preserve his own being according to the dictates of reason alone." By nobility I understand "the desire whereby every individual, according to the dictates of reason alone, endeavors to assist others and make friends of them." So I classify under courage those activities that are directed solely to the advantage of the agent, and those that are directed to the advantage of another I classify under nobility. So self-control, sobriety, and resourcefulness in danger, etc. are kinds of courage; Courtesy [*modestia*] and Mercy [*clementia*] are kinds of nobility.

And now I think I have explained the principal emotions and vacillations that arise from the combination of the three basic emotions—desire, pleasure, and pain—and have clarified them through their first causes. From this it is clear that we are in many respects at the mercy of external causes and are tossed about like the waves of the sea when driven by contrary winds, unsure of the outcome and of our fate. But I have said that I have clarified only the principal conflicts of feeling, not all that can be. For by proceeding in the same manner as above we can readily demonstrate that love is joined with repentance, scorn, shame, and so on. Indeed, from what has been said I think everyone is quite convinced that emotions can be combined with one another in so many ways and give rise to so many variations that they cannot be numbered. But it suffices for my purpose to have enumerated only the principal emotions; for those I have passed over would be a matter of curiosity rather than utility.

However, one further point should be observed concerning love. It frequently happens, while we are enjoying what we were seeking, that from that very enjoyment the body changes to a new condition, as a result of which it is differently determined and different images are activated in it, and at the same time the mind begins to think of and desire other things. For example, when we think of something that is wont to delight us with its taste, we desire to enjoy it, to eat it. But while we are thus enjoying it the stomach is being filled and the body is changing its condition. If therefore, with the body now in a different condition, the image of the said food is fostered by its being set before us, and consequently also the conatus or desire to eat the food, this conatus, or desire, will be opposed by the new condition of the body, and consequently the presence of the food which we used to want will be hateful, and this is what we call Satiety [*fastidium*] and Weariness [*taedium*].

I have passed by those external affections of the body which can be observed in the case of emotions, such as trembling, pallor, sobbing, laughter, and so on, because they are related to the body without any relation to the mind. Finally, with regard to the definitions of emotions there are certain points to be noted, and I shall therefore repeat those definitions here in proper order, accompanied by such observations as I think necessary in each case.

DEFINITIONS OF THE EMOTIONS

1. Desire is the very essence of man insofar as his essence is conceived as determined to any action from any given affection of itself.

Exp We said above in Schol. Pr. 9, III that desire is appetite accompanied by consciousness of itself, and that appetite is the very essence of man insofar as his essence is determined to such actions as contribute to his preservation. But in the same Scholium I also noted that in fact I acknowledge no difference between human appetite and desire. For whether or not a man is conscious of his appetite, the appetite remains one and the same. So to avoid appearing to be guilty of tautology, I declined to explicate desire through appetite; my object was so to define it as to include all the endeavors of human nature that we term appetite, will, desire, or urge. I could merely have said: "Desire is the very essence of man insofar as his essence is conceived as determined to some action"; but then it would not follow from this definition (Pr. 23, II) that the mind can be conscious of its own desire or appetite. Thus, in order to involve the cause of this consciousness it was necessary (by the same Pr.) to add "from any given affection of itself." For by "any affection of the human essence" we understand "any condition [*constitutio*] of the said essence," whether it be innate, whether it be conceived solely through the attribute of Thought or solely through the attribute of Extension, or whether it be related to both attributes together. So here I mean by the word "desire" any of man's endeavors, urges, appetites, and volitions, which vary with man's various states, and are not infrequently so opposed to one another that a man may be drawn in different directions and know not where to turn.

2. Pleasure is man's transition from a state of less perfection to a state of greater perfection.

3. Pain is man's transition from a state of greater perfection to a state of less perfection.

Exp I say "transition," for pleasure is not perfection itself. If a man were to be born with the perfection to which he passes, he would be in possession of it without the emotion of pleasure. This is clearer in the case of pain, the contrary emotion. For nobody can deny that pain consists in the transition to a state of less perfection, not in the less perfection itself, since man cannot feel pain insofar as he participates in any degree of perfection. Nor can we say that pain consists in the privation of greater perfection, for privation is nothing, whereas the emotion of pain is an actuality, which therefore can be nothing other than the actuality of the transition to a state of less perfection; that is, the actuality whereby a man's power of activity is diminished or checked (Schol. Pr. 11, III).

As to the definitions of Cheerfulness, Titillation, Melancholy, and Anguish, I omit them because they are related chiefly to the body, and are only species of pleasure and pain.

4. Wonder is the thought of any thing on which the mind stays fixed because this particular thought has no connection with any others. See Proposition 52 and its Scholium.

Exp   In Schol. Pr. 18, II we demonstrated the reason why the mind, from thinking of one thing, passes immediately on to the thought of another, and that is that in such cases the images are bound together and so ordered that one follows another. This concept cannot cover the case when the image is a strange one. The mind will be kept in contemplation of the said thing until it is determined by other causes to think of other things. So the thought of an unusual thing, considered in itself, is of the same nature as other thoughts, and for this reason I do not count wonder among the emotions; nor do I see why I should do so, since this distraction of the mind arises from no positive cause that distracts it from other things, but only from the lack of a cause for determining the mind, from the contemplation of one thing, to think of other things.

Therefore, as I noted in Schol. Pr. 11, III, I acknowledge only three basic or primary emotions, pleasure, pain, and desire; and I have made mention of wonder only because it is customary for certain emotions derived from the three basic emotions to be signified by different terms when they are related to objects that evoke our wonder. There is an equally valid reason for my adding here a definition of contempt.

5. Contempt is the imagining [*imaginatio*] of some thing that makes so little impact on the mind that the presence of the thing motivates the mind to think of what is not in the thing rather than of what is in the thing. See Schol. Pr. 52, III.

I here pass over the definitions of Veneration and Scorn because, as far as I know, there are no emotions that take their name from them.

6. Love is pleasure accompanied by the idea of an external cause.

Exp   This definition explains quite clearly the essence of love. The definition given by writers who define love as "the lover's wish to be united with the object of his love" expresses not the essence of love, but a property of it; and since these writers have not sufficiently grasped the essence of love, neither have they succeeded in forming any clear conception of its property. This has led to the universal verdict that their definition is very obscure. However, be it noted that when I say that in the case of a lover it is a property to wish to be united with the object of his love, by "wish" I do not mean consent or deliberate intention, that is, free decision (for in Pr. 48, II we proved this to be fictitious), nor again desire to be united with the loved object when it is absent or to continue in its presence when it is there; for love can be conceived without any one particular desire. By "wish" I mean the contentment that is in the lover by reason of the presence of the object of his love, by which the lover's pleasure is strengthened, or at least fostered.

7. Hatred is pain accompanied by the idea of an external cause.

Exp The points here to be noted can be easily perceived from the Explication of the preceding Proposition. See also Schol. Pr. 13, III.

8. Inclination [*propensio*] is pleasure accompanied by the idea of a thing which is indirectly the cause of the pleasure.

9. Aversion [*aversio*] is pain accompanied by the idea of a thing which is indirectly the cause of the pain. (For these see Schol. Pr. 15, III.)

10. Devotion is love toward one at whom we wonder.

Exp We demonstrated in Pr. 52, III that Wonder [*admiratio*] arises from the strangeness of a thing. So if it happens that we often think about the object of our wonder, we shall cease to wonder at it. So we see that the emotion of devotion can easily degenerate into mere love.

11. Derision is pleasure arising from our imagining that there is in the object of our hate something that we despise.

Exp Insofar as we despise a thing that we hate, to that extent we deny existence regarding it (Schol. Pr. 52, III) and to that extent we feel pleasure (Pr. 20, III). But since we are supposing that what a man derides he nevertheless hates, it follows that this pleasure is not unalloyed (Schol. Pr. 47, III).

12. Hope is inconstant pleasure arising from the idea of a thing future or past, of whose outcome we are in some doubt.

13. Fear is inconstant pain arising from the idea of a thing future or past, of whose outcome we are in some doubt.

For these see Schol. 2, Pr. 18, III.

Exp From these definitions it follows that there is no hope without fear and no fear without hope. For he who is in hopeful suspense and has doubts as to the outcome of a thing is assumed to be imagining something that excludes the existence of the hoped-for thing, and so to that extent he feels pain (Pr. 19, III). Consequently, as long as he is in hopeful suspense, he fears as to the outcome. On the other hand, he who is in a state of fear, that is, is unsure of the occurrence of a thing that he hates, is also imagining something that excludes the existence of the said thing, and so (Pr. 20, III) he feels pleasure, and to that extent he entertains hope of its not happening.

14. Confidence is pleasure arising from the idea of a thing future or past, concerning which reason for doubt has been removed.

15. Despair is pain arising from the idea of a thing future or past concerning which reason for doubt has been removed.

Exp Therefore confidence arises from hope and despair from fear when reason for uncertainty as to the outcome of a thing has been removed. This comes about either because man imagines a thing past or future as being at hand and regards it as present, or because he thinks of other things that exclude the existence of those things that were causing his uncertainty. For although we can never be certain as to the outcome of particular things (Cor. Pr. 31, II), it is possible for us not to be doubtful as to their outcome. For we have demonstrated (Schol. Pr. 49, II) that not having doubts concerning a thing is different from being certain of the thing. So it is possible for us to be affected by the same emotion of pleasure or pain from the image of a thing past or future as from the image of a thing present, as we proved in Proposition 18, III, q.v., with Schol.

16. Joy is pleasure accompanied by the idea of a past thing whose outcome was contrary to our fear.

17. Disappointment [*conscientiae morsus*] is pain accompanied by the idea of a past thing whose outcome was contrary to our hope.

18. Pity is pain accompanied by the idea of ill that has happened to another whom we think of as like ourselves. See Schol. Pr. 22 and Schol. Pr. 27, III.

Exp There seems to be no difference between pity and compassion [*misericordia*], unless perhaps pity has reference to a particular occurrence of emotion, while compassion has regard to a set disposition to that emotion.

19. Approbation is love toward one who has benefited another.

20. Indignation is hatred toward one who has injured another.

Exp I know that these words are commonly used with a different meaning. But my purpose is to explain not the meaning of words but the nature of things, and to assign to things terms whose common meaning is not very far away from the meaning I decide to give them. Let this one reminder suffice. As to the cause of these emotions, see Cor. 1, Pr. 27 and Schol. Pr. 22, III.

21. Over-esteem is to think too highly of someone by reason of love.

22. Disparagement [*despectus*] is to think too meanly of someone by reason of hatred.

Exp Over-esteem is therefore a result, or a property, of love, and disparagement of hatred. So over-esteem can also be defined as "love, insofar as it so affects a man that he thinks too highly of the object of his love"; and disparagement as "hatred, insofar as it so affects a man that he thinks too meanly of the object of his hatred." For these see Schol. Pr. 26, III.

23. Envy is hatred, insofar as it so affects a man that he is pained at another's good fortune and rejoices at another's ill-fortune.

Exp The opposite of envy is commonly said to be compassion which therefore, with some distortion of its usual meaning, can be defined thus:

24. Compassion is love, insofar as it so affects a man that he rejoices at another's good and feels pain at another's hurt.

Exp As to envy, see Schol. Pr. 24, III and Schol. Pr. 32, III.

Such are the emotions of pleasure and pain which are accompanied by the idea of an external thing as direct [*per se*] or indirect [*per accidens*] cause. From these I pass on to other emotions which are accompanied by the idea of an internal thing as cause.

25. Self-contentment is pleasure arising from a man's contemplation of himself and his power of activity.

26. Humility is pain arising from a man's contemplation of his own impotence, or weakness.

Exp Self-contentment is the opposite of humility insofar as by the former we understand pleasure that arises from our regarding our power of activity. But insofar as we also understand by it pleasure accompanied by the idea of some deed which we think we have done from free decision of the mind, then its opposite is repentance, which we define thus:

27. Repentance is pain accompanied by the idea of some deed which we believe we have done from free decision of the mind.

Exp We have demonstrated the causes of these emotions in Schol. Pr. 51, III and Prs. 53, 54, 55, III and its Schol. As for free decision of the mind, see Schol. Pr. 35, II. But here we should also note that it is not surprising that all our actions that are customarily called wrong are followed by pain, and those which are said to be right, by pleasure. For we readily understand from what has been said that our upbringing is chiefly responsible for this. By disapproving of wrong actions and frequently rebuking their children when they commit them, and contrariwise by approving and praising right actions, parents have caused the former to be associated with painful feelings and the latter with pleasurable feelings. This is further confirmed by experience. For not all people have the same customs and religion. What some hold as sacred, others regard as profane; what some hold as honorable, others regard as disgraceful. So each individual repents of a deed or exults in it according to his upbringing.

28. Pride is thinking too highly of oneself by reason of self-love.

Exp So pride differs from over-esteem, for the latter is related to an external object, while pride is related to a subject who thinks too highly of himself. However, as over-esteem is an effect or property of love, so is pride of self-love, and so it can also be defined as "love of self, or self-contentment, insofar as it so affects a man that he thinks too highly of himself" (see Schol. Pr. 26, III). This emotion has no opposite, for nobody thinks too meanly of himself by reason of self-hatred. Indeed, nobody thinks too meanly of himself insofar as he thinks this or that is beyond his capability. For whenever a man thinks something is beyond his capability, he necessarily thinks so, and by this belief he is so conditioned that he really cannot do what he thinks he cannot do. For while thinking that he cannot do this or that, he is not determined to do it, and consequently it is impossible that he should do it.

However, if we direct our attention solely to the way that others see him, we can conceive it as possible that a man may think too meanly of himself. For it can happen that a man, regarding with pain his own weakness, should think that everyone despises him, and this while the rest of the world is very far from despising him. Furthermore, a man may think too meanly of himself if he denies of himself in present time something related to future time of which he is not sure, as that he may say that he cannot achieve any certainty, or that he can desire or do nothing that is not wrong or disgraceful, and so on. Again, we can say that a man thinks too meanly of himself when we see that from excessive fear of disgrace he does not dare what others who are his peers dare. So we can take this emotion, which I shall call Self-abasement [*abjectio*], to be the opposite of pride. For as pride arises from self-contentment, so self-abasement arises from humility. Therefore we shall define it as follows:

29. Self-abasement is thinking too meanly of oneself by reason of pain.

Exp   We usually oppose humility to pride, but then we are having regard to the effects of the two emotions rather than their nature. For we usually apply the term "proud" to one who exults overmuch [Schol. Pr. 30, III], who talks only of his own virtues and the faults of others, who expects to take precedence over all, and who goes about with the pomp and style usually affected by those far above him in station. On the other hand, we apply the term "humble" to one who blushes frequently, who confesses his faults and talks of the virtues of others, who gives way to all, and who goes about downcast and careless of his appearance.

Now these emotions, humility and self-abasement, are very rare; for human nature, considered in itself, strives against them as far as it can (Prs. 13 and 54, III). So those who are believed to be most self-abased and humble are generally the most ambitious and envious.

30. Honor is pleasure accompanied by the idea of some action of ours which we think that others praise.

31. Shame is pain accompanied by the idea of some action of ours that we think that others censure.

Exp   For these, see Schol. Pr. 30, III. But one should here observe the difference between shame and bashfulness. Shame is the pain that follows on a deed of which we are ashamed. Bashfulness is the fear or apprehension of shame, whereby a man is restrained from some disgraceful act. The opposite of bashfulness is usually Impudence [*impudentia*], which is not really an emotion, as I shall demonstrate in due course. But the names of emotions, as I have noted, have regard more to usage than to their nature.

Herewith I have completed my proposed task of explicating the emotions of pleasure and pain. I now pass on to those emotions that are related to desire.

32. Longing is desire or appetite for possessing something, a desire fostered by remembrance of the said thing and at the same time checked by remembrance of other things that exclude the existence of the said object of appetite.

Exp   As I have often said, when we recall something we are thereby conditioned to regard it with the same emotion as if the thing were actually present. But in our waking hours, this disposition or conatus is generally restrained by the images of things that exclude the existence of that which we recall. So when we remember a thing that affected us with some kind of pleasure, by that very fact we endeavor to regard it as present along with that same emotion of pleasure; but this conatus is straightway checked by the remembrance of things that exclude the existence of the said thing. Therefore longing is really the opposite pain to the pleasure that arises from the absence of a thing that we hate, concerning which see Schol. Pr. 47, III. But as the word "longing" seems to have regard to desire, I classify this emotion under emotions of desire.

33. Emulation is the desire for something, engendered in us from the fact that we think others to have the same desire.

Exp   When someone flees because he sees others fleeing, or fears because he sees others fearing, or again, on seeing that someone has burnt his hand, draws his hand back and makes a movement of the body as if his own hand were burnt, we say that he is imitating another's emotion, not that he is emulating him. This is not because we realize that the causes of imitation and emulation are different, but because it is the usual practice to call only him emulous who imitates what we judge to be honorable, useful, or pleasant. As to the cause of emulation, see Pr. 27, III and Schol. As to the reason why envy is generally associated with this emotion, see Pr. 32, III and Schol.

34. Gratitude is the desire, or eagerness of love [*amoris studium*], whereby we endeavor to benefit one who, from a like emotion of love, has bestowed a benefit on us. See Pr. 39, and Schol. Pr. 41, III.

35. Benevolence is the desire to benefit one whom we pity. See Schol. Pr. 27, III.

36. Anger is the desire whereby we are urged from hatred to inflict injury on one whom we hate. See Pr. 39, III.

37. Revenge is the desire whereby we are urged from mutual hatred to inflict injury on one who, from like emotion, has injured us. See Cor. 2, Pr. 40, III and Schol.

38. Cruelty, or savageness [*saevitia*], is the desire whereby someone is urged to inflict injury on one whom we love or whom we pity.

Exp   The opposite of cruelty is mercy, which is not a passive emotion but the power of the mind whereby a man controls anger and revenge.

39. Timidity is the desire to avoid a greater evil, which we fear, by a lesser evil. See Schol. Pr. 39, III.

40. Boldness is the desire whereby someone is urged to some dangerous action which his fellows fear to undertake.

41. Cowardice is a term applied to one whose desire is checked by apprehension of a danger which his fellows dare to face.

Exp   So cowardice is simply the fear of some evil which most people are not wont to fear. So I do not classify it as an emotion of desire. Still, I have decided to explain it here because it is the opposite of boldness insofar as we attend to desire.

42. Consternation is a term applied to one whose desire to avoid evil is checked by a feeling of wonder at the evil that he fears.

Exp   So consternation is a kind of cowardice. But since consternation arises from a twofold timorousness, it can therefore more fittingly be defined as "fear that holds a man in such a state of stupefaction and hesitation that he is not able to remove the evil." I say "stupefaction" inasmuch as we mean that his desire to remove the evil is checked by a feeling of wonder. I say "hesitation" insofar as we conceive the said desire to be checked by apprehension of another evil by which he is equally tormented, with the result that he knows not which of the two to avert. For this see Schol. Pr. 39 and Schol. Pr. 52, III. With regard to cowardice and boldness, see Schol. Pr. 51, III.

43. Courtesy [*humanitas*] or Politeness [*modestia*] is desire to do things that please men and avoid things that displease them.

44. Ambition is the immoderate desire for honor.

Exp   Ambition is the desire whereby all emotions (Prs. 27 and 31, III) are encouraged and strengthened; and thus this emotion can scarcely be overcome. For as long as a man is subject to any desire, he is necessarily subject to this one. "The best men," said Cicero, "are particularly led by the hope of renown. Even philosophers, in the books that they write in condemnation of fame, add their names thereto . . ." and so on.[5]

45. Dissipation is the immoderate desire, or also love, of sumptuous living.

46. Drunkenness is the immoderate desire and love of drinking.

47. Avarice is the immoderate desire and love of riches.

48. Lust is also the desire and love of sexual intercourse.

Exp   Whether this desire for sex is moderate or not, it is usually called lust.

These five emotions (as I noted in Schol. Pr. 56, III) have no opposites. For politeness is a species of ambition (concerning which see Schol. Pr. 29, III); and self-control, sobriety, and chastity, too, I have already noted as indicating the power of the mind, not its passivity. And although it is possible that a miser, an ambitious or a timid man may abstain from excessive food, drinking and sex, yet avarice, ambition, and timidity are not the opposites of dissipation, drunkenness, and lust. For the miser generally longs to gorge himself on other people's food and drink. The ambitious man will not exercise any kind of self-control if secrecy is assured; and if he should live in the company of drunkards and libertines, he will be more prone to these vices because he is ambitious. The timid man does what he wants not to do. Although the miser may cast his riches into the sea to avoid death, he nevertheless remains a miser. If a libertine is pained at not being able to indulge himself, he does not on that account cease to be a libertine. Fundamentally, these emotions do not have regard so much to the activities of sumptuous living, drinking, and so on, as to appetite and love. Therefore, these emotions have no opposites except for courage and nobility, with which I shall deal hereafter.

---

[5] [Cicero, *Pro Archia*, II. — S.S.]

I pass over the definitions of jealousy and other vacillations, both because they arise from the combination of emotions which we have already defined and because the majority have no names, which shows that for practical purposes it suffices to know them in a general way. Now it is clear from the definitions of the emotions we have dealt with that they all spring from desire, pleasure, or pain, or rather that they are nothing apart from these three emotions, each of which is wont to appear under various names according to their various contexts and extrinsic characteristics. If now we direct our attention to these basic emotions and to the explanation we have already given of the nature of the mind, we can define emotions, insofar as they are related only to the mind, as follows:

GENERAL DEFINITION OF EMOTIONS

The emotion called a passive experience is a confused idea whereby the mind affirms a greater or less force of existence of its body, or part of its body, than was previously the case, and by the occurrence of which the mind is determined to think of one thing rather than another.

Exp I say in the first place that an emotion, or passivity of the mind, is a "confused idea." For we have demonstrated (Pr. 3, III) that the mind is passive only to the extent that it has inadequate or confused ideas. Next, I say "whereby the mind affirms a greater or less force of existence of its body or part of its body than was previously the case." For all ideas that we have of bodies indicate the actual physical state of our own body rather than the nature of the external body (Cor. 2, Pr. 16, II). Now the idea that constitutes the specific reality of emotion must indicate or express the state of the body or some part of it, which the body or some part of it possesses from the fact that its power of activity or force of existence [*vis existendi*] is increased or diminished, assisted or checked. But it should be noted that when I say "a greater or less force of existence than was previously the case," I do not mean that the mind compares the body's present state with its past state, but that the idea that constitutes the specific reality of emotion affirms of the body something that in fact involves more or less reality than was previously the case. And since the essence of the mind consists in this (Prs. 11 and 13, II), that it affirms the actual existence of its body, and by perfection we mean the very essence of a thing, it therefore follows that the mind passes to a state of greater or less perfection when it comes about that it affirms of its body, or some part of it, something that involves more or less reality than was previously the case. So when I said above that the mind's power of thinking increases or diminishes, I meant merely this, that the mind has formed an idea of its body or some part of it that expresses more or less reality than it had been affirming of it. For the excellence of ideas and the actual power of thinking are measured by the excellence of the object. Lastly, I added "by the occurrence of which the mind is determined to think of one thing rather than another" in order to express the nature of desire in addition to the nature of pleasure and pain as explicated in the first part of the definition.

PART IV
OF HUMAN BONDAGE, OR THE
STRENGTH OF THE EMOTIONS

PREFACE

I assign the term "bondage" to man's lack of power to control and check the emotions. For a man at the mercy of his emotions is not his own master but is subject to fortune, in whose power he so lies that he is often compelled, although he sees the better course, to pursue the worse. In this Part I have set myself the task of demonstrating why this is so, and also what is good and what is bad in emotions. But before I begin, I should like to make a few preliminary observations on perfection and imperfection, and on good and bad.

He who has undertaken something and has brought it to completion[1] will say that the thing is completed; and not only he but everyone who rightly knew, or thought he knew, the intention and aim of the author of that work. For example, if anyone sees a work (which I assume is not yet finished) and knows that the aim of the author is to build a house, he will say that the house is imperfect. On the other hand, as soon as he sees that the work has been brought to the conclusion that its author had intended to give it, he will say that it is perfect. But if anyone sees a work whose like he had never seen before, and he does not know the artificer's intention, he cannot possibly know whether the work is perfect or imperfect.

This appears to have been the original meaning of these terms. But when men began to form general ideas and to devise ideal types of houses, buildings, towers, and so on, and to prefer some models to others, it came about that each called "perfect" what he saw to be in agreement with the general idea he had formed of the said thing, and "imperfect" that which he saw at variance with his own preconceived ideal, although in the artificer's opinion it had been fully completed. There seems to be no other reason why even natural phenomena (those not made by human hand) should commonly be called perfect or imperfect. For men are wont to form general ideas both of natural phenomena and of artifacts, and these ideas they regard as models, and they believe that Nature (which they consider does nothing without an end in view) looks to these ideas and holds them before herself as models. So when they see something occurring in Nature at variance with their preconceived ideal of the thing in question, they believe that Nature has then failed or blundered and has left that thing imperfect. So we see that men are in the habit of calling natural phenomena perfect or imperfect from their own

---

[1] [The Latin term *perfectus*, which is crucial in this Preface, can mean both "perfect" and "completed." For Spinoza the emphasis here is upon completion: that which has been finished or accomplished is perfect; contrarily, that which is not yet completed is imperfect. Spinoza will go on to say that we eventually learn to make evaluative judgments on the basis of what we have come to take as completed specimens of things. The latter now become normative models for further comparison and valuation.]

preconceptions rather than from true knowledge. For we have demonstrated in Appendix, Part I that Nature does not act with an end in view; that the eternal and infinite being, whom we call God, or Nature, acts by the same necessity whereby it exists. That the necessity of his nature whereby he acts is the same as that whereby he exists has been demonstrated (Pr. 16, I). So the reason or cause why God, or nature, acts, and the reason or cause why he exists, are one and the same. Therefore, just as he does not exist for an end, so he does not act for an end; just as there is no beginning or end to his existing, so there is no beginning or end to his acting. What is termed a "final cause" is nothing but human appetite insofar as it is considered as the starting point or primary cause of some thing. For example, when we say that being a place of habitation was the final cause of this or that house, we surely mean no more than this, that a man, from thinking of the advantages of domestic life, had an urge to build a house. Therefore, the need for a habitation insofar as it is considered as a final cause is nothing but this particular urge, which is in reality an efficient cause, and is considered as the prime cause because men are commonly ignorant of the causes of their own urges; for, as I have repeatedly said, they are conscious of their actions and appetites but unaware of the causes by which they are determined to seek something. As to the common saying that Nature sometimes fails or blunders and produces imperfect things, I count this among the fictions with which I dealt in Appendix I.

So perfection and imperfection are in reality only modes of thinking, notions which we are wont to invent from comparing individuals of the same species or kind; and it is for this reason that I previously said (Def. 6, II) that by reality and perfection I mean the same thing. For we are wont to classify all the individuals in Nature under one genus which is called the highest genus, namely, the notion of Entity, which pertains to all the individuals in Nature without exception. Therefore insofar as we classify individuals in Nature under this genus and compare them with one another and find that some have more being or reality than others, to that extent we say some are more perfect than others. And insofar as we attribute to them something involving negation, such as limit, end, impotence and so on, to that extent we call them imperfect because they do not affect our minds as much as those we call perfect, and not because they lack something of their own or because Nature has blundered. For nothing belongs to the nature of anything except that which follows from the necessity of nature of its efficient cause; and whatever follows from the necessity of the nature of its efficient cause must necessarily be so.

As for the terms "good" and "bad," they likewise indicate nothing positive in things considered in themselves, and are nothing but modes of thinking, or notions which we form from comparing things with one another. For one and the same thing can at the same time be good and bad, and also indifferent. For example, music is good for one who is melancholy, bad for one in mourning, and neither good nor bad for the deaf. However, although this is so, these terms ought to be retained. For since we desire to form the idea of a man which we may look to as a model of human nature, we shall find it useful to keep these terms in the sense I have indicated. So in what follows I shall mean by "good" that which we

certainly know to be the means for our approaching nearer to the model of human nature that we set before ourselves, and by "bad" that which we certainly
know prevents us from reproducing the said model. Again, we shall say that men
are more perfect or less perfect insofar as they are nearer to or farther from this
model. For it is important to note that when I say that somebody passes from a
state of less perfection to a state of greater perfection, and vice versa, I do not mean
that he changes from one essence or form to another (for example, a horse is as
completely destroyed if it changes into a man as it would be if it were to change
into an insect), but that we conceive his power of activity, insofar as this is understood through his nature, to be increased or diminished.

Finally, by perfection in general I shall understand reality, as I have said; that
is, the essence of anything whatsoever in as far as it exists and acts in a definite
manner, without taking duration into account. For no individual thing can be said
to be more perfect on the grounds that it has continued in existence over a greater
period of time. The duration of things cannot be determined from their essence,
for the essence of things involves no fixed and determinate period of time. But
any thing whatsoever, whether it be more perfect or less perfect, will always be
able to persist in existing with that same force whereby it begins to exist, so that
in this respect all things are equal.

Definitions

1. By *good* I understand that which we certainly know to be useful to us.

2. By *bad* I understand that which we certainly know to be an obstacle to our
attainment of some good.

For these, see the foregoing preface, toward the end.

3. I call individual things *contingent* insofar as, in attending only to their
essence, we find nothing that necessarily posits their existence or necessarily excludes it.

4. I call individual things *possible* insofar as, in attending to the causes by
which they should be brought about, we do not know whether these causes are
determined to bring them about.

In Schol. 1, Pr. 33, I, I did not differentiate between possible and contingent
because at that point it was unnecessary to distinguish carefully between them.

5. In what follows, by *conflicting emotions* I shall understand those that draw
a man in different directions, although they belong to the same genus, such as dissipation and avarice, which are species of love, and contrary not by nature, but indirectly [*per accidens*].

6. In Schols. 1 and 2, Pr. 18, III I have explained what I mean by emotion toward a thing future, present, and past.

But it should be further noted that just as we cannot distinctly imagine spatial
distance beyond a certain limit, the same is true of time. That is, just as we are
wont to imagine that all those objects more than 200 feet away from us, or whose
distance from our position exceeds what we can distinctly imagine, are the same
distance from us and appear to be in the same plane, so too in the case of objects

whose time of existence is farther away from the present by a longer distance than we are wont to distinctly imagine, we think of them all as equally far from the present, and we refer them to one point of time, as it were.

7. By the *end* for the sake of which we do something, I mean appetite.

8. By *virtue* and *power* I mean the same thing; that is (Pr. 7, III), virtue, insofar as it is related to man, is man's very essence, or nature, insofar as he has power to bring about that which can be understood solely through the laws of his own nature.

Axiom

There is in Nature no individual thing that is not surpassed in strength and power by some other thing. Whatsoever thing there is, there is another more powerful by which the said thing can be destroyed.

P1 *Nothing positive contained in a false idea can be annulled by the presence of what is true, insofar as it is true.*

Proof Falsity consists solely in the privation of knowledge, a privation which is involved in inadequate ideas (Pr. 35, II), and it is not by possessing something positive that they are called false (Pr. 33, II). On the contrary, insofar as they are related to God, they are true (Pr. 32, II). If therefore what is positive in a false idea were to be annulled by the presence of what is true, insofar as it is true, a true idea would be annulled by itself, which is absurd (Pr. 4, III). Therefore . . . etc.

Schol This proposition is more clearly understood from Cor. 2, Pr. 16, II. For imagination [*imaginatio*] is an idea that indicates the present disposition of the human body more than the nature of an external body, not indeed distinctly, but confusedly, whence it comes about that the mind is said to err. For example, when we gaze at the sun, it seems to us to be about 200 feet away; and in this we are deceived as long as we are unaware of its true distance. With knowledge of its distance the error is removed, but not the imagining [*imaginatio*], that is, the idea of the sun that explicates its nature only insofar as the body is affected by it. Thus although we know its true distance, we shall nevertheless see it as being close to us. For as we said in Schol. Pr. 35, II, it is not by reason of our ignorance of its true distance that we see it as being so near, but because the mind conceives the magnitude of the sun insofar as the body is affected by it. In the same way, when the rays of the sun falling on the surface of water are reflected back to our eyes, we see it as if it were in the water although we know its true position. Similarly other imaginings whereby the mind is deceived, whether they indicate the natural disposition of the body or the increase or diminution of its power of activity, are not contrary to what is true and do not disappear at the presence of truth. It does indeed happen that when we mistakenly fear some evil, the fear disappears when we hear the truth. But the contrary also happens; when we fear an evil that is assuredly going to overtake us, the fear likewise disappears on our hearing false tidings. So imaginings do not disappear at the presence of what is true insofar as it is true, but because other imaginings that are stronger supervene to exclude the present existence of the things we imagine, as we demonstrated in Pr. 17, II.

P2   *We are passive insofar as we are a part of Nature which cannot be conceived independently of other parts.*

Proof   We are said to be passive when something arises in us of which we are only the partial cause (Def. 2, III); that is (Def. 1, III), something that cannot be deduced solely from the laws of our own nature. So we are passive insofar as we are a part of Nature which cannot be conceived independently of other parts.

P3   *The force [vis] whereby a man persists in existing is limited, and infinitely surpassed by the power of external causes.*

Proof   This is clear from the Axiom of this Part. In the case of every man there is something else, say A, more powerful than he, and then there is another thing, say B, more powerful than A, and so ad infinitum. Therefore, the power of a man is limited in comparison with something else, and is infinitely surpassed by the power of external causes.

P4   *It is impossible for a man not to be part of Nature and not to undergo changes other than those which can be understood solely through his own nature and of which he is the adequate cause.*

Proof   The power whereby each single thing, and consequently man, preserves its own being is the very power of God, or Nature (Cor. Pr. 24, I), not insofar as it is infinite but insofar as it can be explicated through actual human essence (Pr. 7, III). Therefore, the power of man insofar as it is explicated through his actual essence is part of the infinite power of God, or Nature, that is, of God's essence (Pr. 34, I). This is the first point. Again, if it were possible for man to undergo no changes except those which can be understood solely through his own nature, it would follow (Prs. 4 and 6, III) that he cannot perish but would always necessarily exist; and this would have to follow from a cause whose power is either finite or infinite, namely, either from the power of man alone, in that he would be capable of removing from himself all changes which might arise from external causes, or else from the infinite power of Nature, by which all particular things would be so governed that man could undergo no changes other than those that serve for his preservation. But of these alternatives the first is absurd (by the preceding proposition, whose proof is universal and can be applied to all particular things). Therefore, if it were possible that man could undergo no changes except such as could be understood through man's nature alone, and consequently (as I have already demonstrated) that he should always necessarily exist, this would have to follow from the infinite power of God. Consequently (Pr. 16, I), the entire order of Nature as conceived under the attributes of Extension and Thought would have to be deducible from the necessity of the divine nature insofar as it is considered as affected by the idea of some man. And so it would follow (Pr. 21, I) that man would be infinite, which is absurd (by the first part of this proof). There-fore, it is impossible that man should not undergo any changes except those of which he is the adequate cause.

Cor   Hence it follows that man is necessarily always subject to passive emotions, and that he follows the common order of Nature, and obeys it, and accommo-dates himself to it as far as the nature of things demands.

P5   *The force and increase of any passive emotion and its persistence in existing is defined not by the power whereby we ourselves endeavor to persist in existing, but by the power of external causes compared with our own power.*

Proof   The essence of a passive emotion cannot be explicated through our own essence alone (Defs. 1 and 2, III); that is (Pr. 7, III), the power of a passive emo-tion cannot be defined by the power whereby we endeavor to persist in our own being, but (as we have demonstrated in Pr. 16, II) must necessarily be defined by the power of an external cause compared with our own power.

P6   *The force of any passive emotion can surpass the rest of man's activities or power so that the emotion stays firmly fixed in him.*

Proof   The force and increase of any passive emotion and its persistence in ex-isting is defined by the power of an external cause compared with our own power (by the preceding proposition) and so (Pr. 3, IV) can surpass man's power.

P7   *An emotion cannot be checked or destroyed except by a contrary emotion which is stronger than the emotion which is to be checked.*

Proof   An emotion, insofar as it is related to the mind, is an idea whereby the mind affirms a greater or less force of existence in its body than was previously the case (General Definition of Emotions, near the end of Part III). So when the mind is assailed by an emotion, the body at the same time is affected by an affection whereby its power of acting is increased or diminished. Furthermore, this affec-tion of the body (Pr. 5, IV) receives from its own cause its force for persisting in its own being, and therefore this force cannot be checked or destroyed except by a corporeal cause (Pr. 6, II) which affects the body with an affection contrary to the other (Pr. 5, III) and stronger than it (Ax. IV). So (Pr. 12, II) the mind will be affected by the idea of an affection stronger than and contrary to the earlier one; that is (by the General Definition of Emotions), the mind will be affected by an emotion stronger than and contrary to the previous one, an emotion which will exclude or destroy the existence of the previous one. So an emotion cannot be ei-ther destroyed or checked except by a contrary and stronger emotion.

Cor   An emotion, insofar as it is related to the mind, can neither be checked nor destroyed except through the idea of an affection of the body contrary to and stronger than the affection which we are experiencing. For the emotion we are experiencing can neither be checked nor destroyed except by an emotion stronger than and contrary to it (preceding Pr.), that is, except through the idea of an affection of the body stronger than and contrary to the affection we are experiencing (General Definition of Emotions).

P8   *Knowledge of good and evil is nothing other than the emotion of pleasure or pain insofar as we are conscious of it.*

Proof   We call good or bad that which is advantageous, or an obstacle, to the preservation of our being (Defs. 1 and 2, IV); that is (Pr. 7, III), that which increases or diminishes, helps or checks, our power of activity. Therefore insofar as we perceive some thing to affect us with pleasure or pain (by the definitions of pleasure and pain, q.v., in Schol. Pr. 11, III), we call it good or bad; and so knowledge of good and evil is nothing other than the idea of pleasure or pain which necessarily follows from the emotion of pleasure or pain (Pr. 22, II). But this idea is united to the emotion in the same way as the mind is united to the body (Pr. 21, II); that is (as has been demonstrated in the Scholium to the same Proposition), this idea is not distinct in reality from the emotion, or, in other words (by the General Definition of the Emotions), from the idea of an affection of the body, save only in conception. Therefore, this knowledge of good and evil is nothing other than the emotion itself, insofar as we are conscious of it.

P9   *An emotion whose cause we think to be with us in the present is stronger than it would be if we did not think the said cause to be with us.*

Proof   An imagining [*imaginatio*] is an idea whereby the mind regards a thing as present (see its definition in Schol. Pr. 17, II), but which indicates the disposition of the human body rather than the nature of the external thing (Cor. 2, Pr. 16, II). Therefore, an emotion (by the General Definition of Emotions) is an imagining insofar as it indicates the disposition of the body. Now an imagining (Pr. 17, II) is more intense as long as we think of nothing that excludes the present existence of the external thing. Therefore that emotion, too, whose cause we think to be with us in the present, is more intense or stronger than it would be if we did not think the said cause to be with us.

Schol   When I asserted above in Proposition 18, III that from the image of a thing future or past we are affected by the same emotion as if the thing we are thinking of were present, I deliberately gave warning that this is true only insofar as we attend to the image of the thing; for an image is of the same nature whether or not we picture things as present. But I did not deny that the image becomes feebler when we regard as present to us other things which exclude the present existence of a future thing. I omitted to emphasize this at the time because I had decided to treat of the strength of the emotions in this Part.

Cor   The image of a thing future or past, that is, a thing which we regard as related to our future or past time to the exclusion of present time, is feebler, other things being equal, than the image of a present thing. Consequently, the emotion toward a thing future or past, other things being equal, is weaker than an emotion toward a present thing.

P10   *We are affected toward a future thing which we imagine to be imminent more intensely than if we were to imagine its time of existence to be farther away from the present. We are also affected by remembrance of a thing we imagine to belong to the near past more intensely than if we were to imagine it to belong to the distant past.*

Proof   Insofar as we imagine a thing to be imminent or to belong to the near past, by that very fact we are imagining something that excludes the thing's presence to a less degree than if we were to imagine that its future time of existence was farther from the present or that it happened long ago (as is self-evident). So to that extent (preceding proposition) we are more intensely affected toward it.

Schol   From our note to Definition 6, IV, it follows that with regard to objects that are distant from the present by a longer interval of time than comes within the scope of our imagination, although we know that they are far distant in time from one another, we are affected toward them with the same degree of faintness.

P11   *An emotion toward a thing which we think of as inevitable [necessarius] is more intense, other things being equal, than emotion toward a thing possible, or contingent, that is, not inevitable.*

Proof   Insofar as we imagine a thing to be inevitable, to that extent we affirm its existence. On the other hand, insofar as we imagine a thing not to be inevitable, we deny its existence (Schol. 1, Pr. 33, I), and therefore (Pr. 9, IV) emotion toward an inevitable thing, other things being equal, is more intense than emotion toward something not inevitable.

P12   *Emotion toward a thing which we know not to exist in the present, and which we imagine to be possible, is, other things being equal, more intense than emotion toward a contingent thing.*

Proof   Insofar as we imagine a thing to be contingent, we are not affected by any image of another thing that posits the existence of the former (Def. 3, IV). On the contrary, by hypothesis, we are thinking of things that exclude its present existence. But insofar as we think of a thing as possible in the future, we are thinking of things that posit its existence (Def. 4, IV); that is (Pr. 18, III), things that encourage hope or fear. Therefore, emotion toward a possible thing is more intense.

Cor   Emotion toward a thing which we know not to exist in the present and which we think of as contingent is much feebler than if we were to think of the thing as with us in the present.

Proof   Emotion toward a thing that we imagine to exist in the present is more intense than if we were to imagine it to belong to the future (Cor. Pr. 9, IV), and much stronger than it would be if we were to think of that future time as far distant from the present (Pr. 10, IV). Therefore, emotion toward a thing whose time of existence we imagine to be far distant from the present is much weaker than it would be if we were to imagine the said thing to be present, but is nevertheless (preceding Pr.) more intense than it would be if we were to imagine the said thing to be contingent. So emotion toward a contingent thing is much feebler than it would be if we were to imagine the thing to be with us in the present.

P13   *Emotion toward a contingent thing which we know not to exist in the present is, other things being equal, feebler than emotion toward a thing past.*

Proof   Insofar as we imagine a thing to be contingent, we are not affected by the image of any other thing that posits the existence of the former (Def. 3, IV). On the contrary, by hypothesis, we are imagining things that exclude its present existence. But insofar as we think of the said thing as belonging to the past, to that extent it is assumed that we are thinking of something that brings it back to memory, that is, which activates the image of the thing (Pr. 18, II and Schol.), and therefore to that extent causes us to regard the thing as present (Cor. Pr. 17, II). So (Pr. 9, IV) emotion toward a contingent thing which we know not to exist in the present is, other things being equal, feebler than emotion toward a thing past.

P14   *No emotion can be checked by the true knowledge of good and evil insofar as it is true, but only insofar as it is considered as an emotion.*

Proof   An emotion is an idea whereby the mind affirms a greater or less force of existence of its body than was previously the case (by the General Definition of Emotions), and so (Pr. 1, IV) it contains nothing positive that can be annulled by the presence of what is true. Consequently, true knowledge of good and evil cannot check an emotion by virtue of being true. But insofar as it is an emotion (Pr. 8, IV), if it be stronger than the emotion which is to be checked, to that extent only (Pr. 7, IV) it can check an emotion.

P15   *Desire that arises from the true knowledge of good and evil can be extinguished or checked by many other desires that arise from the emotions by which we are assailed.*

Proof   From the true knowledge of good and evil, insofar as this is an emotion (Pr. 8, IV), there necessarily arises desire (Definition of Emotions 1), whose strength is proportionate to the strength of the emotion from which it arises (Pr. 37, III). But since this desire, by hypothesis, arises from our truly understanding something, it therefore follows in us insofar as we are active (Pr. 3, III), and so must be understood solely through our essence (Def. 2, III). Consequently (Pr. 7, III), its force and increase must be defined solely in terms of human power. Now desires that arise from emotions by which we are assailed are also greater in proportion to the strength of the emotions, and so their force and increase (Pr. 5, IV) must be defined in terms of the power of external causes which indefinitely surpasses our power when compared with it (Pr. 3, IV). So desires that arise from emotions of this kind may be stronger than that desire which arises from the true knowledge of good and evil, and therefore (Pr. 7, IV) are able to check or extinguish it.

P16   *The desire that arises from a knowledge of good and evil insofar as this knowledge has regard to the future can be the more easily checked or extinguished by desire of things that are attractive in the present.*

Proof   Emotion toward a thing that we imagine to be future is feebler than emotion toward something present (Cor. Pr. 9, IV). But desire that arises from the true knowledge of good and evil, even when this knowledge is concerned with things that are good in the present, can be extinguished or checked by any chance desire (by the preceding proposition, whose proof is universally valid). Therefore, desire that arises from the said knowledge insofar as it has regard to the future can be the more easily checked or extinguished . . . etc.

P17   *Desire that arises from the true knowledge of good and evil insofar as this knowledge is concerned with contingent things can be even more easily checked by desire for things which are present.*

Proof   This proposition is proved in the same way as the preceding proposition, from Cor. Pr. 12, IV.

Schol   I think I have thus demonstrated why men are motivated by uncritical belief [*opinio*] more than by true reasoning, and why the true knowledge of good and evil stirs up conflict in the mind and often yields to every kind of passion. Hence the saying of the poet, "I see the better course and approve it, but I pursue the worse course."[2] Ecclesiastes seems to have had the same point in mind when he said: "He who increaseth knowledge increaseth sorrow."[3] My purpose in saying this is not to conclude that ignorance is preferable to knowledge, or that there is no difference between a fool and a wise man in the matter of controlling the emotions. I say this because it is necessary to know both the power of our nature and its lack of power, so that we can determine what reason can and cannot do in controlling the emotions, and in this Part I have said that I shall treat only of human weakness. As for the power of reason over the emotions, it is my intention to treat of that in a separate Part.

P18   *Desire arising from pleasure is, other things being equal, stronger than desire arising from pain.*

Proof   Desire is the very essence of man (Definition of Emotions 1); that is (Pr. 7, III), the conatus whereby man endeavors to persist in his own being. Therefore the desire that arises from pleasure is assisted or increased by the very emotion of pleasure (by Definition of Pleasure, q.v., in Schol. Pr. 11, III); whereas the desire

---

[2] [Ovid, *Metamorphoses* VII, 20. — S.S.]

[3] [*Ecclesiastes* 1:18. — S.S.]

that arises from pain is diminished or checked by the very emotion of pain (same Schol.). So the force of the desire that arises from pleasure must be defined by human power together with the power of an external cause, whereas the desire that arises from pain must be defined by human power alone. Therefore, the former is stronger than the latter.

Schol   I have thus briefly explained the causes of human weakness and inconstancy, and why men do not abide by the precepts of reason. It now remains for me to demonstrate what it is that reason prescribes for us, and which emotions are in harmony with the rules of human reason, and which are contrary to them. But before I embark on the task of proving these things in our detailed geometrical order, it would be well first of all to make a brief survey of the dictates of reason, so that my meaning may be more readily grasped by everyone.

Since reason demands nothing contrary to nature, it therefore demands that every man should love himself, should seek his own advantage (I mean his real advantage), should aim at whatever really leads a man toward greater perfection, and, to sum it all up, that each man, as far as in him lies, should endeavor to preserve his own being. This is as necessarily true as that the whole is greater than its part (Pr. 4, III).

Again, since virtue (Def. 8, IV) is nothing other than to act from the laws of one's own nature, and since nobody endeavors to preserve his own being (Pr. 7, III) except from the laws of his own nature, it follows firstly that the basis of virtue is the very conatus to preserve one's own being, and that happiness consists in a man's being able to preserve his own being. Secondly, it follows that virtue should be sought for its own sake, and that there is nothing preferable to it or more to our advantage, for the sake of which it should be sought. Thirdly, it follows that those who commit suicide are of weak spirit and are completely overcome by external causes opposed to their own nature. Further, it follows from Post. 4, II that we can never bring it about that we should need nothing outside ourselves to preserve our own being and that we should live a life quite unrelated to things outside ourselves. Besides, if we consider the mind, surely our intellect would be less perfect if the mind were in solitude and understood nothing beyond itself. Therefore, there are many things outside ourselves which are advantageous to us and ought therefore to be sought. Of these none more excellent can be discovered than those which are in complete harmony with our own nature. For example, if two individuals of completely the same nature are combined, they compose an individual twice as powerful as each one singly.

Therefore, nothing is more advantageous to man than man. Men, I repeat, can wish for nothing more excellent for preserving their own being than that they should all be in such harmony in all respects that their minds and bodies should compose, as it were, one mind and one body, and that all together should endeavor as best they can to preserve their own being, and that all together they should aim at the common advantage of all. From this it follows that men who are governed by reason, that is, men who aim at their own advantage under the guidance of reason, seek nothing for themselves that they would not desire for the rest of mankind; and so are just, faithful, and honorable.

These are the dictates of reason, which I have decided to set forth in brief at this point before embarking upon their more detailed demonstration. This I have done so that I may, if possible, gain the attention of those who believe that the principle that every man is bound to seek his own advantage is the basis, not of virtue and piety, but of impiety. Now that I have briefly shown that the contrary is the case, I proceed to its proof, using the same method as hitherto.

P19   *Every man, from the laws of his own nature, necessarily seeks or avoids what he judges to be good or evil.*

Proof   Knowledge of good and evil is (Pr. 8, IV) the emotion of pleasure or pain insofar as we are conscious of it, and therefore every man (Pr. 28, III) necessarily seeks what he judges to be good and avoids what he judges to be evil. But this appetite is nothing other than man's very essence or nature (Definition of Appetites, q.v. in Schol. Pr. 9, III and Definition of Emotions 1). Therefore every man, solely from the laws of his own nature, necessarily seeks or avoids . . . etc.

P20   *The more every man endeavors and is able to seek his own advantage, that is, to preserve his own being, the more he is endowed with virtue. On the other hand, insofar as he neglects to preserve what is to his advantage, that is, his own being, to that extent he is weak.*

Proof   Virtue is human power, which is defined solely by man's essence (Def. 8, IV); that is, it is defined solely by the conatus whereby man endeavors to persist in his own being (Pr. 7, III). Therefore, the more every man endeavors and is able to preserve his own being, the more he is endowed with virtue, and consequently (Prs. 4 and 6, III) insofar as he neglects to preserve his own being, to that extent he is weak.

Schol   Therefore nobody, unless he is overcome by external causes contrary to his own nature, neglects to seek his own advantage, that is, to preserve his own being. Nobody, I repeat, refuses food or kills himself from the necessity of his own nature, but from the constraint of external causes. This can take place in many ways. A man kills himself when he is compelled by another who twists the hand in which he happens to hold a sword and makes him turn the blade against his heart; or when, in obedience to a tyrant's command, he, like Seneca,[4] is compelled to open his veins, that is, he chooses a lesser evil to avoid a greater. Or it may come about when unobservable external causes condition a man's imagination and affect his body in such a way that the latter assumes a different nature contrary to the previously existing one, a nature whereof there can be no idea in mind (Pr. 10, III). But that a man from the necessity of his own nature should endeavor to cease to exist or to be changed into another form, is as

---

[4] [Seneca (4 B.C.–A.D. 66), the Roman writer and statesman, committed suicide under political pressure rather than suffer public disgrace. In many of his essays and letters he praised and justified suicide under certain conditions.]

impossible as that something should come from nothing, as anyone can see with a little thought.

P21   *Nobody can desire to be happy, to do well and to live well without at the same time desiring to be, to do, and to live; that is, actually to exist.*

Proof   The proof of this proposition, or rather, the fact itself, is self-evident, and also follows from the definition of desire. For the desire (Definition of Emotions 1) to live happily, to do well and so on is the very essence of man; that is (Pr. 7, III), the conatus whereby every man endeavors to preserve his own being. Therefore nobody can desire . . . etc.

P22   *No virtue can be conceived as prior to this one, namely, the conatus to preserve oneself.*

Proof   The conatus to preserve itself is the very essence of a thing (Pr. 7, III). Thus, if any virtue could be conceived as prior to this one—namely, this conatus— then (Def. 8, IV) the essence of a thing would be conceived as prior to itself, which is obviously absurd. Therefore no virtue . . . etc.

Cor   The conatus to preserve oneself is the primary and sole basis of virtue. For no other principle can be conceived as prior to this one (preceding Pr.), and no virtue can be conceived independently of it (Pr. 21, IV).

P23   *Insofar as a man is determined to some action from the fact that he has in-adequate ideas, he cannot be said, without qualification, to be acting from virtue; he can be said to do so only insofar as he is determined from the fact that he understands.*

Proof   Insofar as a man is determined to action from the fact that he has inade-quate ideas, to that extent (Pr. 1, III) he is passive; that is (Defs. 1 and 2, III), he does something that cannot be perceived solely in terms of his own essence, that is (Def. 8, IV), something that does not follow from his own virtue. But insofar as he is determined to an action from the fact that he understands, to that extent he is active (Pr. 1, III); that is (Def. 2, III), he does something that is perceived solely in terms of his own essence, that is (Def. 8, IV), which follows adequately from his own virtue.

P24   *To act in absolute conformity with virtue is nothing else in us but to act, to live, to preserve one's own being (these three mean the same) under the guidance of reason, on the basis of seeking one's own advantage.*

Proof   To act in absolute conformity with virtue is nothing else (Def. 8, IV) but to act according to the laws of one's own nature. But we are active only insofar as we understand (Pr. 3, III). Therefore, to act from virtue is nothing else in us but to act, to live, and to preserve one's own being under the guidance of reason, on the basis (Cor. Pr. 22, IV) of seeking one's own advantage.

P25   *Nobody endeavors to preserve his being for the sake of some other thing.*

Proof   The conatus whereby each thing endeavors to preserve its own being is defined solely by the essence of the thing itself (Pr. 7, III); given this essence alone, and not from the essence of any other thing, it necessarily follows (Pr. 6, III) that every one endeavors to preserve his own being. Moreover, this proposition is obvious from Cor. Pr. 22, IV. For if a man were to endeavor to preserve his own being for the sake of another thing, then that thing would be the primary basis of his virtue (as is self-evident), which is absurd (by the aforementioned corollary). Therefore nobody . . . etc.

P26   *Whatever we endeavor according to reason is nothing else but to understand; and the mind, insofar as it exercises reason, judges nothing else to be to its advantage except what conduces to understanding.*

Proof   The conatus to preserve itself is nothing but the essence of a thing (Pr. 7, III), which, insofar as it exists as such, is conceived as having a force to persist in existing (Pr. 6, III) and to do those things that necessarily follow from its given nature (see Definition of Appetite in Schol. Pr. 9, III). But the essence of reason is nothing other than our mind insofar as it clearly and distinctly understands (see its Definition in Schol. 2, Pr. 40, II). Therefore (Pr. 40, II), whatever we endeavor according to reason is nothing else but to understand. Again, since this conatus of the mind wherewith the mind, insofar as it exercises reason, endeavors to preserve its own being is nothing else but a conatus to understand (by the first part of this proof), this conatus to understand (Cor. Pr. 22, IV) is therefore the primary and only basis of virtue, and it is not for some further purpose that we endeavor to understand things (Pr. 25, IV). On the contrary, the mind, insofar as it exercises reason, cannot conceive any good for itself except what is conducive to understanding (Def. 1, IV).

P27   *We know nothing to be certainly good or evil except what is really conducive to understanding or what can hinder understanding.*

Proof   The mind, insofar as it exercises reason, seeks nothing else but to understand, and judges nothing else to be to its advantage except what is conducive to understanding (preceding Pr.). But the mind (Prs. 41 and 43, II, and Schol.) possesses no certainty save insofar as it has adequate ideas, or (which is the same thing by Schol. Pr. 40, II) insofar as it exercises reason. Therefore, we do not know anything to be certainly good except what is truly conducive to understanding, or certainly evil except what can hinder understanding.

P28   *The mind's highest good is the knowledge of God, and the mind's highest virtue is to know God.*

Proof   The highest object that the mind can understand is God, that is (Def. 6, I), an absolutely infinite being, and one without whom (Pr. 15, I) nothing can be or be conceived. Thus (Prs. 26 and 27, IV) the mind's utmost advantage or (Def.

1, IV) its highest good is knowledge of God. Again, the mind is active only to the extent that it understands (Prs. 1 and 3, III), and to that extent only (Pr. 23, IV) can it be said without qualification to act from virtue. So the absolute virtue of the mind is to understand. But the highest thing the mind can understand is God (as we have just proved). Therefore, the highest virtue of the mind is to understand or to know God.

P29   *No individual thing whose nature is quite different from ours can either assist or check our power to act, and nothing whatsoever can be either good or evil for us unless it has something in common with us.*

Proof   The power of each individual thing, and consequently of man (Cor. Pr. 10, II), whereby he exists and acts is determined only by another particular thing (Pr. 28, I) whose nature (Pr. 6, II) must be understood through the same attribute as that through which human nature is conceived. So our power to act, in whatever way it be conceived, can be determined, and consequently assisted or checked, by the power of another individual thing which has something in common with us, and not by the power of a thing whose nature is entirely different from our own. And since we call good or evil that which is the cause of pleasure or pain (Pr. 8, IV), that is (Schol. Pr. 11, III), which increases or diminishes, assists or checks our power of activity, a thing whose nature is entirely different from our own can be neither good nor evil for us.

P30   *No thing can be evil for us through what it possesses in common with our nature, but insofar as it is evil for us, it is contrary to us.*

Proof   We call bad that which is the cause of pain (Pr. 8, IV), that is (through Definition of Pain, q.v. in Schol. Pr. 11, III), that which diminishes or checks our power of activity. So if something were bad for us through that which it has in common with us, that thing would be able to diminish or check the very thing that it has in common with us, which is absurd (Pr. 4, III). So nothing can be bad for us through that which it has in common with us. On the contrary, insofar as it is bad—that is (as we have just demonstrated), insofar as it can diminish or check our power of activity—to that extent (Pr. 5, III) it is contrary to us.

P31   *Insofar as a thing is in agreement with our nature, to that extent it is necessarily good.*

Proof   Insofar as a thing is in agreement with our nature, it cannot be bad (preceding Pr.). Therefore, it is necessarily either good or indifferent. If we make the latter assumption, namely, that it is neither good nor bad, then nothing will follow from its nature (Ax. 3, IV)[5] which serves to preserve our nature; that is (by

---

[5] [The standard Latin text of Gebhardt has a reference to Axiom 3 of Part IV. However, in our current text there is only *one* axiom for Part IV. Translators have suggested various corrections; but Gebhardt notes in his critical apparatus that in Spinoza's original draft of the *Ethics* there were probably

hypothesis), which serves to preserve the nature of the thing itself. But this is absurd (Pr. 6, III). Therefore, insofar as it is in agreement with our nature, it is necessarily good.

Cor Hence it follows that the more a thing is in agreement with our nature, the more advantageous it is to us, that is, the more it is good; and, conversely, the more advantageous a thing is to us, to that extent it is in more agreement with our nature. For insofar as it is not in agreement with our nature, it is necessarily either different from our nature or contrary to it. If it is different (Pr. 29, IV), it can be neither good nor bad; but if contrary, it will therefore be contrary also to that which is in agreement with our nature, that is (preceding Pr.), contrary to our good; that is, it will be evil. So nothing can be good save insofar as it is in agreement with our nature. So the more a thing is in agreement with our nature, the more advantageous it is to us, and vice versa.

P32 *Insofar as men are subject to passive emotions, to that extent they cannot be said to agree in nature.*

Proof Things which are said to agree in nature are understood to agree in respect of their power (Pr. 7, III), not in respect of their weakness or negation, and consequently (Schol. Pr. 3, III) not in respect of passive emotions. Therefore men, insofar as they are subject to passive emotions, cannot be said to agree in nature.

Schol This is also self-evident. For he who says that white and black agree only in the fact that neither is red is making an absolute assertion that white and black agree in no respect. So, too, if someone says that stone and man agree only in this respect, that they are both finite, or weak, or that they do not exist from the necessity of their own natures, or that they are indefinitely surpassed by the power of external causes, he is making the general assertion that stone and man agree in no respect. For things that agree only negatively, that is, in what they do not possess, in reality agree in nothing.

P33 *Men can differ in nature insofar as they are assailed by emotions that are passive, and to that extent one and the same man, too, is variable and inconstant.*

Proof The nature or essence of emotions cannot be explicated solely through our own essence or nature (Defs. 1 and 2, III), but must be defined by the potency, that is (Pr. 7, III), the nature, of external causes as compared with our own power. Hence there are as many kinds of each emotion as there are kinds of objects by which we are affected (Pr. 56, III), and men are affected in different ways by one and the same object (Pr. 51, III), and to that extent they differ in nature. Finally, one and the same man (Pr. 51, III) is affected in different ways toward the same object, and to that extent he is variable . . . etc.

---

several axioms for Part IV. In the final version all but one of these axioms were deleted, although in Proposition 31 Spinoza still has Axiom 3 in mind. — S.S.]

P34   *Insofar as men are assailed by emotions that are passive, they can be contrary to one another.*

Proof   A man, Peter, for example, can be the cause of Paul's feeling pain because Peter has something similar to a thing that Paul hates (Pr. 16, III), or because Peter has sole possession of a thing that Paul also loves (Pr. 32, III and Schol.), or for other reasons (for the principal reasons, see Schol. Pr. 55, III). Thus it will come about (Def. of Emotions 7) that Paul will hate Peter. Consequently, it will easily happen (Pr. 40, III, and Schol.) that Peter will hate Paul in return; thus (Pr. 39, III), they will endeavor to injure each other, that is (Pr. 30, IV), they will be contrary to each other. But the emotion of pain is always a passive emotion (Pr. 59, III). Therefore men, insofar as they are assailed by passive emotions, can be contrary to one another.

Schol   I said that Paul hates Peter because he thinks that Peter possesses something that Paul also loves, from which at first sight it seems to follow that these two are injurious to each other as a result of loving the same thing, and consequently of their agreeing in nature. So if this is true, Propositions 30 and 31, IV would be false. But if we examine this question with scrupulous fairness, we find that there is no contradiction at any point. These two do not dislike each other insofar as they agree in nature, that is, insofar as they both love the same thing, but insofar as they differ from each other. For insofar as they both love the same thing, each one's love is thereby fostered (Pr. 31, III); that is (Def. of Emotions 6), each one's pleasure is fostered. Therefore, it is by no means true that insofar as they both love the same thing and agree in nature, they dislike each other. As I have said, the reason for their dislike is none other than that they are assumed to differ in nature. For we are supposing that Peter has an idea of the loved thing as now in his possession, while Paul has an idea of the loved thing lost to him. Hence the latter is affected with pain, while the former is affected with pleasure, and to that extent they are contrary to each other. In this way we can readily demonstrate that all other causes of hatred depend on men being different in nature, and not on a point wherein they agree.

P35   *Insofar as men live under the guidance of reason, to that extent only do they always necessarily agree in nature.*

Proof   Insofar as men are assailed by passive emotions, they can be different in nature (Pr. 33, IV) and contrary to one another (preceding Pr.). But we say that men are active only insofar as they live under the guidance of reason (Pr. 3, III). Thus, whatever follows from human nature, insofar as it is defined by reason, must be understood (Def. 2, III) through human nature alone as its proximate cause. But since everyone, in accordance with the laws of his own nature, aims at what he judges to be good and endeavors to remove what he judges to be evil (Pr. 19, IV), and since furthermore what he judges from the dictates of reason to be good or evil is necessarily good or evil (Pr. 41, II), it follows that insofar as men live under the guidance of reason, to that extent only do they necessarily do the things which are necessarily good for human nature and consequently for every single man; that is (Cor. Pr. 31, IV), which agree with the nature of every single man. So men also are necessarily in agreement insofar as they live under the guidance of reason.

Cor 1   There is no individual thing in the universe more advantageous to man than a man who lives by the guidance of reason. For the most advantageous thing to man is that which agrees most closely with his nature (Cor. Pr. 31, IV); that is (as is self-evident), man. But man acts absolutely according to the laws of his own nature when he lives under the guidance of reason (Def. 2, III), and only to that extent is he always necessarily in agreement with the nature of another man (preceding Pr.). Therefore, among individual things there is nothing more advantageous to man than a man who . . . etc.

Cor 2   It is when every man is most devoted to seeking his own advantage that men are of most advantage to one another. For the more every man seeks his own advantage and endeavors to preserve himself, the more he is endowed with virtue (Pr. 20, IV), or (and this is the same thing [Def. 8, IV]) the greater the power with which he is endowed for acting according to the laws of his own nature; that is (Pr. 3, III), for living by the guidance of reason. But it is when men live by the guidance of reason that they agree most in nature (preceding Pr.). Therefore (preceding Cor.), it is when each is most devoted to seeking his own advantage that men are of most advantage to one another.

Schol   What we have just demonstrated is also confirmed by daily experience with so many convincing examples as to give rise to the common saying: "Man is a God to man." Yet it is rarely the case that men live by the guidance of reason; their condition is such that they are generally disposed to envy and mutual dislike. Nevertheless they find solitary life scarcely endurable, so that for most people the definition "man is a social animal" meets with strong approval. And the fact of the matter is that the social organization of man shows a balance of much more profit than loss. So let satirists deride as much as they like the doings of mankind, let theologians revile them, and let the misanthropists [*melancholici*] heap praise on the life of rude rusticity, despising men and admiring beasts. Men will still discover from experience that they can much more easily meet their needs by mutual help and can ward off ever-threatening perils only by joining forces, not to mention that it is a much more excellent thing and worthy of our knowledge to study the deeds of men than the deeds of beasts. But I shall say more on this subject later on.

P36   *The highest good of those who pursue virtue is common to all, and all can equally enjoy it.*

Proof   To act from virtue is to act by the guidance of reason (Pr. 24, IV), and whatever we endeavor to do in accordance with reason is to understand (Pr. 26, IV). So (Pr. 28, IV) the highest good of those who pursue virtue is to know God; that is (Pr. 47, II and Schol.) a good that is common to all men and can be possessed equally by all men insofar as they are of the same nature.

Schol   Somebody may ask: "What if the highest good of those who pursue virtue were not common to all? Would it not then follow, as above (Pr. 34, IV), that men who live by the guidance of reason, that is (Pr. 35, IV), men insofar as they agree in nature, would be contrary to one another?" Let him take this reply, that it arises not by accident but from the very nature of reason that men's highest good is common to all, because this is deduced from the very essence of man insofar as that is defined by reason, and because man could neither be nor be conceived if he did not have the ability to enjoy this highest good. For it belongs to the essence of the human mind (Pr. 47, II) to have an adequate knowledge of the eternal and infinite essence of God.

P37   *The good which every man who pursues virtue aims at for himself he will also desire for the rest of mankind, and all the more as he acquires a greater knowledge of God.*

Proof   Insofar as men live by the guidance of reason, they are most useful to man (Cor. 1, Pr. 35, IV), and so (Pr. 19, IV) by the guidance of reason we shall necessarily endeavor to bring it about that men should live by the guidance of reason. But the good that every man who lives according to the dictates of reason, that is (Pr. 24, IV), who pursues virtue, seeks for himself is to understand (Pr. 26, IV). Therefore the good which every man who pursues virtue seeks for himself he will also desire for the rest of mankind. Again, desire, insofar as it is related to mind, is the very essence of mind (Def. of Emotions 1). Now the essence of mind consists in knowledge (Pr. 11, II) which involves the knowledge of God (Pr. 47, II), without which (Pr. 15, I) it can neither be nor be conceived. So the more the essence of the mind involves knowledge of God, the greater the desire with which he who pursues virtue desires for another the good which he seeks for himself.

Another Proof   The good which a man seeks for himself, and loves, he will love with greater constancy if he sees others loving the same thing (Pr. 31, III). Thus (Cor. Pr. 31, III) he will endeavor that others should love the same thing. And because this good (preceding Pr.) is common to all, and all can enjoy it, he will therefore endeavor (by the same reasoning) that all should enjoy it, and the more so (Pr. 37, III) the more he enjoys this good.

Schol 1   He who from emotion alone endeavors that others love what he himself loves and live according to his way of thinking acts only by impulse, and therefore incurs dislike, especially from those who have different preferences and who therefore strive and endeavor by that same impulse that others should live according to their way of thinking. Again, since the highest good sought by men under the sway of emotion is often such that only one man can possess it, the result is that men who love it are at odds with themselves; and, while they rejoice to sing the praises of the object of their love, they are afraid of being believed. But he who endeavors to guide others by reason acts not from impulse but from kindly concern, and is entirely consistent with himself.

Whatever we desire and do, whereof we are the cause insofar as we have the idea of God, that is, insofar as we know God, I refer to Religion [*religio*]. The desire to do good which derives from our living by the guidance of reason, I call Piety [*pietas*]. Again, the desire to establish friendship with others, a desire that characterizes the man who lives by the guidance of reason, I call Sense of Honor [*honestas*]; and I use the term "honorable" for what is praised by men who live by the guidance of reason, and "base" for what is opposed to the establishing of friendship. Moreover, I have demonstrated what are the foundations of the state. Again, the difference between true virtue and weakness can readily be apprehended from what has been said above; namely, true virtue is nothing other than to live by the guidance of reason, and so weakness consists solely in this, that a man suffers himself to be led by things external to himself and is determined by them to act in a way required by the general state of external circumstances, not by his own nature considered only in itself.

These are the proofs which I undertook in Schol. Pr. 18, IV to establish. From this it is clear that the requirement to refrain from slaughtering beasts is founded on groundless superstition and womanish compassion rather than on sound reason. The principle of seeking our own advantage teaches us to be in close relationship with men, not with beasts or things whose nature is different from human nature, and that we have the same right over them as they over us. Indeed, since every individual's right is defined by his virtue or power, man's right over beasts is far greater than their rights over man. I do not deny that beasts feel; I am denying that they are on that account debarred from paying heed to our own advantages and from making use of them as we please and dealing with them as best suits us, seeing that they do not agree with us in nature and these emotions are different in nature from human emotions (Schol. Pr. 57, III).

It remains for me to explain what is just, what is unjust, what is sin and what is merit. On these matters, see the following Scholium.

Schol 2 In Appendix Part I, I undertook to explain what is praise, what is blame, what is merit, what is sin, what is just and what is unjust. With regard to praise and blame, I have explained them in Schol. Pr. 29, III. The occasion has now arrived for me to speak of the others. But I must first speak briefly of man in a state of nature and of man in society.

Every man exists by the sovereign natural right, and consequently by the sovereign natural right every man does what follows from the necessity of his nature. So it is by the sovereign natural right that every man judges what is good and what is bad, and has regard for his own advantage according to his own way of thinking (Prs. 19 and 20, IV), and seeks revenge (Cor. 2, Pr. 40, III), and endeavors to preserve what he loves and to destroy what he hates (Pr. 28, III). Now if men lived by the guidance of reason, every man would possess this right of his (Cor. 1, Pr. 35, IV) without any harm to another. But since men are subject to emotions (Cor. Pr. 4, IV) which far surpass the power or virtue of men (Pr. 6, IV), they are therefore often pulled in different directions (Pr. 33, IV) and are contrary to one another (Pr. 34, IV), while needing each other's help (Schol. Pr. 35, IV).

Therefore, in order that men may live in harmony and help one another, it is necessary for them to give up their natural right and to create a feeling of mutual confidence that they will refrain from any action that may be harmful to another.

The way to bring this about (that men who are necessarily subject to passive emotions [Cor. Pr. 4, IV] and are inconstant and variable [Pr. 33, IV] should establish a mutual confidence and should trust one another) is obvious from Pr. 7, IV and Pr. 39, III. There it was demonstrated that no emotion can be checked except by a stronger emotion contrary to the emotion which is to be checked, and that every man refrains from inflicting injury through fear of greater injury. On these terms, then, society can be established, provided that it claims for itself the right that every man has of avenging himself and deciding what is good and what is evil; and furthermore if it has the power to prescribe common rules of behavior and to pass laws to enforce them, not by reason, which is incapable of checking the emotions (Schol. Pr. 17, IV), but by threats.

Now such a society, strengthened by law and by the capacity to preserve itself, is called a State [*civitas*]: and those who are protected by its rights are called Citizens [*cives*]. From this it can readily be understood that in a state of nature there is nothing that is universally agreed upon as good or evil, since every man in a state of nature has regard only to his own advantage and decides what is good and what is bad according to his own way of thinking and only insofar as he has regard to his own advantage, and is not bound by any law to obey anyone but himself. Thus in a state of nature wrongdoing cannot be conceived, but it can be in a civil state where good and bad are decided by common agreement and everyone is bound to obey the state. Wrongdoing is therefore nothing other than disobedience, which is therefore punishable only by the right of the State, and on the other hand obedience is held to be merit in a citizen because he is thereby deemed to deserve to enjoy the advantages of the state.

Again, in a state of nature nobody is by common agreement the owner [*dominus*] of any thing, and in nature there is nothing that can be said to belong to this man rather than that man. Everything belongs to everybody, and accordingly in a state of nature there cannot be conceived any intention to render to each what is his own or to rob someone of what is his. That is, in a state of nature nothing can be said to be just or unjust; this is so only in a civil state, where it is decided by common agreement what belongs to this or that man. From this it is clear that justice and injustice, wrongdoing and merit, are extrinsic notions, not attributes that explicate the nature of the mind. But I have said enough on this subject.

P38   *That which so disposes the human body that it can be affected in more ways, or which renders it capable of affecting external bodies in more ways, is advantageous to man, and proportionately more advantageous as the body is thereby rendered more capable of being affected in more ways and of affecting other bodies in more ways. On the other hand, that which renders the body less capable in these respects is harmful.*

Proof   In proportion as the body is rendered more capable in these respects, so is the mind rendered more capable of apprehension (Pr. 14, II); so that which disposes the body in this way and renders it more capable in these respects is necessarily good or advantageous (Prs. 26 and 27, IV), and the more so as it renders the body more capable in these respects. On the other hand (by inversion of the same Pr. 14, II, and Prs. 26 and 27, IV), that which renders it less capable in these respects is harmful.

P39 *Whatever is conducive to the preservation of the proportion of motion-and-rest, which the parts of the human body maintain toward one another, is good; and those things that effect a change in the proportion of motion-and-rest of the parts of the human body to one another are bad.*

Proof The human body needs many other bodies for its preservation (Post. 4, II). But that which constitutes the form [*forma*] of the human body consists in this, that its parts communicate their motions to one another in a certain fixed proportion (Def. before Lemma 4, q.v. after Pr. 13, II). Therefore, whatever is conducive to the preservation of the proportion of motion-and-rest, which the parts of the human body maintain toward one another, preserves the form of the human body and, consequently (Posts. 3 and 6, II), brings it about that the human body can be affected in many ways and can affect external bodies in many ways, and is, therefore (by preceding Pr.), good. Again, whatever effects a change in the proportion of motion-and-rest of the parts of the human body (by the same Def. II) causes the human body to assume a different form; that is (as is self-evident, and as we noted at the end of the Preface to Part IV), it causes it to be destroyed, and consequently quite incapable of being affected in many ways, and is, therefore, bad (preceding Pr.).

Schol In Part V, I shall explain to what extent these things can hinder or be of service to the mind. But here it should be noted that I understand a body to die when its parts are so disposed as to maintain a different proportion of motion-and-rest to one another. For I do not venture to deny that the human body, while retaining blood circulation and whatever else is regarded as essential to life, can nevertheless assume another nature quite different from its own. I have no reason to hold that a body does not die unless it turns into a corpse; indeed, experience seems to teach otherwise. It sometimes happens that a man undergoes such changes that I would not be prepared to say that he is the same person. I have heard tell of a certain Spanish poet who was seized with sickness, and although he recovered, he remained so unconscious of his past life that he did not believe that the stories and tragedies he had written were his own. Indeed, he might have been taken for a child in adult form if he had also forgotten his native tongue. And if this seems incredible, what are we to say about babies? A man of advanced years believes their nature to be so different from his own that he could not be persuaded that he had ever been a baby if he did not draw a parallel from other cases. But I prefer to leave these matters unresolved, so as not to afford material for the superstitious to raise new problems.

P40 *Whatever is conducive to man's social organization, or causes men to live in harmony, is advantageous, while those things that introduce discord into the state are bad.*

Proof   Whatever things cause men to live in harmony cause them also to live by the guidance of reason (Pr. 35, IV), and so are good (Prs. 26 and 27, IV), while those things that introduce discord are bad (by the same reasoning).

P41   *Pleasure is not in itself bad, but good. On the other hand, pain is in itself bad.*

Proof   Pleasure (Pr. 11, III and Schol.) is an emotion whereby the body's power of activity is increased or assisted. Pain, on the other hand, is an emotion whereby the body's power of activity is diminished or checked. Therefore (Pr. 38, IV) pleasure in itself is good . . . etc.

P42   *Cheerfulness [hilaritas] cannot be excessive; it is always good. On the other hand, melancholy is always bad.*

Proof   Cheerfulness (see its definition in Schol. Pr. 11, III) is pleasure which, insofar as it is related to the body, consists in this, that all parts of the body are affected equally; that is (Pr. 11, III), the body's power of activity is increased or assisted in such a way that all its parts maintain the same proportion of motion-and-rest toward one another. Thus (Pr. 39, IV) cheerfulness is always good, and cannot be excessive. But melancholy (see again its definition in same Schol. Pr. 11, III) is pain, which, insofar as it is related to the body, consists in this, that the body's power of activity is absolutely diminished or checked, and therefore (Pr. 38, IV) it is always bad.

P43   *Titillation [titillatio] can be excessive and bad. But anguish [dolor] can be good to the extent that titillation or pleasure is bad.*

Proof   Titillation is pleasure which, insofar as it is related to the body, consists in one or more of the body's parts being affected more than the rest. (See its definition in Schol. Pr. 11, III.) The power of this emotion can be so great as to surpass the other activities of the body (Pr. 6, IV) and to stay firmly fixed therein, and thus hinder the body's ability to be affected in numerous other ways. So (Pr. 38, IV) it can be bad. Again, anguish [*dolor*] on the other hand, which is pain, cannot be good considered solely in itself (Pr. 41, IV). However, because its force and increase is defined by the power of an external cause compared with our own power (Pr. 5, IV), we can therefore conceive this emotion as having infinite degrees of strength and infinite modes (Pr. 3, IV). Thus, we can conceive it as being able to check titillation so that it does not become excessive, and to that extent (by the first part of this proposition) it would prevent the body from being rendered less capable. Therefore, to that extent it is good.

P44   *Love and desire can be excessive.*

Proof   Love is pleasure (Def. of Emotions 6) accompanied by the idea of an external cause. Therefore, titillation (Schol. Pr. 11, III) accompanied by the idea of an external cause is love, and thus love (by the preceding Pr.) can be excessive. Again, the strength of a desire is in proportion to that of the emotion from which it arises (Pr. 37, III). Therefore, just as an emotion (Pr. 6, IV) can surpass the other activities of man, so too a desire arising from that same emotion can surpass the other desires, and can therefore be excessive in the same way as was the case with titillation in the previous proposition.

Schol Cheerfulness, which I have asserted to be good, is more easily conceived than observed. For the emotions by which we are daily assailed are generally related to some part of the body which is affected more than the rest. Therefore, emotions are as a general rule excessive and keep the mind obsessed with one single object to such an extent that it cannot think of anything else. And although men are subject to numerous emotions, and so few are found who are always assailed by one and the same emotion, yet there are some in whom one and the same emotion stays firmly fixed. For sometimes we see men so affected by one object that they think they have it before them even though it is not present. When this happens to a man who is not asleep, we say he is delirious or mad, and no less mad are those thought to be who are fired with love, dreaming night and day only of their sweetheart or mistress, for they usually provoke ridicule. But when the miser thinks of nothing but gain or money, and the ambitious man of honor, they are not reckoned as mad, for they are usually unpopular and arouse disgust. But in reality avarice, ambition, lust, etc. are kinds of madness, although they are not accounted as diseases.

P45 *Hatred can never be good.*

Proof We endeavor to destroy the man we hate (Pr. 39, III); that is (Pr. 37, IV), we endeavor to do something that is bad. Therefore . . . etc.

Schol Note that here and in what follows, by hatred I mean only hatred toward men.

Cor 1 Envy, derision, contempt, anger, revenge, and the other emotions related to hatred or arising from hatred are bad. This is also clear from Pr. 39, III and Pr. 37, IV.

Cor 2 Whatever we desire as a result of being affected by hatred is base, and, in a state, unjust. This is also clear from Pr. 39, III and from the definitions of base and unjust, q.v. in Schol. Pr. 37, IV.

Schol I make a definite distinction between derision (which in Cor. 1 I said is bad) and laughter. For laughter, and likewise merriment, are pure pleasure, and so, provided that they are not excessive, they are good in themselves (Pr. 41, IV). Certainly nothing but grim and gloomy superstition forbids enjoyment. Why is it less fitting to drive away melancholy than to dispel hunger and thirst? The principle that guides me and shapes my attitude to life is this: no deity, nor anyone else but the envious, takes pleasure in my weakness and my misfortune, nor does he take to be a virtue our tears, sobs, fearfulness, and other such things that are a mark of a weak spirit. On the contrary, the more we are affected with pleasure, the more we pass to state of greater perfection; that is, the more we necessarily participate in the divine nature. Therefore, it is the part of a wise man to make use of things and to take pleasure in them as far as he can (but not to the point of satiety, for that is not taking pleasure). It is, I repeat, the part of a wise man to refresh and invigorate himself in moderation with good food and drink, as also with perfumes, with the beauty of blossoming plants, with dress, music, sporting activities, theaters, and the like, in which every man can indulge without harm to another. For the human body is composed of many parts of various kinds which are continually in need of fresh and varied nourishment so that the entire body may be equally capable of all the functions that follow from its own nature, and consequently that the mind may be equally capable of simultaneously understanding many things. So this manner of life is in closest agreement both with our principles and with common practice. Therefore, of all ways of life, this is the best and is to be commended on all accounts. There is no need for me to deal more clearly or at greater length with this subject.

P46 *He who lives by the guidance of reason endeavors as far as he can to repay with love or nobility another's hatred, anger, contempt, etc. toward himself.*

Proof All emotions of hatred are bad (Cor. 1 preceding Pr.), and thus he who lives by the guidance of reason will endeavor as far as he can not to be assailed by emotions of hatred (Pr. 19, IV), and consequently (Pr. 37, IV) he will also endeavor that another should not suffer these same emotions. But hatred is increased by reciprocal hatred, and can on the other hand be extinguished by love (Pr. 43, III), so that hatred is transformed into love (Pr. 44, III). Therefore, he who lives by the guidance of reason will endeavor to render back love, that is, nobility (for whose definition see Schol. Pr. 59, III), in return for another's hatred, etc.

Schol He who wishes to avenge injuries through reciprocal hatred lives a miserable life indeed. But he who strives to overcome hatred with love is surely fighting a happy and carefree battle. He resists several opponents as easily as one, and stands in least need of fortune's help. Those whom he conquers yield gladly, not through failure of strength but through its increase. All this follows so clearly solely from the definitions of love and intellect that there is no need of detailed proof.

P47 *The emotions of hope and fear cannot be good in themselves.*

Proof The emotions of hope and fear cannot be without pain. For fear is pain (Def. of Emotions 13), and there cannot be hope without fear (see Def. of Emotions 12 and 13, Explications). Therefore (Pr. 41, IV), these emotions cannot be good in themselves, but only insofar as they can check excessive pleasure (Pr. 43, IV).

Schol We should add that these emotions indicate a lack of knowledge and a weakness of mind, and for this reason, too, confidence, despair, joy, and disappointment are also indications of our weakness. For although confidence and joy are emotions of pleasure, they imply a preceding pain, namely, hope and fear. Therefore, the more we endeavor to live by the guidance of reason, the more we endeavor to be independent of hope, to free ourselves from fear, and to command fortune as far as we can, and to direct our actions by the sure counsel of reason.

P48   *The emotions of over-esteem* [existimatio] *and disparagement* [despectus] *are always bad.*

Proof   These emotions (Def. of Emotions 21 and 22) are opposed to reason, and so (Prs. 26 and 27, IV) are bad.

P49   *Over-esteem is apt to render its recipient proud.*

Proof   If we see that someone by reason of love has too high an opinion of us, we are inclined to exult (Schol. Pr. 41, III), that is, to be affected with pleasure (Def. of Emotions 30), and we readily believe whatever good we hear said of us (Pr. 25, III). Thus, we shall think too highly of ourselves through self-love; that is (Def. of Emotions 28), we shall be inclined to pride.

P50   *In the man who lives by the guidance of reason, pity is in itself bad and disadvantageous.*

Proof   Pity is pain (Def. of Emotions 18) and therefore in itself it is bad (Pr. 41, IV). Now the good that follows from it (that we endeavor to free from distress one whom we pity [Cor. 3, Pr. 27, III]) we desire to do solely from the dictates of reason (Pr. 37, IV), and it is only from the dictates of reason that we desire to do something that we certainly know to be good (Pr. 27, IV). So in the man who lives by the guidance of reason pity in itself is bad and disadvantageous.

Cor   Hence it follows that the man who lives by the dictates of reason endeavors, as far as he can, not to be touched by pity.

Schol   He who rightly knows that all things follow from the necessity of the divine nature and happen in accordance with the eternal laws and rules of Nature will surely find nothing deserving of hatred, derision, or contempt nor will he pity anyone. Rather, as far as the virtue of man extends, he will endeavor to do well, as the saying goes, and be glad. Furthermore, he who is easily touched by the emotion of pity and is moved by another's distress or tears often does something which he later regrets, both because from emotion we do nothing that we certainly know to be good and because we are easily deceived by false tears. Now I emphasize that I am here speaking of the man who lives by the guidance of reason. For he who is moved neither by reason nor by pity to render help to others is rightly called inhuman. For (Pr. 27, III) he seems to be unlike a man.

P51   *Approbation* [favor] *is not opposed to reason; it can agree with reason and arise from it.*

Proof   Approbation is love toward one who has benefited another (Def. of Emotions 19); thus it can be related to the mind insofar as the mind is said to be active (Pr. 59, III), that is (Pr. 3, III), insofar as it understands. Therefore it is in agreement with reason . . . etc.

Another Proof   He who lives by the guidance of reason desires for another, too, the good that he seeks for himself (Pr. 37, IV). Therefore, as a result of seeing someone do good to another, his own conatus to do good is assisted; that is (Schol. Pr. 11, III), he will feel pleasure accompanied (by hypothesis) by the idea of him who has benefited another and so he feels well-disposed toward him (Def. of Emotions 19).

Schol   Indignation, as we have defined it (Def. of Emotions 20), is necessarily evil (Pr. 45, IV). But it should be noted that when the sovereign power, through its duty to safeguard peace, punishes a citizen who has injured another, I am not saying that it is indignant with citizen. It punishes him not because it is stirred by hatred to destroy the citizen, but from a sense of duty [*pietate*].

P52   *Self-contentment [acquiescentia in se ipso] can arise from reason, and only that self-contentment which arises from reason is the highest there can be.*

Proof   Self-contentment is the pleasure arising from a man's contemplation of himself and his power of activity (Def. of Emotions 25). Now man's true power of activity, or his virtue, is reason itself (Pr. 3, III), which man regards clearly and distinctly (Prs. 40 and 43, II). Therefore self-contentment arises from reason. Again, in contemplating himself a man perceives clearly and distinctly, that is, adequately, only what follows from his power of activity (Def. 2, III), that is (Pr. 3, III), what follows from his power of understanding. So the greatest self-contentment there can be arises only from this contemplation.

Schol   In fact self-contentment is the highest good we can hope for. For (as we proved in Pr. 25, IV) nobody endeavors to preserve his own being for the sake of something else. And because this self-contentment is increasingly fostered and strengthened by praise (Cor. Pr. 53, III), and on the other hand is increasingly disturbed by blame (Cor. Pr. 55, III), honor [*gloria*] is the greatest incentive, and we can scarcely endure life in disgrace.

P53   *Humility is not a virtue; that is, it does not arise from reason.*

Proof   Humility is the pain arising from a man's contemplation of his own weakness (Def. of Emotions 26). Now insofar as a man knows himself by true reason, to that extent he is assumed to understand his own essence, that is (Pr. 7, III), his own power. Therefore if a man, in contemplating himself, perceives some weakness in himself, this does not arise from his understanding himself but (Pr. 55, III) from the checking of his power of activity. Now if we suppose that a man conceives his own weakness from understanding something more powerful than himself, by the knowledge of which he measures his own power of activity, we are conceiving only that the man understands himself distinctly; that is (Pr. 26,

IV), that his power of activity is assisted. Therefore the humility, or the pain, that arises from a man's contemplation of his own weakness, does not arise from true contemplation or reason, and is not a virtue but a passive emotion.

P54 *Repentance is not a virtue, i.e., it does not arise from reason; he who repents of his action is doubly unhappy or weak.*

Proof The first part of this Proposition is proved in the same way as the preceding proposition. The second part is evident simply from the definition of this emotion (Def. of Emotions 27). For the subject suffers himself to be overcome first by a wicked desire [*cupiditas*], and then by pain.

Schol As men seldom live according to the dictates of reason, these two emotions, humility and repentance, and also hope and fear, bring more advantage than harm; and thus, if sin we must, it is better to sin in their direction. For if men of weak spirit should all equally be subject to pride, and should be ashamed of nothing and afraid of nothing, by what bonds could they be held together and bound? The mob is fearsome, if it does not fear. So it is not surprising that the prophets, who had regard for the good of the whole community, and not of the few, have been so zealous in commending humility, repentance, and reverence. And in fact those who are subject to these emotions can be far more readily induced than others to live by the guidance of reason in the end, that is, to become free men and enjoy the life of the blessed.

P55 *Extreme pride, or self-abasement, is extreme ignorance of oneself.*

Proof This is clear from Definition of Emotions 28 and 29.

P56 *Extreme pride, or self-abasement, indicates extreme weakness of spirit.*

Proof The primary basis of virtue is to preserve one's own being (Cor. Pr. 22, IV), and this by the guidance of reason (Pr. 24, IV). So he who is ignorant of himself is ignorant of the basis of all the virtues, and consequently of all the virtues. Again, to act from virtue is nothing else but to act from the guidance of reason (Pr. 24, IV), and he who acts from the guidance of reason must necessarily know that he acts from the guidance of reason (Pr. 43, II). Therefore, he whose ignorance of himself (and consequently as I have just demonstrated, of all the virtues) is extreme, acts least of all from virtue; that is (as is evident from Def. 8, IV), he is most impotent in spirit. And so (by the preceding Pr.) extreme pride or self-abasement indicates extreme weakness of spirit.

Cor Hence it clearly follows that the proud and the self-abased are most subject to emotions.

Schol But self-abasement can be more easily corrected than pride, since the latter is an emotion of pleasure, while the former is an emotion of pain. So the latter is stronger than the former (Pr. 18, IV).

P57   *The proud man loves the company of parasites or flatterers, and hates the company of those of noble spirit.*

Proof   Pride is the pleasure arising from a man's thinking too highly of himself (Def. of Emotions 28 and 6), a belief which the proud man will endeavor to foster as much as he can (Schol. Pr. 13, III). So the proud love the company of parasites and flatterers (I omit their definitions as being too well-known) and shun the company of those of noble spirit, who value them according to their deserts.

Schol   It would be tedious to recount here all the ills that spring from pride, for the proud are subject to all the emotions, though to love and pity least of all. But I must not omit here to mention that the term "proud" is also applied to a man who thinks too meanly of others, and so in this sense pride should be defined as the pleasure arising from false belief, in that a man thinks himself above others. And the self-abasement which is the opposite of this pride should be defined as the pain arising from false belief, in that a man thinks himself beneath others. Now on this basis we readily conceive that the proud man is necessarily envious (Schol. Pr. 55, III) and hates most those who are praised for their virtues—a hatred that cannot easily be conquered by their love and kindness (Schol. Pr. 41, III)—and finds pleasure only in the company of those who humor his weakness of spirit and turn his folly to madness.

Although self-abasement is the opposite of pride, the self-abased man is very close to the proud man. For since his pain arises from judging his own weakness by the power or virtue of others, his pain will be assuaged, that is, he will feel pleasure, if his thoughts are engaged in contemplating other people's faults. This is the origin of the proverb: "The consolation of the wretched is to have fellows in misfortune." On the other hand, he will be more pained in proportion as he thinks himself lower than others. Hence it comes about that the self-abased are more prone to envy than all others, and that they, more than any, endeavor to keep watch on men's deeds with a view to criticizing rather than correcting them, and they end up by praising only self-abasement and exulting in it even while still preserving the appearance of self-abasement.

Now these results follow from this emotion with the same necessity as it follows from the nature of a triangle that its angles are equal to two right angles, and I have already stated that it is only in respect of the good of man that I call these and similar emotions evil. But the laws of Nature have regard to the universal order of Nature, of which man is a part. I have thought first to note this in passing lest anyone should think that my intention here has been to recount the faults and absurdities of mankind rather than to demonstrate the nature and properties of things. As I said in the Preface to Part III, I consider human emotions and their properties on the same footing with other natural phenomena. And surely human emotions indicate, if not human power, at any rate the power and intricacy of Nature to no less a degree than many other things that evoke our wonder and whose contemplation gives pleasure. But I am going on to point out what features in our emotions bring advantage or harm to men.

P58   *Honor is not opposed to reason, but can arise from it.*

Proof   This is evident from Def. of Emotions 30, and from the definition of honorable, for which see Schol. 1, Pr. 37, IV.

Schol   Vainglory, as it is called, is the self-contentment that is fostered only by popular esteem and ceases with it; that is (Schol. Pr. 52, IV), the highest good which everyone loves, ceases. So it happens that he who exults in popular esteem has the daily burden of anxiously striving, acting and contriving to preserve his reputation. For the populace is fickle and inconstant, and unless a reputation is preserved it soon withers away. Indeed, since all are eager to capture the applause of the populace, each is ready to decry another's reputation. As a result, since the prize at stake is what is esteemed the highest good, there arises a fierce desire to put down one's rivals in whatever way one can, and he who finally emerges victorious prides himself more on having hindered another than on having gained an advantage for himself. So this kind of glory, or self-contentment, is really vain because it is nothing.

As to what is to be remarked about Shame [*pudor*], this can readily be gathered from our account of compassion and repentance. I shall merely add this, that shame, like pity, although not a virtue, can be good insofar as it is an indication that the man who feels ashamed has a desire to live honorably, just as is the case with anguish, which is said to be good insofar as it indicates that the injured part has not yet putrefied. Therefore, although the man who is ashamed of some deed is in fact pained, he is nearer perfection than the shameless man who has no desire to live honorably.

I have now completed my undertaking to deal with the emotions of pleasure and pain. As for desires, they are, of course, good or evil insofar as they arise from good or evil emotions. But in truth all desires insofar as they are engendered in us from passive emotions, are blind (as can easily be gathered from a reading of Schol. Pr. 44, IV) and would be ineffective if men could readily be induced to live only according to the dictates of reason, as I shall now demonstrate in brief.

P59   *In the case of all actions to which we are determined by a passive emotion, we can be determined thereto by reason without that emotion.*

Proof   To act from reason is nothing else but to do what follows from the necessity of our own nature considered solely in itself (Pr. 3 and Def. 2, III). Now pain is bad to the extent that it diminishes or checks this power of action (Pr. 41, IV). Therefore, we cannot be determined from this emotion to any action that we could not do if we were guided by reason. Moreover, pleasure is bad to the extent that it hinders a man's capacity for action (Prs. 41 and 43, IV), and to that extent also we cannot be determined to any action that we could not do if we were guided by reason. Finally, insofar as pleasure is good, it is in agreement with reason (for it consists in this, that a man's power of activity is increased or assisted), and it is a passive emotion only insofar as a man's power of activity is not increased to such a degree that he adequately conceives himself and his actions (Pr. 3, III and Schol.) Therefore, if a man affected with pleasure were brought to such a degree of perfection that he were adequately to conceive himself and his actions, he would be capable, indeed, more capable, of those same actions to which he is now determined by passive emotions. Now all emotions are related to pleasure, pain, or desire (see Explication of Def. of Emotions 4), and desire is merely the endeavor to act (Def. of Emotions 1). Therefore, in the case of all actions to which we are determined by a passive emotion, we can be guided thereto by reason alone, without the emotion.

Another Proof   Any action is said to be bad insofar as it arises from our having been affected with hatred or some evil emotion (Cor. 1, Pr. 45, IV). But no action, considered solely in itself, is good or evil (as we demonstrated in the Preface, Part IV), but one and the same action can be now good, now evil. Therefore, we can be guided by reason to that same action which is now bad, that is, which arises from an evil emotion (Pr. 19, IV).

Schol   An example will make this clearer. The act of striking a blow, insofar as it is considered physically and insofar as we look only to the fact that a man raises an arm, clenches his fist and violently brings his arm down, is a virtue, conceived as resulting from the structure of the human body. So if a man, stirred by anger or hatred, is determined to clench his fist or move his arm, this happens because (as we demonstrated in Part II), one and the same action can be associated with any images whatsoever. And so we can be determined to one and the same action both from images of things which we conceive confusedly and from those we conceive clearly and distinctly. It is therefore clear that if men could be guided by reason, all desire that arises from passive emotion would be ineffective [*nullius esset usus*].

Now let us see why desire that arises from an emotion, that is, a passive emotion, is called blind.

P60   *Desire that arises from the pleasure or pain that is related to one or more, but not to all, parts of the body takes no account of the advantage of the whole man.*

Proof   Let it be supposed that part A of the body is so strengthened by the force of some external cause that it prevails over the other parts (Pr. 6, IV). This part will not endeavor to abate its own strength in order that other parts of the body may perform their function, for then it would have to possess the force or power to abate its own strength, which is absurd (Pr. 6, III). Therefore that part of the body, and consequently the mind too (Prs. 7 and 12, III), will endeavor to preserve the existing condition. Therefore, the desire that arises from such an emotion of pleasure takes no account of the whole. Now if we suppose on the other hand that part A is checked so that the other parts prevail over it, it can be proved in the same way that desire arising from pain likewise takes no account of the whole.

Schol   Therefore, since pleasure is usually related to one part of the body (Schol. Pr. 44, IV), we usually desire to preserve our being without taking account of our entire well-being. There is also the fact that the desires by which we are most enslaved (Cor. Pr. 9, IV) take into account only the present, not the future.

P61   *Desire that arises from reason cannot be excessive.*

Proof   Desire (Def. of Emotions 1), considered absolutely, is man's very essence insofar as he is conceived as determined in any manner to some action. Therefore desire that arises from reason, that is (Pr. 3, III), desire that is engendered in us insofar as we are active, is man's very essence of nature insofar as it is conceived as determined to such actions as are adequately conceived through man's essence alone (Def. 2, III). So if this desire could be excessive, human nature, considered absolutely, could exceed itself, that is, it could do more than it can do, which is a manifest contradiction. Therefore, this desire cannot be excessive.

P62   *Insofar as the mind conceives things in accordance with the dictates of reason, it is equally affected whether the idea be of the future, in the past, or the present.*

Proof   Whatsoever the mind conceives under the guidance of reason, it conceives under the same form of eternity or necessity (Cor. 2, Pr. 44, II), and is affected with the same certainty (Pr. 43, II and Schol.). Therefore, whether the idea be of the future, the past, or the present, the mind conceives the thing with the same necessity and is affected with the same certainty; and whether the idea be of the future, the past, or the present, it will nevertheless be equally true (Pr. 41, II); that is (Def. 4, II), it will nevertheless always have the same properties of an adequate idea. Therefore, insofar as the mind conceives things according to the dictates of reason, it is affected in the same way, whether the idea be of a thing future, past, or present.

Schol   If we could have an adequate knowledge of the duration of things and could determine by reason the periods of their existence, we should regard things future with the same emotion as things present, and the mind would seek the good that it conceives as future just as much as present good. Consequently, it would necessarily prefer a future greater good to a lesser present good, and would by no means seek that which is good in the present but the cause of future evil, as we shall later demonstrate. But we can have only a very inadequate knowledge of the duration of things (Pr. 31, II), and we determine the periods of existence of things by imagination alone (Schol. Pr. 44, II), which is more strongly affected by the image of a thing present than of a thing future. Thus it comes about that the true knowledge we have of good and evil is only abstract or universal, and the judgment that we make concerning the order of things and the connection of causes so that we may determine what is good or bad for us in the present pertains more to the imagination than to reality. So it is not surprising that desire that arises from a knowledge of good and evil, insofar as this knowledge has reference to the future, can be more readily checked by desire of things that are attractive in the present. See Pr. 16, IV.

P63   *He who is guided by fear, and does good so as to avoid evil, is not guided by reason.*

Proof   All emotions that are related to the mind insofar as it is active, that is (Pr. 3, III), emotions that are related to reason, are emotions of pleasure and desire only (Pr. 59, III). Therefore (Def. of Emotions 13), he who is guided by fear and does good through fear of evil is not guided by reason.

Schol   The superstitious, who know how to censure vice rather than to teach virtue, and who are eager not to guide men by reason but to restrain them by fear so that they may shun evil rather than love virtue, have no other object than to make others as wretched as themselves. So it is not surprising that they are generally resented and hated.

Cor   Through the desire that arises from reason we pursue good directly and shun evil indirectly.

Proof   The desire that arises from reason can arise only from an emotion of pleasure that is not passive (Pr. 59, III), that is, from a pleasure that cannot be excessive (Pr. 61, IV), and not from pain; and therefore this pleasure (Pr. 8, IV) arises from knowledge of good, not of evil. So by the guidance of reason we directly aim at the good, and only to that extent do we shun evil.

Schol   This corollary can be illustrated by the example of the sick man and the healthy man. The sick man eats what he dislikes through fear of death. The healthy man takes pleasure in his food and thus enjoys a better life than if he were to fear death and directly seek to avoid it. Likewise the judge who condemns a man to death not through hatred or anger but solely through love of public welfare is guided only by reason.

P64   *Knowledge of evil is inadequate knowledge.*

Proof   Knowledge of evil is pain itself (Pr. 8, IV) insofar as we are conscious of it. Now pain is a transition to a state of less perfection (Def. of Emotions 3), which therefore cannot be understood through man's essence itself (Prs. 6 and 7, III) and so is a passive emotion (Def. 2, III) which depends on inadequate ideas (Pr. 3, III). Consequently knowledge of it (Pr. 29, II)—that is, knowledge of evil—is inadequate knowledge.

Cor   Hence it follows that if the human mind had only adequate ideas, it could not form any notion of evil.

P65   *By the guidance of reason we pursue the greater of two goods and the lesser of two evils.*

Proof   The good that prevents us from enjoying a greater good is in reality an evil; for evil and good are terms used (as I have demonstrated in the Preface to Part IV) insofar as we compare things with one another, and by the same reasoning a lesser evil is in reality a good. Therefore (Cor. Pr. 63, IV), by the guidance of reason we aim at or pursue only the greater good and the lesser evil.

Cor   Under the guidance of reason we pursue a lesser evil for a greater good, and we reject a lesser good which is the cause of a greater evil. For what is here called the lesser evil is in reality a good, and the good on the other hand an evil. There-fore, we choose the former and reject the latter (Cor. Pr. 63, IV).

P66   *Under the guidance of reason we seek a future greater good in preference to a lesser present good, and a lesser present evil in preference to a greater future evil.*

Proof   If the mind could have an adequate knowledge of what is to come, it would be affected by the same emotion toward a future thing as toward a present thing (Pr. 62, IV). Thus insofar as we have regard to reason itself, as we assume we are doing in this proposition, a thing is the same whether it is supposed to be a greater good or evil in the future or in the present. Therefore (Pr. 65, IV), we seek a future greater good in preference to a lesser present good . . . etc.

Cor   Under the guidance of reason we choose a present lesser evil which is the cause of a future greater good, and we reject a present lesser good which is the cause of a future greater evil. This corollary is related to the preceding proposi-tion, just as Cor. Pr. 65 to Pr. 65.

Schol   If these statements be compared with what we have demonstrated in this Part up to Pr. 18 with reference to the strength of the emotions, we shall readily see the difference between the man who is guided only by emotion or belief and the man who is guided by reason. The former, whether he will or not, performs actions of which he is completely ignorant. The latter does no one's will but his own, and does only what he knows to be of greatest importance in life, which he therefore desires above all. So I call the former a slave and the latter a free man, of whose character and manner of life I have yet a few things to say.

P67   *A free man thinks of death least of all things, and his wisdom is a medita-tion of life, not of death.*

Proof   A free man, that is, he who lives solely according to the dictates of reason, is not guided by fear of death (Pr. 63, IV), but directly desires the good (Cor. Pr. 63, IV); that is (Pr. 24, IV), to act, to live, to preserve his own being in accordance with the principle of seeking his own advantage. So he thinks of death least of all things, and his wisdom is a meditation upon life.

P68   *If men were born free, they would form no conception of good and evil so long as they were free.*

Proof   I have said that a free man is he who is guided solely by reason. There-fore, he who is born free and remains free has only adequate ideas and thus has no conception of evil (Cor. 64, IV), and consequently no conception of good (for good and evil are correlative).

Schol   It is clear from Pr. 4, IV that the hypothesis in this proposition is false and cannot be conceived except insofar as we have regard solely to the nature of man, or rather, to God not insofar as he is infinite but only insofar as he is the cause of man's existence. This and other truths that we have already demonstrated seem to be what Moses intended by his history of the first man. For in that narrative no other power of God is conceived save that whereby he created man; that is, the power whereby he had regard only for man's advantage. And this is the point of the story that God forbade the free man to eat of the tree of the knowledge of good and evil, saying that as soon as he should eat of it he would straightway fear death instead of desiring to live. Again, the story goes that when man had found woman, who agreed entirely with his own nature, he realized that there could be nothing in Nature more to his advantage than woman. But when he came to believe that the beasts were like himself, he straightway began to imitate their emotions (Pr. 27, III) and to lose his freedom, which the Patriarchs later regained under the guidance of the spirit of Christ, that is, the idea of God, on which alone it depends that a man should be free and should desire for mankind the good that he desires for himself, as I have demonstrated above (Pr. 37, IV).

P69 *The virtue of a free man is seen to be as great in avoiding dangers as in over-coming them.*

Proof An emotion cannot be checked or removed except by a contrary emotion stronger than the emotion which is to be checked (Pr. 7, IV). But blind daring [*caeca audacia*] and fear are emotions that can be conceived as equally strong (Prs. 5 and 3, IV). Therefore the virtue or strength of mind (for its definition see Schol. Pr. 59, III) needed to check daring must be equally as great as that needed to check fear; that is (Def. of Emotions 40 and 41), the free man avoids dangers by that same virtue as that whereby he attempts to overcome them.

Cor Therefore, for a free man timely retreat is as much a mark of courage as is fighting; that is, the free man chooses flight by the same courage or spiritedness as he chooses battle.

Schol I have explained in Schol. Pr. 59, III what courage is, or what I understand by it. By danger I mean everything that can be the cause of some evil, such as pain, hatred, discord, etc.

P70 *The free man who lives among ignorant people tries as far as he can to avoid receiving favors from them.*

Proof Every man judges what is good according to his own way of thinking (Schol. Pr. 39, III). Thus the ignorant man who has conferred a favor on someone will value it according to his own way of thinking, and if he sees that the recipient values it less, he will feel pain (Pr. 42, III). Now the free man tries to establish friendship with others (Pr. 37, IV) and not to repay men with favors that are equivalent in their eyes. Rather he tries to guide himself and others by the free judgment of reason and to do only those things that he himself knows to be of primary importance. Therefore, to avoid both the hatred of the ignorant and the need to comply with their expectations, and so as to make reason his sole ruler, he will endeavor as far as he can to avoid their favors.

Schol I say, "as far as he can"; for men, however ignorant, are still men, who in time of need can bring human help, than which nothing is more valuable. So it often happens that it is necessary to accept a favor from them, and consequently to return it so as to give them satisfaction. Furthermore, we should exercise caution even in avoiding their favors so as to avoid appearing to despise them or to be reluctant through avarice to repay them, thus giving offense by the very attempt to escape their hatred. Thus in avoiding favors one should take account of what is advantageous and honorable.

P71 *Only free men are truly grateful to one another.*

Proof Only free men are truly advantageous to one another and united by the closest bond of friendship (Pr. 35, IV and Cor. 1), and are equally motivated by love in endeavoring to benefit one another (Pr. 37, IV). And thus (Def. of Emotions 34) only free men are truly grateful to one another.

Schol The gratitude mutually exhibited by men who are governed by blind desire is more in the nature of a bargain or inducement than gratitude. Moreover, ingratitude is not an emotional state. Nevertheless, ingratitude is base, because it generally is a sign that a man is affected with excessive hatred, anger, pride, or avarice, etc. For if out of stupidity a man knows not how to repay benefits, he is not an ungrateful man; and far less so is he who is not won over by the gifts of a loose woman to serve her lust, nor by the gifts of a thief to conceal his thefts, nor by the gifts of anyone of like character. On the contrary, he shows a steadfast spirit, in that he refuses to be corrupted by gifts to his own hurt or that of society.

P72 *The free man never acts deceitfully, but always with good faith.*

Proof If the free man, insofar as he is free, were to act deceitfully, he would be doing so in accordance with the dictates of reason (for it is in this respect only that we term him free), and thus to act deceitfully would be a virtue (Pr. 24, IV), and consequently (by the same proposition), in order to preserve his own being, it would be better for every man to act deceitfully, that is (as is self-evident), it would be better for men to agree in words only, but to be contrary to one another in reality, which is absurd (Cor. Pr. 31, IV). Therefore the free man . . . etc.

Schol The question may be asked: "What if a man could by deception free himself from imminent danger of death? Would not consideration for the preservation of his own being be decisive in persuading him to deceive?" I reply in the same way, that if reason urges this, it does so for all men; and thus reason urges men in general to join forces and to have common laws only with deceitful intention; that is, in effect, to have no laws in common at all, which is absurd.

P73 *The man who is guided by reason is more free in a state where he lives under a system of law than in solitude where [he] obeys only himself.*

Proof The man who is guided by reason is not guided to obey out of fear (Pr. 63, IV), but insofar as he endeavors to preserve his own being according to the dictates of reason—that is (Schol. Pr. 66, IV), insofar as he endeavors to live freely—he desires to take account of the life and the good of the community (Pr. 37, IV), and consequently (as I have pointed out in Schol. 2, Pr. 37, IV) to live according to the laws of the state. Therefore, the man who is guided by reason desires to adhere to the laws of the state so that he may live more freely.

Schol   These and similar observations that we have made concerning the true freedom of man are related to strength of mind, that is (Pr. 59, III), courage and nobility. I do not think it worthwhile at this point to give separate proof of all the properties of strength of mind, and far less to show that the strong-minded man hates nobody, is angry with nobody, envies nobody, is indignant with nobody, despises nobody, and is in no way prone to pride. For these points and all that concern the true way of life and religion are readily proved from Prs. 37 and 46, IV, to wit, that hatred is to be conquered by returning love, and that every man who is guided by reason aims at procuring for others, too, the good that he seeks for himself. Furthermore, as we have noted in Schol. Pr. 50, IV and elsewhere, the strong-minded man has this foremost in his mind, that everything follows from the necessity of the divine nature, and therefore whatever he thinks of as injurious or bad, and also whatever seems impious, horrible, unjust, and base arises from his conceiving things in a disturbed, fragmented, and confused way. For this reason his prime endeavor is to conceive things as they are in themselves and to remove obstacles to true knowledge, such as hatred, anger, envy, derision, pride, and similar emotions that we have noted. And so he endeavors, as far as he can, to do well and to be glad, as we have said.

In the next Part, I shall pass on to demonstrate the extent to which human virtue can achieve these objectives, and the nature of its power.

APPENDIX

In this Part my exposition of the right way of living is not arranged so that it can be seen at one view. The proofs are scattered so as to meet the convenience of logical deduction one from another. So I propose to gather them together here, and arrange them under their main headings.

1. All our endeavors or desires follow from the necessity of our nature in such a way that they can be understood either through it alone as their approximate cause, or insofar as we are a part of Nature, a part that cannot be adequately conceived through itself independently of the other individual parts.

2. Desires that follow from our nature in such a way that they can be understood through it alone are those that are related to the mind insofar as the mind is conceived as consisting of adequate ideas. The other desires are related to the mind only insofar as it conceives things inadequately; and their force and increase must be defined not by human power but by the power of things external to us. So the former are rightly called active emotions, the latter passive emotions. For the former always indicate our power, the latter our weakness and fragmentary knowledge.

3. Our active emotions, that is, those desires that are defined by man's power, that is, by reason, are always good; the other desires can be either good or evil.

4. Therefore it is of the first importance in life to perfect the intellect, or reason, as far as we can, and the highest happiness or blessedness for mankind consists in this alone. For blessedness is nothing other than that self-contentment that arises from the intuitive knowledge of God. Now to perfect the intellect is also nothing other than to understand God and the attributes and actions of God that follow from the necessity of his nature. Therefore for the man who is guided by reason, the final goal, that is, the highest Desire whereby he strives to control all the others, is that by which he is brought to an adequate conception of himself and of all things that can fall within the scope of his understanding.

5. So there is no rational life without understanding, and things are good only insofar as they assist a man to enjoy the life of the mind, which is defined by understanding. Those things only do we call evil which hinder a man's capacity to perfect reason and to enjoy a rational life.

6. But since all those things of which man is the efficient cause are necessarily good, nothing evil can befall a man except from external causes, namely, insofar as he is a part of the whole of Nature, whose laws human nature is constrained to obey, and to which it must conform in almost an infinite number of ways.

7. A man is bound to be a part of Nature and to follow its universal order; but if he dwells among individuals who are in harmony with man's nature, by that very fact his power of activity will be assisted and fostered. But if he be among individuals who are by no means in harmony with his nature, he will scarcely be able to conform to them without a great change in himself.

8. Whatsoever in nature we deem evil, that is, capable of hindering us from being able to exist and to enjoy a rational life, it is permissible for us to remove in whatever seems the safer way. On the other hand, whatever we deem good, that is, advantageous for preserving our being and for enjoying a rational life, it is permissible for us to take for our use and to use it as we please. And as an absolute rule, it is permissible by the highest natural right for everyone to do what he judges to be to his own advantage.

9. Nothing can be more in harmony with the nature of anything than other individuals of the same species, and so (see No. 7) there is nothing more advantageous to man for preserving his own being and enjoying a rational life than a man who is guided by reason. Again, since among particular things we know of nothing more excellent than a man who is guided by reason, nowhere can each individual display the extent of his skill and genius more than in so educating men that they come at last to live under the sway of their own reason.

10. Insofar as men feel envy or some other emotion of hatred toward one another, they are contrary to one another; consequently, the more powerful they are, the more they are to be feared than other individuals of Nature.

11. Nevertheless men's hearts are conquered not by arms but by love and nobility.

12. It is of the first importance to men to establish close relationships and to bind themselves together with such ties as may most effectively unite them into

one body, and, as an absolute rule, to act in such a way as serves to strengthen friendship.

13. But to this end skill and watchfulness are needed. For men are changeable (few there are who live under the direction of reason) and yet for the most part envious, and more inclined to revenge than to compassion. So it needs an unusually powerful spirit to bear with each according to his disposition and to restrain oneself from imitating their emotions. On the other hand, those whose skill is to criticize mankind and to censure vice rather than to teach virtue, and to shatter men's spirit rather than strengthen it, are a stumbling block both to themselves and to others. Hence many men, over-impatient and with false religious zeal, have chosen to live among beasts rather than among men, just as boys or young men, unable patiently to endure the upbraidings of their parents, run away to join the army, and prefer the hardships of war and tyrannical discipline to the comfort of home and parental admonition, and suffer any burdens to be imposed on them so long as they can spite their parents.

14. So although men for the most part allow lust to govern all their actions, the advantages that follow from living in their society far exceed the disadvantages. Therefore it is better to endure their injuries with patience, and to apply oneself to such measures as promote harmony and friendship.

15. Conduct that brings about harmony is that which is related to justice, equity, and honorable dealing. For apart from resenting injustice and unfairness, men also resent what is held to be base, or contempt for the accepted customs of the state. But for winning their love the most important factors are those that are concerned with religion and piety, for which see Schols. 1 and 2, Pr. 37, and Schol. Pr. 46 and Schol. Pr. 73, IV.

16. Harmony is also commonly produced by fear, but then it is untrustworthy. Furthermore, fear arises from weakness of spirit, and therefore does not belong to the use of reason. Neither does pity, although it bears the appearance of piety.

17. Again, men are won over by generosity, especially those who do not have the wherewithal to produce what is necessary to support life. Yet it is far beyond the power and resources of a private person to come to the assistance of everyone in need. For the wealth of a private person is quite unequal to such a demand. It is also a practical impossibility for one man to establish friendship with all. Therefore the care of the poor devolves upon society as a whole, and looks only to the common good.

18. The care to be taken in accepting favors and in returning them must be of quite a different kind, for which see Schol. Pr. 70 and Schol. Pr. 71, IV.

19. Furthermore, love of a mistress, that is, sexual lust that arises from physical beauty, and in general all love that acknowledges any other cause than freedom of the spirit, easily passes in hatred unless (and this is worse) it be a kind of madness, and then it is fostered by discord rather than harmony.

20. As for marriage, it is certain that this is in agreement with reason if the desire for intercourse be engendered not simply by physical beauty but also by love of begetting children and rearing them wisely, and if, in addition, the love of both

man and woman has for its cause not merely physical beauty but especially freedom of the spirit.

21. Flattery, too, produces harmony, but at the cost of base servility, or through perfidy. None are more taken in by flattery than the proud, who want to be foremost, but are not.

22. In self-abasement there is a false appearance of piety and religion. And although self-abasement is opposed to pride, the self-abased man is closest to the proud man. See Schol. Pr. 57, IV.

23. Shame, too, contributes to harmony, but only in matters that cannot be concealed. Again, since shame is species of pain, it does not concern the use of reason.

24. The other painful emotions toward men are directly opposed to justice, equity, honor, piety, and religion; and although indignation seems to bear an outward show of equity, it is a lawless state of society where each is permitted to pass judgment on another's deeds and assert his own or another's right.

25. Courtesy, that is, the desire to please men as determined by reason, is related to piety (as we have said in Schol. 1, Pr. 37, IV). But if it arises from emotion, it is ambition, or the desire whereby under a false cover of piety men generally stir up discord and quarrelling. For he who desires to help others by word or deed to enjoy the highest good along with him, will strive above all to win their love, but not to evoke their admiration so that some system of philosophy may be named after him, nor to afford any cause whatsoever for envy. Again, in ordinary conversation he will beware of talking about the vices of mankind and will take care to speak only sparingly of human weakness, but will dwell on human virtue, or power, and the means to perfect it, so that men may thus endeavor as far as they can to live in accordance with reason's behest, not from fear or dislike, but motivated only by the emotion of pleasure.

26. Except for mankind, we know of no individual thing in Nature in whose mind we can rejoice, and with which we can unite in friendship or some kind of close tie. So whatever there is in Nature external to man, regard for our own advantage does not require us to preserve it, but teaches us to preserve or destroy it according to its varying usefulness, or to adapt it to our own use in whatever way we please.

27. The advantage that we get from things external to us, apart from the experience and knowledge we gain from observing them and changing them from one form to another, is especially the preservation of the body, and in this respect those things above all are advantageous which can so feed and nourish the body that all its parts can efficiently perform their function. For as the body is more capable of being affected in many ways and of affecting external bodies in many ways, so the mind is more capable of thinking (see Prs. 38 and 39, IV). But there appear to be few things of this kind in Nature; wherefore to nourish the body as it should be one must use many foods of different kinds. For the human body is composed of numerous parts of different natures, which need a continual supply of food of various sorts so that the whole body is equally capable of all that can

follow from its nature, and consequently that the mind too is equally capable of conceiving many things.

28. Now to provide all this the strength of each single person would scarcely suffice if men did not lend mutual aid to one another. However, money has supplied a token for all things, with the result that its image is wont to obsess the minds of the populace, because they can scarcely think of any kind of pleasure that is not accompanied by the idea of money as its cause.

29. But this vice is characteristic only of those who seek money not through poverty nor to meet their necessities, but because they have acquired the art of money-making, whereby they raise themselves to a splendid estate. They feed the body from habit, but thriftily, because they believe that what they spend on preserving the body is lost to their goods. But those who know the true use of money set the limit of their wealth solely according to their needs, and live content with little.

30. Since those things are good which assist the parts of the body to perform their function, and pleasure consists in this, that a man's power is assisted or increased insofar as he is composed of mind and body, all those things that bring pleasure are good. On the other hand, since things do not act with the object of affecting us with pleasure, and their power of acting is not adjusted to suit our needs, and, lastly, since pleasure is usually related to one part of the body in particular, the emotions of pleasure (unless one exercises reason and care), and consequently the desires that are generated from them, can be excessive. There is this further point, that from emotion we place prime importance on what is attractive in the present, and we cannot feel as strongly about the future. See Schol. Pr. 44 and Schol. Pr. 60, IV.

31. But superstition on the other hand seems to assert that what brings pain is good and what brings pleasure is bad. But, as we have already said (Schol. Pr. 45, IV), nobody but the envious takes pleasure in my weakness and my misfortune. For the more we are affected with pleasure, the more we pass to a state of greater perfection, and consequently the more we participate in the divine nature. Nor can pleasure ever be evil when it is controlled by true regard for our advantage. Now he who on the other hand is guided by fear and does good in order to avoid evil is not guided by reason.

32. But human power is very limited and is infinitely surpassed by the power of external causes, and so we do not have absolute power to adapt to our purposes things external to us. However, we shall patiently bear whatever happens to us that is contrary to what is required by consideration of our own advantage, if we are conscious that we have done our duty and that our power was not extensive enough for us to have avoided the said things, and that we are a part of the whole of Nature whose order we follow. If we clearly and distinctly understand this, that part of us which is defined by the understanding, that is, the better part of us, will be fully resigned and will endeavor to persevere in that resignation. For insofar as we understand, we can desire nothing but that which must be, nor, in an absolute sense, can we find contentment in anything but truth. And so insofar as we rightly understand these matters, the endeavor of the better part of us is in harmony with the order of the whole of Nature.

PART V

OF THE POWER OF THE INTELLECT, OR OF HUMAN FREEDOM

PREFACE

I pass on finally to that part of the *Ethics* which concerns the method or way leading to freedom. In this part, then, I shall be dealing with the power of reason, pointing out the degree of control reason has over the emotions, and then what is freedom of mind, or blessedness, from which we shall see how much to be preferred is the life of the wise man to the life of the ignorant man. Now we are not concerned here with the manner or way in which the intellect should be perfected, nor yet with the science of tending the body so that it may correctly perform its functions. The latter is the province of medicine, the former of logic. Here then, as I have said, I shall be dealing only with the power of the mind or reason. Above all I shall be showing the degree and nature of its command over the emotions in checking and controlling them. For I have already demonstrated that we do not have absolute command over them.

Now the Stoics thought that the emotions depend absolutely on our will, and that we can have absolute command over them. However, with experience crying out against them they were obliged against their principles to admit that no little practice and zeal are required in order to check and control emotions. One of them tried to illustrate this point with the example of two dogs, if I remember correctly, one a house dog, and the other a hunting dog; in the end he succeeded in training the house dog to hunt and the hunting dog to refrain from chasing hares.

This view is much favored by Descartes. He maintained that the soul or mind is united in a special way with a certain part of the brain called the pineal gland, by means of which the mind senses all movements that occur in the body, as well as external objects, and by the mere act of willing it can move the gland in various ways. He maintained that this gland is suspended in the middle of the brain in such a way that it can be moved by the slightest motion of the animal spirits. He further maintained that the number of different ways in which the gland can be suspended in the middle of the brain corresponds with the number of different ways in which the animal spirits can impinge upon it, and that, furthermore, as many different marks can be imprinted on the gland as there are external objects impelling the animal spirits toward it. As a result, if by the will of the soul, which can move it in various ways, the gland is later suspended in that particular way in which it had previously been suspended by a particular mode of agitation of the spirits, then the gland will impel and determine the animal spirits in the same way as they had previously been acted upon by a similar mode of suspension of the gland. He furthermore maintained that every single act of willing is by nature united to a particular motion of the gland. For example, if anyone wills to gaze at a distant object, this act of willing will bring about the dilation of the pupil.

But if he thinks only of dilating the pupil, it will be useless for him to will this, because the motion of the gland which serves to impel the spirits toward the optic nerve in a manner that will bring about dilation or contraction of the pupil has not been joined by nature to the act of willing its contraction or dilation, but only to the act of willing to gaze at distant or near objects. Finally, he maintained that although each motion of this gland seems to have been connected through nature from the beginning of our lives to particular thoughts, these motions can be joined to other thoughts through training, and this he endeavors to prove in Article 50, Part I of *On the Passions of the Soul*. From this he concludes that there is no soul so weak that it cannot, through good guidance, acquire absolute power over its passions. For these passions are defined by him as "perceptions, or feelings, or disturbances of the soul, which are related to the soul as species, and which are produced (note well!), preserved and strengthened through some motion of the spirits." (See Article 27, Part 1, *On the Passions of the Soul*.) But as we are able to join any motion of the gland, and consequently of the spirits, to any act of willing, and as the determination of the will depends only on our own power, if therefore we determine our will by the sure and firm decisions in accordance with which we want to direct the actions of our lives, and if to these decisions we join the movements of the passions which we want to have, we shall acquire absolute command over our passions.

Such is the view of this illustrious person (as far as I can gather from his own words), a view which I could scarcely have believed to have been put forward by such a great man, had it been less ingenious. Indeed, I am lost in wonder that a philosopher who had strictly resolved to deduce nothing except from self-evident bases and to affirm nothing that he did not clearly and distinctly perceive, who had so often censured the Scholastics for seeking to explain obscurities through occult qualities, should adopt a theory more occult than any occult quality. What, I ask, does he understand by the union of mind and body? What clear and distinct conception does he have of thought closely united to a certain particle of matter? I should have liked him, indeed, to explain this union through its proximate cause. But he had conceived mind as so distinct from body that he could assign no one cause either of this union or of mind itself, and found it necessary to have recourse to the cause of the entire universe, that is, God. Again, I should like to know how many degrees of motion mind can impart to that pineal gland of his, and by what force it can hold it suspended. For I know not whether this gland can be moved about more slowly or more quickly by the mind than by animal spirits, and whether the movements of the passions which we have joined in a close union with firm decisions cannot again be separated from those decisions by corporeal causes, from which it would follow that, although the mind firmly decides to face danger and joins to that decision the motions of boldness, when the danger appears, the gland may assume such a form of suspension that the mind can think only of flight. And surely, since will and motion have no common standard, there cannot be any comparison between the power or strength of the mind and body, and consequently the strength of the latter cannot possibly be determined by the strength of the former. There is the additional fact that this gland is not to be found located in the middle of the brain in such a way that it can be driven about so easily and in so many ways, nor do all nerves extend as far as the cavities of the brain.

Finally, I omit all Descartes's assertions about the will and its freedom, since I have already abundantly demonstrated that they are false. Therefore, since the power of the mind is defined solely by the understanding, as I have demonstrated above, we shall determine solely by the knowledge of the mind the remedies for the emotions—remedies which I believe all men experience but do not accurately observe nor distinctly see—and from this knowledge we shall deduce all that concerns the blessedness of the mind.

Axioms

1. If two contrary actions are instigated in the same subject, a change must necessarily take place in both or in the one of them until they cease to be contrary.

2. The power of an effect is defined by the power of the cause insofar as its essence is explicated or defined through the essence of its cause.

This Axiom is evident from Pr. 7, III.

P1 *The affections of the body, that is, the images of things, are arranged and connected in the body in exactly the same way as thoughts and the ideas of things are arranged and connected in the mind.*

Proof The order and connection of ideas is the same (Pr. 7, II) as the order and connection of things, and, vice versa, the order and connection of things is the same (Cor. Pr. 6 and Pr. 7, II) as the order and connection of ideas. Therefore, just as the order and connection of ideas in the mind occurs in accordance with the order and connection of the affections of the body (Pr. 18, II), so, vice versa (Pr. 2, III), the order and connection of the affections of the body occurs in just the way that thoughts and the ideas of things are arranged and connected in the mind.

P2 *If we remove an agitation of the mind, or emotion, from the thought of its external cause, and join it to other thoughts, then love or hatred toward the external cause, and also vacillations, that arise from these emotions will be destroyed.*

Proof That which constitutes the form of love or hatred is pleasure or pain accompanied by the idea of an external cause (Def. of Emotions 6 and 7). So when the latter is removed, the form of love or hatred is removed with it; and thus these emotions, and those that arise from them, are destroyed.

P3 *A passive emotion ceases to be a passive emotion as soon as we form a clear and distinct idea of it.*

Proof A passive emotion is a confused idea (Gen. Def. of Emotions). So if we form a clear and distinct idea of the emotion, this idea is distinguishable only in concept from the emotion insofar as the latter is related only to mind (Pr. 21, 11 and Schol.); and so the emotion will cease to be passive (Pr. 3, III).

Cor So the more an emotion is known to us, the more it is within our control, and the mind is the less passive in respect of it.

P4 *There is no affection of the body of which we cannot form a clear and distinct conception.*

Proof What is common to all things can only be conceived adequately (Pr. 38, II), and thus (Pr. 12 and Lemma 2 which comes after Schol. Pr. 13, II) there is no affection of the body of which we cannot form a clear and distinct conception.

Cor Hence it follows that there is no emotion of which we cannot form a clear and distinct conception. For an emotion is the idea of an affection of the body (Gen. Def. of Emotions), which must therefore involve some clear and distinct conception (preceding Pr.).

Schol Since there exists nothing from which some effect does not follow (Pr. 36, I), and all that follows from an idea that is adequate in us is understood by us clearly and distinctly (Pr. 40, II), it therefore follows that everyone has the power of clearly and distinctly understanding himself and his emotions, if not absolutely, at least in part, and consequently of bringing it about that he should be less passive in respect of them. So we should pay particular attention to getting to know each emotion, as far as possible, clearly and distinctly, so that the mind may thus be determined from the emotion to think those things that it clearly and distinctly perceives, and in which it finds full contentment. Thus the emotion may be detached from the thought of an external cause and joined to true thoughts. The result will be that not only are love, hatred, etc. destroyed (Pr. 2, V) but also that the appetites or desires that are wont to arise from such an emotion cannot be excessive (Pr. 61, IV). For it is very important to note that it is one and the same appetite through which a man is said both to be active and to be passive. For example, we have shown that human nature is so constituted that everyone wants others to live according to his way of thinking (Cor. Pr. 31, III). Now this appetite in a man who is not guided by reason is a passive emotion which is called ambition, and differs to no great extent from pride. But in a man who lives according to the dictates of reason it is an active emotion, or virtue, which is called piety (Schol. 1, Pr. 37, IV and second proof of that same Proposition). In this way all appetites or desires are passive emotions only insofar as they arise from inadequate ideas, and they are accredited to virtue when they are aroused or generated by adequate ideas. For all desires whereby we are determined to some action can arise both from adequate and from inadequate ideas (Pr. 59, IV). To return to the point from which I digressed, there is available to us no more excellent remedy for the emotions than that which consists in a true knowledge of them, since there is no other power of the mind than the power of thought and of forming adequate ideas, as I have shown above (Pr. 3, III).

P5 *An emotion toward a thing which we imagine merely in itself, and not as necessary, possible, or contingent, is the greatest of all emotions, other things being equal.*

Proof   An emotion toward a thing that we imagine to be free is greater than an emotion toward a necessary thing (Pr. 49, III), and consequently still greater than an emotion toward a thing that we imagine to be possible or contingent (Pr. 11, IV). But to imagine something as free can be nothing else than to imagine it merely in itself, while we are ignorant of the causes by which it has been determined to act (Schol. Pr. 35, II). Therefore, an emotion toward a thing that we imagine merely in itself is greater, other things being equal, than an emotion toward a necessary, possible, or contingent thing, and consequently it is the greatest of all emotions.

P6   *Insofar as the mind understands all things as governed by necessity, to that extent it has greater power over emotions, i.e., it is less passive in respect of them.*

Proof   The mind understands all things to be governed by necessity (Pr. 29, I) and to be determined to exist and to act by an infinite chain of causes (Pr. 28, I). And so (preceding Pr.) to that extent the mind succeeds in becoming less passive to the emotions that arise from things, and (Pr. 48, III) less affected toward the things themselves.

Schol   The more this knowledge (namely, that things are governed by necessity) is applied to particular things which we imagine more distinctly and more vividly, the greater is this power of the mind over the emotions, as is testified by experience. For we see that pain over the loss of some good is assuaged as soon as the man who has lost it realizes that that good could not have been saved in any way. Similarly, we see that nobody pities a baby because it cannot talk or walk or reason, and because it spends many years in a kind of ignorance of self. But if most people were born adults and only a few were born babies, then everybody would feel sorry for babies because they would then look on infancy not as a natural and necessary thing but as a fault or flaw in Nature. There are many other examples of this kind that we might note.

P7   *Emotions which arise or originate from reason are, if we take account of time, more powerful than those that are related to particular things which we regard as absent.*

Proof   We do not look on a thing as absent by reason of the emotion with which we think of it, but by reason of the body being affected by another emotion which excludes the existence of the said thing (Pr. 17, II). Therefore, the emotion that is related to a thing that we regard as absent is not of a kind to overcome the rest of man's activities and power (see Pr. 6, IV). On the contrary, its nature is such that it can be checked in some way by those affections which exclude the existence of its external cause (Pr. 9, IV). But an emotion that arises from reason is necessarily related to the common properties of things (see Def. of Reason in Schol. 2, Pr. 40, II) which we regard as being always present (for there can be nothing that excludes their present existence) and which we always think of in the same way (Pr. 38, II). Therefore, such an emotion always remains the same. Consequently (Ax. 1, V), emotions which are contrary to it and are not fostered by their external causes must adapt themselves to it more and more until they are no longer contrary; and to that extent an emotion that arises from reason is more powerful.

P8   *The greater the number of causes that simultaneously concur in arousing an emotion, the greater the emotion.*

Proof   Several causes acting together are more effective than if they were fewer (Pr. 7, III). So (Pr. 5, IV) the more simultaneous causes there are in arousing an emotion, the stronger will be the emotion.

Schol   This Proposition is also obvious from Ax. 2, V.

P9   *An emotion that is related to several different causes, which the mind regards together with the emotion itself, is less harmful, and we suffer less from it and are less affected toward each individual cause, than if we were affected by another equally great emotion which is related to only one or to a few causes.*

Proof   An emotion is bad or harmful only insofar as the mind is thereby hindered from being able to think (Prs. 26 and 27, IV). Thus, an emotion whereby the mind is determined to regard several objects simultaneously is less harmful than another equally great emotion which so keeps the mind in the contemplation of only one or few objects that it cannot think of anything else. This is the first point. Again, because the essence of the mind, that is (Pr. 7, III), its power, consists only in thought (Pr. 11, II), it follows that the mind is less passive through an emotion by which it is determined to regard several things all together than through an equally great emotion which keeps the mind engrossed in the contemplation of only one or few objects. This is the second point. Finally, this emotion (Pr. 48, III), insofar as it is related to several external causes, is also less toward each cause.

P10   *As long as we are not assailed by emotions that are contrary to our nature, we have the power to arrange and associate affections of the body according to the order of the intellect.*

Proof   Emotions that are contrary to our nature, that is (Pr. 30, IV), which are bad, are bad to the extent that they hinder the mind from understanding (Pr. 27, IV). Therefore, as long as we are not assailed by emotions contrary to our nature, the power of the mind whereby it endeavors to understand things (Pr. 26, IV) is not hindered, and thus it has the ability to form clear and distinct ideas, deducing them from one another (Schol. 2, Pr. 40 and Schol. Pr. 47, II). Consequently (Pr. 1, V), in this case we have the ability to arrange and associate affections of the body according to the order of the intellect.

Schol   Through the ability to arrange and associate rightly the affections of the body we can bring it about that we are not easily affected by bad emotions. For (Pr. 7, V) greater force is required to check emotions arranged and associated according to intellectual order than emotions that are uncertain and random.

Therefore the best course we can adopt, as long as we do not have perfect knowledge of our emotions, is to conceive a right method of living, or fixed rules of life, and to commit them to memory and continually apply them to particular situations that are frequently encountered in life, so that our casual thinking is thoroughly permeated by them and they are always ready to hand. For example, among our practical rules, we laid down (Pr. 46, IV and Schol.) that hatred should be conquered by love or nobility, and not repaid with reciprocal hatred. Now in order that we may have this precept of reason always ready to hand we should think about and frequently reflect on the wrongs that are commonly committed among mankind, and the best way and method of warding them off by nobility of character. For thus we shall associate the image of a wrong with the presentation of this rule of conduct, and it will always be at hand for us (Pr. 18, II) when we suffer a wrong. Again, if we always have in readiness consideration of our true advantage and also of the good that follows from mutual friendship and social relations, and also remember that supreme contentment of spirit follows from the right way of life (Pr. 52, IV), and that men, like everything else, act from the necessity of their nature, then the wrong, or the hatred that is wont to arise from it, will occupy just a small part of our imagination and will easily be overcome. Or if the anger that is wont to arise from grievous wrongs be not easily overcome, it will nevertheless be overcome, though not without vacillation, in a far shorter space of time than if we had not previously reflected on these things in the way I have described, as is evident from Prs. 6, 7, and 8, V. We ought, in the same way, to reflect on courage to banish fear; we should enumerate and often picture the everyday dangers of life, and how they can best be avoided and overcome by resourcefulness and strength of mind.

But it should be noted that in arranging our thoughts and images we should always concentrate on that which is good in every single thing (Cor. Pr. 63, IV and Pr. 59, III) so that in so doing we may be determined to act always from the emotion of pleasure. For example, if anyone sees that he is devoted overmuch to the pursuit of honor, let him reflect on its proper function, and the purpose for which it ought to be pursued, and the means by which it can be attained, and not on its abuse and hollowness and the fickleness of mankind and the like, on which nobody reflects except from a morbid disposition. It is by thoughts like these that the most ambitious especially torment themselves when they despair of attaining the honor that they covet, and in vomiting forth their anger they try to make some show of wisdom. It is therefore certain that those who raise the loudest outcry about the abuse of honor and about worldly vanity are most eager for honor. Nor is this trait confined to the ambitious: it is shared by all who meet with adverse fortune and are weak in spirit. For the miser, too, who is in poverty, does not cease to talk of the abuse of money and the vices of the rich, with the result that he merely torments himself and makes it clear that he resents not only his own poverty but also the wealth of others. So, too, those who have been ill-received by a sweetheart are obsessed by thoughts of the fickleness and deceitfulness of women and the other faults commonly attributed to them, but immediately forget about all this as soon as they again find favor with their sweetheart. Therefore, he who aims solely from love of freedom to control his emotions and appetites will strive his best to familiarize himself with virtues and their causes and to fill his mind with the joy that arises from the true knowledge of them, while refraining from dwelling on men's faults and abusing mankind and deriving pleasure from a false show of freedom. He who diligently follows these precepts and practices them (for they are not difficult) will surely within a short space of time be able to direct his actions for the most part according to reason's behest.

P11   *In proportion as a mental image is related to more things, the more frequently does it occur—i.e., the more often it springs to life—and the more it engages the mind.*

Proof   In proportion as an image or emotion is related to more things, the more causes there are by which it can be aroused and fostered, all of which the mind, by hypothesis, regards simultaneously as a result of the emotion. And so the emotion thereby occurs more frequently—i.e., springs to life more often—and engages the mind the more (Pr. 8, V).

P12   *Images are more readily associated with those images that are related to things which we clearly and distinctly understand than they are to others.*

Proof   Things that are clearly and distinctly understood are either the common properties of things or deductions made from them (see Def. of Reason in Schol. 2, Pr. 40, II) and consequently they are more often before the mind (preceding Pr.). So it is more likely that we should regard other things in conjunction with these than in conjunction with different things, and consequently (Pr. 18, II) that they should more readily be associated with these than with others.

P13   *The greater the number of other images with which an image is associated, the more often it springs to life.*

Proof   The greater the number of images with which an image is associated, the more causes there are by which it can be aroused (Pr. 18, II).

P14   *The mind can bring it about that all the affections of the body—i.e., images of things—be related to the idea of God.*

Proof   There is no affection of the body of which the mind cannot form a clear and distinct conception (Pr. 4, V), and so the mind can bring it about (Pr. 15, I) that they should all be related to the idea of God.

P15   *He who clearly and distinctly understands himself and his emotions loves God, and the more so the more he understands himself and his emotions.*

Proof   He who clearly and distinctly understands himself and his emotions feels pleasure (Pr. 53, III) accompanied by the idea of God (preceding Pr.). So (Def.

of Emotions 6) he loves God, and, by the same reasoning, the more so the more he understands himself and his emotions.

P16   *This love toward God is bound to hold chief place in the mind.*

Proof   This love is associated with all the affections of the body (Pr. 14, V), and is fostered by them all (Pr. 15, V), and so (Pr. 11, V) it is bound to hold chief place in the mind.

P17   *God is without passive emotions, and he is not affected with any emotion of pleasure or pain.*

Proof   All ideas, insofar as they are related to God, are true (Pr. 32, III), that is (Def. 4, II), they are adequate. Thus (Gen. Def. of Emotions), God is without passive emotions. Again, God cannot pass to a state of greater or less perfection (Cor. 2, Pr. 20, I), and so (Def. of Emotions 2 and 3) he is not affected with any emotion of pleasure or pain.

Cor   Strictly speaking, God does not love or hate anyone. For God (preceding Pr.) is not affected with any emotion of pleasure or pain, and consequently (Def. of Emotions 6 and 7) he neither loves nor hates anyone.

P18   *Nobody can hate God.*

Proof   The idea of God which is in us is adequate and perfect (Prs. 46 and 47, II). Therefore, insofar as we contemplate God, we are active (Pr. 3, III). Consequently (Pr. 59, III), there can be no pain accompanied by the idea of God; that is (Def. of Emotions 7), nobody can hate God.

Cor   Love toward God cannot turn to hatred.

Schol   It may be objected that in understanding God to be the cause of all things we thereby consider God to be the cause of pain. To this I reply that insofar as we understand the causes of pain, it ceases to be a passive emotion (Pr. 3, V); that is (Pr. 59, III), to that extent it ceases to be pain. So insofar as we understand God to be the cause of pain, to that extent we feel pleasure.

P19   *He who loves God cannot endeavor that God should love him in return.*

Proof   If a man were so to endeavor, he would therefore desire (Cor. Pr. 17, V) that God whom he loves should not be God, and consequently (Pr. 19, III) he would desire to feel pain, which is absurd (Pr. 28, III). Therefore he who loves God . . . etc.

P20   *This love toward God cannot be tainted with emotions of envy or jealousy, but is the more fostered as we think more men to be joined to God by this same bond of love.*

Proof   This love toward God is the highest good that we can aim at according to the dictates of reason (Pr. 28, IV) and is available to all men (Pr. 36, IV), and we desire that all men should enjoy it (Pr. 37, IV). Therefore (Def. of Emotions 23), it cannot be stained by the emotion of envy, nor again by the emotion of jealousy (Pr. 18, V and Def. of Jealousy, q.v. in Schol. Pr. 36, III). On the contrary (Pr. 31, III), it is the more fostered as we think more men to be enjoying it.

Schol   We can in the same way demonstrate that there is no emotion directly contrary to this love by which this love can be destroyed; and so we may conclude that this love toward God is the most constant of all emotions, and insofar as it is related to the body it cannot be destroyed except together with the body. As to its nature insofar as it is related solely to the mind, this we shall examine later on.

With this I have completed the account of all the remedies for the emotions; that is, all that the mind, considered solely in itself, can do against the emotions. From this it is clear that the power of the mind over the emotions consists:

1. In the very knowledge of the emotions (Schol. Pr. 4, V).

2. In detaching the emotions from the thought of their external cause, which we imagine confusedly. (See Pr. 2 together with Schol. Pr. 4, V.)

3. In the matter of time, in respect of which the affections that are related to things we understand are superior to those which are related to things that we conceive in a confused or fragmentary way (Pr. 7, V).

4. In the number of causes whereby those affections are fostered which are related to the common properties of things, or to God (Prs. 9 and 11, V).

5. Lastly, in the order wherein the mind can arrange its emotions and associate them one with another (Schol. Pr. 10 and also Prs. 12, 13, 14, V).

But in order that this power of the mind over the emotions may be better understood, it is important to note that we call emotions strong when we compare the emotion of one man with that of another, and when we see one man more than another assailed by the same emotion, or when we compare with one another the emotions of the same man and find that the same man is affected or moved by one emotion more than by another. For (Pr. 5, IV) the strength of every emotion is defined by the power of an external cause as compared with our own power. Now the power of the mind is defined solely by knowledge, its weakness or passivity solely by the privation of knowledge; that is, it is measured by the extent to which its ideas are said to be inadequate. Hence it follows that that mind is most passive whose greatest part is constituted by inadequate ideas, so that it is characterized more by passivity than by activity. On the other hand, that mind is most active whose greatest part is constituted by adequate ideas, so that even if the latter mind contains as many inadequate ideas as the former, it is characterized by those ideas which are attributed to human virtue rather than by those that point to human weakness.

Again, it should be noted that emotional distress and unhappiness have their origin especially in excessive love toward a thing subject to considerable instability, a thing which we can never completely possess. For nobody is disturbed or anxious about any thing unless he loves it, nor do wrongs, suspicions, enmities, etc. arise except from love toward things which nobody can truly possess.

So from this we readily conceive how effective against the emotions is clear and distinct knowledge, and especially the third kind of knowledge (for which see

Schol. Pr. 47, II) whose basis is the knowledge of God. Insofar as they are passive emotions, if it does not completely destroy them (Pr. 3, and Schol. Pr. 4, V), at least it brings it about that they constitute the least part of the mind (Pr. 14, V). Again, it begets love toward something immutable and eternal (Pr. 15, V) which we can truly possess (Pr. 45, II), and which therefore cannot be defiled by any of the faults that are to be found in the common sort of love, but can continue to grow more and more (Pr. 15, V) and engage the greatest part of the mind (Pr. 16, V) and pervade it.

And now I have completed all that concerns this present life; for, as I said at the beginning of this Scholium, in this brief account I have covered all the remedies against the emotions. This everyone can see who gives his mind to the contents of this Scholium, and likewise to the definitions of the mind and its emotions, and lastly to Prs. 1 and 3, III. So it is now time to pass on to those matters that concern the duration of the mind without respect to the body.

P21 *The mind can exercise neither imagination nor memory save while the body endures.*

Proof It is only while the body endures that the mind expresses the actual existence of its body and conceives the affections of the body as actual (Cor. Pr. 8, II). Consequently (Pr. 26, II), it does not conceive any body as actually existing save while its own body endures. Therefore (see Def. of Imagination in Schol. Pr. 17, II), it cannot exercise either imagination or memory save while the body endures (see Def. of Memory in Schol. Pr. 18, II).

P22 *Nevertheless, there is necessarily in God an idea which expresses the essence of this or that human body under a form of eternity* [sub specie aeternitatis].

Proof God is the cause not only of the existence of this or that human body but also of its essence (Pr. 25, I), which must therefore necessarily be received through God's essence (Ax. 4, I) by a certain eternal necessity (Pr. 16, I), and this conception must necessarily be in God (Pr. 3, II).

P23 *The human mind cannot be absolutely destroyed along with body, but something of it remains, which is eternal.*

Proof In God there is necessarily a conception, or idea, which expresses the essence of the human body (preceding Pr.) and which therefore is necessarily something that pertains to the essence of the human mind (Pr. 13, II). But we assign to the human mind the kind of duration that can be defined by time only insofar as the mind expresses the actual existence of the body, an existence that is explicated through duration and can be defined by time. That is, we do not assign duration to the mind except while the body endures (Cor. Pr. 8, II). However, since that which is conceived by a certain eternal necessity through God's essence is nevertheless a something (preceding Pr.), this something, which pertains to the essence of mind, will necessarily be eternal.

Schol   As we have said, this idea, which expresses the essence of the body under a form of eternity, is a definite mode of thinking which pertains to the essence of mind, and which is necessarily eternal. Yet it is impossible that we should remember that we existed before the body, since neither can there be any traces of this in the body nor can eternity be defined by time, or be in any way related to time. Nevertheless, we feel and experience that we are eternal. For the mind senses those things that it conceives by its understanding just as much as those which it has in its memory. Logical proofs are the eyes of the mind, whereby it sees and observes things. So although we have no recollection of having existed before the body, we nevertheless sense that our mind, insofar as it involves the essence of the body under a form of eternity, is eternal, and that this aspect of its existence cannot be defined by time, that is, cannot be explicated through duration. Therefore, our mind can be said to endure, and its existence to be defined by a definite period of time, only to the extent that it involves the actual existence of the body, and it is only to that extent that it has the power to determine the existence of things by time and to conceive them from the point of view of duration.

P24   *The more we understand particular things, the more we understand God.*

Proof   This is evident from Cor. Pr. 25, I.

P25   *The highest conatus of the mind and its highest virtue is to understand things by the third kind of knowledge.*

Proof   The third kind of knowledge proceeds from the adequate idea of certain of God's attributes to the adequate knowledge of the essence of things (see its definition in Schol. 2, Pr. 40, II), and the more we understand things in this way, the more we understand God (preceding Pr.). Therefore (Pr. 28, IV), the highest virtue of the mind, that is (Def. 8, IV), its power or nature, or its highest conatus (Pr. 7, III), is to understand things by this third kind of knowledge.

P26   *The more capable the mind is of understanding things by the third kind of knowledge, the more it desires to understand things by this same kind of knowledge.*

Proof   This is evident; for insofar as we conceive the mind to be capable of understanding things by the third kind of knowledge, to that extent we conceive it as determined to understand things by that same kind of knowledge. Consequently (Def. of Emotions 1), the more the mind is capable of this, the more it desires it.

P27   *From this third kind of knowledge there arises the highest possible contentment of mind.*

Proof   The highest virtue of the mind is to know God (Pr. 28, IV), that is, to understand things by the third kind of knowledge (Pr. 25, V), and this virtue is all the greater the more the mind knows things by the third kind of knowledge (Pr. 24, V). So he who knows things by this third kind of knowledge passes to the highest state of human perfection, and consequently (Def. of Emotions 2) is affected by the highest pleasure, this pleasure being accompanied (Pr. 43, II) by the idea of himself and his own virtue. Therefore (Def. of Emotions 25), from this kind of knowledge there arises the highest possible contentment.

P28   *The conatus, or desire, to know things by the third kind of knowledge cannot arise from the first kind of knowledge, but from the second.*

Proof   This proposition is self-evident. For whatever we understand clearly and distinctly, we understand either through itself or through something else which is conceived through itself. That is, ideas which are clear and distinct in us or which are related to the third kind of knowledge (Schol. 2, Pr. 40, II) cannot follow from fragmentary or confused ideas which (same Schol.) are related to the first kind of knowledge, but from adequate ideas, that is (same Schol.), from the second or third kind of knowledge. Therefore (Def. of Emotions 1), the desire to know things by the third kind of knowledge cannot arise from the first kind of knowledge, but from the second.

P29   *Whatever the mind understands under a form of eternity it does not understand from the fact that it conceives the present actual existence of the body, but from the fact that it conceives the essence of the body under a form of eternity.*

Proof   Insofar as the mind conceives the present existence of its body, to that extent it conceives a duration that can be determined by time, and only to that extent does it have the power to conceive things in relation to time (Pr. 21, V and Pr. 26, II). But eternity cannot be explicated through duration (Def. 8, I and its explication). Therefore, to that extent the mind does not have the power to conceive things under a form of eternity. But since it is the nature of reason to conceive things under a form of eternity (Cor. 2, Pr. 44, II), and since it belongs to the nature of mind, too, to conceive the essence of the body under a form of eternity (Pr. 23, V), and since there belongs to the essence of mind nothing but these two ways of conceiving (Pr. 13, II), it follows that this power to conceive things under a form of eternity pertains to the mind only insofar as it conceives the essence of the body under a form of eternity.

Schol   We conceive things as actual in two ways: either insofar as we conceive them as related to a fixed time and place, or insofar as we conceive them to be contained in God and to follow from the necessity of the divine nature. Now the things that are conceived as true or real in this second way, we conceive under a form of eternity, and their ideas involve the eternal and infinite essence of God, as we demonstrated in Pr. 45, II. See also its Scholium.

P30   *Our mind, insofar as it knows both itself and the body under a form of eternity, necessarily has a knowledge of God, and knows that it is in God and is conceived through God.*

Proof   Eternity is the very essence of God insofar as this essence involves necessary existence (Def. 8, I). Therefore, to conceive things under a form of eternity is to conceive things insofar as they are conceived through God's essence as real entities; that is, insofar as they involve existence through God's essence. Therefore, our mind, insofar as it knows itself and the body under a form of eternity, necessarily has knowledge of God, and knows . . . etc.

P31   *The third kind of knowledge depends on the mind as its formal cause insofar as the mind is eternal.*

Proof   The mind conceives nothing under a form of eternity except insofar as it conceives the essence of its body under a form of eternity (Pr. 29, V), that is (Prs. 21 and 23, V), except insofar as the mind is eternal. Therefore (preceding Pr.), insofar as it is eternal, it has knowledge of God, knowledge which is necessarily adequate (Pr. 46, II). Therefore, the mind, insofar as it is eternal, is capable of knowing all the things that can follow from this given knowledge of God (Pr. 40, II); that is, of knowing things by the third kind of knowledge (see its definition in Schol. 2, Pr. 40, II), of which the mind is therefore (Def. 1, III) the adequate or formal cause insofar as it is eternal.

Schol   So the more each man is advanced in this kind of knowledge, the more clearly conscious he is of himself and of God, that is, the more perfect and blessed he is, as will become even more evident from what is to follow. But here it should be noted that although we are at this point certain that the mind is eternal insofar as it conceives things under a form of eternity, yet, to facilitate the explanation and render more readily intelligible what I intend to demonstrate, we shall consider the mind as if it were now beginning to be and were now beginning to understand things under a form of eternity, as we have been doing up to now. This we may do without any danger of error, provided we are careful to reach no conclusion except from premises that are quite clear.

P32   *We take pleasure in whatever we understand by the third kind of knowledge, and this is accompanied by the idea of God as cause.*

Proof   From this kind of knowledge there arises the highest possible contentment of mind (Pr. 27, V), that is (Def. of Emotions 25), the highest possible pleasure, and this is accompanied by the idea of oneself, and consequently (Pr. 30, V) also by the idea of God, as cause.

Cor   From the third kind of knowledge there necessarily arises the intellectual love of God [*amor Dei intellectualis*]. For from this kind of knowledge there arises (preceding Pr.) pleasure accompanied by the idea of God as cause, that is (Def. of Emotions 6), the love of God not insofar as we imagine him as present (Pr. 29, V) but insofar as we understand God to be eternal. And this is what I call the intellectual love of God.

P33   *The intellectual love of God which arises from the third kind of knowledge is eternal.*

Proof   The third kind of knowledge is eternal (Pr. 31, V and Ax. 3, I), and therefore (by the same Ax. 3, I) the love that arises from it is also necessarily eternal.

Schol   Although this love toward God has had no beginning (preceding Pr.), it yet has all the perfections of love just as if it had originated in the manner we supposed in the Corollary to the preceding Proposition. There is no difference, except that the mind has possessed from eternity those perfections which we then supposed to be accruing to it, accompanied by the idea of God as eternal cause. If pleasure consists in the transition to a state of greater perfection, blessedness must surely consist in this, that the mind is endowed with perfection itself.

P34   *It is only while the body endures that the mind is subject to passive emotions.*

Proof   Imagining is the idea whereby the mind regards some thing as present (see its definition in Schol. Pr. 17, II), an idea which, however, indicates the present state of the body rather than the nature of an external thing (Cor. 2, Pr. 16, II). Therefore, an emotion (Gen. Def. of Emotions) is an imagining insofar as it indicates the present state of the body. So (Pr. 21, V) it is only while the body endures that the mind is subject to passive emotions.

Cor   Hence it follows that no love is eternal except for intellectual love [*amor intellectualis*].

Schol   If we turn our attention to the common belief entertained by men, we shall see that they are indeed conscious of the eternity of the mind, but they confuse it with duration and assign it to imagination or to memory, which they believe to continue after death.

P35   *God loves himself with an infinite intellectual love.*

Proof   God is absolutely infinite (Def. 6, I); that is (Def. 6, II), God's nature enjoys infinite perfection, accompanied (Pr. 3, II) by the idea of itself, that is (Pr. 11 and Def. 1, I), by the idea of its own cause; and that is what, in Cor. Pr. 32. V, we declared to be intellectual love.

P36   *The mind's intellectual love toward God is the love of God wherewith God loves himself not insofar as he is infinite, but insofar as he can be explicated through the essence of the human mind considered under a form of eternity. That is, the mind's intellectual love toward God is part of the infinite love wherewith God loves himself.*

Proof   This, the mind's love, must be related to the active nature of the mind (Cor. Pr. 32, V and Pr. 3, III), and is therefore an activity whereby the mind regards itself, accompanied by the idea of God as cause (Pr. 32, V and Cor.); that is (Cor. Pr. 25, I and Cor. Pr. 11, II), an activity whereby God, insofar as he can be explicated through the human mind, regards himself, accompanied by the idea of himself. And therefore (preceding Pr.) this love of God is part of the infinite love wherewith God loves himself.

Cor   Hence it follows that God, insofar as he loves himself, loves mankind, and, consequently, that the love of God toward men and the mind's intellectual love toward God are one and the same.

Schol   From this we clearly understand in what our salvation or blessedness or freedom consists, namely, in the constant and eternal love toward God, that is, in God's love toward men. This love or blessedness is called glory in the Holy Scriptures, and rightly so. For whether this love be related to God or to the mind, it can properly be called spiritual contentment, which in reality cannot be distinguished from glory (Def. of Emotions 25 and 30). For insofar as it is related to God, it is (Pr. 35, V) pleasure (if we may still use this term) accompanied by the idea of himself, and this is also the case insofar as it is related to the mind (Pr. 27, V). Again, since the essence of our mind consists solely in knowledge, whose principle and basis is God (Pr. 15, I and Schol. Pr. 47, II), it follows that we see quite clearly how and in what way our mind, in respect of essence and existence, follows from the divine nature and is continuously dependent on God.

I have thought this worth noting here in order to show by this example the superiority of that knowledge of particular things which I have called "intuitive" or "of the third kind," and its preferability to that abstract knowledge which I have called "knowledge of the second kind."

For although I demonstrated in a general way in Part I that everything (and consequently the human mind, too) is dependent on God in respect of its essence and of its existence, that proof, although legitimate and exempt from any shadow of doubt, does not so strike the mind as when it is inferred from the essence of each particular thing which we assert to be dependent on God.

P37   *There is nothing in Nature which is contrary to this intellectual love, or which can destroy it.*

Proof   This intellectual love follows necessarily from the nature of the mind insofar as that is considered as an eternal truth through God's nature (Prs. 33 and 29, V). Therefore, if there were anything that was contrary to this love, it would be contrary to truth, and consequently that which could destroy this love could cause truth to be false, which, as is self-evident, is absurd. Therefore, there is nothing in Nature . . . etc.

Schol   The Axiom in Part IV is concerned with particular things insofar as they are considered in relation to a definite time and place, of which I think no one can be in doubt.

P38   *The greater the number of things the mind understands by the second and third kinds of knowledge, the less subject it is to emotions that are bad, and the less it fears death.*

Proof   The essence of the mind consists in knowledge (Pr. 11, II). Therefore, the greater the number of things the mind knows by the second and third kinds of knowledge, the greater is the part of it that survives (Prs. 23 and 29, V), and consequently (preceding Pr.) the greater is that part of it that is not touched by emotions contrary to our nature; that is (Pr. 30, IV), by emotions that are bad. Therefore, the greater the number of things the mind understands by the second and third kinds of knowledge, the greater is that part of it that remains unimpaired, and consequently the less subject it is to emotions . . . etc.

Schol Hence we understand that point which I touched upon in Schol. Pr. 39, IV and which I promised to explain in this part, namely that death is less hurtful in proportion as the mind's clear and distinct knowledge is greater, and consequently the more the mind loves God. Again, since (Pr. 27, V) from the third kind of knowledge there arises the highest possible contentment, hence it follows that the human mind can be of such a nature that that part of it that we have shown to perish with the body (Pr. 21, V) is of no account compared with that part of it that survives. But I shall be dealing with this at greater length in due course.

P39 *He whose body is capable of the greatest amount of activity has a mind whose greatest part is eternal.*

Proof He whose body is capable of the greatest amount of activity is least assailed by emotions that are evil (Pr. 38, IV), that is (Pr. 30, IV), by emotions that are contrary to our nature. Thus (Pr. 10, V) he has the capacity to arrange and associate the affections of the body according to intellectual order and consequently to bring it about (Pr. 14, V) that all the affections of the body are related to God. This will result (Pr. 15, V) in his being affected with love toward God, a love (Pr. 16, V) that must occupy or constitute the greatest part of the mind. Therefore (Pr. 33, V), he has a mind whose greatest part is eternal.

Schol Since human bodies are capable of a great many activities, there is no doubt that they can be of such a nature as to be related to minds which have great knowledge of themselves and of God, and whose greatest and principal part is eternal, with the result that they scarcely fear death. But in order that this may be more clearly understood, it should here be remarked that our lives are subject to continual variation, and as the change is for the better or worse, so we are said to be fortunate or unfortunate. For he who passes from being a baby or child into being a corpse is said to be unfortunate; while, on the other hand, to have been able to pass the whole of one's life with a healthy mind in a healthy body is regarded as a mark of good fortune. And in fact he who, like a baby or a child, has a body capable of very little activity and is most dependent on external causes, has a mind which, considered solely in itself, has practically no consciousness of itself, of God, or of things, while he whose body is capable of very considerable activity has a mind which, considered solely in itself, is highly conscious of itself and of God and of things. In this life, therefore, we mainly endeavor that the body of childhood, as far as its nature allows and is conducive thereto, should develop into a body that is capable of a great many activities and is related to a mind that is highly conscious of itself, of God, and of things, and in such a way that everything relating to its memory or imagination should be of scarcely any importance in comparison with its intellect, as I have already stated in the Scholium to the preceding Proposition.

P40   *The more perfection a thing has, the more active and the less passive it is. Conversely, the more active it is, the more perfect it is.*

Proof   The more perfect a thing is, the more reality it has (Def. 6, II); consequently (Pr. 3, III and Schol.), the more active it is and the less passive. This proof proceeds in the same manner in inverse order, from which it follows that a thing is the more perfect as it is more active.

Cor   Hence it follows that the part of the mind that survives, of whatever extent it may be, is more perfect than the rest. For the eternal part of the mind (Prs. 23 and 29, V) is the intellect, through which alone we are said to be active (Pr. 3, III), whereas that part which we have shown to perish is the imagination (Pr. 21, V), through which alone we are said to be passive (Pr. 3, III and Gen. Def. of Emotions). Therefore, the former (preceding Pr.), of whatever extent it be, is more perfect than the latter.

Schol   This is what I had resolved to demonstrate concerning the mind insofar as it is considered without reference to the existence of the body. It is clear from this, and also from Pr. 21, I and other propositions, that our mind, insofar as it understands, is an eternal mode of thinking which is determined by another eternal mode of thinking, and this again by another, and so on ad infinitum, with the result that they all together constitute the eternal and infinite intellect of God.

P41   *Even if we did not know that our mind is eternal, we should still regard as being of prime importance piety and religion and, to sum up completely, everything which in Part IV we showed to be related to courage and nobility.*

Proof   The first and only basis of virtue, that is, of the right way of life (Cor. Pr. 22 and Pr. 24, IV), is to seek one's own advantage. Now in order to determine what reason prescribes as advantageous we took no account of the mind's eternity, a topic which we did not consider until Part V. So although at that point we were unaware that the mind is eternal, we regarded as being of prime importance whatever is related to courage and nobleness. So even if now we were unaware of the mind's eternity, we should still regard the said precepts of reason as being of prime importance.

Schol   The common belief of the multitude seems to be quite different. For the majority appear to think that they are free to the extent that they can indulge their lusts, and that they are giving up their rights to the extent that they are required to live under the commandments of the divine law. So they believe that piety and religion, in fact everything related to strength of mind, are burdens which they hope to lay aside after death, when they will receive the reward of their servitude, that is, of piety and religion. And it is not by this hope alone, but also and especially by fear of incurring dreadful punishment after death, that they are induced to live according to the commandments of the divine law as far as their feebleness and impotent spirit allows. And if men did not have this hope and this fear, and if they believed on the contrary that minds perish with bodies and that they, miserable creatures, worn out by the burden of piety, had no prospect of further existence, they would return to their own inclinations and decide to shape their lives according to their lusts, and to be ruled by fortune rather than by themselves. This seems to me no less absurd than if a man, not believing that he can sustain his body on good food forever, were to decide to glut himself on poisons and deadly fare; or, on realizing that the mind is not eternal or immortal, he preferred to be mad and to live without reason. Such attitudes are so absurd that they are scarcely worth recounting.

P42 *Blessedness is not the reward of virtue, but virtue itself. We do not enjoy blessedness because we keep our lusts in check. On the contrary, it is because we enjoy blessedness that we are able to keep our lusts in check.*

Proof   Blessedness consists in love toward God (Pr. 36, V and Schol.), a love that arises from the third kind of knowledge (Cor. Pr. 32. V), and so this love (Prs. 59 and 3, III) must be related to the mind insofar as the mind is active; and therefore it is virtue itself (Def. 8, IV). That is the first point. Again, the more the mind enjoys this divine love or blessedness, the more it understands (Pr. 32, V); that is (Cor. Pr. 3, V), the more power it has over the emotions and (Pr. 38, V) the less subject it is to emotions that are bad. So the mind's enjoyment of this divine love or blessedness gives it the power to check lusts. And since human power to keep lusts in check consists solely in the intellect, nobody enjoys blessedness because he has kept his emotions in check. On the contrary, the power to keep lusts in check arises from blessedness itself.

Schol   I have now completed all that I intended to demonstrate concerning the power of the mind over the emotions and concerning the freedom of the mind. This makes clear how strong the wise man is and how much he surpasses the ignorant man whose motive force is only lust. The ignorant man, besides being driven hither and thither by external causes, never possessing true contentment of spirit, lives as if he were unconscious of himself, God, and things, and as soon as he ceases to be passive, he at once ceases to be at all. On the other hand, the wise man, insofar as he is considered as such, suffers scarcely any disturbance of spirit, but being conscious, by virtue of a certain eternal necessity, of himself, of God and of things, never ceases to be, but always possesses true spiritual contentment.

If the road I have pointed out as leading to this goal seems very difficult, yet it can be found. Indeed, what is so rarely discovered is bound to be hard. For if salvation were ready to hand and could be discovered without great toil, how could it be that it is almost universally neglected? All things excellent are as difficult as they are rare.

End

TREATISE ON THE EMENDATION OF THE INTELLECT

Scholars agree that the brief Treatise on the Emendation of the Intellect *(TIE)* *is the earliest piece of philosophical writing that we have from Spinoza. It probably dates from the period immediately after his excommunication, between 1657 and 1660. The treatise is unfinished, and it is likely that Spinoza set it aside as his work on the more substantial* Short Treatise on God, Man, and His Well-Being *progressed. The latter too was left unfinished. Still, these two works exhibit Spinoza's first attempts at a philosophical system, and while later books, especially the* Ethics, *correct and extend these early efforts, the two are valuable glimpses of his mature thought.*

The TIE is often compared with Descartes' Discourse on Method, *first published in 1636, and the comparison is apt. Indeed, Spinoza was most likely influenced by Descartes' short introduction to his system. Like the latter, the TIE is an autobiographical work, more personal than most of Spinoza's writings. It sets questions of goals and methods in an ethical context and is largely epistemological in content. Descartes'* Discourse *is itself indebted to Augustine, and he in turn to Plato and Aristotle. In a sense, then, Spinoza's little work is his* protrepticus, *his introduction to and apology for the new scientific philosophy, for reason and for the life of reason. It is a sketch for a justification of the philosophical life, reminiscent of the Plato of* Phaedo *and* Republic *and the Aristotle of* Nicomachean Ethics X, *drawn through the lens of Latin Stoicism.*

The immediate autobiographical context for the TIE includes Spinoza's excommunication in 1656, his subsequent disengagement from his family's mercantile business and from the Jewish community in Amsterdam, and his more intense involvement with his rationalist, radical friends. By 1661 Spinoza was well known as a Cartesian and as a lens grinder skilled at producing optical lenses. He was associated with rational critics of Scripture like Juan de Prado, Isaac La Peyrère, and Uriel da Costa. Spinoza was a member of the circle around Franciscus Van den Enden, a frequent participant in Collegiant meetings, and an expert in Cartesian philosophy. There is reason to believe that Spinoza's critical spirit and attraction to the revolutionary science of his day were not new. They had been cultivated since his teenage years and came to a head with his public expulsion from the Jewish community. By that time, 27 July 1656, Spinoza had been a student and disciple of Van den Enden for some time and an advocate of tolerance, rational critique, and religious freedom. His traditional Jewish education, thorough as it was, had turned, when he was fourteen or fifteen years old, into this new set of commitments. The result was a view of God, nature, and the human good more rational and more universal than the traditional establishment could bear.

By 1657 Spinoza's exile was at least sufficient to cut him off from his teachers R. Saul Morteira and R. Manasseh ben Israel and to intensify his radical intellectual friendships with thinkers such as Van den Enden, Lodewijk Meyer, Adriaan Koerbagh, Pieter Balling, Simon de Vries, and Jarig Jelles. He probably lived with Van den Enden for a time, for he was the latter's prize student, and it was at his school that he had first become acquainted with the philosophy of Descartes and much else. He turned to lens grinding to earn a living, increased his scholarly associations by spending time at the university in Leiden, and frequently attended the meetings of the religiously radical Protestant group, the Collegiants.

The TIE, one might speculate, is the first literary product of this intense activity, hence its rather personal and programmatic qualities. It is a work marked by three significant features. First, in it Spinoza valorizes the life of reason and in particular scientific reason and the attainment of a knowledge of nature. Second, Spinoza distinguishes four modes of cognition, two of which, associated with imagination and sensation, are inadequate and defective, and the remaining two of which, involving deductive reasoning and intuitive reason, are the height of human achievement. Finally, Spinoza discusses the requirements of definition, distinguishing the definition of eternal essences from those of dependent and contingent ones. At this point, the text breaks off. It is a beginning, but only that. Some believe Spinoza abandoned the work when other tasks became more compelling; others, however, believe he left the TIE when he came to doubt the fruitfulness of its method. In years to come, the *Ethics* would mark a new beginning—working from new principles and in a new way.

M.L.M.

NOTICE TO THE READER
(by the Editors of the *Opera Posthuma*)

This "Treatise on the Emendation of the Intellect, etc.," which in its unfinished state we here present to you, dear reader, was written by our author many years ago. He always intended to finish it, but, distracted by his other occupations and taken from us by death, he did not succeed in bringing it to the desired conclusion. But since it contains many excellent and useful things which we are convinced will be of considerable interest to an earnest seeker after truth, we did not wish to deprive you of them. That you may the more readily excuse occasional obscurities and lack of polish that appear in places in the text, we have thought it proper that you, too, should be made aware of these circumstances.

TREATISE ON THE EMENDATION OF THE INTELLECT
AND ON THE WAY BY WHICH IT IS
BEST DIRECTED TO THE
TRUE KNOWLEDGE OF THINGS

1 After experience had taught me the hollowness and futility of everything that is ordinarily encountered in daily life, and I realised that all the things which were the source and object of my anxiety held nothing of good or evil in themselves save insofar as the mind was influenced by them, I resolved at length to enquire whether there existed a true good, one which was capable of communicating itself and could alone affect the mind to the exclusion of all else, whether, in fact, there was something whose discovery and acquisition would afford me a continuous and supreme joy to all eternity.

2 I say 'I resolved at length,' for at first sight it seemed ill-advised to risk the loss of what was certain in the hope of something at that time uncertain. I could well see the advantages that derive from honour and wealth, and that I would be forced to abandon their quest if I were to devote myself to some new and different objective. And if in fact supreme happiness were to be found in the former, I must inevitably fail to attain it, whereas if it did not lie in these objectives and I devoted myself entirely to them, then once again I would lose that highest happiness.

3 I therefore debated whether it might be possible to arrive at a new guiding principle—or at least the sure hope of its attainment—without changing the manner and normal routine of my life. This I frequently attempted, but in vain. For the things which for the most part offer themselves in life, and which, to judge from their actions, men regard as the highest good, can be reduced to these three headings: riches, honour, and sensual pleasure. With these three the mind is so distracted that it is quite incapable of thinking of any other good. With regard to

4 sensual pleasure, the mind is so utterly obsessed by it that it seems as if it were absorbed in some good, and so is quite prevented from thinking of anything else. But after the enjoyment of this pleasure there ensues a profound depression which, if it does not completely inhibit the mind, leads to its confusion and enervation. The pursuit of honour and wealth, too, engrosses the mind to no small

5 degree, especially when the latter is sought exclusively for its own sake,[a] for it is then regarded as the highest good. Even more so is the mind obsessed with honour, for this is always regarded as a good in itself and the ultimate end to which everything is directed. Then again, in both these cases, there is no repentance as

---

All notes are Spinoza's.

[a] This could be explained more fully and clearly by making a distinction between wealth that is sought for its own sake, for the sake of honour, for sensual pleasure, for health, or for the advancement of the sciences and the arts. But this is reserved for its proper place, such a detailed investigation being inappropriate here.

in the case of sensual pleasure. The more each of them is possessed, the more our joy is enhanced, and we are therefore more and more induced to increase them both. But if it should come about that our hopes are disappointed, there ensues a profound depression. And finally, honour has this great drawback, that to attain it we must conduct our lives to suit other men, avoiding what the masses avoid and seeking what the masses seek.

So when I saw that all these things stood in the way of my embarking on a new 6 course, and were indeed so opposed to it that I must necessarily choose between the one alternative and the other, I was forced to ask what was to my greater advantage; for, as I have said, I seemed set on losing a certain good for the sake of an uncertain good. But after a little reflection, I first of all realised that if I abandoned the old ways and embarked on a new way of life, I should be abandoning a good that was by its very nature uncertain—as we can clearly gather from what has been said—in favour of one that was uncertain not of its own nature (for I was seeking a permanent good) but only in respect of its attainment. Then persistent 7 meditation enabled me to see that, if only I could be thoroughly resolute, I should be abandoning certain evils for the sake of a certain good. For I saw that my situation was one of great peril and that I was obliged to seek a remedy with all my might, however uncertain it might be, like a sick man suffering from a fatal malady who, foreseeing certain death unless a remedy is forthcoming, is forced to seek it, however uncertain it be, with all his might, for therein lies all his hope. Now all those objectives that are commonly pursued not only contribute nothing to the preservation of our being but even hinder it, being frequently the cause of the destruction of those who gain possession of them, and invariably the cause of the destruction of those who are possessed by them.[b] For there are numerous examples 8 of men who have suffered persecution unto death because of their wealth, and also of men who have exposed themselves to so many dangers to acquire riches that they have finally paid for their folly with their lives. Nor are there less numerous examples of men who, to gain or preserve honour, have suffered a most wretched fate. Finally, there are innumerable examples of men who have hastened their death by reason of excessive sensual pleasure.

These evils, moreover, seemed to arise from this, that all happiness or unhap- 9 piness depends solely on the quality of the object to which we are bound by love. For strife will never arise on account of that which is not loved; there will be no sorrow if it is lost, no envy if it is possessed by another, no fear, no hatred—in a word, no emotional agitation, all of which, however, occur in the case of the love of perishable things, such as all those of which we have been speaking. But love 10 towards a thing eternal and infinite feeds the mind with joy alone, unmixed with any sadness. This is greatly to be desired, and to be sought with all our might. However, it was not without reason that I used these words, 'If only I could be earnestly resolute,' for although I perceived these things quite clearly in my mind, I could not on that account put aside all greed, sensual pleasure, and desire for esteem.

---

[b] This is to be demonstrated at greater length.

11   This one thing I could see, that as long as my mind was occupied with these thoughts, it turned away from those other objectives and earnestly applied itself to the quest for a new guiding principle. This was a great comfort to me, for I saw that those evils were not so persistent as to refuse to yield to remedies. And although at first these intermissions were rare and of very brief duration, nevertheless, as the true good became more and more discernible to me, these intermissions became more frequent and longer, especially when I realised that the acquisition of money, sensual pleasure, and esteem is a hindrance only as long as they are sought on their own account, and not as a means to other things. If they are sought as means, they will then be under some restriction, and far from being hindrances, they will do much to further the end for which they are sought, as I shall demonstrate in its proper place.

12   At this point I shall only state briefly what I understand by the true good, and at the same time what is the supreme good. In order that this may be rightly understood, it must be borne in mind that good and bad are only relative terms, so that one and the same thing may be said to be good or bad in different respects, just like the terms perfect and imperfect. Nothing, when regarded in its own nature, can be called perfect or imperfect, especially when we realise that all things that come into being do so in accordance with an eternal order and Nature's fixed laws.

13   But human weakness fails to comprehend that order in its thought, and meanwhile man conceives a human nature much stronger than his own, and sees no reason why he cannot acquire such a nature. Thus he is urged to seek the means that will bring him to such a perfection, and all that can be the means of his attaining this objective is called a true good, while the supreme good is to arrive at the enjoyment of such a nature, together with other individuals, if possible. What that nature is we shall show in its proper place; namely, the knowledge of the union which the mind has with the whole of Nature.[c]

14   This, then, is the end for which I strive, to acquire the nature I have described and to endeavour that many should acquire it along with me. That is to say, my own happiness involves my making an effort to persuade many others to think as I do, so that their understanding and their desire should entirely accord with my understanding and my desire. To bring this about, it is necessary[d] (1) to understand as much about Nature as suffices for acquiring such a nature, and (2) to establish such a social order as will enable as many as possible to reach this goal

15   with the greatest possible ease and assurance. Furthermore, (3) attention must be paid to moral philosophy and likewise the theory of the education of children; and since health is of no little importance in attaining this end, (4) the whole science of medicine must be elaborated. And since many difficult tasks are rendered easy by contrivance, and we can thereby gain much time and convenience in our daily lives, (5) the science of mechanics is in no way to be despised.

---

[c] This is explained more fully in its proper place.

[d] Note that here I am only concerned to enumerate the sciences necessary to our purpose, without regard to their order.

But our first consideration must be to devise a method of emending the intel- 16
lect and of purifying it, as far as is feasible at the outset, so that it may succeed in
understanding things without error and as well as possible. So now it will be evident to everyone that my purpose is to direct all the sciences to one end and goal,[e]
to wit (as we have said), the achievement of the highest human perfection. Thus
everything in the sciences which does nothing to advance us towards our goal
must be rejected as pointless — in short, all our activities and likewise our thoughts
must be directed to this end.

But since we have to continue with our lives while pursuing this end and en- 17
deavouring to bring down the intellect into the right path, our first priority must
be to lay down certain rules for living, as being good rules. They are as follows:

1. To speak to the understanding of the multitude and to engage in all those
   activities that do not hinder the attainment of our aim. For we can gain no
   little advantage from the multitude, provided that we accommodate ourselves as far as possible to their level of understanding. Furthermore, in this
   way they will give a more favourable hearing to the truth.
2. To enjoy pleasures just so far as suffices to preserve health.
3. Finally, to seek as much money or any other goods as are sufficient for sus-
   taining life and health and for conforming with those social customs that
   do not conflict with our aim.

Having laid down these rules, I shall embark upon the first and most important 18
task, emending the intellect and rendering it apt for the understanding of things
in a manner appropriate to the achievement of our purpose. To this end our natural order of exposition requires that I should here recapitulate all the modes of
perceiving which I have hitherto employed in confidently affirming or denying
something, so that I may select the best of all, and at the same time begin to know
my powers and the nature which I desire to perfect.

If I examine them carefully, they can all be classified under four headings. 19

1. There is the perception we have from hearsay, or from some sign conven-
   tionally agreed upon.
2. There is the perception we have from casual experience; that is, experience
   that is not determined by intellect, but is so called because it chances thus
   to occur, and we have experienced nothing else that contradicts it, so that
   it remains in our minds unchallenged.
3. There is the perception we have when the essence of a thing is inferred from
   another thing, but not adequately. This happens either when we infer a
   cause from some effect[f] or when an inference is made from some universal
   which is always accompanied by some property.

---

[e] In the sciences there is only one end, to which all must be directed.

[f] In such a case, we understand nothing about the cause except what we consider in the effect.
This is sufficiently evident from the fact that the cause is then explained only in very general terms:

4. Finally, there is the perception we have when a thing is perceived through its essence alone, or through knowledge of its proximate cause.

20   All these I shall illustrate with examples. By hearsay alone I know the date of my birth, who my parents were, and things of that sort, which I have never doubted. By casual experience I know that I shall die; this I affirm because I have seen that others like me have died, although they have not all lived to the same age nor have they died from the same disease. Again, by casual experience I know that oil has the property of feeding fire, and water of extinguishing it. I know too that a dog is a barking animal and man a rational animal. And it is in this way that I know almost everything that is of practical use in life.

21   We deduce one thing from another as follows. When we clearly perceive that we sense such-and-such a body and no other, then from this, I say, we clearly infer that the soul is united to the body,[g] a union which is the cause of such-and-such a sensation. But from this[h] we cannot positively understand what is that sensation and union. Or, after I have come to know the nature of vision and realise that it has the property of making us see one and the same thing as smaller at a distance than if we were to see it near at hand, we infer that the sun is bigger than it appears, and other similar instances.

22   Finally, a thing is perceived through its essence alone when, from the fact that I know something, I know what it is to know something; or, from the fact that I know the essence of the soul, I know that it is united to the body. By the same kind of knowledge we know that two and three are five, and that if two lines are parallel to a third line, they are parallel to one another, and so on. But the things that I have hitherto been able to know by this kind of knowledge have been very few.

23   For the better understanding of all this, I shall make use of a single example, as follows. Three numbers are given; a fourth number is required, which is to the third as the second to the first. Here tradesmen generally tell us that they know what to do to find the fourth number, for they have not forgotten the procedure which they merely learned without proof from their teachers. Others formulate a universal axiom from their experience with simple numbers when the fourth number is self-evident, as in the case of the numbers 2, 4, 3, 6. Here they find that

---

e.g., 'Therefore there is something; therefore there is some power,' etc. Or again from the fact that the cause is expressed negatively: 'Therefore there is not this, or that,' etc. In the second case something clearly conceived is ascribed to the cause by reason of the effect, as we shall show by an example. But it is only the properties, not the particular essence of the thing.

g From this example one can clearly see what I have just noted. For by this union we understand nothing beyond the sensation itself; that is, the effect from which we inferred a cause of which we have no understanding.

h Such a conclusion, although it be certain, is not to be relied on without great caution; for unless we take great care, we shall immediately fall into error. When things are conceived in this abstract way and not through their true essence, they are at once confused by the imagination. For to the things that they conceive abstractly, separately, and confusedly, men apply terms which they use to signify other more familiar things. Consequently, they imagine the former things in the same way as they are wont to imagine the things to which they originally applied these terms.

when the second is multiplied by the third and the product is divided by the first, the answer is 6. Seeing that the same number is produced which they knew to be the proportional number without going through the procedure, they conclude that this procedure is always a good way to find the fourth proportional. But mathematicians, because of the force of the demonstration of Proposition 19 of Book 7 of Euclid, know what numbers are proportional to one another from the nature and property of proportion, which tells us that the product of the first and fourth numbers is equal to the product of the second and third. However, they do not see the adequate proportionality of the given numbers, and if they do see it, they see it not by the force of that proposition but intuitively, without going through any procedure.

To choose from these the best mode of perceiving, we should briefly enumerate the means necessary to attain our end, as follows:

1. To have an exact knowledge of our nature which we wish to perfect, and at the same time to know as much of the nature of things as is necessary.
2. Therefrom to infer correctly the differences, agreements and oppositions of things.
3. To conceive aright the extent to which things can, and cannot, be acted upon.
4. To compare this result with the nature and power of man.

From this the highest degree of perfection that man can attain will readily be made manifest.

With these considerations in mind, let us see which mode of perceiving we ought to choose.

As to the first mode, it is self-evident that from hearsay, besides the considerable degree of uncertainty therein, we perceive nothing of the essence of the thing, as our example makes clear. And since a thing's individual existence is not known unless its essence is known (as will later be seen), we can clearly infer from this that any degree of certainty that we have from hearsay must be excluded from the sciences. For no one can ever be affected by mere hearsay unless his own understanding has already preceded it.

As to the second mode, again[i] it cannot be said to contain the idea of the proportion which it seeks. Besides its considerable uncertainty and indefiniteness, no one will in this way perceive anything in natural things except their accidents, which are never clearly understood unless their essences are first known. Hence this mode, too, must be excluded.

As for the third mode, we can in some sense say that we have the idea of the thing, and also that we can make inferences without danger of error. Yet it is not in itself the means of our acquiring our perfection.

---

[i] Here I shall discuss experience at some greater length, and examine the method of proceeding of Empiricists and the new philosophers.

29   Only the fourth mode comprehends the adequate essence of the thing, and is without danger of error. So this is the one we must chiefly adopt. Therefore we shall proceed to explain how it is to be employed, so that we may understand by this kind of knowledge what is unknown, and also may do this as directly as pos-

30   sible. That is, now that we know what kind of knowledge is necessary for us, we must describe the way and method by which we may come to know by this kind of knowledge the things that are needful to be known.

To this end, the first point to consider is that this is not a case of an enquiry extending to infinity. That is, to find the best method of seeking the truth, there is no need of another method for seeking the method of seeking the truth, and there is no need of a third method to seek the second method, and so on to infinity. For in that way we should never arrive at knowledge of the truth, or indeed at any knowledge. The case is analogous to that of material tools, where the same kind of argument could be employed. To work iron, a hammer is needed, and to have a hammer, it must be made. For this purpose there is need of another hammer and other tools, and again to get these there is need of other tools, and so on to infinity. In this way one might try to prove, in vain, that men have no power to work iron.

31   But the fact is that at first, with the tools they were born with, men succeeded, however laboriously and imperfectly, in making some very simple things; and when these were made they made other more complex things with less labour and greater perfection; and thus advancing gradually from the simplest works to the making of tools, and from tools to other works and other tools, they have reached a point where they can make very many complex things with little labour. In just the same way the intellect by its inborn power[j] makes intellectual tools for itself by which it acquires other powers for other intellectual works,[k] and from these works still other tools—or capacity for further investigation—and thus makes steady progress until it reaches the summit of wisdom.

32   That this is the case with the intellect will readily be seen, provided we understand what is the method of seeking truth, and what are those innate tools which are all the intellect needs for making other tools from them so as to progress further. To demonstrate this I proceed as follows.

33   A true idea[l] (for we do have a true idea) is something different from its object (ideatum). A circle is one thing, the idea of a circle another. For the idea of a circle is not something having a circumference and a centre, as is a circle, nor is the idea of a body itself a body. And since it is something different from its object, it will also be something intelligible through itself. That is, in respect of its formal essence the idea can be the object of another objective essence, which in turn, regarded in itself, will also be something real and intelligible, and so on indefinitely.

---

[j] By inborn power I mean that which is not caused in us by external causes, as I shall later explain in my Philosophy.

[k] Here they are called works. In my Philosophy, I shall explain what they are.

[l] Note that here we shall endeavour to demonstrate not only what has just been said, but also the correctness of our procedure so far, and likewise other points of primary importance.

For example, Peter is something real. Now the true idea of Peter is the objec-   34
tive essence of Peter and is in itself something real, something entirely different
from Peter. So since the idea of Peter is something real, having its own individual
essence, it will also be something intelligible, that is, the object of another idea
which has in itself objectively everything that the idea of Peter has formally. And
in turn the idea of the idea of Peter again has its own essence, which can also be
the object of another idea, and so on without end. This anyone can experience
for himself when he realises that he knows what Peter is, and also that he knows
that he knows, and again that he knows that he knows that he knows, and so on.
From this it is evident that, to understand the essence of Peter, it is not necessary
to understand the idea of Peter, and far less the idea of Peter. This is no more than
to say that, in order to know, I need not know that I know, and far less do I need
to know that I know that I know. It is no more necessary than, in order to understand the essence of a triangle, one needs to understand the essence of a triangle,
one needs to understand the essence^m of a circle. Indeed, in the case of these ideas
it is the other way round; for in order to know that I know, it is necessary that I
must first know.

Hence it is evident that certainty is nothing else than the objective essence it-   35
self; that is to say, the way in which we become aware of the formal essence is certainty itself. And from this again it is evident that for the certainty of truth no other
sign is needed but to have a true idea. For, as we have shown, in order to know,
there is no need for me to know that I know. From this, again, it is clear that no
one can know what the highest certainty is unless he has an adequate idea or the
objective essence of some thing. For certainty and objective essence are the same.

Since truth, then, needs no sign, and to have the objective essences of things,   36
or—which is the same thing—their ideas, is enough to remove all doubt, it follows that the true method does not consist in seeking a sign of truth after acquiring ideas; the true method is the path whereby truth itself, or the objective
essences of things, or ideas (all these mean the same) is to be sought^n in proper
order.

Again, method must necessarily be discourse about reasoning or intellection.   37
That is, method is not reasoning itself which leads to the understanding of the
causes of things, and far less is it the understanding of the causes of things. It is
the understanding of what is a true idea, distinguishing it from other kinds of perception and examining its nature, so that we may thereby come to know our power
of understanding and may so train the mind that it will understand according to
that standard all that needs to be understood, laying down definite rules as aids,
and also ensuring that the mind does not waste its energy on useless pursuits.

From this we may conclude that method is nothing but reflexive knowledge,   38
or the idea of an idea; and because there is no idea of an idea unless there is first

---

^m Note that we are not here inquiring as to how the first objective essence is innate in us. For that
   topic belongs to the investigation of Nature, where these matters are dealt with more fully and
   where we also demonstrate that there is no affirmation or negation or act of will apart from the idea.

^n The nature of this seeking in the soul is explained in my Philosophy.

an idea, there will be no method unless there is first an idea. So a good method will be one which shows how the mind is to be directed according to the standard of a given true idea. Again, since the relation between two ideas is the same as the relation between the formal essences of those ideas, it follows that the reflexive knowledge of the idea of the most perfect Being will be more excellent than the reflexive knowledge of other ideas. That is, the most perfect method will be one which shows how the mind should be directed according to the standard of a given idea of the most perfect Being.

39   From this one can readily understand how the mind, as it understands more things, at the same time acquires other tools which facilitate its further understanding. For, as may be gathered from what has been said, there must first of all exist in us a true idea as an innate tool, and together with the understanding of this idea there would likewise be an understanding of the difference between this perception and all other perceptions. Herein consists one part of our method. And since it is self-evident that the more the mind understands of Nature, the better it understands itself, it clearly follows that this part of our method will become that much more perfect as the mind understands more things, and will become then most perfect when the mind attends to, or reflects upon, the knowledge of the most perfect Being.

40   Then again, the more things the mind knows, the better it understands both its own powers and the order of Nature. Now the better it understands its own powers, the more easily it can direct itself and lay down rules for its own guidance; and the better it understands the order of Nature, the more easily it can restrain itself from useless pursuits. And it is in this, as we have said, that the whole of our method consists.

41   Moreover, an idea is situated in the context of thought exactly as is its object in the context of reality. Therefore, if there were something in Nature having no interrelation with other things, and if there were also granted its objective essence (which must agree entirely with its formal essence), then this idea likewise would have no interrelation° with other ideas; that is, we could make no inference regarding it. On the other hand, those things that do have interrelation with other things—as is the case with everything that exists in Nature—will be intelligible, and their objective essences will also have that same interrelation; that is, other ideas will be deduced from them, and these in turn will be interrelated with other ideas, and so the tools for further progress will increase. This is what we were endeavouring to demonstrate.

42   Furthermore, from the point just mentioned—that the idea must entirely agree with its formal essence—it is again evident that, for the human mind to reproduce a faithful image of Nature, it must draw all its ideas from that idea which represents the source and origin of the whole of Nature, so that this may likewise become the source of other ideas.

43   Here it may seem surprising that, having said that the good method is one which demonstrates how the mind is to be directed according to the standard of

---

° To be interrelated with other things is to produce, or be produced by, other things.

a given true idea, I resort to reasoning to prove this point, which appears to indicate that it is not self-evident. So the question can be raised as to whether our reasoning is sound. If our reasoning is sound, we have to begin from a given idea, and since to begin from a given idea is something that needs proving, we ought again to prove the validity of our reasoning, and then again the validity of that reasoning, and so on ad infinitum.

To this I reply that if anyone in his investigation of Nature had by some chance   44
advanced in this way—that is, by acquiring other ideas in proper order according to the standard of a given true idea—he would never have doubted[p] his own truth (inasmuch as truth, as we have said, reveals its own self), and all would have progressed smoothly for him. But since this rarely or never happens, I have been constrained to posit those guidelines, so that what we cannot acquire by chance, we may yet acquire by deliberate planning, and also in order to make it clear that, for the validation of truth and sound reasoning, we need no other instruments than truth and sound reasoning. For it is by sound reasoning that I have validated sound reasoning, and still continue so to do. Furthermore, it is this way of thinking that   45
men usually adopt in their own internal meditations.

That the proper order is rarely employed in the investigation of Nature is due to prejudices whose causes I shall later explain in my Philosophy. A further reason, as I shall later show, is the need for a considerable capacity to make accurate distinctions, a very laborious task. And finally, there is the matter of the human condition, which, as has already been shown, is highly unstable. There are yet other reasons, which we shall not pursue.

If anyone perchance should ask why at the very outset I adopted that arrange-   46
ment in demonstrating the truths of Nature—for does not truth reveal its own self?—I reply by urging him not to reject these things as false because of paradoxes which will occasionally occur here and there. Let him first please to consider the arrangement of our demonstration, and he will then be convinced that we have arrived at the truth. This explains the reason why I began as I did.

But if after this there is some sceptic who still entertains doubt both as to the   47
first truth itself and all the deductions we shall make according to the standard of the first truth, then surely either he is speaking contrary to his own consciousness or else we shall have to declare that there are men whose minds are also blinded either from birth or by reason of their prejudices, that is, through some accident that has befallen them. For they are not even aware of their own selves. If they affirm or doubt something, they do not know that they are doubting or affirming. They say that they know nothing, and they say that they are ignorant of this very fact of knowing nothing. And they do not even say this without qualification; for they are afraid that, in saying they know nothing, they are declaring that they exist, so that in the end they have to maintain silence lest they should perchance say something that has the savour of truth.

Finally, although in matters relating to the usages of life and society neces-   48
sity has compelled them to suppose their existence, to seek their own good and

---

[p] Just as here, too, we do not doubt our truth.

frequently to affirm and deny things on oath, it is quite impossible to discuss the sciences with them. If a proof is presented to them, they do not know whether the argumentation is valid or not. If they deny, grant or oppose, they do not know that they deny, grant or oppose. So they must be regarded as automata, completely lacking in mind.

49   Let us now return to our theme. Up to the present, we have in the first place established the end to which we strive to direct all our thoughts. Second, we have learned which is the best mode of perception that will help us to attain our perfection. Third, we have learned which is the path our mind should first take in order to make a good beginning, and that is, to proceed to its enquiry by fixed rules, taking as its standard some given true idea. To do this correctly, our method must enable us, first, to distinguish a true idea from all other perceptions and to restrain the mind from those other perceptions; second, to lay down rules for perceiving things unknown according to the aforementioned standard; third, to establish an orderly procedure which will enable us to avoid useless toil. Having discovered this method, we realised, fourthly, that this method would be most perfect when we possessed the idea of a most perfect Being. So at the outset this must be our chief objective, to arrive at the knowledge of such a Being as speedily as possible.

50   Let us then make a beginning with the first part of the method, which is, as we have said, to distinguish and separate the true idea from other perceptions, and to keep the mind from confusing false, fictitious, and doubtful ideas with true ideas. Here I intend to dwell on this subject at some length so as to engage my readers in the study of so important a topic, and also because there are many who, failing to attend to the distinction between a true perception and all other perceptions, have come to doubt even their true perceptions. Their condition is like that of men who, when they were awake, did not doubt that they were awake, but having once in their dreams—as is often the case—felt certain that they were wide awake and later found this to be untrue, doubted even their waking experiences. This comes about because they have never distinguished between dreaming and being awake.

51   But I must first warn the reader that I shall not here be discussing the essence of every perception, explaining it through its proximate cause, for this pertains to Philosophy. I shall confine myself to discussing what the method demands; that is, what are the circumstances with which the fictitious, the false, and the doubtful perception are concerned, and how we may be delivered from each of them. Let our first inquiry, then, deal with the fictitious idea.

52   Every perception has for its object either a thing considered as existing or solely the essence of a thing. Now since in most cases fictions are concerned with things considered as existing, I shall deal first with that situation—that is, where the existence of some action is the sole object of the fiction, and the thing which is supposed to be so acting is comprehensible by intellect, or is posited as such. For example, I make up the idea that Peter, whom I well know, is on his way home, is coming to visit me, or the like.q Here I ask, with what is such an idea concerned?

---

q See later on what we shall have to say about hypotheses. These are clearly understood by us, but the
   fiction consists in our saying that the hypotheses are actually true of the heavenly bodies.

I see that it is concerned only with what is possible, not with what is necessary, nor with what is impossible.

I call a thing impossible if its nature implies that it would be a contradiction 53 for it to exist; necessary, if its nature implies that it would be a contradiction for it not to exist; and possible, if, by its very nature, neither its existence nor its nonexistence implies a contradiction, the necessity or impossibility of its existence being dependent on causes which are unknown to us while we are assuming its existence. So if its necessity or impossibility, which are dependent on external causes, were known to us, it could not then be for us the subject of any fiction.

Hence it follows that if there is a God, or some omniscient being, such a be- 54 ing cannot engage in any fiction. For in our own case, knowing as I do that I exist,[r] my existence or nonexistence cannot be a matter of fiction for me; nor again can I engage in the fiction of an elephant that can pass through the eye of a needle; nor, knowing the nature of God,[s] can his existence or nonexistence be a matter of fiction for me. The same applies to the Chimera, whose nature implies its nonexistence. From this it is evident, as I have said, that eternal truths do not allow of the fiction of which we are here speaking.[t]

But before proceeding further, I must first observe in passing that the differ- 55 ence between the essence of one thing and the essence of another thing is the same as that which holds between the actuality or existence of the one thing and the actuality or existence of the other. So if we were to conceive the existence of Adam, for example, under the general category of existence, this would be the same as if, to conceive his essence, we were to focus our attention on the nature of being, so that we end up by defining Adam as a being. Thus the more generally existence is conceived, the more confusedly it is conceived and the more readily it can be ascribed to any one thing. Conversely, the more singularly existence is conceived, the more clearly it is then understood, and the less likely we are to ascribe it (when we are not attending to the order of Nature) to anything other than the thing itself. This is worth noting.

We must now proceed to consider those cases which are loosely called fictions 56 in common parlance even though we clearly understand that the reality is not as we feign it to be. For example, although I know that the earth is round, nothing prevents my saying to somebody that the earth is a hemisphere, like half an orange on a plate, or saying that the sun moves round the earth, and the like. If we

---

[r] Since a thing, when once it is understood, manifests itself, we need only an example without further proof. The same is true of its contradictory, which needs only to be examined to expose its falsity, as will later become clear when we shall be discussing the fiction that concerns essence.

[s] Note that, although many may say that they doubt the existence of God, they have in mind nothing but a word, or some fictitious idea they call God. This does not accord with the nature of God, as I shall later demonstrate in its proper place.

[t] I shall also presently demonstrate that eternal truths do not admit of fiction of any kind. By an eternal truth I mean one which, if it is affirmative, will never be able to be negative. Thus it is a first and eternal truth that 'God is,' but that 'Adam thinks' is not an eternal truth. That 'there is no Chimera' is an eternal truth, but not that 'Adam does not think.'

consider these cases, we shall find nothing that is not consistent with what we have already said, provided that we note that, first, we have occasionally fallen into errors of which we are now conscious; and second, that we can entertain the fictitious idea, or at least the thought, that others have fallen into the same error, or may so do, as we once did. This fiction, I say, is feasible for us as long as we see no impossibility and no necessity therein. So when I say to somebody that the earth is not round, and the like, I do no more than to recall to mind an error which I perchance have made, or into which I might have fallen, and thereafter I feign, or think, that the person to whom I tell this is as yet a victim of this same error or is capable of falling into it. As I have said, I can engage in this fiction only as long as I see that no impossibility and no necessity lies therein. For had I understood this to be so, there would have been no room whatsoever for fiction, and it would have to be said that I had done no more than utter words.

57　It remains for us now furthermore to consider the kind of suppositions that are made in connection with problems: for these, too, not infrequently involve impossibilities. For example, we may say, "Let us suppose that this burning candle is not now burning," or "Let us suppose that it is burning in some imaginary space where there are no bodies." Such suppositions are quite commonly made, although the latter example is obviously understood to be impossible. But in such cases there is no question of fiction. In the first case I have done no more than recall to memory[u] another candle which was not burning (or I have conceived this candle without a flame), and my thoughts of the latter candle I now transfer to the former, dismissing the flame from my mind. In the second case I merely withdraw my thoughts from the surrounding bodies so that the mind concentrates its attention on the candle alone, regarded in itself. This leads to the conclusion that the candle contains in itself no cause for its own destruction, so that, if there were no surrounding bodies, this candle and likewise its flame would remain immutable, or some such conclusion. Here, then, there is no question of fiction; there are really mere assertions,[v] and no more.

58　Let us now pass on to those fictions which are concerned either with essences alone or with essences combined with some actuality or existence. With regard to these it must especially be noted that, the less the mind understands while yet perceiving more things, the greater its capacity to form fictions; and the more it understands, the less its capacity to form fictions. For example, just as we saw above that while we are actually thinking, it cannot be for us a fictional idea that

---

[u] Later, when we shall be speaking of fictions concerning essences, it will be manifest that fiction never invents or presents to the mind anything new; it recalls to mind only things that are in the brain or the imagination, and the mind attends to all these together in a confused way. For example, the uttering of words and a tree are recalled to memory, and when the mind attends to them in a confused way without distinction, it forms the notion of a tree speaking. The same applies to existence, especially when, as we have said, it is conceived in a very general way as entity, for it is then liable to be attached to all things that occur together in memory. This is a very important point.

[v] This is also the case with hypotheses which are formed to explain the regular movements which accord with celestial phenomena, except that, if the hypotheses are actually applied to the celestial movement, an inference is drawn as to the nature of the heavens, which may nevertheless be quite different. For one may conceive many other causes to explain these movements.

we are thinking or not thinking, so too, when we have come to know the nature of body, we cannot entertain the idea of an infinite fly; or when we have come to know the nature of the soul,ʷ we cannot entertain the idea that it is square—though anything can be put into words. But as we have said, the less men know of Nature, the more easily they can fashion numerous fictitious ideas, as that trees speak, that men can change instantaneously into stones or springs, that ghosts appear in mirrors, that something can come from nothing, even that gods can change into beasts or men, and any number of such fantasies.

Someone may perhaps think that the limits of fiction are set by fiction, not by intellection. That is, when I have formed a fictitious idea and then, by some sort of freedom, assented to its existence in reality, this has the consequence that I cannot thereafter think it in any other way. For instance, when I have engaged in the fiction (to speak as they do) that body has a certain nature, and of my own free will I convince myself that this is so in reality, I can no longer entertain the idea, say, of an infinite fly; and when I have formed an idea of the essence of the soul, I can no longer conceive it as square, and so forth. 59

But this view must be examined. First, either they deny or they grant that we have the capacity to understand something. If they grant this, then it must follow that what they say about fiction also applies to intellection. If they deny it, then let us, who know that we know something, consider what they are saying. They are in fact saying that the soul can be conscious of and perceive, in a variety of ways, not its own self nor things that exist, but only things that are neither in themselves nor anywhere at all; that is, the soul can by its unaided power create sensations or ideas which are not ideas of things. So to some extent they are likening the soul to God. Further, they are saying that we, or our soul, possess a freedom of such a kind that it can constrain our own selves, or the soul's self—nay, it can constrain its own freedom. For after it has formed some fictitious idea and given assent thereto, it cannot think it or fashion it in any other way, and is even compelled by that fictitious idea to form all its other thoughts so as not to conflict with the original fiction—just as here, too, their own fictitious idea compels them to allow the absurdities which I am here reviewing. We shall waste no time on demonstrations to refute this nonsense. 60

But leaving them to their delusions, we shall endeavour to draw from our discussion with them something true and to our purpose, namely, that when the mind attends to a thing that is both fictitious and false by its very nature, so as to ponder over it and achieve understanding, and then deduces from it in proper order what is to be deduced, it will easily detect its falsity;ˣ and if the fictitious idea 61

ʷ It often happens that a man recalls to mind this term 'soul' and at the same time forms some material image. Now when these two things are presented together in his mind, he is prone to think that he imagines and forms the idea of a material soul, failing to distinguish between word and reality. Here I ask my readers not to be too hasty to refute what I have said, which I hope they will refrain from doing provided that they pay close attention to the examples, and also to what follows.

ˣ Although I seem to infer this from experience, and someone may deny its cogency because no proof is attached, he may take this if he wants one. Since there can be nothing in Nature contrary to her laws and all things happen in accordance with her fixed laws, so that definite effects are produced

is by its own nature true, when the mind attends to it so as to understand it, and begins to deduce from it in proper order the conclusions that follow from it, it will proceed smoothly without any interruption — just as we have seen that, in the case of the false fiction just mentioned, the intellect immediately applied itself to exposing its absurdity and the absurdities that follow from it.

62   We need therefore be in no way apprehensive about engaging in fiction provided that we clearly and distinctly perceive what is really the case. If we were perchance to say that men are suddenly changed into beasts, this is a statement of a very general kind, such that there would be in the mind no conception, that is, no idea or connection of subject with predicate. For if there were such, the mind would at that time see the means and causes, the 'how' and the 'why' such a thing took place. Then again, no attention is given to the nature of the subject and predicate.

63   Furthermore, provided that the first idea is not fictitious and all the other ideas are deduced from it, the hasty tendency to form fictitious ideas will gradually disappear. Then again, since a fictitious idea cannot be clear and distinct but only confused, and since all confusion arises from mind's having only partial knowledge of a complete whole or a unity composed of many constituents — failing to distinguish between the known and the unknown, and also attending at the same time without any distinction to the many constituents contained in a single thing — it follows, first, that if the idea is of a thing completely simple, it can only be clear and distinct. For such a thing would have to be known not in part, but

64   either wholly or not at all. Secondly, it follows that if a thing composed of many constituents is divided in thought into all its simplest parts, and attention is given to each part separately, then all confusion will disappear. Thirdly, it follows that a fictitious idea cannot be simple, but is formed by the blending of various confused ideas of various things and actions existing in Nature; or, as better expressed, fiction results from attending at the same time, without assent, to various ideas of this kind.[y] For if fiction were simple, it would be clear and distinct, and consequently true. And if it were formed from the blending of distinct ideas, their composition would also be clear and distinct, and therefore true. For example, once we know the nature of a circle and also that of a square, we cannot compound the two and make a square circle, or a square soul and the like.

65   Let us then once more sum up briefly and see why we need in no way fear that fiction may be confused with true ideas. For as to the first case we mentioned earlier, i.e., when a thing is clearly conceived, we saw that if the thing which is clearly conceived, and also its existence, is in itself an eternal truth, we cannot engage in any fiction regarding such a thing. But if the existence of the thing conceived is not an eternal truth, we need only to ensure that the existence of the thing is

---

by definite laws in unalterable sequence, it follows that when the soul conceives a thing truly, it will proceed to produce in thought those same effects. See below, where I discuss the false idea.

[y] Fiction, considered in itself, does not much differ from dreaming, except that those causes which their senses present to the waking, from which they infer that those presentations are not presented at that time by things external to them, are not presented in dreaming. Now error, as will soon be manifest, is dreaming while awake, and if it reaches a certain pitch, it is called madness.

compared with its essence, while at the same time attending to the order of Nature. As to the second case of fiction, which we said to consist in attending simultaneously, without assenting, to various confused ideas of various things and actions existing in Nature, we again saw that a completely simple thing cannot be the object of fiction, but only of intellect. And the same is true of a composite thing provided we attend to its simplest component parts. Indeed, these things cannot be the subject of fiction involving any actions that are not true, for at the same time we shall be compelled to consider how and why such a thing came about.

With these matters thus understood, let us now pass on to the investigation of   66
the false idea so as to see with what it is concerned, and how we may guard ourselves against falling into false perceptions. Neither of these objectives will now afford us any difficulty after our investigation of the fictitious idea. For between these ideas there is no difference except that the false idea implies assent; that is (as we have already noted), while the ideas are presented to the mind, there are no causes presented from which it can infer (as in the case of fiction) that they do not arise from things extraneous. It is practically the same as dreaming with one's eyes open or while wide awake. Therefore the false idea is like the fictitious idea in that it is concerned with, or (as better expressed) has reference to, the existence of a thing whose essence is known, or it is concerned with an essence.

The false idea that has reference to existence is emended in the same way as the   67
fictitious idea. For if the nature of the known thing implies necessary existence, we cannot possibly be deceived regarding the existence of that thing. If the existence of the thing is not an eternal truth (as is its essence) and the necessity or impossibility of its existence depends on external causes, then follow the same course which we indicated in our discussion of fiction, for it can be emended in the same way.

As for the kind of false idea that is related to essences, and also to actions, such   68
perceptions are necessarily always confused, being compounded of various confused perceptions of things existing in Nature, as when men are convinced that divinities are present in woods, in images, in animals and other things, that there are bodies whose mere composition gives rise to intelligence, that corpses can reason, walk and speak, that God can be deceived, and the like. But ideas which are clear and distinct can never be false; for ideas of things which are clearly and distinctly conceived either are absolutely simple or are compounded of absolutely simple ideas—that is, deduced from absolutely simple ideas. But that an absolutely simple idea cannot be false is obvious to everyone, provided that he knows what is truth or understanding, and likewise what is falsity.

As to what constitutes the specific character of truth, it is certain that a true   69
thought is distinguishable from a false thought not merely by its extrinsic relation but more particularly by an intrinsic characteristic. If an architect conceives a building in proper fashion, although such a building has never existed nor is ever likely to exist, his thought is nevertheless a true thought, and the thought is the same whether the building exists or not. On the other hand, if someone says, for example, that Peter exists, while yet not knowing that Peter exists, that thought in respect to the speaker is false, or, if you prefer, not true, although Peter really exists. The statement 'Peter exists' is true only in respect of one who knows for certain that Peter exists.

70   Hence it follows that there is something real in ideas through which the true are distinguished from the false, and this must now be the subject of our inquiry so that we may possess the best standard of truth (for we have said that we ought to determine our thoughts according to the standard of a given true idea, and method consists in reflexive knowledge) and may get to know the properties of the intellect. Nor must we say that the difference between true and false ideas derives from the fact that a true thought is to know things through their first causes— wherein it would indeed be very different from a false thought as we have explained it above. For a thought is also said to be true when it involves as its object the essence of some basic principle which is uncaused and is known through itself and in itself.

71   Therefore the specific character of a true thought must be intrinsic to the thought itself without reference to other thoughts. Nor does it acknowledge its object as cause, but must depend on the very power and nature of the intellect. For let us suppose that the intellect has perceived some new entity which has never existed, as some conceive the intellect of God before he created things (a perception which obviously could not have arisen from any object), and that from such a perception it deduces other perceptions in logical order. All those thoughts would be true and would not be determined by any external object, but would depend entirely on the power and nature of the intellect. Therefore that which constitutes the specific character of a true thought must be sought in that very same thought and deduced from the nature of intellect.

72   So to investigate this question, let us set before us a true idea whose object we are absolutely certain depends on our power of thought, there being no object to it in Nature; for such an idea, as is clear from what has been said, will more easily enable us to pursue the enquiry we have in view. For example, to form the concept of a sphere, I invent a cause at will, namely, that a semicircle rotates about its centre, and a sphere, as it were, is produced by this rotation. Now this is, of course, a true idea, and although we know that in Nature no sphere has ever been produced in this way, this is nevertheless a true perception and a very convenient way of forming the concept of a sphere. Now, we should observe that this perception affirms that a semicircle rotates, an affirmation that would be false were it not conjoined with the concept of a sphere, or else with a cause determining such motion; that is, in short, if this were a completely isolated affirmation. For in that case the mind would not be extending its affirmation to anything beyond the motion of the semicircle, and neither is this contained in the concept of a semicircle nor does it originate from the conception of a cause determining the motion. Therefore the falsity consists solely in this, that something is affirmed of a thing when it is not contained in the conception we have formed of the thing, as in this case motion or rest is affirmed of the semicircle. Hence it follows that simple thoughts are bound to be true, such as the simple idea of a semicircle, of motion, of quantity, and so on. Whatever of affirmation is contained in these thoughts is coextensive with their concept, and extends no further. Therefore we may form simple ideas at will without any danger of error.

It remains, then, only to inquire by what power the mind can form these sim- 73
ple ideas, and what is the extent of this power; for once this is discovered we shall
easily see what is the highest knowledge we can attain. It is certain that this power
of the mind does not extend to infinity; for when we affirm of a thing something
that is not contained in the concept we form of the thing, this indicates that our
perception is defective, or in other words that we have thoughts or ideas that are,
as it were, mutilated and fragmentary. For we saw that the motion of the semicircle is false when taken in isolation, but true if it is conjoined with the concept of
a sphere, or the concept of some cause determining such motion. Now if it is in
the nature of a thinking being, as seems apparently to be the case, to form true or
adequate thoughts, it is certain that inadequate ideas arise in us from this, that we
are part of some thinking being, some of whose thoughts constitute our mind in
their entirety, and some only in part.

But we have yet to consider another case, which was not worth raising when 74
dealing with fiction, and wherein one can go far astray. This happens when certain things presented in the imagination are also in the intellect; that is, are clearly
and distinctly conceived. For then, when the distinct is not differentiated from the
confused, the result is that certainty, i.e., a true idea, is mixed up with the nondis-
tinct. For example, certain Stoics perhaps heard the word 'soul,' and also that it is
immortal, which things they imagined only confusedly. They also imagined, and
at the same time understood, that the most subtle bodies penetrate all other bodies and are penetrated by none. Since all these things were presented together in
the imagination and were accompanied by the certainty of this axiom, they forthwith became convinced that the mind consists of those most subtle bodies, that
those most subtle bodies cannot be divided, and so on.

But we are delivered from this error, too, as long as we make an effort to ex- 75
amine all our perceptions according to the standard of a given true idea, being on
our guard, as we initially said, against those perceptions that we have from hearsay
or from casual experience. In addition, this kind of mistake arises from their conceiving things in too abstract a way; for it is sufficiently clear in itself that what I
conceive in its true object I cannot apply to any other object. Finally, this mistake
also arises from their failure to understand the primary elements of Nature as a
whole, so that, proceeding without due order and confusing Nature with abstractions (although these are true axioms), they fall into confusion and distort the order of Nature. However, if we proceed with the least possible abstraction and
begin at the earliest stage from the primary elements—that is, from the source
and origin of Nature—we need in no way fear this kind of mistake.

As for our knowledge of the origin of Nature, we need have no fear of confus- 76
ing it with abstractions. For when things are conceived in an abstract way (as is
the case with all universals), they always have a wider extension in the intellect
than is really possessed by their particular exemplifications existing in Nature.
Again, since there are many things in Nature whose difference is so slight as to be
hardly perceptible to the intellect, it can easily come about that they are confused
if they are conceived in an abstract way. But since, as we shall later see, the origin

of Nature can neither be conceived in an abstract or universal way, nor can it have a wider extension in the intellect than in reality, nor has it any resemblance to things mutable, we need fear no confusion as to its idea, provided we possess the standard of truth as before shown. For this entity is unique and infinite;[z] that is, it is total being, beyond which there is no being.[a]

77   So much for the false idea. It remains for us to enquire into the doubtful idea, that is, to consider what are the things that can lead us to doubt, and also how that doubt may be removed. I am speaking of genuine doubt in the mind, not the sort of doubt that we frequently encounter when somebody verbally asserts that he doubts, although he mentally does not doubt. The correction of the latter is not the province of our method; rather does it pertain to an enquiry into obstinacy and its emendation.

78   Doubt, then, never arises in the soul through the thing itself which is the object of doubt. That is, if there should be only one idea in our consciousness, whether true or false, there will be neither doubt nor certainty, but only a certain kind of awareness. For an idea in itself is nothing but a certain awareness. Doubt arises through another idea, which is not so clear and distinct that we can infer from it any certainty as to the thing which is doubted. That is, the idea which causes us to doubt is not clear and distinct. For example, if someone has never been led, whether by experience or in any other way, to reflect upon the deceptiveness of the senses, he will never entertain doubt as to whether the sun is greater or smaller than it appears. Hence country folk are frequently surprised when they hear that the sun is much greater than the earth's sphere. But reflection on the deceptiveness of the senses induces doubt.[b] If, after being in doubt, a man acquires true knowledge of the senses and of the manner whereby through their means distant things are represented, then the doubt is in turn removed.

79   Hence it follows that it is only when we do not have a clear and distinct idea of God that we can cast doubt on our true ideas on the grounds of the possible existence of some deceiving God who misleads us even in things most certain. That is, this can happen only if, attending to the knowledge we have of the origin of all things, we find nothing there to convince us that he is not a deceiver, with the same conviction that we have when, attending to the nature of a triangle, we find that its three angles are equal to two right angles. But if we do possess such knowledge of God as we have of a triangle, all doubt is removed. And just as we can attain such knowledge of a triangle although not knowing for sure whether some arch-deceiver is misleading us, so too can we attain such knowledge of God although not knowing for sure whether there is some arch-deceiver. Provided we

---

[z] These are not attributes of God, displaying his essence, as I shall make clear in my Philosophy.

[a] This has already been demonstrated above. For is such a being did not exist, it could never be produced, and so the mind could understand more than Nature could furnish, which has been shown above to be false.

[b] That is to say, a man knows that the senses have sometimes deceived him, but he knows this only confusedly, for he does not know in what way the senses deceive him.

have that knowledge, it will suffice, as I have said, to remove all doubt that we may have concerning clear and distinct ideas.

Furthermore, if anyone follows the correct procedure, investigating first what should be first investigated without any interruption in the interconnection of things, and if he knows how to define problems precisely before seeking to solve them, he will never have anything but the most certain ideas, that is, clear and distinct ideas. For doubt is nothing but the suspension of judgment in respect of some affirmation or denial which would be made but that something comes to mind which, being outside our understanding, must render imperfect our knowledge of the thing in question. We may therefore conclude that doubt always arises from want of order in the investigation. 80

These are the matters which I promised to set forth in this first part of our Method. But to omit nothing that can advance our knowledge of the intellect and its powers, I shall add a few words on memory and forgetting. Here the most important point to be considered is that memory is strengthened both by the aid of the intellect and also without its aid. As to the first case, the more intelligible a thing is, the more easily it is retained; the less intelligible, the more easily it is forgotten. For example, if I give someone a list of unconnected words, he will find it much more difficult to retain them than if I were to give him the same words in the form of a story. 81

It is also strengthened without the aid of the intellect, namely, through the force wherewith the imagination, or what is termed the common sense, is affected by some singular corporeal thing. I say 'singular,' for the imagination is affected by singular things only. For example, if someone reads just one love story, he will retain it very well as long as he does not read many others of the same kind, for then it flourishes alone in his imagination. But if he reads several of the same kind, he will imagine them all together, and they will easily be confused. I say 'corporeal,' for the imagination is affected only by bodies. Since, then, the memory is strengthened not only by the intellect but also independently of the intellect, we may conclude that it is something different from the intellect, and that the intellect considered in itself does not involve either memory or forgetting. 82

What, then, is memory? It is nothing but the sensation of impressions in the brain together with the thought of the determinate duration^c of the sensation. This is further demonstrated by recollection, for in this the soul thinks of that sensation, but without the notion of a continuous duration; and thus the idea of that sensation is not identical with the duration of the sensation, that is, with memory itself. The question as to whether the ideas themselves undergo some corruption will be discussed in my Philosophy. 83

---

c But if the duration is indeterminate, the memory of the thing is imperfect, as each of us seems also to have learned naturally. For it often happens that, to confirm our belief in what someone is telling us, we ask when and where it occurred. And although ideas, too, have their own duration in the mind, since we are accustomed to determine duration with the help of some measure of motion which also involves the imagination, we still do not see in memory anything which appertains solely to the mind.

If this seems quite absurd to anyone, it will be enough for our purpose that he should reflect that, the more singular a thing is, the more easily it is retained, as is evident from the example of the comedy just mentioned. And again, the more intelligible a thing is, the more easily it is retained. Hence we cannot fail to retain a thing that is most singular and sufficiently intelligible.

84   Thus we have distinguished between the true idea and other perceptions, and we have established that the fictitious, the false, and other ideas have their origin in the imagination, that is, in certain sensations that are (so to speak) fortuitous and unconnected, arising not from the power of the mind but from external causes, in accordance as the body, dreaming or waking, receives various motions. Or if you wish, you may here understand by imagination whatever you please, as long as it is something different from the intellect, and the soul has a passive relation to it. It matters not how you understand it, now that we know that it is something random, and that the soul is passive to it, while we also know how we may be delivered from it with the aid of the intellect. And so let no one be surprised that, without as yet having proved that there is such a thing as body and other important matters, I speak of the imagination, the body, and its constitution. For, as I have said, it matters not how I understand it, now that I know that it is something random, and so on.

85   But we have demonstrated that a true idea is simple or compounded of simple ideas, and that it shows how and why something is the case, or has been so, and that its ideal effects in the soul correspond to the specific reality of its object. This is identical with the saying of the ancients that true science proceeds from cause to effect, except that, as far as I know, they never conceived the soul, as we are here doing, as acting according to fixed laws, a sort of spiritual automaton.

86   From these demonstrations, as far as was possible in the initial stages of our enquiry, we have acquired knowledge of our intellect, and such a standard of the true idea that we no longer fear we may confuse true ideas with false or fictitious ideas. Nor again will we wonder why we understand some things that do not in any way fall within the scope of the imagination, and why there are in the imagination some things that are completely opposed to the intellect, while there are other things which agree with the intellect. For we know that the operations by which imaginings are produced are subject to other laws which are quite different from the laws of the intellect, and that in relation to imagining, the soul has only a passive rôle.

87   From this we may also see how easily those who have not made a careful distinction between imagination and intellection may fall into grave errors, such as, for instance, that extension must be localised, that it must be finite, that its parts are really distinct from one another, that it is the first and only foundation of all things, that it occupies more space at one time than at another, and many other beliefs of this kind, all of which are completely opposed to truth, as we shall demonstrate in its proper place.

88   Then again, since words are a part of the imagination—that is, since many of our concepts are formed according to the haphazard composition of words in memory from some disposition of the body—there can be no doubt that words

no less than imagination can bring about many grave errors unless we exercise great caution in that respect. Add to this that words owe their formation to the whim and understanding of the common people, so that they are merely symbols of things as they are in the imagination, not in the intellect. This is evident from the fact that men have often devised negative terms for all those things that are only in the intellect and not in the imagination (e.g., incorporeal, infinite, etc.), and they also express negatively many things that are really affirmative, and conversely (e.g., uncreated, independent, infinite, immortal, etc.).[d] The reason for this is that the contraries of these words are much more easily imagined, and so they occurred first to the early generations, and they used them as positive terms.

Furthermore, we avoid another frequent cause of confusion, one that prevents the intellect from reflecting on itself; viz., by failing to distinguish between imagination and intellection, we think that the things we more easily imagine are clearer to us, and we think that we understand what we imagine. Thus we put first what should be put later, and so the true order of procedure is reversed and there can be no legitimate conclusion drawn.

To move on in turn to the second part[e] of this Method, I shall first set forth our aim in this Method, and then the means of attaining it. Our aim, then, is to have clear and distinct ideas, that is, such as originate from pure mind and not from fortuitous motions of the body. Next, so that all ideas may be subsumed under one, we shall endeavour to connect and arrange them in such a manner that our mind, as far as possible, may reproduce in thought the reality of Nature, both as to the whole and as to its parts.

As to the first point, our ultimate aim, as we have already said, requires that a thing be conceived either through its essence alone or through its proximate cause. That is, if the thing is in itself, or, as is commonly said, self-caused, then it will have to be understood solely through its essence; if the thing is not in itself and needs a cause for its existence, then it must be understood through its proximate cause. For in fact knowledge of the effect is nothing other than to acquire a more perfect knowledge of the cause.[f]

Therefore, as long as we are engaged in an enquiry into real things, it will never be permissible for us to draw a conclusion from what is abstract, and we shall take great care not to mix the things that are merely in the intellect with those things that are in reality. The most secure conclusion is to be drawn from some particular affirmative essence, i.e., from a true and legitimate definition. For, starting

89

90

91

92

93

---

d We affirm and deny many things because the nature of words, not the nature of things, suffers us to do so; and in our ignorance of the latter, we may easily take the false to be true.

e The principal rule of this part, as follows from the first part, is to review all the ideas which we discover in us as originating from pure intellect, so that they may be distinguished from those we imagine. This distinction will have to be elicited from the properties of each, that is, imagination and intellection.

f Note that this leads to the conclusion that we cannot properly understand anything of Nature without at the same time extending our knowledge of the first cause, or God.

94 from universal axioms alone, the intellect cannot descend to particulars, since axioms are of infinite extension and do not determine the intellect to contemplate one particular thing rather than another. So the correct path to discovery is to develop our thinking from the basis of some given definition, and progress will be more successful and easier as a thing is better defined. Therefore the whole of this second part of our method hinges on this alone: getting to know the conditions of a good definition, and then devising a way to discover them. I shall therefore first discuss the conditions of definition.

95 For a definition to be regarded as complete, it must explain the inmost essence of the thing, and must take care not to substitute for this any of its properties. To explicate this, passing over other examples so as not to appear bent on exposing the errors of others, I shall choose only the example of an abstract thing where the manner of definition is unimportant, a circle, say. If this is defined as a figure in which the lines drawn from the centre to the circumference are equal, it is obvious that such a definition by no means explains the essence of a circle, but only one of its properties. And although, as I have said, this is a matter of little importance when it is a question of figures and other mental constructs, it is nevertheless a matter of prime importance when it is a question of physical and real beings. For the properties of things are not understood as long as their essences are not known; and if the latter are neglected, this is bound to distort the interconnections made by our intellect which ought to reproduce the interconnections of Nature, and we shall go far astray from our goal.

96 So if we are to be delivered from this fault, the following requirements must be satisfied in definition.

1. If the thing be a created thing, the definition, as we have said, must include its proximate cause. For example, according to this rule a circle would have to be defined as follows: a figure described by any line of which one end is fixed and the other movable. This definition clearly includes the proximate cause.

2. The conception or definition of the thing must be such that all the properties of the thing, when regarded by itself and not in conjunction with other things, can be deduced from it, as can be seen in the case of this definition of a circle. For from it we clearly deduce that all the lines drawn from the centre to the circumference are equal.

That this is a necessary requirement of a definition is so self-evident to one who pays attention that it does not seem worthwhile spending time in demonstrating it, nor again in showing that according to this second requirement every definition must be affirmative. I am speaking of intellectual affirmation, disregarding verbal affirmation, which, because of poverty of language, may sometimes be expressed negatively, although understood affirmatively.

97 The requirements for the definition of an uncreated thing are as follows:

1. That it should exclude every cause; that is, that the thing should need nothing else for its explanation besides its own being.

2. That, given the definition of the thing, there should remain no room for the question: Does it exist?
3. That, as far as the mind is concerned, it should contain no substantives that can be put in adjectival form; that is, it should not be explicated through any abstractions.
4. And finally (although it is not really necessary to make this observation), it is required that all its properties can be deduced from its definition.

All these points are evident if careful attention is paid.

I have also stated that the best basis for drawing a conclusion will be a partic- 98
ular affirmative essence. For the more individualised an idea is, the more distinct it is, and therefore the clearer it is. Hence our most important task is to seek knowledge of particular things.

As to the ordering of all our perceptions and their proper arrangement and uni- 99
fication, it is required that, as soon as is possible and reason demands, we should ask whether there is a being—and also what kind of being—which is the cause of all things so that its essence represented in thought is also the cause of all our ideas. Then our mind, as we have said, will reproduce Nature as closely as possible; for it will possess in the form of thought the essence, order, and unity of Nature. Hence we can see that it is above all necessary for us always to deduce our ideas from physical things, i.e., from real beings, advancing, as far as we can, in accordance with the chain of causes from one real being to another real being, and in such a manner as never to get involved with abstractions and universals, neither inferring something real from them nor inferring them from something real. For in either case the true progress of the intellect is interrupted.

But it should be noted that by the series of causes and real beings I do not here 100
mean the series of mutable particular things, but only the series of fixed and eternal things. It would be impossible for human limitation to grasp the series of mutable particular things, not only because they are innumerable but also because of the infinite number of factors affecting one and the same thing, each of which can be the cause of the existence or nonexistence of the thing. For the existence of mutable particular things has no connection with their essence; that is (as we have said), their existence is not an eternal truth.

But neither is there any need for us to understand their series. For the essences 101
of particular mutable things are not to be elicited from their series or order of existing, which would furnish us with nothing but their extrinsic characteristics, their relations, or, at the most, their circumstances. All these are far from the inmost essence of things. This essence is to be sought only from the fixed and eternal things, and at the same time from the laws inscribed in these things as in their true codes, which govern the coming into existence and the ordering of all particular things. Indeed, these mutable particular things depend so intimately and essentially (so to phrase it) on the fixed things that they can neither be nor be conceived without them. Hence, although these fixed and eternal things are singular, by reason of their omnipresence and wide-ranging power they will be to us like universals, i.e., the genera of the definitions of particular mutable things, and the proximate causes of all things.

102   But this being so, there appears to be no small difficulty to surmount before we can arrive at the knowledge of these particular things. For to conceive them all at once is a task far beyond the powers of the human intellect. And, as we have said, the order wherein one thing may be understood before another is not to be sought from their position in the series of existing, nor again from eternal things. For in the latter case all these things are by nature simultaneous. Therefore we must resort to other aids apart from those employed in understanding the eternal things and their laws. However, this is not the appropriate place to give an account of those aids, nor do we need to do so until we have acquired a sufficient knowledge of the eternal things and their infallible laws, and have gained an understanding of the nature of our senses.

103   Before we embark upon an enquiry into our knowledge of particular things, it will be timely for us to treat of those aids, all of which will serve to assist us in knowing how to use our senses and to conduct experiments under fixed rules and proper arrangement, such as will suffice to determine the thing which is the object of our enquiry. From these we may finally infer what are the laws of eternal things that govern the thing's production, and may gain an insight into its inmost nature, as I shall duly show. Here, to return to our theme, I shall confine my efforts to setting forth what seems necessary to enable us to attain to knowledge of eternal things, and to frame their definitions on the terms previously explained.

104   To achieve this, we must recall what we said earlier, namely, that when the mind attends to some thought so as to examine it and to deduce from it in proper order what can legitimately be deduced, if it is false, the mind will detect its falsity; but if it is true, the mind will proceed fruitfully without interruption to deduce truths from it. This, I say, is what our purpose requires. For our thoughts cannot be determined on any other foundation.

105   If, therefore, we wish to investigate the first of all things, there has to be some foundation which may direct our thoughts there. Next, since method is reflexive knowledge itself, the foundation which is to give direction to our thoughts can be nothing other than knowledge of what constitutes the specific reality of truth, and knowledge of the intellect, its properties and powers. For when this is acquired, we shall have a foundation from which we shall deduce our thoughts, and a path by which the intellect, according to its capacity, may attain knowledge of eternal things, taking into account, of course, the powers of the intellect.

106   But if, as has been demonstrated in the first part, it pertains to the nature of thought to form true ideas, we must here enquire what we understand by the faculties and power of the intellect. Now since the chief part of our Method is to achieve a good understanding of the powers of the intellect and its nature, we are necessarily constrained (through considerations set out in this second part of our

107   Method) to deduce these simply from the definition of thought and intellect. But so far we have not had any rules for finding definitions; and since we cannot treat of these rules without knowing the nature or definition of the intellect and its power, it follows that either the definition of the intellect must be self-evident or we cannot understand anything. But that definition is not absolutely self-evident.

Nevertheless, since its properties—like everything we have from the intellect—can be clearly and distinctly perceived only if their nature is known, the definition of intellect will become self-evident if we attend to its properties that we do understand clearly and distinctly. So let us here enumerate the properties of the intellect, consider them, and begin a discussion of our innate tools.[g]

The properties of the intellect which I have chiefly noted and clearly understand are as follows: 108

1. That it involves certainty; that is, it knows that things are in reality as they are contained in the intellect in the form of thought.

2. That it perceives some things, or forms some ideas, independently, and some ideas it forms from other ideas. To wit, it forms the idea of quantity independently without attending to other thoughts, but it forms ideas of motion only by attending to the idea of quantity.

3. The ideas that it forms independently express infinity, but determinate ideas are formed from other ideas. For if it perceives the idea of a quantity through a cause, then it determines that idea through the idea of a quantity, as when it perceives that a body is formed from the motion of a plane, a plane from the motion of a line, and a line from the motion of a point. These perceptions do not serve for the understanding of quantity, but only to determine it. This is evident from the fact that we conceive these quantities as formed, as it were, from motion, whereas motion is not perceived unless quantity is perceived; and again we can prolong the motion to form a line of infinite extent, which we could not do if we did not possess the idea of infinite quantity.

4. It forms positive ideas before negative ones.

5. It perceives things not so much under duration as under some form of eternity, and as being of infinite number. Or rather, in its perception of things, it attends neither to number nor duration. But when it imagines things, it perceives them as being of fixed number, with determinate duration and quantity.

6. The clear and distinct ideas that we form seem to follow solely from the necessity of our nature in such a way as to seem to depend absolutely on our power alone. But with confused ideas the contrary is the case; they are often formed without our consent.

7. There are many ways in which the mind can determine the ideas that the intellect forms from other ideas. For example, to determine the plane of an ellipse, the mind supposes that a pencil attached to a string moves about two centres, or alternatively it conceives an infinite number of points always maintaining the same fixed relation to a given straight line, or a cone cut in an oblique plane so that the angle of inclination is greater than the angle at the vertex of the cone. There are innumerable other ways.

---

[g] See above, section 31.

8. Ideas are the more perfect as they express a greater degree of perfection of an object. For we do not admire the architect who has designed a chapel as much as one who has designed a splendid temple.

109   Other things that are referred to thought, such as love, joy, and so on, I shall not pause to consider; for they are neither relevant to our purpose, nor again can they be conceived unless the intellect is perceived. For if perception is entirely removed, all these are removed.

110   False and fictitious ideas have nothing positive (as we have abundantly shown) through which they are called false or fictitious; they are considered as such only from the defectiveness of our knowledge. Therefore false and fictitious ideas, as such, can teach us nothing concerning the essence of thought; this is to be sought from those positive properties just reviewed. That is, we must now establish some common basis from which these properties necessarily follow; a basis which, when given, necessarily entails these properties, and which, when removed, removes them all.

The rest is lacking.

SHORT TREATISE ON GOD, MAN, AND HIS WELL-BEING

The Short Treatise on God, Man, and His Well-Being *is the second work of Spinoza's early period. It was probably in hand by 1662. At the end of a long letter to Henry Oldenburg, largely taken up with Spinoza's comments on scientific points in a recent book by Robert Boyle, Spinoza refers to a "short work" that he has written on the question of the origin of things and a first cause; the letter (Ep6) was written in early 1662. In addition, there is a reference to a "certain Dutch writing" that speaks of God as the whole universe, written by a Cartesian associated with Van den Enden, among others, in the journal of a Danish visitor to the Low Countries, Olaus Borch; the journal entry is for 3 April 1662. It is tempting to take this Dutch work to be the* Short Treatise, *the only work of Spinoza's written in Dutch. Some scholars also conjecture that the two Dutch versions of the* Short Treatise *are translations of an original Latin text by Spinoza, now lost.*

By 1662, then, Spinoza had sketched the main lines of the new view—his "philosophy"—about God, the human mind, and nature that he had referred to in the TIE. By this time, he had moved from Amsterdam to Rijnsburg, a small village just outside of Leiden, and enjoyed its relative solitude. Rijnsburg was known for its tolerance, and it was close to the university, where he had met friends and folk of common spirit, Adriaan Koerbagh among them. The Short Treatise, *begun in Amsterdam, was continued in this new environment. It is the work of a devoted student of the Cartesian philosophy who was, at the same time, striking out on his own paths.*

The structure of Spinoza's Ethics *is already suggested in the* Short Treatise. *It begins with metaphysics and theology, turns to epistemology and psychology, and ends with ethics and religion. More precisely, Spinoza begins by proving God's existence, eventually discusses the roles of the senses, reason, and the passions in human conduct, and concludes with a eulogy to the life devoted to the love of God, to knowing God and achieving a comprehensive scientific-philosophical understanding of Nature. Like the earlier TIE, the core of the* Short Treatise *is an ancient commitment to the life of* eudaimonia, *an intellectual life that satisfied the scriptural mandate to* imitatio dei *and the philosophical-Stoic desire for harmonious, natural living. But if the structure is traditionally classical, the core that unites Spinoza's classicism with his biblical affinities is the commitment to the identity of God and Nature. Virtually all that is novel in the* Short Treatise *flows from or at least circulates around this deep belief.*

Still the treatise leaves this commitment insufficiently grounded, and Spinoza came to realize this deficiency. Central to his naturalism, to his denial of free will, to his account of human emotions and action, the identity of God with Nature is a strong and determinative principle. It demanded justification and clarification beyond what it received, as did other claims, like the account of the difference between thought and extension and hence of the relation between mind and body. The overall character of Spinoza's understanding of religion, metaphysics, nature, and ethics had taken shape, but its fine lineaments needed elaboration. The project occupied him in the quiet of Rijnsburg and the company of friends and colleagues.

We include in this volume the First Book of the Short Treatise.

M.L.M.

CONTENTS

THE FIRST BOOK

Treating of God and What Pertains to Him, Contains the Following Chapters

FIRST PART
On God

CHAPTER I
That God Exists

As regards the first, namely, whether there is a God, this, we say, can be proved.

I. In the first place, a priori thus:

  1. Whatever we clearly and distinctly know to belong to the nature[1] of a thing, we can also truly affirm of that thing. Now we can know clearly and distinctly that existence belongs to the nature of God;

  Therefore . . .

  Otherwise also thus:

  2. The essence of things are from all eternity, and unto all eternity shall remain immutable;

  The existence of God is essence;

  Therefore . . .

II. A posteriori, thus:

  If man has an idea of God, then God[2] must exist *formaliter*;

  Now, man has an idea of God;

  Therefore . . .

The first we prove thus:

  If there is an idea of God, then the cause thereof must exist *formaliter*, and contain in itself all that the idea has *objective*;

  Now there is an idea of God;

  Therefore . . .

Spinoza's notes are indicated by numerals. Notes indicated by letters and enclosed in brackets are those of translator A. Wolf (main annotator for this work) and Michael L. Morgan.

[1] Understand the definite nature through which a thing is what it is, and which can by no means be removed from it without at the same time destroying that thing: thus, for instance, it belongs to the essence of a mountain that it should have a valley, or the essence of a mountain is that it has a valley; this is truly eternal and immutable, and must always be included in the concept of a mountain, even if it never existed, or did not exist now.

[2] From the definition which follows in chapter 2, namely, that God has infinite attributes, we can prove his existence thus: Whatever we clearly and distinctly see to belong to the nature of a thing, that we can also with truth affirm of that thing; now to the nature of a being that has infinite attributes belongs existence, which is an attribute; therefore . . . To assert that this may well be affirmed of the idea, but not of the thing itself, is false: for the Idea does not really consist of the attribute which belongs to this being, so that that which is affirmed is [affirmed] neither of the thing, nor of that which is affirmed of the thing; so that there is a great difference between the Idea and the *Ideatum*: therefore what is affirmed of the thing is not affirmed of the Idea, and vice versa.

In order to prove the first part of this argument we state the following principles, namely:

1. That the number of knowable things is infinite;
2. That a finite understanding cannot apprehend the infinite;
3. That a finite understanding, unless it is determined by something external, cannot through itself know anything; because, just as it has no power to know all things equally, so little also has it the power to begin or to commence to know this, for instance, sooner than that, or that sooner than this. Since, then, it can do neither the one nor the other it can know nothing.

The first (or the major premiss) is proved thus:

If the imagination of man were the sole cause of his ideas, then it would be impossible that he should be able to apprehend anything, but he can apprehend something;
Therefore . . .

The first[a] is proved by the first principle, namely, *that the knowable things are infinitely numerous.* Also, following the second principle, man cannot know all, because the human understanding is finite, and if not determined by external things to know this sooner than that, and that sooner than this, then according to the third principle it should be impossible for it to know anything.[3]

---

[a] [Instead of this paragraph B has the following: "Again, since according to the first principle the knowable things are infinite, and according to the second principle the finite understanding cannot comprehend everything, and according to the third principle it has not the power to know this sooner than that, and that sooner than this, it would be impossible for it to know anything, if it were not determined thereto by external things. —A.W.]

[3] Further, to say that this idea is a fiction, this also is false: for it is impossible to have this [idea] if it [the *ideatum*] does not exist; this is shown on pages 37–8, and we also add the following:

It is quite true that when an idea has first come to us from a particular thing, and we have generalised it *in abstracto*, then our understanding may fancy various things about it, and we can add to it many other attributes abstracted from other things. But it is impossible to do this without a prior knowledge of the things themselves from which these abstractions have been made. Once, however, it is assumed that this idea [of God] is a fiction, then all *other ideas* that we have must be fictions no less. If this is so, *whence* comes it that we find such a great difference among them? For as regards *some* we see that it is impossible they should exist; e.g., all monsters supposed to be composed of two natures, such as an animal that should be both a bird and a horse, and the like, for which it is impossible to have a place in Nature, which we find differently constituted; *other ideas* may, but need not, exist; whether, however, they exist or do not exist, their essence is always necessary; such is the idea of a triangle, and that of the love in the soul apart from the body, etc.; so that even if I at first thought that I had imagined these, I am nevertheless compelled afterwards to say that they are, and would be, the same no less even if neither I nor anybody had ever thought about them. They are, consequently, not merely imagined by me, and must also have outside me a *subjectum* other than myself, without which *subjectum* they cannot be. In addition to these there is yet *a third idea*, and it is an only one; this one carries with it necessary existence, and not, like the foregoing, the mere possibility of existence: for, in the case of those, their essence was indeed necessary, but not their existence, while in its case, both its existence and its essence are necessary, and it is nothing without them. I therefore see now that the truth, essence, or existence of anything never depends on

From all this the second point is proved, namely, *that the cause of a man's ideas is not his imagination but some external cause, which compels him to apprehend one thing sooner than another,* and it is no other than this, that the things whose *essentia objectiva* is in his understanding exist *formaliter,* and are nearer to him than other things. If, then, man has the idea of God, it is clear that God must exist *formaliter,* though not *eminenter,* as there is nothing more real or more excellent beside or outside him. Now, that man has the idea of God, this is clear, because he knows his attributes,[4] which attributes cannot be derived from [man] himself, because he is imperfect. And that he knows these attributes is evident from this, namely, that he knows that the infinite cannot be obtained by putting together divers finite parts; that there cannot be two infinites, but *only one;* that it is perfect and immutable, for we know that nothing seeks, of itself, its own annihilation, and also that it cannot change into anything better,[5] because it is perfect, which it would not be in that case, or also that such a being cannot be subjected to anything outside it, since it is omnipotent, and so forth.

From all this, then, it follows clearly that we can prove both a priori and a posteriori that God exists. Better, indeed, a priori. For things which are proved in the latter way [a posteriori] must be proved through their external causes, which is a

---

me: for, as was shown with reference to the second kind of ideas, they are what they are independently of me, whether as regards their essence alone, or as regards both essence and existence. I find this to be true also, indeed much more so, of this third unique idea; not only does it not depend on me, but on the contrary, he alone must be the *subjectum* of that which I affirm of him. Consequently, if he did not exist, I should not be able to assert anything at all about him; although this can be done in the case of other things, even when they do not exist. He must also be, indeed, the *subjectum* of all other things.

From what has been said so far it is clearly manifest that the idea of infinite attributes in the perfect being is no fiction; we shall, however, still add the following:

According to the foregoing consideration of Nature, we have so far not been able to discover more than two attributes only which belong to this all-perfect being. And these give us nothing adequate to satisfy us that this is all of which this perfect being consists, quite the contrary, we find in us *a something* which openly tells us not only of more, but of infinite perfect attributes, which must belong to this perfect being before he can be said to be perfect. And whence comes this idea of perfection? This *something* cannot be the outcome of these two [attributes]: for two can only yield two, and not an infinity. Whence then? From myself, never; else I must be able to give what I did not possess. Whence, then, but from the infinite attributes themselves which tell us *that* they are, without however telling us, at the same time, *what* they are: for only of two do we know what they are.

4 *His attributes;* it is better [to say], because he knows what is proper to God; for these things [infinity, perfection, etc.] are no attributes of God. Without these, indeed, God could not be God, but it is not through them [that he is God], since they show nothing substantial, but are only like adjectives which require substantives or their explanation.

5 The cause of this change would have to be either outside, or in it. It cannot be outside, because no substance which, like this, exists through itself depends on anything outside it; therefore it is not *subject to change through it.* Nor can it be in it: because no thing, much less this, desires its own undoing; all undoing comes from outside.[b]

b [Again, that there can be no finite substance is clear from this, because in that case it would necessarily have to have something which it had from nothing: which is impossible; for whence has it that wherein it differs from God? Certainly not from God; for he has nothing imperfect or finite, etc.: whence, therefore, but from nothing? (in B)] manifest imperfection in them, inasmuch as they cannot make themselves known through themselves, but only through external causes. God, however, who is the first cause of all things, and also the cause of himself [*causa sui*], makes himself known through himself. Hence one need not attach much importance to the saying of Thomas Aquinas, namely, that God could not be proved a priori because he, forsooth, has no cause.

CHAPTER II
What God Is

Now that we have proved above *that* God is, it is time to show *what* he is. Namely, we say that he is *a being of whom all or infinite attributes are predicated,*[6] *of which attributes every one is infinitely perfect in its kind.* Now, in order to express our views clearly, we shall premise the four following propositions:

1. That there is no finite substance,[7] but that every substance must be infinitely perfect in its kind, that is to say, that in the infinite understanding of God no substance can be more perfect than that which already exists in Nature.
2. That there are not two like substances.
3. That one substance cannot produce another.

---

[6] The reason is this, since *Nothing* can have no attributes, the *All* must have all attributes; and just as *Nothing* has no attribute because it is Nothing, so that which is *Something* has attributes because it is *Something.* Hence, the more it is Something, the more attributes it must have, and consequently God being the most perfect, and all that is Anything, he must also have infinite, perfect, and all attributes.

[7] Once we can prove that there can be no *Finite Substance,* then all *substance* must without limitation belong to the divine being. We do it thus: 1. It must either have limited itself or *some other* must have limited it. It could not have done so itself, because having been infinite it would have had to change its whole essence. Nor can it be limited by another: for this again must be either finite or infinite; the former is impossible, therefore the latter; therefore it [i.e., the other thing] is God. He must, then, have made it finite because he lacked either the power or the will [to make it infinite]: but the first [supposition] is contrary to his omnipotence, the second is contrary to his goodness. 2. That *there can be no finite substance* is clear from this, namely, that, if so, it would necessarily have something which it would have from Nothing, which is impossible. For whence can it derive that wherein it differs from God? Certainly not from God, for he has nothing imperfect or finite, etc. So, whence then but from Nothing? Therefore there is no substance other than infinite. Whence it follows, *that there cannot be two like infinite substances;* for to posit such necessitates limitation. And from this, again, it follows *that one substance cannot produce another;* thus: The cause that we might suppose to produce this substance must have the same attribute[c] as the one produced, and also either just as much perfection or more or less. The first supposition is not possible, because there would then be two like [substances]. The second also not, because in that case there would be a finite [substance]. Nor the third, because something cannot come from nothing.—Moreover, if the finite[d] came from the infinite, then the infinite[e] would also be finite, etc. Therefore one substance can not produce another. And from this, again, it follows *that all substance must exist "formaliter,"* for if it did not exist, there would be no possibility for it to come into existence.

[c] [B: attributes.]

[d] [B: infinite.]

[e] [B: the cause.]

4. That in the infinite understanding of God there is no other substance than that which is *formaliter* in Nature.

As regards the first, namely, that there is no finite substance, etc., should any one want to maintain the opposite, we would ask the following question, namely, whether this substance is finite through itself, whether it has made itself thus finite and did not want to make itself less finite; or whether it is thus finite through its cause, which cause either could not or would not give more? The first [alternative] is not true, because it is impossible that a substance should have wanted to make itself finite, especially a substance which had come into existence through itself. Therefore, I say, it is made finite by its cause, which is necessarily God. Further, if it is finite through its cause, this must be so either because its cause could not give more, or because it would not give more. That he should not have been able to give more would contradict his omnipotence;[8] that he should not have been willing to give more, when he could well do so, savours of ill-will, which is nowise in God, who is all goodness and perfection.

As regards the second, *that there are not two like substances,* we prove this on the ground that each substance is perfect in its kind; for if there were two alike they would necessarily limit one another, and would consequently not be infinite, as we have already shown before.

As to the third, namely, *that one substance cannot produce another:* should any one again maintain the opposite, we ask whether the cause, which is supposed to produce this substance, has or has not the same attributes as the produced [substance]. The latter is impossible, because something cannot come from nothing; therefore the former. And then we ask whether in the attribute which is presumed to be the cause of this produced [substance], there is just as much perfection as in the produced substance, or less, or more. Less, we say, there cannot be, for the reasons given above. More, also not, we say, because in that case this second one would be finite, which is opposed to what has already been proved by us. Just as much, then; they are therefore alike, and are two like substances, which clearly conflicts with our previous demonstration. Further, that which is created is by no means produced from Nothing, but must necessarily have been produced from something existing. But that something should have come forth from this, and that it should nonetheless have this something even after it has issued from it, that

---

[8] To say to this *that the nature of the thing required such [limitation] and that it could not therefore be otherwise,* that is no reply: for the nature of a thing can require nothing while it does not exist. Should you say that one may, nevertheless, see what belongs to the nature of a thing which does not exist: that is true as regards its existence, but by no means as regards its essence. And herein lies the difference between *creating* and *generating.* To create is to posit a thing *quo ad essentiam et existentiam simul* [i.e., to give a thing both essence and existence]; while in the case of generation a thing comes forth *quo ad existentiam solam* [i.e., it only receives existence]. And therefore there is now in Nature no creation but only generation. So that when God creates he creates at once the nature of the thing with the thing itself. He would therefore show ill-will if (from lack of will, and not of power) he created the thing in such a way that it should not agree with its cause in essence and existence. However, what we here call creation can really not be said ever to have taken place, and it is only mentioned to indicate what we can say about it, if we distinguish between *creating* and *generating.*

we cannot grasp with our understanding. Lastly, if we would seek the cause of the substance which is the origin of the things which issue from its attribute, then it behoves us to seek also the cause of that cause, and then again the cause of that cause, *et sic in infinitum*; so that if we must necessarily stop and halt somewhere, as indeed we must, it is necessary to stop at this only substance.

As regards the fourth, *that there is no substance or attribute in the infinite understanding of God other than what exists "formaliter" in Nature*, this can be, and is, proved by us: (1) from the infinite power of God, since in him there can be no cause by which he might have been induced to create one sooner or more than another; (2) from the simplicity of his will; (3) because he cannot omit to do what is good, as we shall show afterwards; (4) because it would be impossible for that which does not now exist to come into existence, since one substance cannot produce another. And, what is more, in that case there would be more infinite substances not in existence than there are in existence, which is absurd. From all this it follows then: that of Nature all in all is predicated, and that consequently Nature consists of infinite attributes, each of which is perfect in its kind. And this is just equivalent to the definition usually given of God.

Against what we have just said, namely, that there is no thing in the infinite understanding of God but what exists *formaliter* in Nature, some want to argue in this way: If God has created all, then he can create nothing more; but that he should be able to create nothing more conflicts with his omnipotence; therefore . . .

Concerning the first, we admit that God can create nothing more. And with regard to the second, we say that we own, if God were not able to create all that could be created, then it would conflict with his omnipotence; but that is by no means the case if he cannot create what is self-contradictory; as it is, to say that he has created all, and also that he should be able to create still more. Assuredly it is a far greater perfection in God that he has created all that was in his infinite understanding than if he had not created it, or, as they say, if he had never been able to create it. But why say so much about it? Do they not themselves argue thus,[9] or must they not argue thus from God's omniscience: If God is omniscient then he can know nothing more; but that God can know nothing more is incompatible with his perfection; therefore . . . ? But if God has all in his understanding, and, owing to his infinite perfection, can know nothing more, well then, why can we not say that he has also created all that he had in his understanding, and has made it so that it exists or should exist *formaliter* in Nature?

Since, then, we know that all alike is in the infinite understanding of God, and that there is no cause why he should have created this sooner and more than that, and that he could have produced all things in a moment, so let us see, for once, whether we cannot use against them the same weapons which they take up against us; namely, thus:

If God can never create so much that he cannot create more, then he can never create what he can create; but that he cannot create what he can create is self-contradictory. Therefore . . .

---

[9] That is, whenever we make them argue from this admission, namely, *that God is omniscient*, then they cannot but argue thus.

Now the reasons why we said that all these attributes, which are in Nature, are but one single being, and by no means different things (although we can know them clearly and distinctly the one without the other, and the other without another), are these:

1. Because we have found already before that there must be an infinite and perfect being, by which nothing else can be meant than such a being of which all in all must be predicated. Why? [Because] to a being which has any essence attributes must be referred, and the more essence one ascribes to it, the more attributes also must one ascribe to it, and consequently if a being is infinite then its attributes also must be infinite, and this is just what we call a perfect^f being.

2. Because of the unity which we see everywhere in Nature. If there were different beings in it[10] then it would be impossible for them to unite with one another.

3. Because although, as we have already seen, one substance cannot produce another, and if a substance does not exist it is impossible for it to begin to exist, we see, nevertheless, that in no substance (which we nonetheless know to exist in Nature), when considered separately, is there any necessity to be real, since existence does not pertain to its separate essence.[11] So it must necessarily follow that Nature, which results from no causes, and which we nevertheless know to exist, must necessarily be a perfect being to which existence belongs.

From all that we have so far said it is evident, then, that we posit extension as an attribute of God; and this seems not at all appropriate to a perfect being: for since extension is divisible, the perfect being would have to consist of parts, and this is altogether inapplicable to God, because he is a simple being. Moreover, when extension is divided it is passive, and with God (who is never passive, and cannot be affected by any other being, because he is the first efficient cause of all) this can by no means be the case.

To this we reply: (1) that "part" and "whole" are not true or real entities, but only "things of reason," and consequently there are in Nature[12] neither whole nor

---

^f   [B: an infinite.]

10   That is, if there were different substances which were not connected in one only being, then their union would be impossible, because we see clearly that they have nothing at all in common, it is so with thought and extension of which we nevertheless consist.

11   That is, if no substance can be other than real, and yet existence does not follow from its essence, when it is considered by itself, it follows that it is not something independent, but must be something, that is, an attribute, of another thing, namely, the one, only, and universal being. Or thus: All substance is real, and when a substance is considered by itself its existence does not follow from its essence; therefore, no existing substance can be known through itself, but it must belong to something else. That is, when with our understanding we consider "substantial" Thought and ["substantial"] Extension, then we consider them only in their essence and not as existing, that is [we do not consider] that their existence necessarily pertains to their essence. When, however, we prove [of each] that it is an attribute of God, we thereby prove a priori that it exists, and a posteriori (as regards extension alone) [we prove its existence] from the modes which must necessarily have it for their *subjectum.*

12   In Nature, that is, in "substantial" Extension; for if this were divided its nature and being would be at once annihilated, as it exists only as infinite extension, or, which comes to the same, it exists only as a whole.

But should you say: is there, in extension, no part prior to all its modes? I say, certainly not. But you may say, since there is motion in matter, it must be in some part of matter, for it cannot be in

parts. (2) A thing composed of different parts must be such that the parts thereof, taken separately, can be conceived and understood one without another. Take, for instance, a clock which is composed of many different wheels, cords, and other things; in it, I say, each wheel, cord, etc., can be conceived and understood separately, without the composite whole being necessary thereto. Similarly also in the case of water, which consists of straight oblong particles, each part thereof can be conceived and understood, and can exist without the whole; but extension, being a substance, one cannot say of it that it has parts, since it can neither diminish nor increase, and no parts thereof can be understood apart, because by its nature it must be infinite. And that it must be such, follows from this, namely, because if it were not such, but consisted of parts, then it would not be infinite by its nature, as it is said to be; and it is impossible to conceive parts in an infinite nature, since by their nature all parts are finite.ʲ Add to this still: if it consisted of different parts then it should be intelligible that supposing some parts thereof to be annihilated, extention might remain all the same, and not be annihilated together with the annihilation of some of its parts; this is clearly contradictory in what is infinite by its own nature and can never be, or be conceived, as limited or finite. Further, as regards the parts in Nature, we maintain that division, as has also been said already before, never takes place in substance, but always and only in the mode of substance. Thus, if I want to divide water, I only divide the mode of substance, and not substance itself. And whether this mode is that of water or something else it is always the same.ᵏ

Division, then, or passivity, always takes place in the mode; thus when we say that man passes away or is annihilated, then this is understood to apply to man only insofar as he is such a composite being, and a mode of substance, and not the substance on which he depends.

Moreover, we have already stated, and we shall repeat it later, that outside God there is nothing at all, and that he is an *Immanent Cause*. Now, passivity, whenever

---

the whole, because this is infinite; and whither shall it be moved, when there is nothing outside it? Therefore it must be in a part. My answer is: Motion alone does not exist, but only motion and rest together; and this is in the whole, and must be in it, because there is no part in extension. Should you, however, say that there is, then tell me: if you divide the whole of extension then, as regards any part which you cut off from it in thought, can you also separate it in nature from all [other] parts; and supposing this has been done, I ask, what is there between the part cut offᵍ and the rest? You must say, a vacuum, or another body, or something of extension itself; there is no fourth possibility. The first will not do, because there is no vacuum, something positive and yet no body; nor the second, because then there would exist a mode, which cannot be, sinceʰ extension as extension is without and prior to all modes. Therefore the third; and then there is no part but only the whole of extension.ⁱ

ᵍ [B: separated.]

ʰ [B: therefore.]

ⁱ [B: but extension one and indivisible.]

ʲ [B: because all the parts would have to be infinite by their nature.]

ᵏ [B: When, therefore, I divide water I do not divide the substance, but only that mode of the substance, which substance, however, variously modified, is always the same.]

the agent and the patient are different entities, is a palpable imperfection, because the patient must necessarily be dependent on that which has caused the passivity from outside; it has, therefore, no place in God, who is perfect. Furthermore, of such an agent who acts in himself it can never be said that he has the imperfection of a patient, because he is not affected by another; such, for instance, is the case with the understanding, which, as the philosophers also assert, is the cause of its ideas, since, however, it is an immanent cause, what right has one to say that it is imperfect, howsoever frequently it is affected by itself?[1] Lastly, since substance is [the cause] and the origin of all its modes, it may with far greater right be called an agent than a patient. And with these remarks we consider all adequately answered.

It is further objected, that there must necessarily be a first cause which sets body in motion, because when at rest it is impossible for it to set itself in motion. And since it is clearly manifest that rest and motion exist in Nature, these must, they think, necessarily result from an external cause. But it is easy for us to reply to this; for we concede that, if body were a thing existing through itself, and had no other attributes than length, breadth, and depth, then, if it really rested there would be in it no cause whereby to begin to move itself; but we have already stated before *that Nature is a being of which all attributes are predicated*, and this being so, it can be lacking in nothing wherewith to produce all that there is to be produced.

Having so far discussed what God is, we shall say but a word, as it were, about his attributes: that those which are known to us consist of two only, namely, *Thought* and *Extension*; for here we speak only of attributes which might be called the *proper attributes* of God, through which we come to know him [as he is] in himself, and not [merely] as he acts [towards things] outside himself. All else, then, that men ascribe to God beyond these two attributes, all that (if it otherwise pertains to him) must be either an "extraneous denomination," such as *that he exists through himself*, is *Eternal, One, Immutable*, etc., or, I say, has reference to his activity, such as that he is a *cause, predestines*, and *rules* all things: all which are properties of God, but give us no information as to what he is. But how and in what manner these attributes can nevertheless have a place in God we shall explain in the following chapters. But, for the better understanding of this and in further exposition thereof, we have thought it well and have decided to add the following arguments consisting of a [Dialogue].

[First] Dialogue

Between the Understanding, Love, Reason, and Desire

LOVE: I see, Brother, that both my essence and perfection depend on your perfection; and since the perfection of the object which you have conceived is your perfection, while from yours again mine proceeds, so tell me now, I pray you,

---

[1] [B: And although the understanding, as the philosophers say, is a cause of its ideas, yet, since it is an immanent cause, etc.]

whether you have conceived such a being as is supremely perfect, not capable of being limited by any other, and in which I also am comprehended.

UNDERSTANDING: I for my part consider Nature only in its totality as infinite, and supremely perfect, but you, if you have any doubts about it, ask Reason, she will tell you.

REASON: To me the truth of the matter is indubitable, for if we would limit Nature then we should, absurdly enough, have to limit it with a mere Nothing;[m] we avoid this absurdity by stating that it is *One Eternal Unity, infinite, omnipotent*, etc., that is, that Nature is infinite and that all is contained therein; and the negative of this we call Nothing.

DESIRE: Ah indeed! It is wondrously congruous to suppose that *Unity* is in keeping with the *Difference* which I observe everywhere in Nature. But how? I see that thinking substance has nothing in common with *extended substance*, and that the one limits [not] the other; and if, in addition to these substances, you want to posit yet a third one which is perfect in all respects, then look how you involve yourself in manifest contradictions; for if this third one is placed outside the first two, then it is wanting in all the attributes which belong to those two, but this can never be the case with a whole outside of which there is nothing. Moreover if this being is omnipotent and perfect, then it must be such because it has made itself, and not because another has made it; that, however, which could produce both itself and yet another besides would be even more omnipotent. And lastly, if you call it omniscient then it is necessary that it should know itself; and, at the same time, you must know that the knowledge of oneself alone is less than the knowledge of oneself together with the knowledge of other substances. All these are manifest contradictions. I would, therefore, have advised Love to rest content with what I show her, and to look about for no other things.

LOVE: What now, O dishonourable one, have you shown me but what would result in my immediate ruin. For, if I had ever united myself with what you have shown me, then from that moment I should have been persecuted by the two arch-enemies of the human race, namely, *Hatred* and *Remorse*, and sometimes also by *Oblivion*; and therefore I turn again to Reason only to proceed and stop the mouths of these foes.

REASON: What you say, O Desire, that there are different substances, that, I tell you, is false; for I see clearly that there is but *One, which exists through itself, and is a support to all other attributes*. And if you will refer to the material and the mental as substances, in relation to the modes which are dependent on them, why then, you must also call them modes in relation to the substance on which they depend: for they are not conceived by you as existing through themselves. And in the same way that willing, feeling, understanding, loving, etc., are different modes of that which you call a thinking substance, in which you bring together and unite all these in one,[n] so I also conclude, from your own proofs, that *Both Infinite*

---

[m] [A and B continue: moreover under the following attributes, namely, that it is *One, Eternal, infinite through itself*; we avoid . . .]

[n] [A: All which you bring to one, and make one from all these; B: to which you bring all and make them into one.]

Extension and Thought together with all other infinite attributes (or, according to your usage, other *substances*) are only modes of the *One, Eternal, Infinite Being, who exists through himself;* and from all these we posit, as stated, *An Only One* or a *Unity* outside which nothing can be imagined to be.°

DESIRE: Methinks I see a very great confusion in this argument of yours; for, it seems you will have it that *the whole must be something outside of or apart from its parts,* which is truly absurd. For all philosophers are unanimous in saying that *"whole" is a second notion, and that it is nothing in Nature apart from human thought.* Moreover, as I gather from your example, you confuse *whole* with *cause:* for, as I say, the whole only consists of and [exists] through its parts, and so it comes that you represent the *thinking power* as a thing on which the Understanding, Love, etc., depend. But you cannot call it a *Whole,* only a *Cause of the Effects* just named by you.

REASON: I see decidedly how you muster all your friends against me, and that, after the method usually adopted by those who oppose the truth, you are designing to achieve by quibbling what you have not been able to accomplish with your fallacious reasoning. But you will not succeed in winning Love to your side by such means. Your assertion, then, is, *that the cause (since it is the Originator of the effects) must therefore be outside these.* But you say this because you only know of the *transeunt* and not of the *immanent cause,* which by no means produces anything outside itself, as is exemplified by the Understanding, which is the cause of its ideas. And that is why I called the understanding (insofar as, or because, its ideas depend on it[P]) a *cause;* and on the other hand, since it consists of its ideas, a *whole:* so also *God is both an Immanent Cause with reference to his works or creatures, and also a whole, considered from the second point of view.*

Second Dialogue

Between Erasmus and Theophilus Relating Partly to the Preceding, Partly to the Following Second Part

ERASMUS: I have heard you say, Theophilus, that God is a *cause of all things,* and, at the same time, that he can be *no other* than an *Immanent* cause. Now, if he is an *immanent cause* of *all things,* how then can you call him a *remote[q] cause?* For, that is impossible in the case of an Immanent cause.

THEOPHILUS: When I said that God is a remote[q] cause, I only said it with reference to the things [which God has produced mediately, and not with reference to those] which God (without any other conditions beyond his mere existence) has produced immediately; but on no account did I mean to call him a remote[q] cause absolutely: as you might also have clearly gathered from my remarks. For, I also said that in some respects we can call him a remote cause.

° [B: . . . One, Eternal, self-subsisting Being in which all is one and united, and outside which unity nothing can be imagined to be.]

P [A: It depends on its ideas.]

q [B: prior.]

ERASMUS: I understand now adequately what you want to say; but I note also that you have said, *that the effect of the immanent cause remains united with its cause in such a way that together they constitute a whole.* Now, if this is so, then, methinks, God cannot be an immanent cause. For, if he and that which is produced by him together form a whole, then you ascribe to God at one time more essence than at another time. I pray you, remove these doubts for me.

THEOPHILUS: If, Erasmus, you want to extricate yourself from this confusion, then mark well what I am going to tell you now. The essence of a thing does not increase through its union with another thing with which it constitutes a whole; on the contrary, the first remains unchanged. I will give you an illustration, so that you may understand me the better. An image-carver has made from wood various forms after the likeness of the parts of the human body; he takes one of these, which has the form of a human breast, joins it to another, which has the form of a human head, and of these two he makes a whole, which represents the upper part of a human body; would you therefore say that the essence of the head has increased because it has been joined to the breast? That would be erroneous, because it is the same that it was before. For the sake of greater clearness let me give you another illustration, namely, an idea that I have of a triangle, and another resulting from an extension of one of the angles, which extended or extending angle is necessarily equal to the two interior opposite angles, and so forth. These, I say, have produced a new idea, namely, that the three angles of the triangle are equal to two right angles. This idea is so connected with the first, that it can neither be, nor be conceived without the same.[r] Mark well now that although the new idea is joined to the preceding one, the essence of the preceding idea does not undergo any change in consequence; on the contrary, it remains without the slightest change. The same you may also observe in every idea which produces love in itself: this love in no way adds to the essence of the idea. But why multiply illustrations? since you can see it clearly in the subject which I have been illustrating and which we are discussing now. I have distinctly stated that all attributes, which depend on no other cause, and whose definition requires no genus pertain to the essence of God; and since the created things are not competent to establish an attribute, they do not increase the essence of God, however intimately they become united to him. Add to this, that "whole" is but a thing of Reason, and does not differ from the general except in this alone that the general results from various Disconnected individuals, the Whole, from various United individuals; also in this, that the General only comprises parts of the same kind, but the Whole, parts both the same and different in kind.[s]

ERASMUS: So far as this is concerned you have satisfied me. But, in addition to this, you have also said, that *the effect of the inner cause cannot perish so long*

---

[r] [A continues: And of all ideas which any one has we make a whole, or (which is the same) a thing of reason, which we call *Understanding.*]

[s] [B: . . . the general results from various unconnected individuals of the same kind; but the whole from various connected individuals different as well as the same in kind.]

as its cause lasts; this, I well see, is certainly true, but if this is so, then how can God be an inner cause of all things, seeing that many things perish? After your previous distinction you will say, that *God is really a cause of the effects which he has produced immediately, without any other conditions except his attributes alone; and that these cannot perish so long as their cause endures; but that you do not call God an inner cause of the effects whose existence does not depend on him immediately, but which have come into being through some other thing, except insofar as their causes do not operate, and cannot operate, without God, nor also outside him,* and that for this reason also, since they are not produced immediately by God, they can perish. But this does not satisfy me. For I see that you conclude, that the human understanding is immortal, because it is a product which God has produced in himself. Now it is impossible that more than the attributes of God should have been necessary in order to produce such an understanding; for, in order to be a being of such supreme perfection, it must have been created from eternity, just like all other things which depend immediately on God. And I have heard you say so, if I am not mistaken. And this being so, how will you reconcile this without leaving over any difficulties?

THEOPHILUS: It is true, Erasmus, that the things (for the existence of which no other thing is required, except the attributes of God) which have been created immediately by him have been created from eternity. It is to be remarked, however, that although in order that a thing may exist there is required a special modification and a thing beside the attributes of God, for all that, God does not cease to be able to produce a thing immediately. For, of the necessary things which are required to bring things into existence, some are there in order that they should produce the thing, and others in order that the thing should be capable of being produced. For example, I want to have light in a certain room; I kindle a light, and this lights up the room through itself; or I open a window [shutter], now this act of opening does not itself give light, but still it brings it about that the light can enter the room. Likewise in order to set a body in motion another body is required that shall have all the motion that is to pass from it to the other. But in order to produce in us an idea of God there is no need for another special thing that shall have what is to be produced in us, but only such a body in *Nature* whose idea is necessary in order to represent God immediately. This you could also have gathered from my remarks: for I said that God is only known through himself, and not through something else. However, I tell you this, that so long as we have not such a clear idea of God as shall unite us with him in such a way that it will not let us love anything beside him, we cannot truly say that we are united with God, so as to depend immediately on him. If there is still anything that you may have to ask, leave it for another time; just now circumstances require me to attend to other matters. Farewell.

ERASMUS: Nothing at present, but I shall ponder what you have just told me till the next opportunity. God be with you.

CHAPTER III
That God Is a Cause of All Things

We shall now begin to consider those attributes [of God] which we called *Propria*.[13] And, first of all, how God *is a cause of all things.*

Now, we have already said above *that one substance cannot produce another;* and *that God is a being of whom all attributes are predicated;* whence it clearly follows that all other things can by no means be, or be understood, apart from or outside him. Wherefore we may say with all reason *that God is a cause of all things.*

As it is usual to divide the efficient cause in eight divisions, let me, then, inquire how and in what sense God is a cause.

First, then, we say that he is an *emanative* or *productive cause of his works;* and, insofar as there is activity, *an active or operating cause,* which we regard as one and the same, because they involve each other.

Secondly, he is an *immanent,* and not a *transeunt cause,* since all that he produces is within himself, and not outside him, because there is nothing outside him.

Thirdly, God is a *free cause,* and not a *natural* cause, as we shall make clear and manifest when we come to consider *whether God can omit to do what he does,* and then it will also be explained wherein *true freedom* consists.

Fourthly, God is a cause *through himself,* and not *by accident;* this will become more evident from the discussion on Predestination.

Fifthly, God is a *principal cause of his works which he has created immediately,* such as movement in matter, etc.; in which there is no place for a subsidiary [instrumental] cause, since this is confined to particular things; as when he dries the sea by means of a strong wind, and so forth in the case of all particular things in Nature.

The subsidiary provoking cause is not [found] *in God,* because there is nothing outside him to incite him. The *predisposing cause,* on the other hand, is his perfection itself; through it he is a cause of himself, and, consequently, of all other things.

Sixthly, God alone is *the first or Initial cause,* as is evident from our foregoing proof.

Seventhly, God is also *a Universal cause,* but only insofar as he produces various things; otherwise this can never be predicated of him, as he needs no one in order to produce any results.

Eighthly, God is the *proximate cause* of the things that are infinite, and immutable, and which we assert to have been created immediately by him, but, in one sense, he is the remote cause of all particular things.

---

[13] The [attributes] following are called *Propria,* because they are only Adjectives, which cannot be understood without their Substantives. That is to say, without them God would indeed be no God, but still it is not they that constitute God; for they reveal nothing of the character of a Substance, through which alone God exists.

CHAPTER IV
On God's Necessary Activity

We deny that God can omit to do what he does, and we shall also prove it when we treat of Predestination; when we will show that all things necessarily depend on their causes. But, in the second place, this conclusion also follows from the perfection of God; for it is true, beyond a doubt, *that God can make everything just as perfect as it is conceived in his Idea*; and just as things that are conceived by him cannot be conceived by him more perfectly than he conceives them, so all things can be made by him so perfect that they cannot come from him in a more perfect condition. Again, when we conclude that God could not have omitted to do what he has done, we deduce this from his perfection; because, in God, it would be an imperfection to be able to omit to do what he does; we do not, however, suppose that there is a subsidiary provoking cause in God that might have moved him to action, for then he were no God.

But now, again, there is the controversy whether, namely, of all that is in his Idea, and which he can realise so perfectly, whether, I say, he could omit to realise anything, and whether such an omission would be a perfection in him. Now, we maintain that, since all that happens is done by God, it must therefore necessarily be predetermined by him, otherwise he would be mutable, which would be a great imperfection in him. And as this predetermination by him must be from eternity, in which eternity there is no before or after, it follows irresistibly that God could never have predetermined things in any other way than that in which they are determined now, and have been from eternity, and that God could not have been either before or without these determinations. Further, if God should omit to do anything, then he must either have some cause for it, or not; if he has, then it is necessary that he should omit doing it; if he has not, then it is necessary that he should not omit to do it; this is self-evident. Moreover, in a created thing it is a perfection to exist and to have been produced by God, for, of all imperfection, nonexistence is the greatest imperfection; and since God desires the welfare and perfection of all things, it would follow that if God desired that a certain thing should not exist, then the welfare and perfection of this thing must be supposed to consist in its nonexistence, which is self-contradictory. That is why we deny *that God can omit to do what he does.* Some regard this as blasphemy, and as a belittling of God; but such an assertion results from a misapprehension of what constitutes *true freedom*; this is by no means what they think it is, namely, the ability to do or to omit to do something good or evil; but *true freedom is only, or no other than* [the status of being] *the first cause*, which is in no way constrained or coerced by anything else, and which through its perfection alone is the cause of all perfection; consequently, if God could omit to do this, he would not be perfect: for the ability to omit doing some good, or accomplishing some perfection in what he does, can have no place in him, except through defect.

That God alone is the only free cause is, therefore, clear not only from what has just been said, but also from this, namely, that there is no external cause outside him to force or constrain him; all this is not the case with created things.

Against this it is argued thus: The good is only good because God wills it, and this being so, he can always bring it about that evil should be good. But such reasoning is about as conclusive as if I said: It is because God wills to be God that he is God; therefore it is in his power not to be God, which is absurdity itself. Furthermore, when people do anything, and they are asked why they do it, their answer is, because it is what justice demands. If the question is then put, why justice, or rather the first cause of all that is just, makes such a demand, then the answer must be, because justice wills it so. But, dear me, I think to myself, could Justice really be other than just? By no means, for then it could not be Justice. Those, however, who say that God does all that he does because it is good in itself, these, I say, may possibly think that they do not differ from us. But that is far from being the case, since they suppose that there is something before God to which he has duties or obligations, namely, a cause [through] which [God] desires that this shall be good, and, again, that that shall be just.

Then comes the further controversy, namely, whether God, supposing all things had been created by him in some other way from eternity, or had been ordered and predetermined to be otherwise than they now are, whether, I say, he would then be just as perfect as he is now. To this it may serve as an answer, that if Nature had, from all eternity, been made different from what it is now, then, from the standpoint of those who ascribe to God will and understanding, it would necessarily follow that God had a different will and a different understanding then, in consequence of which he would have made it different; and so we should be compelled to think that God has a different character now from what he had then, and had a different character then from what he has now; so that, if we assume he is most perfect now, we are compelled to say that he would not have been so had he created all things differently. All these things, involving as they do palpable absurdities, can in no way be attributed to God, who now, in the past, and unto all eternity, is, has been, and will remain immutable. We prove this also from the definition that we have given of a free cause, which is not one that can do or omit to do anything, but is only such as is not dependent on anything else, so that whatever God does is done and carried into effect by him as the freest cause. If, therefore, he had formerly made things different from what they are now, it would needs follow that he was at one time imperfect, which is false. For, since God is the first cause of all things, there must be something in him, through which he does what he does, and omits not to do it. Since we say that *Freedom* does not consist in [having the choice of] doing or not doing something, and since we have also shown that that which makes him [God] do anything can be nothing else than his own perfection, we conclude that, *had it not been that his perfection made him do all this, then the things would not exist, and could not come into existence, in order to be what they are now.* This is just like saying: *if God were imperfect then things would be different from what they are now.*

So much as regards the first [attribute]; we shall now pass on to the second attribute, which we call a *proprium* of God, and see what we have to say about it, and so on to the end.

CHAPTER V
On Divine Providence

The second attribute, which we call a *proprium* [of God] is his Providence, which to us is nothing else than the *striving* which we find in the whole of Nature and in individual things to maintain and preserve their own existence. For it is manifest that no thing could, through its own nature, seek its own annihilation, but, on the contrary, that every thing has in itself a striving to preserve its condition, and to improve itself. Following these definitions of ours we, therefore, posit a *general* and a *special providence*. The general [*providence*] is that through which all things are produced and sustained insofar as they are parts of the whole of Nature. The *special providence* is the striving of each thing separately to preserve its existence [each thing, that is to say], considered not as a part of Nature, but as a whole [by itself]. This is explained by the following example: All the limbs of man are provided for, and cared for, insofar as they are parts of man, this is *general* providence; while *special* [*providence*] is the striving of each separate limb (as a whole in itself, and not as a part of man) to preserve and maintain its own well-being.

CHAPTER VI
On Divine Predestination

The third attribute, we say, is divine predestination.

1. We proved before that God cannot omit to do what he does; that he has, namely, made everything so perfect that it cannot be more perfect.

2. And, at the same time, that without him nothing can be, or be conceived.

It remains to be seen now whether there are in Nature any accidental things, that is to say, whether there are any things which may happen and may also not happen. Secondly, whether there is any thing concerning which we cannot ask why it is.

Now that there are no accidental things we prove thus: That which has no cause to exist cannot possibly exist; that which is accidental has no cause: therefore . . .

The first is beyond all dispute; the second we prove thus: If any thing that is accidental has a definite and certain cause why it should exist, then it must necessarily exist; but that it should be both accidental and necessary at the same time, is self-contradictory; Therefore . . .

Perhaps some one will say, that *an accidental thing* has indeed no definite and certain cause, but an accidental one. If this should be so, it must be so either *in sensu diviso* or *in sensu composito*, that is to say, either the existence of the cause is accidental, and not its being a cause; or it is accidental that a certain thing (which indeed must necessarily exist in Nature) should be the cause of the occurrence of that accidental thing. However, both the one and the other are false.

For, as regards the first, if the accidental something is accidental because [the existence of] its cause is accidental, then that cause must also be accidental, because the cause which has produced it is also accidental, *et sic in infinitum.*

And since it has already been proved, *that all things depend on one single cause*, this cause would therefore also have to be accidental: which is manifestly false.

As regards the second: if the cause were no more compelled to produce one thing than another, that is, [if the cause were no more compelled] to produce this something than not to produce it, then it would be impossible at once both that it should produce it and that it should not produce it, which is quite contradictory.

Concerning the second [question raised] above, *whether there is no thing in Nature about which one cannot ask why it is*, this remark of ours shows that we have to inquire through what cause a thing is real; for if this [cause] did not exist it were impossible that the thing should exist. Now, we must look for this cause either in the thing or outside the thing. If, however, any one should ask for a rule whereby to conduct this inquiry, we say that none whatever seems necessary. For if existence pertains to the nature of a thing, then it is certain that we must not look outside it for its cause; but if such is not the case, then we must always look outside the thing for its cause. Since, however, the first pertains to God alone, it is thereby proved (as we have already also proved before) that God alone is the first cause of all things. From this it is also evident that this or that will of man (since the existence of the will does not pertain to its essence) must also have an external cause, by which it is necessarily caused; that this is so is also evident from all that we have said in this chapter; and it will be still more evident when, in the second part, we come to consider and discuss the freedom of man.

Against all this others object: how is it possible that God, who is said to be supremely perfect, and the sole cause, disposer, and provider of all, nevertheless permits such *confusion* to be seen everywhere in Nature? Also, why has he not *made man so as not to be able to sin?*

Now, in the first place, it cannot be rightly said that there is *confusion in Nature*, since nobody knows all the causes of things so as to be able to judge accordingly. This objection, however, originates in this kind of ignorance, namely, that they have set up general Ideas, with which, they think, particular things must agree if they are to be perfect. These *Ideas*, they state, are in the understanding of God, as many of *Plato's* followers have said, namely, that these *general Ideas* (such as Rational, Animal, and the like) *have been created by God*; and although those who follow *Aristotle* say, indeed, that these things are not *real* things, only things of Reason, they nevertheless regard them frequently as [real] things, since they have clearly said that his providence does not extend to particular things, but only to kinds; for example, God has never exercised his providence over Bucephalus, etc., but only over the whole genus Horse. They say also that God has no knowledge of particular and transient things, but only of the general, which, in their opinion, are imperishable. We have, however, rightly considered this to be due to their ignorance. For it is precisely the particular things, and they alone, that have a cause, and not the general, because they are nothing.

God then is the cause of, and providence over, particular things only. If particular things had to conform to some other Nature, then they could not conform to their own, and consequently could not be what they truly are. For example, if God had made all human beings like Adam before the fall, then indeed he would only have created Adam, and no Paul nor Peter; but no, it is just perfection in God, that he gives to all things, from the greatest to the least, their essence, or, to express it better, that he has all things perfectly in himself.

As regards the other [objection], *why God has not made mankind so that they should not sin*, to this it may serve [as an answer], that whatever is said about sin is only said with reference to us, that is, as when we compare two things with each other, or [consider one thing] from different points of view. For instance, if some- one has made a clock precisely in order to strike and to show the hours, and the mechanism quite fulfils the aims of its maker, then we say that it is good, but if it does not do so, then we say that it is bad, notwithstanding that even then it might still be good if only it had been his intention to make it irregular and to strike at wrong times.

We say then, in conclusion, that Peter must, as is necessary, conform to the Idea of Peter, and not to the Idea of *Man*; good and evil, or sin, these are only modes of thought, and by no means things, or anything that has reality, as we shall very likely show yet more fully in what follows. For all things and works which are in Nature are perfect.

CHAPTER VII
On the Attributes Which Do Not Pertain to God

Here we shall take up the consideration of those attributes[14] which are commonly attributed to God, but which, nevertheless, do not pertain to him; as also of those through which it is sought to prove the existence of God, though in vain; and also of the rules of accurate definition.

For this purpose, we shall not trouble ourselves very much about the ideas that people commonly have of God, but we shall only inquire briefly into what the Philosophers can tell us about it. Now these have defined God as *a being existing through or of himself, cause of all things, Omniscient, Almighty, eternal, simple, infinite, the highest good, of infinite compassion*, etc. But before we approach this inquiry, let us just see what admissions they make to us.

In the first place, they say that it is impossible to give a true or right definition of God, because, according to their opinion, there can be no definition except *per genus et differentiam*, and as God is not a species of any genus, he cannot be de- fined rightly, or according to the rules.

---

[14] As regards the attributes of which God consists, they are only infinite substances, each of which must of itself be infinitely perfect. That this must necessarily be so, we are convinced by clear and distinct reasons. It is true, however, that up to the present only two of all these infinites are known to us through their own essence; and these are thought and extension. All else that is commonly ascribed to God is not any attribute of his, but only certain modes which may be attributed to him either in consideration of all, that is, *all* his attributes, or in consideration of *one* attribute. In con- sideration of *all* [it is said], for instance, that he is eternal, self-subsisting, infinite, cause of all things, immutable. In consideration of *one* [it is said], for instance, that he is omniscient, wise, etc., which pertains to thought, and, again, that he is omnipresent, fills all, etc., which pertains to extension.

In the second place, they say that God cannot be defined, because the definition must describe the thing itself and also positively; while, according to their standpoint, our knowledge of God cannot be of a positive, but only of a negative kind; therefore no proper definition can be given of God.

They also say, besides, that God can never be proved a priori, because he has no cause, but only by way of probability, or from his effects.

Since by these assertions of theirs they admit sufficiently that their knowledge of God is very little and slight, let us now proceed to examine their definition.

In the first place, we do not see that they give us in it any *attribute* or attributes through which it can be known what the thing (God) is, but only some *propria* or properties which do, indeed, belong to a thing, but never explain what the thing is. For although *self-subsisting, being the cause of all things, highest good, eternal and immutable*, etc., are peculiar to God alone, nevertheless, from those properties we cannot know what that being, to whom these properties pertain, is, and what attributes he has.

It is now also time for us to consider the things which they ascribe to God, and which do not, however, pertain to him,[15] such as *omniscient, merciful, wise*, and so forth, which things, since they are only certain modes of the thinking thing, and can by no means be, or be understood without the substances whose modes they are, can, consequently, also not be attributed to him, who *is a Being subsisting without the aid of anything, and solely through himself.*

Lastly, they call him *the highest good*; but if they understand by it something different from what they have already said, namely, that God *is immutable, and a cause of all things*, then they have become entangled in their own thought, or are unable to understand themselves. This is the outcome of their misconception of good and evil, for they believe that man himself, and not God, is the cause of his sins and wickedness—which, according to what we have already proved, cannot be the case, else we should be compelled to assert that man is also the cause of himself. However, this will appear yet more evident when we come to consider the will of man.

It is necessary that we should now unravel their specious arguments wherewith they seek to excuse their ignorance in Theology.

First of all, then, they say *that a correct definition must consist of a "genus"* and *"differentia."* Now, although all the Logicians admit this, I do not know where they get it from. And, to be sure, if this must be true, then we can know nothing whatever. For if it is through a definition consisting of *genus* and *differentia* that we can first get to know a thing perfectly, then we can never know perfectly the highest *genus*, which has no *genus* above it. Now then: If the highest *genus*, which is the cause of our knowledge of all other things, is not known, much less, then, can the other things be understood or known which are explained by that *genus*. However, since we are free, and do not consider ourselves in any way tied to their assertions, we shall, in accordance with true logic, propose other rules of definition, namely, on the lines of our division of Nature.

---

[15] That is to say, when he is considered as all that he is, or with regard to all his attributes; *see* on this point page 211 *n.* 14.

Now we have already seen that the attributes (or, as others call them, substances) are things, or, to express ourselves better and more aptly, [constitute] a being which subsists through itself, and therefore makes itself known and reveals itself through itself.

As to the other things, we see that they are but modes of the attributes, without which also they can neither be, nor be understood. Consequently definitions must be of two kinds (or sorts):

1. The first, namely, are those of attributes, which pertain to a self-subsisting being, these need no genus, or anything, through which they might be better understood or explained: for, since they exist as attributes of a self-subsisting being, they also become known through themselves.

2. The second [kind of definitions] are those [of things] which do not exist through themselves, but only through the attributes whose modes they are, and through which, as their *genus*, they must be understood.

And this is [all that need be said] concerning their statement about definitions. As regards the other [assertion], namely, that God can [not] be known by us adequately, this has been sufficiently answered by D. des Cartes in his answers to the objections relating to these things.

And the third [assertion], namely, that God cannot be proved a priori, has also already been answered by us. Since God is the cause of himself, it is enough that we prove him through himself, and such a proof is also much more conclusive than the a posteriori proof, which generally rests only on external causes.

CHAPTER VIII

On *Natura Naturans*

Here, before we proceed to something else, we shall briefly divide the whole of Nature—namely, into *Natura naturans* and *Natura naturata*. By *Natura naturans* we understand a being that we conceive clearly and distinctly through itself, and without needing anything beside itself (like all the attributes which we have so far described), that is, God. The Thomists likewise understand God by it, but their *Natura naturans* was a being (so they called it) beyond all substances.

The *Natura naturata* we shall divide into two, a general, and a particular. The *general* consists of all the modes which depend immediately on God, of which we shall treat in the following chapter; the *particular* consists of all the particular things which are produced by the general mode. So that the *Natura naturata* requires some substance in order to be well understood.

CHAPTER IX

On *Natura Naturata*

Now, as regards the general *Natura naturata*, or the modes, or creations which depend on, or have been created by, God immediately, of these we know no more than two, namely, *motion* in matter,[16] and the *understanding* in the thinking thing. These, then, we say, have been from all eternity, and to all eternity will remain immutable. A work truly as great as becomes the greatness of the work-master.

All that specially concerns *Motion*, such as that it *has been from all eternity, and to all eternity will remain immutable; that it is infinite in its kind; that it can neither be, nor be understood through itself,* but only by means of Extension, — all this, I say, since it [Motion] more properly belongs to a treatise on Natural Science rather than here, we shall not consider in this place, but we shall only say this about it, that it is *a Son, Product, or Effect* created immediately by God.

As regards the *Understanding* in the thinking thing, this, like the first, is also a *Son, Product, or immediate Creation* of God, also created by him from all eternity, and remaining immutable to all eternity. It has but one function, namely, to understand clearly and distinctly all things at all times; which produces invariably an infinite or most perfect satisfaction, which cannot omit to do what it does. Although what we have just said is sufficiently self-evident, still, we shall prove it more clearly afterwards in our account of the Affects of the Soul, and shall therefore say no more about it here.

CHAPTER X
What Good and Evil Are

In order to explain briefly what good and evil are in themselves, we shall begin thus:

Some things are in our understanding and not in Nature, and so they are also only our own creation, and their purpose is to understand things distinctly: among these we include all relations, which have reference to different things, and these we call *Entia Rationis* [things of reason]. Now the question is, whether good and evil belong to the *Entia Rationis* or to the *Entia Realia* [real things]. But since good and evil are only relations, it is beyond doubt that they must be placed among the *Entia Rationis*; for we never say that something is good except with reference to something else which is not so good, or is not so useful to us as some other thing. Thus we say that a man is bad, only in comparison with one who is better, or also that an apple is bad, in comparison with another which is good or better.

All this could not possibly be said, if that which is better or good, in comparison with which it [the bad] is so called, did not exist.

Therefore, when we say that something is good, we only mean that it conforms well to the general Idea which we have of such things. But, as we have already said before, the things must agree with their particular Ideas, whose essence must be a perfect essence, and not with the general [Ideas], since in that case they would not exist.

---

[16] *Note.* —What is here said about motion in matter is not said seriously. For the Author still intends to discover the cause thereof, as he has already done to some extent a posteriori. But it can stand just as it is, because nothing is based upon it, or dependent thereon. [B omits this note.]

As to confirming what we have just said, the thing is clear to us; but still, to conclude our remarks, we will add yet the following proofs:

All things which are in Nature, are either things or actions. Now good and evil are neither things nor actions. Therefore good and evil do not exist in Nature.

For, if good and evil are things or actions, then they must have their definitions. But good and evil (as, for example, the goodness of Peter and the wickedness of Judas) have no definitions apart from the essence of Judas or Peter, because this alone exists in Nature, and they cannot be defined without their essence. Therefore, as above — it follows that good and evil are not things or actions which exist in Nature.

Principles of Cartesian Philosophy

Spinoza is often depicted as a solitary rebel. This is a caricature. In fact, he was one of a group of radical thinkers, deeply involved in the new science and in Cartesian philosophy, who gathered around Franciscus Van den Enden. Others included Lodewijk Meyer, Johan Bouwmeester, Pieter Balling, Simon de Vries, and Jarig Jelles. Spinoza participated with others in what was notorious as a Cartesian revolution, the mechanical philosophy. He, like his friends, was committed to determinism, the condition of human passivity, the intellectual love of God, and more.

The Principles of Cartesian Philosophy *is the most explicit evidence of Spinoza's interest and expertise in Descartes. One of two works published by Spinoza during his lifetime, it appeared in 1663. While living in Rijnsburg, Spinoza acted as a professional tutor, and one of his pupils in Cartesian philosophy was a nineteen-year-old Leiden University student, Johannes Caesarius. According to Spinoza's friend Lodewijk Meyer in his introduction to the 1663 edition, Spinoza's Amsterdam friends had encouraged him to publish the materials on Descartes that he had dictated to Caesarius. In them, Spinoza had recast Descartes' philosophical thinking into a synthetic or demonstrative form both to clarify Descartes' intentions and to secure the details of the system. The result is a work that reveals as much about Spinoza's own thinking as it does about Cartesian philosophy. It was, after all, written on the heels of the TIE and during a period in which Spinoza was still at work on the* Short Treatise, *fully in the spirit of the rest of his philosophical and scientific enquiries.*

Clearly Spinoza is convinced that mathematics is the exemplary science and that presenting philosophical results in a mathematical or geometrical form best reflects their certitude. Descartes'* Principles of Philosophy, *published in 1644, was Descartes' attempt to present in this form (that is, synthetically) the views he had come to in the 1630s—in the* Meditations, Discourse, *and essays on optics, astronomy, and geometry—in a more discursive or analytic way. Spinoza's own presentation advances Descartes' achievement. Originally it dealt with Part 2 of Descartes'* Principles *and the beginning of Part 3. At his friends' request, Spinoza added a presentation of Part 1. He did it rather quickly, however, and apologized for its haste.*

Spinoza was explicit about Caesarius' shortcomings, at least at this early stage in his education; he was after all only nineteen. For this reason, Spinoza studiously avoided discussion of his own views which he thought too advanced and for which Caesarius was not yet prepared. His comments on Part 1 and indeed the finished product were, in the end, prepared for his friends and associates and others attuned to the new philosophy. Ostensibly a work of pure exposition and clarification, the published book reveals some differences between Spinoza and

216

Descartes as well as Spinoza's way of clarifying the point of Cartesian philosophy and science. Like John Rawls' account of Kantian moral philosophy, Principles of Cartesian Philosophy is about both its subject and its author.

When the work was published, Spinoza had already moved from Rijnsburg, near Leiden, to the village of Voorburg, outside The Hague. Shortly after the move, he visited Amsterdam for several weeks in order to prepare the lessons on Descartes for publication. Having spent two weeks writing his account of Part 1, he arranged Lodewijk Meyer's assistance in editing the book and writing its preface. Eventually Spinoza appended some comments on the metaphysics of Part 1 and his own thoughts on these matters; these were published in an appendix, the "Cogitata Metaphysica," or "Metaphysical Thoughts." Meyer was careful in his preface to point out where Spinoza differed from Descartes—for example, on mind as a substance and on the freedom of the will. But Meyer was selective; there were many differences of organization and presentation as well as these central differences in substance.

The Principles of Cartesian Philosophy is an important document for a number of reasons. Spinoza's exposition of Cartesian philosophy reflects his interest in the details of science as well as in its foundations. Second, his own "Cogitata Metaphysica," when compared with his exposition of Part 1 and with his later work, expresses the primary role of God in his thinking and the importance of the modal notions of necessity and contingency and the concepts of eternity and duration. Finally, the work confirms Spinoza's role as an expert in and advocate of Cartesianism and its special character as a model of the new philosophy.

We include in this volume Part 1 of Principles of Cartesian Philosophy.

M.L.M.

CONTENTS

PRINCIPLES OF CARTESIAN PHILOSOPHY

PREFACE

To the honest reader, Lodewijk Meyer gives greetings

It is the unanimous opinion of all who seek wisdom beyond the common lot that the best and surest way to discover and to teach truth is the method used by mathematicians in their study and exposition of the sciences, namely, that whereby conclusions are demonstrated from definitions, postulates, and axioms. And indeed rightly so. Because all sure and sound knowledge of what is unknown can be elicited and derived only from what is already known with certainty, this latter must first be built up from the ground as a solid foundation on which thereafter to construct the entire edifice of human knowledge, if that is not to collapse of its own accord or give way at the slightest blow. That the things familiar to mathematicians under the title of definitions, postulates, and axioms are of this kind cannot be doubted by anyone who has even the slightest acquaintance with that noble discipline. For definitions are merely the perspicuous explanations of the terms and names by which matters under discussion are designated, whereas postulates and axioms—that is, the common notions of the mind—are statements so clear and lucid that no one who has simply understood the words aright can possibly refuse assent.

But although this is so, you will find that with the exception of mathematics hardly any branch of learning is treated by this method. Instead, a totally different method is adopted, whereby the entire work is executed by means of definitions and logical divisions interlinked in a chain, with problems and explanations interspersed here and there. For almost all who have applied themselves to establishing and setting out the sciences have believed, and many still do believe, that the mathematical method is peculiar to mathematics and is to be rejected as inapplicable to all other branches of learning.

In consequence, nothing of what they produce is demonstrated with conclusive reasoning. They try to advance arguments that depend merely on likelihood and probability, and in this way they thrust before the public a great medley of great books in which you may look in vain for solidity and certainty. Disputes and strife abound, and what one somehow establishes with trivial arguments of no real weight is soon refuted by another, demolished and shattered with the same weapons. So where the mind, eager for unshakable truth, had thought to find for its labors a placid stretch of water that it could navigate with safety and success, thereafter attaining the haven of knowledge for which it yearned, it finds itself tossed on a stormy sea of opinion, beset on all sides with tempests of dispute, hurled about and carried away on waves of uncertainty, endlessly, with no hope of ever emerging therefrom.

Yet there have not been lacking some who have thought differently and, taking pity on the wretched plight of Philosophy, have distanced themselves from this universally adopted and habitual way of treating the sciences and have entered upon a new and indeed an arduous path bristling with difficulties, so as to leave to posterity the other parts of Philosophy, besides mathematics, demonstrated with mathematical method and with mathematical certainty. Of these, some have arranged in mathematical order and passed on to the world of letters a philosophy already accepted and customarily taught in the schools, whereas others have thus treated a new philosophy, discovered by their own exertions. For a long time, the many who undertook this task met with no success, but at last there arose that brightest star of our age, René Descartes. After bringing forth by a new method from darkness to light whatever had been inaccessible to the ancients, and in addition whatever could be wanting in his own age, he laid the unshakable foundations of philosophy on which numerous truths could be built with mathematical order and certainty, as he himself effectively proved, and as is clearer than the midday sun to all who have paid careful attention to his writings, for which no praise is too great.

Although the philosophical writings of this most noble and incomparable man exhibit the mathematical manner and order of demonstration, yet they are not composed in the style commonly used in Euclid's *Elements* and other geometrical works, the style wherein Definitions, Postulates, and Axioms are first enunciated, followed by Propositions and their demonstrations. They are arranged in a very different way, which he calls the true and best way of teaching, the Analytic way. For at the end of his "Reply to Second Objections,"[1] he acknowledges two modes of conclusive proof. One is by analysis, "which shows the true way by which a thing is discovered methodically and, as it were, a priori"; the other is by synthesis, "which employs a long series of definitions, postulates, axioms, theorems and problems, so that if any of the conclusions be denied, it can be shown immediately that this is involved in what has preceded, and thus the reader, however reluctant and obstinate, is forced to agree."

However, although both kinds of demonstration afford a certainty that lies beyond any risk of doubt, not everyone finds them equally useful and convenient. There are many who, being quite unacquainted with the mathematical sciences and therefore completely ignorant of the synthetic method in which they are arranged and of the analytic method by which they were discovered, are neither able themselves to understand nor to expound to others the things that are discussed and logically demonstrated in these books. Consequently, many who, either carried away by blind enthusiasm or influenced by the authority of others, have become followers of Descartes have done no more than commit to memory his opinions and doctrines. When the subject arises in conversation, they can only prate and chatter without offering any proof, as was once and still is the case with the followers of the Peripatetic philosophy. Therefore, to provide them with some assistance, I have often wished that someone, skilled both in the analytic and synthetic arrangement and thoroughly versed in Descartes's writings and expert in his philosophy, should set his hand to this task, and undertake to arrange in synthetic order what Descartes wrote in analytic order, demonstrating it in the way familiar to geometricians. Indeed, though fully conscious of my incompetence

---

Notes without brackets are Spinoza's. Bracketed notes are those of Steven Barbone and Lee Rice (main annotators for this work) and translator Samuel Shirley.

[1] [See AT7, 155–156; cf. the slight variation in the French version at AT9, 121–122. —S.B./L.R.]

and unfitness for such a task, I have frequently thought of undertaking it myself and have even made a start. But other distractions, which so often claim my attention, have prevented its completion.

I was therefore delighted to hear from our Author that, while teaching Descartes's philosophy to a certain pupil of his, he had dictated to him the whole of Part II of the *Principia* and some of Part III, demonstrated in that geometric style, and also the principal and more difficult questions that arise in metaphysics and remain unresolved by Descartes, and that, at the urgent entreaties and pleadings of his friends, he has permitted these to be published as a single work, corrected and amplified by himself. So I also commended this same project, at the same time gladly offering my services, if needed, to get this published. Furthermore I urged him—indeed, besought him—to set out Part I of the *Principia* as well in like order to precede the rest, so that the work, as thus arranged from its very beginning, might be better understood and give greater satisfaction. When he saw how reasonable was this proposal, he could not refuse the pleas of a friend and likewise the good of the reader. He further entrusted to my care the entire business both of printing and of publishing because he lives in the country far from the city and so cannot give it his personal attention.[2]

Such then, honest reader, are the contents of this little book, namely, Parts I and II of Descartes's *Principia Philosophiae* together with a fragment of Part III, to which we have added, as an appendix, our Author's *Cogitata Metaphysica*. But when we here say Part I of the *Principia*, and the book's title so announces, we do not intend it to be understood that everything Descartes says there is here set forth as demonstrated in geometric order. The title derives only from its main contents, and so the chief metaphysical themes that were treated by Descartes in his *Meditations* are taken from that book (omitting all other matters that concern Logic and are related and reviewed only in a historical way). To do this more effectively, the Author has transposed word for word almost the entire passage at the end of the "Reply to the Second Set of Objections," which Descartes arranged in geometric order.[3] He first sets out all Descartes's definitions and inserts Descartes's propositions among his own, but he does not place the axioms immediately after the definitions; he brings them in only after Proposition 4, changing their order so as to make it easier to prove them, and omitting some that he did not require.

Although our Author is well aware that these axioms (as Descartes himself says in Postulate 7) can be proved as theorems and can even more neatly be classed as propositions, and although we also asked him to do this, being engaged in more important affairs he had only the space of two weeks to complete this work, and that is why he could not satisfy his own wishes and ours. He does at any rate add a brief explanation that can serve as a demonstration, postponing for another occasion a lengthier proof, complete in all respects, with view to a new edition to follow this hurried one. To augment this, we shall also try to persuade him to

---

[2] [It appears from Ep12, however, that Spinoza was able to make corrections to the page proofs.]
[3] [AT7, 160–170.]

complete Part III in its entirety, "Concerning the Visible World" (of which we give here only a fragment, since the Author ended his instruction at this point and we did not wish to deprive the reader of it, little as it is). For this to be properly executed, some propositions concerning the nature and property of Fluids will need to be inserted at various places in Part II, and I shall then do my best to persuade the Author to do this at the time.

It is not only in setting forth and explaining the Axioms that our Author frequently diverges from Descartes but also in proving the Propositions themselves and the other conclusions, and he employs a logical proof far different from that of Descartes. But let no one take this to mean that he intended to correct the illustrious Descartes in these matters, but that our Author's sole purpose in so doing is to enable him the better to retain his already established order and to avoid increasing unduly the number of Axioms. For the same reason, he has also been compelled to prove many things that Descartes propounded without proof, and to add others that he completely omitted.

However, I should like it to be particularly noted that in all these writings, in Parts I and II and the fragment of Part III of the *Principia* and also in the *Cogitata Metaphysica*, our Author has simply given Descartes's opinions and their demonstrations just as they are found in his writings, or such as should validly be deduced from the foundations laid by him. For having undertaken to teach his pupil Descartes's philosophy, his scruples forbade him to depart in the slightest degree from Descartes's views or to dictate anything that did not correspond with, or was contrary to, his doctrines. Therefore no one should conclude that he here teaches either his own views or only those of which he approves. For although he holds some of the doctrines to be true, and admits that some are his own additions, there are many he rejects as false, holding a very different opinion.[4]

Of this sort, to single out one of many, are statements concerning the Will in the Scholium to Proposition 15 of Part I of the *Principia* and in Chapter 12, Part II of the Appendix, although they appear to be laboriously and meticulously proved. For he does not consider the Will to be distinct from the Intellect, far less endowed with freedom of that kind. Indeed, in making these assertions, as is clear from Part 4 of the *Discourse on Method*, the "Second Meditation," and other passages, Descartes merely assumes, and does not prove, that the human mind is an absolutely thinking substance. Although our Author does indeed admit that there is in Nature a thinking substance, he denies that this constitutes the essence of the human mind.[5] He maintains that, just as Extension is not determined by any limits, so Thought, too, is not determined by any limits. And therefore, just as the human body is not Extension absolutely, but only as determined in a particular way in accordance with the laws of extended Nature through motion and rest, so too the human mind or soul is not Thought absolutely, but only as determined in a particular way in accordance with the laws of thinking Nature through ideas,

---

[4] [Meyer notes three main differences: the substantiality of the human soul, the distinction between the will and intellect, and the freedom to suspend judgment. Spinoza notes his differences with Descartes; see Ep2, 63.]

[5] [Cf. E2P11.]

and one concludes that this must come into existence when the human body begins to exist. From this definition, he thinks it is not difficult to prove that Will is
not distinct from Intellect, far less is it endowed with the freedom that Descartes
ascribes to it.[6] Indeed, he holds that a faculty of affirming and denying is quite fictitious, that affirming and denying are nothing but ideas, and that other faculties
such as Intellect, Desire, etc., must be accounted as figments, or at least among
those notions that men have formed through conceiving things in an abstract way,
such as humanity, stoniness, and other things of that kind.

Here, too, we must not omit to mention that assertions found in some passages,
that this or that surpasses human understanding, must be taken in the same sense
(i.e., as giving only Descartes's opinion). This must not be regarded as expressing
our Author's own view. All such things, he holds, and many others even more sublime and subtle, can not only be conceived by us clearly and distinctly but can
also be explained quite satisfactorily, provided that the human intellect can be
guided to the search for truth and the knowledge of things along a path different
from that which was opened up and leveled by Descartes. And so he holds that
the foundations of the sciences laid by Descartes and the superstructure that he
built thereon do not suffice to elucidate and resolve all the most difficult problems that arise in metaphysics. Other foundations are required if we seek to raise
our intellect to that pinnacle of knowledge.

Finally, to bring my preface to a close, we should like our readers to realize
that all that is here treated is given to the public for the sole purpose of searching
out and disseminating truth and to urge men to the pursuit of a true and genuine
philosophy. And so in order that all may reap therefrom as rich a profit as we sincerely desire for them, before they begin reading we earnestly beg them to insert
omitted passages in their proper place and carefully to correct printing errors that
have crept in. Some of these are such as may be an obstacle in the way of perceiving the force of the demonstration and the Author's meaning, as anyone will
readily gather from looking at them.

THE PRINCIPLES OF PHILOSOPHY
DEMONSTRATED IN THE
GEOMETRIC MANNER

PART 1

Prolegomenon

Before coming to the Propositions and their Demonstrations, I have thought it
helpful to give a concise account as to why Descartes doubted everything, the way

---

[6] [Cf. E2P48; E2P49 Cor and Schol.]

in which he laid the solid foundations of the sciences, and finally the means by which he freed himself from all doubts. I should indeed have arranged all this in mathematical order had I not considered that the prolixity involved in this form of presentation would be an obstacle to the proper understanding of all those things that ought to be beheld at a single glance, as in the case of a picture.

Descartes, then, so as to proceed with the greatest caution in his enquiry, attempted:

1. to put aside all prejudice,
2. to discover the foundations on which everything should be built,
3. to uncover the cause of error,
4. to understand everything clearly and distinctly.

To achieve his first, second, and third aims, he proceeded to call everything into doubt, not indeed like a Skeptic whose sole aim is to doubt, but to free his mind from all prejudice so that he might finally discover the firm and unshakable foundations of the sciences, which, if they existed, could thus not escape him. For the true principles of the sciences ought to be so clear and certain that they need no proof, are placed beyond all hazard of doubt, and without them nothing can be demonstrated. These principles, after a lengthy period of doubting, he discovered. Now when he had found them, it was not difficult for him to distinguish true from false, to uncover the cause of error, and so to take precautions against assuming as true and certain what was false and doubtful.

To achieve his fourth and final aim, that of understanding everything clearly and distinctly, his chief rule was to enumerate the simple ideas out of which all others are compounded and to scrutinize each one separately. For when he could perceive simple ideas clearly and distinctly, he would doubtless understand with the same clarity and distinctness all the other ideas compounded from those simple ideas. Having thus outlined my program, I shall briefly explain in what manner he called everything into doubt, discovered the true principles of the sciences, and extricated himself from the difficulties of doubt.

Doubt Concerning All Things

First, then, he reviewed all those things he had gathered from his senses—the sky, the earth, and the like, and even his own body—all of which he had hitherto regarded as belonging to reality. And he doubted their certainty because he had found that the senses occasionally deceived him, and in dreams he had often been convinced that many things truly existed externally to himself, discovering afterward that he had been deluded. And finally there was the fact that he had heard others, even when awake, declare that they felt pain in limbs they had lost long before.[7] Therefore he was able to doubt, not without reason, even the existence of his

---

[7] [The first two arguments are given in Med1, 13–15 (AT7, 18–20) and PPH1A4, whereas the third is not given until Med6, 50 (AT7, 76–77).]

own body. From all these considerations he could truly conclude that the senses are not a very strong foundation on which to build all science, for they can be called into doubt; certainty depends on other principles of which we can be more sure. Continuing his enquiry, in the second place he turned to the consideration of all universals, such as corporeal nature in general, its extension, likewise its figure, quantity, etc., and also all mathematical truths. Although these seemed to him more certain than any of the things he had gathered from his senses, yet he discovered a reason for doubting them.[8] For others had erred even concerning these. And there was a particularly strong reason, an ancient belief, fixed in his mind, that there was an all-powerful God who had created him as he was, and so may have caused him to be deceived even regarding those things that seemed very clear to him.[9] This, then, is the manner in which he called everything into doubt.

The Discovery of the Foundation of All Science

Now in order to discover the true principles of the sciences, he proceeded to enquire whether he had called into doubt everything that could come within the scope of his thought; thus he might find out whether there was not perchance still something left that he had not yet doubted. For if in the course of thus doubting he should find something that could not be called into doubt either for any of the previous reasons or for any other reason, he quite rightly considered that this must be established as a foundation on which he could build all his knowledge.[10] And although he had already, as it seemed, doubted everything—for he had doubted not only what he had gathered from his senses but also what he had perceived by intellect alone—yet there was still something left to be examined, namely, himself who was doing the doubting, not insofar as he consisted of head, hands, and other bodily parts (since he had doubted these) but only insofar as he was doubting, thinking, etc. Examining this carefully, he realized that he could not doubt it for any of the foregoing reasons. For whether he is dreaming or awake as he thinks, nevertheless he thinks, and is.[11] And although others, or even he himself, had erred with regard to other matters; nevertheless, because they were erring, they were. He could imagine no author of his being so cunning as to deceive him on that score; for it must be granted that he himself exists as long as it is supposed that he is being deceived. In short, whatever other reason for doubting be devised, there could be adduced none of such a kind as not at the same time to make him most certain of his existence. Indeed, the more reasons are adduced for doubting, the more arguments are simultaneously adduced to convince him of his own existence. So, in whatever direction he turns in order to doubt, he is nevertheless compelled to utter these words: "I doubt, I think, therefore I am."[12]

---

8 [Med1, 15 (AT7, 20).]
9 [Med1, 15–16 (AT7, 21–22).]
10 [Med2, 17 (AT7, 24).]
11 [Med2, 17–18 (AT7, 24–25).]
12 [Med2, 18 (AT7, 25); *Discourse on Method* 4 (AT6, 32–33).]

Thus, in laying bare this truth, at the same time he also discovered the foundation of all the sciences, and also the measure and rule for all other truths—that whatever is perceived as clearly and distinctly as this, is true.[13]

It is abundantly clear from the preceding that there can be no other foundation for the sciences than this; everything else can quite easily be called into doubt, but this can by no means be doubted. However, with regard to this foundation, it should be particularly noted that the statement, "I doubt, I think, therefore I am," is not a syllogism with the major premise omitted. If it were a syllogism, the premises should be clearer and better known than the conclusion 'Therefore I am', and so 'I am' would not be the prime basis of all knowledge. Furthermore, it would not be a certain conclusion, for its truth would depend on universal premises which the Author had already called into doubt. So 'I think, therefore I am' is a single independent proposition, equivalent to the following—'I am, while thinking'.

To avoid confusion in what follows (for this is a matter that must be perceived clearly and distinctly), we must next know what we are. For when this has been clearly and distinctly understood, we shall not confuse our essence with others. In order to deduce this from what has gone before, our Author proceeds as follows.

He recalls to mind all thoughts that he once had about himself, that his soul is something tenuous like the wind or fire or the ether, infused among the denser parts of his body; that his body is better known to him than his soul; and that he perceives the former more clearly and distinctly.[14] And he realizes that all this is clearly inconsistent with what he has so far understood. For he was able to doubt his body, but not his own essence insofar as he was thinking. Furthermore, he perceived these things neither clearly nor distinctly, and so, in accordance with the requirements of his method, he ought to reject them as false. Therefore, understanding that such things could not pertain to him insofar as he was as yet known to himself, he went on to ask what was that, pertaining peculiarly to his essence, which he had not been able to call into doubt and which had compelled him to conclude his own existence. Of this kind there were—that he wanted to take precautions against being deceived, that he desired to understand many things, that he doubted everything that he could not understand, that up to this point he affirmed one thing only and everything else he denied and rejected as false, that he imagined many things even against his will, and, finally, that he was conscious of many things as proceeding from his senses. Because he could infer his existence with equal certainty from each of these points and could list none of them as belonging to the things that he had called into doubt, and finally, because all these things can be conceived under the same attribute, it follows that all these things are true and pertain to his nature. And so whenever he said, "I think," all the following modes of thinking were understood—doubting, understanding, affirming, denying, willing, non-willing, imagining, and sensing.[15]

---

[13] [Spinoza follows the *Discourse on Method*, rather than the *Meditations* or PPH, in deriving this principle directly from the *cogito*.]

[14] [Med2, 18 (AT7, 25–26).]

[15] [This enumeration is taken from Med2, 20 (AT7, 28).]

Here it is important to note the following points, which will prove to be very useful later on when the distinction between mind and body is discussed. First, these modes of thinking are clearly and distinctly understood independently of other matters that are still in doubt. Second, the clear and distinct conception we have of them would be rendered obscure and confused if we were to intermingle with them any of the matters of which we are still in doubt.

Liberation from All Doubts

Finally, to achieve certainty about what he had called into doubt and to remove all doubt, he proceeds to enquire into the nature of the most perfect Being, and whether such exists. For when he realizes that there exists a most perfect Being by whose power all things are produced and preserved and to whose nature it is contrary that he should be a deceiver, then this will remove the reason for doubting that resulted from his not knowing the cause of himself. For he will know that the faculty of distinguishing true from false was not given to him by a supremely good and truthful God in order that he might be deceived. And so mathematical truths, or all things that seem to him most evident, cannot be in the least suspect.[16] Then, to remove the other causes for doubting, he goes on to enquire how it comes about that we sometimes err. When he discovered that this arises from our using our free will to assent even to what we have perceived only confusedly, he was immediately able to conclude that he can guard against error in the future provided that he gives assent only to what he clearly and distinctly perceives. This is something that each individual can easily obtain of himself because he has the power to control the will and thereby bring it about that it is restrained within the limits of the intellect.[17] But since in our earliest days we have been imbued with many prejudices from which we are not easily freed, in order that we may be freed from them and accept nothing but what we clearly and distinctly perceive, he goes on to enumerate all the simple notions and ideas from which all our thoughts are compounded and to examine them one by one, so that he can observe in each of them what is clear and what is obscure. For thus he will easily be able to distinguish the clear from the obscure and to form clear and distinct thoughts. So he will easily discover the real distinction between soul and body, and what is clear and what is obscure in the deliverance of our senses, and lastly wherein dreaming differs from waking.[18] Thereafter he could no longer doubt that he was awake nor could he be deceived by his senses. Thus he freed himself from all doubts listed previously.

However, before I here make an end, I think I ought to satisfy those who argue as follows: "Because the existence of God is not self-evident to us, it seems that we can never be certain of anything, nor can it ever be known to us that God exists. For from premises that are uncertain (and we have said that, as long as we do not know our own origin), nothing certain can be concluded."

---

16 [Med3, 34–35 (AT7, 51–52); Med5, 46–47 (AT7, 70–71).]

17 [Med4, 35–42 (AT7, 52–62).]

18 [Med6, 47–59 (AT7, 71–90).]

To remove this difficulty, Descartes replies in the following manner. From the fact that we do not as yet know whether the author of our origin may have created us such as to be deceived even in those matters that appear to us most certain, it by no means follows that we can doubt those things that we understand clearly and distinctly through themselves or through a process of reasoning, that is, as long as we are paying attention to it. We can doubt only those things previously demonstrated to be true, which we may remember when we are no longer attending to the reasoning from which we deduced them, and which we have thus forgotten. Therefore, although the existence of God can be known not through itself but only through something else, we can nevertheless attain certain knowledge of God's existence provided that we carefully attend to all the premises from which we conclude it. See *Principia* Part 1 Article 13, and "Reply to Second Objections," No. 3, and at the end of the "Fifth Meditation."

However, because some do not find this reply satisfactory, I shall give another. When we were speaking previously of the certainty and sureness of our existence, we saw that we concluded it from the fact that, in whatever direction we turned the mind's eye, we did not find any reason for doubting that did not by that very fact convince us of our existence. This was so whether we were considering our own nature, whether we were imagining the author of our nature to be a cunning deceiver—in short, whatever reason for doubting we invoked, external to ourselves. Hitherto we had not found this to be so in the case of any other matter. For example, while attending to the nature of a triangle, although we are compelled to conclude that its three angles are equal to two right angles, we cannot reach this same conclusion if we suppose that we may be deceived by the author of our nature. Yet this very supposition assured us of our existence with the utmost certainty. So it is not the case that, wherever we turn the mind's eye, we are compelled to conclude that the three angles of a triangle are equal to two right angles; on the contrary, we find a reason for doubting it in that we do not possess an idea of God such as to render it impossible for us to think that God is a deceiver. For one who does not possess the true idea of God—which at the moment we suppose we do not possess—may quite as easily think that his author is a deceiver as think that he is not a deceiver, just as one who does not have the idea of a triangle may indifferently think its angles are equal or not equal to two right angles.

Therefore we concede that, except for our existence, we cannot be absolutely certain of anything, however earnestly we attend to its demonstration, as long as we do not have the clear and distinct conception of God that makes us affirm that God is supremely truthful, just as the idea we have of a triangle makes us conclude that its three angles are equal to two right angles. But we deny that, for this reason, we cannot attain knowledge of anything. For, as is evident from all that has already been said, the whole matter hinges on this alone, that we are able to form such a conception of God as so disposes us that it is not as easy for us to think that God is a deceiver as to think that he is not a deceiver, a conception that compels us to affirm that he is supremely truthful. When we have formed such an idea, the reason for doubting mathematical truths will be removed. For in whatever direction we now turn the mind's eye with the purpose of doubting one of these truths, we shall not find anything that itself does not make us conclude that this truth is most certain, just as was the case with regard to our existence.

For example, if after discovering the idea of God we attend to the nature of a triangle, its idea will compel us to affirm that its three angles are equal to two right angles, whereas if we attend to the idea of God, this too will compel us to affirm that he is supremely truthful, the author and continuous preserver of our nature, and therefore that he is not deceiving us with regard to this truth. And attending to the idea of God (which we now suppose we have discovered), it will be just as impossible for us to think that he is a deceiver as to think, when attending to the idea of a triangle, that its three angles are not equal to two right angles. And just as we can form such an idea of a triangle in spite of not knowing whether the author of our nature is deceiving us, so too we can achieve a clear idea of God and set it before us even though also doubting whether the author of our nature is deceiving us in all things. And provided we possess this idea, in whatever way we may have acquired it, it will be enough to remove all doubts, as has just now been shown.

So having made these points, I reply as follows to the difficulty that has been raised. It is not as long as we do not know of God's existence (for I have not spoken of that) but as long as we do not have a clear and distinct idea of God, that we cannot be certain of anything. Therefore, if anyone wishes to argue against me, his argument will have to be as follows: "We cannot be certain of anything until we have a clear and distinct idea of God. But we cannot have a clear and distinct idea of God as long as we do not know whether the author of our nature is deceiving us. Therefore, we cannot be certain of anything as long as we do not know whether the author of our nature is deceiving us, etc." To this I reply by conceding the major premise and denying the minor. For we do have a clear and distinct idea of a triangle, although we do not know whether the author of our nature is deceiving us; and granted that we have such an idea of God, as I have just shown at some length, we cannot doubt his existence or any mathematical truth.

With this as preface, I now enter upon the work itself.

Definitions

1. Under the word *Thought*, I include all that is in us and of which we are immediately conscious. Thus all operations of the will, intellect, imagination, and senses are thoughts. But I have added 'immediately' so as to exclude those things that are their consequences. For example, voluntary motion has thought for its starting point, but in itself it is still not thought.

2. By the word *Idea*, I understand the specific form [*forma*] of a thought, through the immediate perception of which I am conscious of that same thought.

So whenever I express something in words while understanding what I am saying, this very fact makes it certain that there is in me the idea of that which is meant by those words. And so I do not apply the term 'ideas' simply to images depicted in the fantasy; indeed I do not here term these 'ideas' at all, insofar as they are depicted in the corporeal fantasy (i.e., in some part of the brain) but only insofar as they communicate their form to the mind itself when this is directed toward that part of the brain.

3. By the *objective reality of an idea*, I understand the being of that which is presented through the idea, insofar as it is in the idea.[19]

In the same way one can speak of 'objective perfection' or 'objective art', etc. For whatever we perceive as being in the objects of ideas is objectively in the ideas themselves.

4. When things are, in themselves, such as we perceive them to be, they are said to be *formally* in the objects of ideas, and *eminently* when they are not just such in themselves as we perceive them to be but are more than sufficient to account fully for our perception.

Note that when I say that the cause contains eminently the perfections of its effect, I mean that the cause contains the perfections of the effect with a higher degree of excellence than does the effect itself. See also Axiom 8.

5. Everything in which there is something that we perceive as immediately inhering in a subject, or through which there exists something that we perceive (i.e., some property, quality or attribute whose real idea is in us), is called *substance*. For of substance itself, taken precisely, we have no other idea than that it is a thing in which there exists formally or eminently that something which we perceive (i.e., that something which is objectively in one of our ideas).

6. Substance in which thought immediately inheres is called *Mind* [*Mens*].

I here speak of 'Mind' rather than 'Soul' [*anima*] because the word 'soul' is equivocal, and is often used to mean a corporeal thing.

7. Substance that is the immediate subject of extension and of accidents that presuppose extension, such as figure, position, and local motion, is called *Body*.

Whether what is called Mind and what is called Body is one and the same substance, or two different substances, is something to be enquired into later.

8. Substance that we understand through itself to be supremely perfect, and in which we conceive nothing at all that involves any defect or limitation of perfection, is called *God*.

9. When we say that something is contained in the nature or conception of some thing, that is the same as saying that it is true of that thing or can be truly affirmed of it.[20]

10. Two substances are said to be distinct in reality when each one can exist without the other.

We have here omitted the Postulates of Descartes because in what follows we do not draw any conclusions from them. But we earnestly ask readers to read them through and to think them over carefully.[21]

---

[19] [Cf. Med3, 27–28 (AT7, 40–41).]

[20] [In each of the preceding eight definitions a word or phrase has been italicized to indicate the *definiendum*, but in this definition and the next there is no text italicized. It appears reasonable to assume that Def9 has as *definiendum contained in the nature or conception of some thing* and Def10 *distinct in reality*.]

[21] [The seven postulates (AT7, 162–164) or *demandes* in the French version (AT9, 125–127) are not postulates in the Euclidean sense but are requests from Descartes to his readers to ponder carefully what can be doubted, the preceding definitions, and especially the distinction between clear, distinct perception and obscure, confused perception.]

Axioms[22]

1. We arrive at the knowledge and certainty of some unknown thing only through the knowledge and certainty of another thing that is prior to it in certainty and knowledge.

2. There are reasons that make us doubt the existence of our bodies.

This has in fact been shown in the Prolegomenon, and so is here posited as an axiom.

3. If we have anything besides mind and body, this is less known to us than mind and body.

It should be noted that these axioms do not affirm anything about things external to us, but only such things as we find within ourselves insofar as we are thinking things.

P1   *We cannot be absolutely certain of anything as long as we do not know that we exist.*

Proof   This proposition is self-evident; for he who absolutely does not know that he is likewise does not know that he is a being affirming or denying, that is, that he certainly affirms or denies.

Here it should be noted that although we may affirm or deny many things with great certainty while not attending to the fact that we exist, unless this is presupposed as indubitable, everything could be called into doubt.

P2   *'I am' must be self-evident.*

Proof   If this be denied, it will therefore be known only through something else, the knowledge and certainty of which will be prior in us to the statement 'I am' (Ax. 1). But this is absurd (Pr. 1). Therefore it must be self-evident. Q.E.D.

P3   *'I am', insofar as the 'I' is a thing consisting of body, is not a first principle and is not known through itself.*

Proof   There are certain things that make us doubt the existence of our body (Ax. 2). Therefore (Ax. 1) we shall not attain certainty of this except through the knowledge and certainty of something else that is prior to it in knowledge and certainty. Therefore the statement 'I am', insofar as 'I' am a thing consisting of body, is not a first principle and is not known through itself. Q.E.D.

P4   *'I am' cannot be the first known principle except insofar as we think.*

Proof   The statement 'I am a corporeal thing, or a thing consisting of body' is not a first-known principle (Pr. 3), nor again am I certain of my existence insofar as I

---

22 [The first three axioms are not taken from Descartes; but Meyer, in his preface, has mentioned that Spinoza would expound Descartes's opinions and demonstrations "just as they are found in his writings, or such as should validly be deduced from the foundations laid by him."]

consist of anything other than mind and body. For if we consist of anything different from mind and body, this is less well known to us than body (Ax. 3). Therefore 'I am' cannot be the first known thing except insofar as we think. Q.E.D.

Cor   From this it is obvious that mind, or a thinking thing, is better known than body.

But for a fuller explanation read Part 1 of the *Principia* Arts. 11 and 12.

Schol   Everyone perceives with the utmost certainty that he affirms, denies, doubts, understands, imagines, etc., or that he exists as doubting, understanding, affirming, etc.—in short, as thinking. Nor can this be called into doubt. Therefore the statement 'I think' or 'I am, as thinking' is the unique (Pr. 1) and most certain basis of all philosophy. Now in order to achieve the greatest certainty in the sciences, our aim and purpose can be no other than this, to deduce everything from the strongest first principles and to make the inferences as clear and distinct as the first principles from which they are deduced. It therefore clearly follows that we must consider as most certainly true everything that is equally evident to us and that we perceive with the same clearness and distinctness as the already discovered first principle, and also everything that so agrees with this first principle and so depends on it that we cannot doubt it without also having to doubt this first principle.

But to proceed with the utmost caution in reviewing these matters, at the first stage I shall admit as equally evident and equally clearly and distinctly perceived by us only those things that each of us observes in himself insofar as he is engaged in thinking. Such are, for example, that he wills this or that, that he has definite ideas of such-and-such a kind, and that one idea contains in itself more reality and perfection than another—namely, that the one that contains objectively the being and perfection of substance is far more perfect than one that contains only the objective perfection of some accident, and, finally, that the idea of a supremely perfect being is the most perfect of all. These things, I say, we perceive not merely with equal sureness and clarity but perhaps even more distinctly; for they affirm not only that we think but also how we think.

Further, we shall also say that those things that cannot be doubted without at the same time casting doubt on this unshakable foundation of ours are also in agreement with this first principle. For example, if anyone should doubt whether something can come from nothing, he will be able at the same time to doubt whether we, as long as we are thinking, are. For if I can affirm something of nothing—in effect, that nothing can be the cause of something—I can at the same time and with the same right affirm thought of nothing, and say that I, as long as I am thinking, am nothing. Because I find this impossible, it will also be impossible for me to think that something may come from nothing.

With these considerations in mind, I have decided at this point to list here in order those things that at present seem to us necessary for future progress, and to add to the number of axioms. For these are indeed set forth by Descartes as axioms at the end of his "Reply to the Second Set of Objections," and I do not aim at greater accuracy than he. However, not to depart from the order we have been pursuing,

I shall try to make them somewhat clearer, and to show how one depends on another and all on this one first principle, 'I am, while thinking', or how their certainty and reasonableness is of the same degree as that of the first principle.

Axioms Taken from Descartes

4. There are different degrees of reality or being; for substance has more reality than accident or mode, and infinite substance, more than finite substance. Therefore there is more objective reality in the idea of substance than in the idea of accident, and in the idea of infinite substance than in the idea of finite substance.[23]

This axiom is known simply from contemplating our ideas, of whose existence we are certain because they are modes of thinking. For we know how much reality or perfection the idea of substance affirms of substance, and how much the idea of mode affirms of mode. This being so, we also necessarily realize that the idea of substance contains more objective reality than the idea of some accident, etc. See Scholium Pr. 4.

5. A thinking thing, if it knows of any perfections that it lacks, will immediately give these to itself, if they are within its power.[24]

This everyone observes in himself insofar as he is a thinking thing. Therefore (Scholium Pr. 4) we are most certain of it. And for the same reason, we are just as certain of the following:

6. In the idea or concept of every thing, there is contained either possible or necessary existence. (See Axiom 10, Descartes.)

Necessary existence is contained in the concept of God, or a supremely perfect being; for otherwise he would be conceived as imperfect, which is contrary to what is supposed to be conceived. Contingent or possible existence is contained in the concept of a limited thing.

7. No thing, nor any perfection of a thing actually existing, can have nothing, or a nonexisting thing, as the cause of its existence.

I have demonstrated in the Scholium Pr. 4 that this axiom is as clear to us as is 'I am, when thinking'.

8. Whatever there is of reality or perfection in any thing exists formally or eminently in its first and adequate cause.[25]

By 'eminently' I understand: when the cause contains all the reality of the effect more perfectly than the effect itself. By 'formally': when the cause contains all the reality of the effect equally perfectly.

This axiom depends on the preceding one. For if it were supposed that there is nothing in the cause, or less in the cause than in the effect, then nothing in the cause would be the cause of the effect. But this is absurd (Ax. 7). Therefore it is not the case that anything whatsoever can be the cause of a certain effect; it must

---

[23] [Cf. Med3, 27–28 (AT7, 40–42).]

[24] [Cf. Med3, 32–33 (AT7, 48).]

[25] [Cf. Med3, 28 (AT7, 40–41).]

be precisely a thing in which there is eminently or at least formally all the perfection that is in the effect.

9. The objective reality of our ideas requires a cause in which that same reality is contained not only objectively but also formally or eminently.[26]

This axiom, although misused by many, is universally admitted, for when somebody conceives something new, everyone wants to know the cause of this concept or idea. Now when they can assign a cause in which is contained formally or eminently as much reality as is contained objectively in that concept, they are satisfied. This is made quite clear by the example of a machine, which Descartes adduces in Art. 17 Part 1 *Principia*.[27] Similarly, if anyone were to ask whence it is that a man has the ideas of his thought and of his body, no one can fail to see that he has them from himself, as containing formally everything that his ideas contain objectively. Therefore if a man were to have some idea that contained more of objective reality than he himself contained of formal reality, then of necessity we should be driven by the natural light to seek another cause outside the man himself, a cause that contained all that perfection formally or eminently. And apart from that cause no one has ever assigned any other cause that he has conceived so clearly and distinctly.

Furthermore, as for the truth of this axiom, it depends on the previous ones. By Axiom 4 there are different degrees of reality or being in ideas. Therefore (Ax. 8) they need a more perfect cause in accordance with their degree of perfection. But because the degrees of reality that we observe in ideas are not in the ideas insofar as they are considered as modes of thinking but insofar as one presents substance and another merely a mode of substance—or, in brief, insofar as they are considered as images of things—hence it clearly follows that there can be granted no other first cause of ideas than that which, as we have just shown, all men understand clearly and distinctly by the natural light, namely, one in which is contained formally or eminently the same reality that the ideas have objectively.[28]

To make this conclusion more clearly understood, I shall illustrate it with one or two examples. If anyone sees some books (imagine one to be that of a distinguished philosopher and the other to be that of some trifler) written in one and the same hand, and if he pays no attention to the meaning of the words (i.e., insofar as they are symbols) but only to the shape of the writing and the order of the letters, he will find no distinction between them such as to compel him to seek different causes for them. They will appear to him to have proceeded from the same cause and in the same manner. But if he pays attention to the meaning of the words and of the language, he will find a considerable distinction between them. He will therefore conclude that the first cause of the one book was very different from the first cause of the other, and that the one cause was in fact more

---

[26] [Cf. Med3, 28 (AT7, 41–42).]

[27] [Cf. Rep1, AT7, 104–106.]

[28] We are also certain of this because we experience it ourselves insofar as we are thinking. See preceding Scholium.

perfect than the other to the extent that the meaning of the language of the two books, or their words considered as symbols, are found to differ from one another.

I am speaking of the first cause of books, and there must necessarily be one although I admit—indeed, I take for granted—that one book can be transcribed from another, as is self-evident.

The same point can also be clearly illustrated by the example of a portrait, let us say, of some prince. If we pay attention only to the materials of which it is made, we shall not find any distinction between it and other portraits such as to compel us to look for different causes. Indeed, there will be nothing to prevent us from thinking that it was copied from another likeness, and that one again from another, and so ad infinitum. For we shall be quite satisfied that there need be no other cause for its production. But if we attend to the image insofar as it is the image of something, we shall immediately be compelled to seek a first cause such as formally or eminently contains what that image contains representatively. I do not see what more need be said to confirm and elucidate this axiom.

10. To preserve a thing, no lesser cause is required than to produce it in the first place.

From the fact that at this moment we are thinking, it does not necessarily follow that we shall hereafter be thinking. For the concept that we have of our thought does not involve, or does not contain, the necessary existence of the thought. I can clearly and distinctly conceive the thought even though I suppose it not to exist.[29] Now the nature of every cause must contain in itself or involve the perfection of its effect (Ax. 8). Hence it clearly follows that there must be something in us or external to us that we have not yet understood, whose concept or nature involves existence, and that is the reason why our thought began to exist and also continues to exist. For although our thought began to exist, its nature and essence does not on that account involve necessary existence any the more than before it existed, and so in order to persevere in existing it stands in need of the same force that it needs to begin existing. And what we here say about thought must be said about every thing whose essence does not involve necessary existence.

11. Of every thing that exists, it can be asked what is the cause or reason why it exists. See Descartes, Axiom 1.

Because to exist is something positive, we cannot say that it has nothing for its cause (Ax. 7). Therefore we must assign some positive cause or reason why it exists. And this must be either external (i.e., outside the thing itself) or else internal (i.e., included in the nature and definition of the existing thing itself).

The four propositions that follow are taken from Descartes.

P5   *The existence of God is known solely from the consideration of his nature.*

Proof   To say that something is contained in the nature or concept of a thing is the same as to say that it is true of that thing (Def. 9). But necessary existence is

---

[29] This is something everyone discovers in himself, insofar as he is a thinking thing.

236 Principles of Cartesian Philosophy

contained in the concept of God (Ax. 6). Therefore it is true to say of God that there is necessary existence in him, or that he exists.[30]

Schol From this proposition there follow many important consequences. Indeed, on this fact alone—that existence pertains to the nature of God, or that the concept of God involves necessary existence just as the concept of a triangle involves its three angles being equal to two right angles, or that his existence, just like his essence, is an eternal truth—depends almost all knowledge of the attributes of God through which we are brought to love of him and to the highest blessedness. Therefore it is much to be desired that mankind should come round to our opinion on this subject.

I do indeed admit that there are some prejudices that prevent this from being so easily understood by everyone.[31] If anyone, moved by goodwill and by the simple love of truth and his own true advantage, comes to look at the matter closely and to reflect on what is contained in the "Fifth Meditation" and the end of "Replies to the First Set of Objections," and also on what we say about Eternity in Chapter 1 Part 2 of our Appendix, he will undoubtedly understand the matter quite clearly and will in no way be able to doubt whether he has an idea of God (which is, of course, the first foundation of human blessedness). For when he realizes that God is completely different in kind from other things in respect of essence and existence, he will at once see clearly that the idea of God is far different from the ideas of other things. Therefore there is no need to detain the reader any longer on this subject.

P6 *The existence of God is proved a posteriori from the mere fact that the idea of him is in us.*

Proof The objective reality of any of our ideas requires a cause in which that same reality is contained not just objectively but formally or eminently (Ax. 9). Now we do have the idea of God (Defs. 2 and 8), and the objective reality of this idea is not contained in us either formally or eminently (Ax. 4), nor can it be contained in anything other than God himself (Def. 8). Therefore this idea of God, which is in us, requires God for its cause, and therefore God exists (Ax. 7).[32]

Schol There are some who deny that they have any idea of God, and yet, as they declare, they worship and love him. And though you were to set before them the definition of God and the attributes of God, you will meet with no more success than if you were to labor to teach a man blind from birth the differences of colors as we see them. However, except to consider them as a strange type of creature halfway between man and beast, we should pay small heed to their words. How else, I ask, can we show the idea of some thing than by giving its definition and explaining its attributes? Because this is what we are doing in the case of the idea

---

[30] [Cf. Med5, 43–46 (AT7, 65–69); E1P11Dem1; KV1/1/1–2.]

[31] Read *Principia* Part 1 Art. 16.

[32] [Cf. Med3, 28–31 (AT7, 40–45).]

of God, there is no reason for us to be concerned over the words of men who deny the idea of God simply on the grounds that they cannot form an image of him in their brain.

Furthermore, we should note that when Descartes quotes Axiom 4 to show that the objective reality of the idea of God is not contained in us either formally or eminently, he takes for granted that everyone knows that he is not an infinite substance, that is, supremely intelligent, supremely powerful, etc., and this he is entitled to do. For he who knows that he thinks, also knows that he doubts many things and that he does not understand everything clearly and distinctly.

Finally, we should note that it also follows clearly from Definition 8 that there cannot be a number of Gods, but only one God, as we clearly demonstrate in Proposition 11 of this Part, and in Part 2 of our Appendix, Chapter 2.

P7   *The existence of God is also proved from the fact that we ourselves exist while having the idea of him.*

Proof   If I had the force to preserve myself, I would be of such a nature that I would involve necessary existence (Lemma 2). Therefore (Corollary Lemma 1) my nature would contain all perfections. But I find in myself, insofar as I am a thinking thing, many imperfections—as that I doubt, desire, etc.—and of this I am certain (Scholium Pr. 4). Therefore I have no force to preserve myself. Nor can I say that the reason I now lack those perfections is that I now will to deny them to myself, for this would be clearly inconsistent with Lemma 1, and with what I clearly find in myself (Ax. 5).

Further, I cannot now exist, while I am existing, without being preserved either by myself—if indeed I have that force—or by something else that does have that force (Axioms 10 and 11). But I do exist (Scholium Pr. 4), and yet I do not have the force to preserve myself, as has just now been proved. Therefore I am preserved by something else. But not by something else that does not have the force to preserve itself (by the same reasoning whereby I have just demonstrated that I am not able to preserve myself). Therefore it must be by something else that has the force to preserve itself; that is (Lemma 2), something whose nature involves necessary existence; that is (Corollary Lemma 1), something that contains all the perfections that I clearly understand to pertain to a supremely perfect being. Therefore a supremely perfect being exists; that is (Def. 8), God exists. Q.E.D.

Schol   To demonstrate this proposition Descartes assumes the following two axioms:

1. That which can effect what is greater or more difficult can also effect what is less.
2. It is a greater thing to create or (Ax. 10) to preserve substance than the attributes or properties of substance.

What he means by these axioms I do not know. For what does he call easy, and what difficult? Nothing is said to be easy or difficult in an absolute sense, but only with respect to its cause. So one and the same thing can be said at the same time to be easy and difficult in respect of different causes.[33] Now if, of things that can be effected by the same cause, he calls those difficult that need great effort and those easy that need less (e.g., the force that can raise fifty pounds can raise twenty-five pounds twice as easily) then surely the axiom is not absolutely true, nor can he prove from it what he aims to prove. For when he says, "If I had the force to preserve myself, I should also have the force to give myself all the perfections that I lack" (because this latter does not require as much power), I would grant him that the strength that I expend on preserving myself could effect many other things far more easily had I not needed it to preserve myself, but I deny that, as long as I am using it to preserve myself,[34] I can direct it to effecting other things however much easier, as can clearly be seen in our example.

And the difficulty is not removed by saying that, because I am a thinking thing, I must necessarily know whether I am expending all my strength in preserving myself, and whether this is also the reason why I do not give myself the other perfections. For—apart from the fact that this point is not at issue, but only how the necessity of this proposition follows from this axiom—if I knew this, I should be a greater being and perhaps require greater strength than I have so as to preserve myself in that greater perfection. Again, I do not know whether it is a greater task to create or preserve substance than to create or preserve its attributes. That is, to speak more clearly and in more philosophic terms, I do not know whether a substance, so as to preserve its attributes, does not need the whole of its virtue and essence with which it may be preserving itself.

But let us leave this and examine further what our noble Author here intends; that is, what he understands by 'easy' and what by 'difficult'. I do not think, nor can I in any way be convinced, that by 'difficult' he understands that which is impossible (and therefore cannot be conceived in any way as coming into being), and by 'easy', that which does not imply any contradiction (and therefore can readily be conceived as coming into being)—although in the "Third Meditation" he seems at first glance to mean this when he says: "Nor ought I to think that perhaps those things that I lack are more difficult to acquire than those that are already in me. For on the contrary it is obvious that it was far more difficult for me, a thinking thing or substance, to emerge from nothing than . . .", etc.[35] This would not be consistent with the Author's words nor would it smack of his genius. For, passing over the first point, there is no relationship between the possible and the impossible, or between the intelligible and the nonintelligible, just as there is no relationship between something and nothing, and power has no more to do with impossible things than creation and generation, with nonentities; so there can be no comparison between them. Besides, I can compare things and understand

---

[33] Take as only one example the spider, which easily weaves a web that men would find very difficult to weave. On the other hand, men find it quite easy to do many things that are perhaps impossible for angels.

[34] [I have diverged from the punctuation of Gebhardt.—S.S.]

[35] [Cf. Med3, 32–33 (AT7, 48).]

their relationship only when I have a clear and distinct conception of them all. So I deny that it follows that he who can do the impossible can also do the possible. What sort of conclusion, I ask, would this be? That if someone can make a square circle, he will also be able to make a circle wherein all the lines drawn from the center to the circumference are equal. Or if someone can bring it about that 'nothing' can be acted upon, and can use it as material to produce something, he will also have the power to make something from something. For, as I have said, there is no agreement, or analogy, or comparison or any relationship whatsoever between these things and things like these. Anyone can see this, if only he gives a little attention to the matter. Therefore I think this quite irreconcilable with Descartes's genius.

But if I attend to the second of the two axioms just now stated, it appears that what he means by 'greater' and 'more difficult' is 'more perfect', and by 'lesser' and 'easier', 'less perfect'. Yet this, again, seems very obscure, for there is here the same difficulty as before. As before, I deny that he who can do the greater can, at the same time and with the same effort (as must be supposed in the proposition), do the lesser.

Again, when he says: "It is a greater thing to create or preserve substance than its attributes," surely he cannot understand by attributes that which is formally contained in substance and differs from substance itself only by conceptual abstraction. For then it would be the same thing to create substance as to create attributes. Nor again, by the same reasoning, can he mean the properties of substance which necessarily follow from its essence and definition.

Far less can he mean—and yet he appears to—the properties and attributes of another substance. For instance, if I say that I have the power to preserve myself, a finite thinking substance, I cannot for that reason say that I also have the power to give myself the perfections of infinite substance, which differs totally in essence from my essence. For the force or essence whereby I preserve myself in my being is quite different in kind from the force or essence whereby absolutely infinite substance preserves itself, and from which its powers and properties are distinguishable only by abstract reason.[36] So even though I were to suppose that I preserve myself, if I wanted to conceive that I could give myself the perfections of absolutely infinite substance, I should be supposing nothing other than this, that I could reduce my entire essence to nothing and create an infinite substance anew. This would be much more, surely, than merely to suppose that I can preserve myself, a finite substance.

Therefore, because by the terms 'attributes' or 'properties' he can mean none of these things, there remain only the qualities that substance itself contains eminently (as this or that thought in the mind, which I clearly perceive to be lacking in me), but not the qualities that another substance contains eminently (as this or that motion in extension; for such perfections are not perfections for me,

---

[36] Note that the force by which substance preserves itself is nothing but its essence, differing from it only in name. This will be a particular feature of our discussion in the Appendix, concerning the power of God.

a thinking thing, and therefore they are not lacking to me). But then what Descartes wants to prove—that if I am preserving myself, I also have the power to give myself all the perfections that I clearly see as pertaining to a most perfect being—can in no way be concluded from this axiom, as is quite clear from what I have said previously. However, not to leave the matter unproved, and to avoid all confusion, I have thought it advisable first of all to demonstrate the following Lemmas, and thereafter to construct on them the proof of Proposition 7.

Lemma 1   The more perfect a thing is by its own nature, the greater the existence it involves, and the more necessary is the existence. Conversely, the more a thing by its own nature involves necessary existence, the more perfect it is.

Proof   Existence is contained in the idea or concept of everything (Ax.6). Then let it be supposed that A is a thing that has ten degrees of perfection. I say that its concept involves more existence than if it were supposed to contain only five degrees of perfection. Because we cannot affirm any existence of nothing (see Scholium Pr. 4), in proportion as we in thought subtract from its perfection and therefore conceive it as participating more and more in nothing, to that extent we also deny the possibility of its existence. So if we conceive its degrees of perfection to be reduced indefinitely to nought or zero, it will contain no existence, or absolutely impossible existence. But, on the other hand, if we increase its degrees of perfection indefinitely, we shall conceive it as involving the utmost existence, and therefore the most necessary existence. That was the first thing to be proved. Now since these two things can in no way be separated (as is quite clear from Axiom 6 and the whole of Part 1 of this work), what we proposed to prove in the second place clearly follows.

Note 1. Although many things are said to exist necessarily solely on the grounds that there is given a cause determined to produce them, it is not of this that we are here speaking; we are speaking only of that necessity and possibility that follows solely from consideration of the nature or essence of a thing, without taking any account of its cause.

Note 2. We are not here speaking of beauty and other 'perfections', which, out of superstition and ignorance, men have thought fit to call perfections; by perfection I understand only reality or being. For example, I perceive that more reality is contained in substance than in modes or accidents. So I understand clearly that substance contains more necessary and more perfect existence than is contained in accidents, as is well established from Axioms 4 and 6.

Cor   Hence it follows that whatever involves necessary existence is a supremely perfect being, or God.

Lemma 2   The nature of one who has the power to preserve himself involves necessary existence.

Proof   He who has the force to preserve himself has also the force to create himself (Ax. 10); that is (as everyone will readily admit), he needs no external cause to exist, but his own nature alone will be a sufficient cause of his existence, either possibly (Ax. 10) or necessarily. But not possibly; for then (through what I have demonstrated with regard to Axiom 10) from the fact that he now existed it would not follow that he would thereafter exist (which is contrary to the hypothesis). Therefore necessarily; that is, his nature involves necessary existence. Q.E.D.

Cor God can bring about every thing that we clearly perceive, just as we perceive it.

Proof All this follows clearly from the preceding proposition. For there God's existence was proved from the fact that there must exist someone in whom are all the perfections of which there is an idea in us. Now there is in us the idea of a power so great that by him alone in whom it resides there can be made the sky, the earth, and all the other things that are understood by me as possible. Therefore, along with God's existence, all these things, too, are proved of him.

P8 *Mind and body are distinct in reality.*

Proof Whatever we clearly perceive can be brought about by God just as we perceive it (Cor. Pr. 7). But we clearly perceive mind, that is (Def. 6), a thinking substance, without body, that is (Def. 7), without any extended substance (Prs. 3 and 4); and conversely we clearly perceive body without mind, as everyone readily admits. Therefore, at least through divine power, mind can be without body and body without mind.[37]

Now substances that can be without one another are distinct in reality (Def. 10). But mind and body are substances (Defs. 5, 6, and 7) that can exist without one another, as has just been proved. Therefore mind and body are distinct in reality.

See Proposition 4 at the end of Descartes's "Replies to the Second Set of Objections," and the passages in *Principia* Part 1 from Arts. 22–29. For I do not think it worthwhile to transcribe them here.

P9 *God is a supremely understanding being.*

Proof If you deny this, then God will understand either nothing or not everything, that is, only some things. But to understand only some things and to be ignorant of the rest supposes a limited and imperfect intellect, which it is absurd to ascribe to God (Def. 8). And that God should understand nothing either indicates a lack of intellection in God — as it does with men who understand nothing — and involves imperfection (which, by the same definition, cannot be the case with God), or else it indicates that it is incompatible with God's perfection that he should understand something. But because intellection is thus completely denied of God, he will not be able to create any intellect (Ax. 8). Now because intellect is clearly and distinctly perceived by us, God can be its cause (Cor. Pr. 7). Therefore it is far from true that it is incompatible with God's perfection for him to understand something. Therefore he is a supremely understanding being. Q.E.D.

---

[37] [Cf. Med6, 51 (AT7, 78).]

Schol   Although it must be granted that God is incorporeal, as is demonstrated in Pr. 16, this must not be taken to mean that all the perfections of extension are to be withdrawn from him. They are to be withdrawn from him only to the extent that the nature and properties of extension involve some imperfection. The same point is to be made concerning God's intellection, as is admitted by all who seek wisdom beyond the common run of philosophers, and as will be fully explained in our Appendix Part 2 Chapter 7.

P10   *Whatever perfection is found in God, is from God.*

Proof   If you deny this, suppose that there is in God some perfection that is not from God. It will be in God either from itself, or from something different from God. If from itself, it will therefore have necessary existence, not merely possible existence (Lemma 2 Pr. 7), and so (Corollary Lemma 1 Pr. 7) it will be something supremely perfect, and therefore (Def. 8) it will be God. So if it be said that there is in God something that is from itself, at the same time it is said that this is from God. Q.E.D. But if it be from something different from God, then God cannot be conceived through himself as supremely perfect, contrary to Definition 8. Therefore whatever perfection is found in God, is from God. Q.E.D.

P11   *There cannot be more than one God.*

Proof   If you deny this, conceive, if you can, more than one God (e.g., A and B). Then of necessity (Pr. 9) both A and B will have the highest degree of understanding; that is, A will understand everything, himself and B, and in turn B will understand himself and A. But because A and B necessarily exist (Pr. 5), therefore the cause of the truth and the necessity of the idea of B, which is in A, is B; and conversely the cause of the truth and the necessity of the idea of A, which is in B, is A. Therefore there will be in A a perfection that is not from A, and in B a perfection that is not from B. Therefore (Pr. 10) neither A nor B will be a God, and so there cannot be more than one God. Q.E.D.

Here it should be noted that, from the mere fact that something of itself involves necessary existence—as is the case with God—it necessarily follows that it is unique. This is something that everyone can see for himself with careful thought, and I could have demonstrated it here, but not in a manner as comprehensible to all as is done in this proposition.

P12   *All things that exist are preserved solely by the power of God.*

Proof   If you deny this, suppose that something preserves itself. Therefore (Lemma 2 Pr. 7) its nature involves necessary existence. Thus (Corollary Lemma 1 Pr. 7) it would be God, and there would be more than one God, which is absurd (Pr. 11). Therefore everything that exists is preserved solely by the power of God. Q.E.D.

Cor 1   God is the creator of all things.

Proof   God preserves all things (Pr. 12); that is (Ax. 10), he has created, and still continuously creates, everything that exists.

Cor 2   Things of themselves do not have any essence that is the cause of God's knowledge. On the contrary, God is also the cause of things with respect to their essence.

Proof   Because there is not to be found in God anything of perfection that is not from God (Pr. 10), things of themselves will not have any essence that can be the cause of God's knowledge. On the contrary, because God has created all things wholly, not generating them from something else (Pr. 12 with Cor. 1), and because the act of creation acknowledges no other cause but the efficient cause (for this is how I define 'creation'), which is God, it follows that before their creation things were nothing at all, and therefore God was also the cause of their essence. Q.E.D.

It should be noted that this corollary is also evident from the fact that God is the cause or creator of all things (Cor. 1) and that the cause must contain in itself all the perfections of the effect (Ax. 8), as everyone can readily see.

Cor 3   Hence it clearly follows that God does not sense, nor, properly speaking, does he perceive. For his intellect is not determined by anything external to himself; all things derive from him.

Cor 4   God is prior in causality to the essence and existence of things, as clearly follows from Corollaries 1 and 2 of this Proposition.

P13   *God is supremely truthful, and not at all a deceiver.*[38]

Proof   We cannot attribute to God anything in which we find any imperfection (Def. 8); and because (as is self-evident) all deception or will to deceive proceeds only from malice or fear, and fear supposes diminished power while malice supposes privation of goodness, no deception or will to deceive is to be ascribed to God, a being supremely powerful and supremely good. On the contrary, he must be said to be supremely truthful and not at all a deceiver. Q.E.D. See "Replies to the Second Set of Objections," No. 4.[39]

P14   *Whatever we clearly and distinctly perceive is true.*

Proof   The faculty of distinguishing true from false, which is in us (as everyone can discover in himself, and as is obvious from all that has already been proved) has been created and is continuously preserved by God (Pr. 12 with Cor.), that is, by a being supremely truthful and not at all a deceiver (Pr. 13), and he has not bestowed on us (as everyone can discover in himself) any faculty for holding aloof

---

[38] I have not included this axiom among the axioms because it was not at all necessary. I had no need of it except for the proof of this proposition alone, and furthermore, as long as I did not know God's existence, I did not wish to assume as true anything more than what I could deduce from the first known thing, 'I am', as I said in the Scholium to Proposition 4. Again, I have not included among my definitions the definitions of fear and malice because everyone knows them, and I have no need of them except for this one proposition.

[39] [AT7, 142–147.]

from, or refusing assent to, those things that we clearly and distinctly perceive. Therefore if we were to be deceived in regard to them, we should be deceived entirely by God, and he would be a deceiver, which is absurd (Pr. 13). So whatever we clearly and distinctly perceive is true. Q.E.D.

Schol   Because those things to which we must necessarily assent when they are clearly and distinctly perceived by us are necessarily true, and because we have a faculty for withholding assent from those things that are obscure or doubtful or are not deduced from the most certain principles—as everyone can see in himself—it clearly follows that we can always take precautions against falling into error and against ever being deceived (a point that will be understood even more clearly from what follows), provided that we make an earnest resolution to affirm nothing that we do not clearly and distinctly perceive or that is not deduced from first principles clear and certain in themselves.

P15   *Error is not anything positive.*

Proof   If error were something positive, it would have as its cause only God, by whom it must be continuously created (Pr. 12). But this is absurd (Pr. 13). Therefore error is not anything positive. Q.E.D.

Schol   Because error is not anything positive in man, it can be nothing else than the privation of the right use of freedom (Schol. Pr. 14). Therefore God must not be said to be the cause of error, except in the sense in which we say that the absence of the sun is the cause of darkness, or that God, in making a child similar to others except for sight, is the cause of blindness. He is not to be said to be the cause of error in giving us an intellect that extends to only a few things. To understand this clearly, and also how error depends solely on the misuse of the will, and, finally, to understand how we may guard against error, let us recall to mind the modes of thinking that we possess, namely, all modes of perceiving (sensing, imagining, and pure understanding) and modes of willing (desiring, misliking, affirming, denying, and doubting); for they can all be subsumed under these two headings.

Now with regard to these modes we should note, first, that insofar as the mind understands things clearly and distinctly and assents to them, it cannot be deceived (Pr. 14); nor again can it be deceived insofar as it merely perceives things and does not assent to them. For although I may now perceive a winged horse, it is certain that this perception contains nothing false as long as I do not assent to the truth that there is a winged horse, nor again as long as I doubt whether there is a winged horse. And because to assent is nothing but to determine the will, it follows that error depends only on the use of the will.

To make this even clearer, we should note, secondly, that we have the power to assent not only to those things that we clearly and distinctly perceive but also to those things that we perceive in any other way. For our will is not determined by any limits. Everyone can clearly see this if only he attends to the following point, that if God had wished to make infinite our faculty of understanding, he would not have needed to give us a more extensive faculty of willing than that which we already possess in order to enable us to assent to all that we understand. That which we already possess would be sufficient for assenting to an infinite number of things.[40] And in fact experience tells us, too, that we assent to many things that we have not deduced from sure first principles. Furthermore, these considerations make it clear that if the intellect extended as widely as the faculty of willing, or if the faculty of willing could not extend more widely than the intellect, or if, finally, we could restrict the faculty of willing within the limits of the intellect, we would never fall into error (Pr. 14).

But the first two possibilities lie beyond our power, for they would involve that the will should not be infinite and the intellect created finite. So it remains for us to consider the third possibility, namely, whether we have the power to restrict our faculty of willing within the limits of the intellect. Now because the will is free to determine itself, it follows that we do have the power to restrict the faculty of assenting within the limits of the intellect, therefore bringing it about that we do not fall into error. Hence it is quite manifest that our never being deceived depends entirely on the use of the freedom of the will. That our will is free is demonstrated in Art. 39 Part 1 of the *Principia* and in the "Fourth Meditation," and is also shown at some length by me in the last chapter of my Appendix. And although, when we perceive a thing clearly and distinctly, we cannot refrain from assenting to it, that necessary assent depends not on the weakness but simply on the freedom and perfection of the will. For to assent to the truth is a perfection in us (as is self-evident), and the will is never more perfect and more free than when it completely determines itself. Because this can occur when the mind understands something clearly and distinctly, it will necessarily give itself this perfection at once (Ax. 3). Therefore we by no means understand ourselves to be less free because we are not at all indifferent in embracing truth. On the contrary, we take it as certain that the more indifferent we are, the less free we are.

So now it remains only to be explained how error is nothing but privation with respect to man, whereas with respect to God it is mere negation. This will easily be seen if we first observe that our perceiving many things besides those that we clearly understand makes us more perfect than if we did not perceive them. This is clearly established from the fact that, if it were supposed that we could perceive nothing clearly and distinctly but only confusedly, we should possess nothing more perfect than this perceiving things confusedly, nor would anything else be expected of our nature. Furthermore, to assent to things, however confused, insofar as it is also a kind of action, is a perfection. This will also be obvious to everyone if he supposes, as previously, that it is contrary to man's nature to perceive things clearly and distinctly. For then it will become quite clear that it is far better for a man to assent to things, however confused, and to exercise his freedom, than to remain always indifferent, that is (as we have just shown), at the lowest grade of freedom. And if we also turn our attention to the needs and convenience

---

[40] [Cf. Med4, 38 (AT7, 56–57).]

of human life, we shall find this absolutely necessary, as experience teaches each of us every day.

Therefore, because all the modes of thinking that we possess are perfect insofar as they are regarded in themselves alone, to that extent that which constitutes the form of error cannot be in them. But if we attend to the way in which modes of willing differ from one another, we shall find that some are more perfect than others in that some render the will less indifferent (i.e., more free) than others. Again, we shall also see that, as long as we assent to confused things, we make our minds less apt to distinguish true from false, thereby depriving ourselves of the highest freedom. Therefore to assent to confused things, insofar as this is something positive, does not contain any imperfection or the form of error; it does so only insofar as we thus deprive our own selves of the highest freedom that is within reach of our nature and is within our power. So the imperfection of error will consist entirely merely in the privation of the highest freedom, a privation that is called error. Now it is called privation because we are deprived of a perfection that is compatible with our nature, and it is called error because it is our own fault that we lack this perfection, in that we fail to restrict the will within the limits of the intellect, as we are able to do. Therefore, because error is nothing else with respect to man but the privation of the perfect or correct use of freedom, it follows that it does not lie in any faculty that he has from God, nor again in any operation of his faculties insofar as this depends on God.[41] Nor can we say that God has deprived us of the greater intellect that he might have given us and has thereby brought it about that we could fall into error. For no thing's nature can demand anything from God, and nothing belongs to a thing except what the will of God has willed to bestow on it. For nothing existed, or can even be conceived, prior to God's will (as is fully explained in our Appendix Part 2 Chapters 7 and 8). Therefore God has not deprived us of a greater intellect or a more perfect faculty of understanding any more than he has deprived a circle of the properties of a sphere, and a circumference of the properties of a spherical surface.

So because none of our faculties, in whatever way it be considered, can point to any imperfection in God, it clearly follows that the imperfection in which the form of error consists is privation only with respect to man. When related to God as its cause, it can be termed not privation, but only negation.

P16   *God is incorporeal.*

Proof   Body is the immediate subject of local motion (Def. 7). Therefore if God were corporeal, he would be divided into parts; and this, since it clearly involves imperfection, it is absurd to affirm of God (Def. 8).

Another Proof   If God were corporeal, he could be divided into parts (Def. 7). Now either each single part could subsist of itself, or it could not. If the latter, it would be like the other things created by God, and thus, like every created thing, it would be continuously created by the same force by God (Pr. 10 and Ax. 11),

---

[41] [Med4, 36–39 (AT7, 54–58).]

and would not pertain to God's nature any more than other created things, which is absurd (Pr. 5). But if each single part exists through itself, each single part must also involve necessary existence (Lemma 2 Pr. 7), and consequently each single part would be a supremely perfect being (Cor. Lemma 2 Pr. 7). But this, too, is absurd (Pr. 11). Therefore God is incorporeal. Q.E.D.

P17   *God is a completely simple being.*

Proof   If God were composed of parts, the parts (as all will readily grant) would have to be at least prior in nature to God, which is absurd (Cor. 4 Pr. 12). Therefore he is a completely simple being. Q.E.D.

Cor   Hence it follows that God's intelligence, his will or decree, and his power are not distinguished from his essence, except by abstract reasoning.

P18   *God is immutable.*

Proof   If God were mutable, he could not change in part, but would have to change with respect to his whole essence (Pr. 17). But the essence of God exists necessarily (Prs. 5, 6, and 7). Therefore God is immutable. Q.E.D.

P19   *God is eternal.*

Proof   God is a supremely perfect being (Def. 8), from which it follows that he exists necessarily (Pr. 5). If now we attribute to him limited existence, the limits of his existence must necessarily be understood, if not by us, at any rate by God himself (Pr. 9), because he has understanding in the highest degree. Therefore God will understand himself (i.e. [Def. 8], a supremely perfect being) as not existing beyond these limits, which is absurd (Pr. 5). Therefore God has not a limited but an infinite existence, which we call eternity. See Chapter 1 Part 2 of our Appendix. Therefore God is eternal. Q.E.D.

P20   *God has preordained all things from eternity.*

Proof   Because God is eternal (Pr. 19), his understanding is eternal, because it pertains to his eternal essence (Cor. Pr. 17). But his intellect is not different in reality from his will or decree (Cor. Pr. 17). Therefore when we say that God has understood things from eternity, we are also saying that he has willed or decreed things thus from eternity. Q.E.D.

Cor   From this proposition it follows that God is in the highest degree constant in his works.

P21   *Substance extended in length, breadth, and depth exists in reality, and we are united to one part of it.*

Proof   That which is extended, as it is clearly and distinctly perceived by us, does not pertain to God's nature (Pr. 16), but it can be created by God (Cor. Pr. 7 and Pr. 8). Furthermore, we clearly and distinctly perceive (as everyone can discover in himself, insofar as he thinks) that extended substance is a sufficient cause for producing in us pleasure, pain, and similar ideas or sensations, which are continually produced in us even against our will. But if we wish to suppose some other cause for our sensations apart from extended substance—say, God or an angel—we immediately destroy the clear and distinct concept that we have. Therefore,[42] as long as we correctly attend to our perceptions so as to allow nothing but what we clearly and distinctly perceive, we shall be altogether inclined, or by no means uninclined, to accept that extended substance is the only cause of our sensations, and therefore to affirm that the extended thing exists, created by God. And in this we surely cannot be deceived (Pr. 14 with Schol.). Therefore it is truly affirmed that substance extended in length, breadth, and depth exists. This was the first point.[43]

Furthermore, among our sensations, which must be produced in us (as we have already proved) by extended substance, we observe a considerable difference, as when I say that I sense or see a tree or when I say that I am thirsty, or in pain, etc. But I clearly see that I cannot perceive the cause of this difference unless I first understand that I am closely united to one part of matter, and not so to other parts. Because I clearly and distinctly understand this, and I cannot perceive it in any other way, it is true (Pr. 14 with Schol.) that I am united to one part of matter. This was the second point. We have therefore proved what was to be proved.[44]

Note: Unless the reader here considers himself only as a thinking thing, lacking body, and unless he puts aside as prejudices all the reasons that he previously entertained for believing that body exists, his attempts to understand this proof will be in vain.

End of Part 1

---

[42] See the proof to Proposition 14 and the Scholium to Proposition 15.
[43] [Cf. Med6, 51–52 (AT7, 78–80).]
[44] [See Med6, 52–53 (AT7, 80–81).]

THE LETTERS

Correspondence to and from an author can be an invaluable aid to the reconstruction of his life and the understanding of his thought. So it is with Spinoza's letters. Although the political and ecclesiastical persecution of the time led the original editors of the Opera Posthuma—his friends Lodewijk Meyer, Georg Schuller, and Johan Bouwmeester—to delete personal matters and disregard letters of a personal nature, the letters that we have do help us to understand Spinoza's biography. And many of the letters include important questions about issues of philosophical, theological, and scientific interest and Spinoza's responses to those questions. Without the correspondence, the depths of Spinoza's life and thought would be much more obscure indeed.

The correspondence spans the years from 1661 to 1676 and includes letters to and from a variety of correspondents. The Opera Posthuma contained seventy-four letters in the Latin edition of 1677. The collected works published by J. Van Vloten and J. P. N. Land in 1882 added ten letters and ordered them chronologically; their numbering has become standard. The Gebhardt edition of 1925 added two letters, 30a and 67a, thus bringing the currently accepted total to eighty-six letters.

The period between 1661 and 1665 includes an important correspondence between Spinoza and Henry Oldenburg, secretary of the Royal Society in London from 1662. Among the letters is Spinoza's lengthy discussion of Robert Boyle's treatise on nitre, which Oldenburg had sent to Spinoza (Ep6), and Spinoza's critique of the experimentalism that underlay Boyle's mechanical philosophy. Other letters deal with God, attributes, and additional metaphysical matters, as well as questions about knowledge. In 1665, Spinoza outlines to Oldenburg his reasons for writing a treatise on Scripture and what Oldenburg calls his views about "angels, prophecy, and miracles" (Ep30). Later that fall, on 20 November 1665, Spinoza writes to Oldenburg about parts and wholes, and using the metaphor of a tiny worm living in the blood, he clarifies how and why he holds that both the human body and the human mind are parts of Nature. After a hiatus of about ten years, the correspondence with Oldenburg is revived in 1675–1676 and includes a heated discussion of the Theological-Political Treatise, Spinoza's views expressed in it and in his Ethics, and the implications for moral and religious life.

Oldenburg was a friend, although not as personal or close a one as men like Simon de Vries, Lodewijk Meyer, Pieter Balling, Johan Bouwmeester, and Jarig Jelles. There are letters to and from these more intimate friends as well, dealing with a whole range of topics. Among them is the famous and important letter "on the infinite" (Ep12), written to Meyer on 20 April 1663. In later years Spinoza came to know Walther Ehrenfried von Tschirnhaus, a German aristocrat studying in Leiden and a person familiar with philosophers and scientists throughout Europe. Their correspondence of nine letters, between 1674 and 1676, discussed,

249

among other topics, the important issue of free will and causal determinism, an issue also treated in the correspondence with Georg Hermann Schuller, the Amsterdam physician who may very well have introduced Spinoza to Tschirnhaus.

Not only do the letters cover a wide range of issues and engage a variety of correspondents, from close friends to acquaintances; they also differ in tone and detail. Often Spinoza is asked to clarify or defend himself. In his letters with John Hudde, an Amsterdam friend interested in optics and an elected political official, he discusses the proofs for God's necessary existence (Ep34–35). The correspondence with J. Louis Fabritius, professor of theology and philosophy at Heidelberg, concerns the offer to Spinoza to teach at that university and his refusal in 1673 (Ep47–48). These letters are respectful and businesslike. Different in tone are the letters from Alfred Burgh and Nicholas Steno, old friends who wrote to Spinoza in 1675, seeking to convert him to Roman Catholicism, as they themselves had been converted. There is an aggressiveness and edge to this exchange that is not present in the more collegial letters among other friends, a tension characteristic too of the earlier correspondence of 1664–1665 with the grain merchant Willem van Blyenburgh, about God, anthropomorphism, and human freedom (Ep18–24).

The technicality and abstractness of Spinoza's philosophical work have a crystalline power that keeps the man at a distance. The letters give us access to that man and the concrete reality of his life and work.

In this edition we have included twenty-nine of Spinoza's letters. These deal, in one way or another, with philosophical issues of significance for reading the Ethics. Anyone interested in Spinoza's correspondence on political and religious matters and the interpretation of Scripture should consult Spinoza: The Letters, *edited by Steven Barbone, Lee Rice, and Jacob Adler (Hackett Publishing Company, 1995).*

M.L.M.

THE LETTERS

OF CERTAIN LEARNED MEN
TO B.D.S.
AND THE AUTHOR'S REPLIES
CONTRIBUTING NOT A LITTLE TO THE
ELUCIDATION OF HIS OTHER WORKS

LETTER 1
To the most esteemed B.d.S., from Henry Oldenburg

[Known only from the O.P. The original is lost.]

Most illustrious Sir, esteemed friend,

With such reluctance did I recently tear myself away from your side when visiting you at your retreat in Rijnsburg, that no sooner am I back in England than I am endeavouring to join you again, as far as possible, at least by exchange of letters. Substantial learning, combined with humanity and courtesy—all of which nature and diligence have so amply bestowed on you—hold such an allurement as to gain the affection of any men of quality and of liberal education. Come then, most excellent Sir, let us join hands in unfeigned friendship, and let us assiduously cultivate that friendship with devotion and service of every kind. Whatever my poor resources can furnish, consider as yours. As to the gifts of mind that you possess, let me claim a share in them, as this cannot impoverish you.

At Rijnsburg we conversed about God, about infinite Extension and Thought, about the difference and agreement of these attributes, and about the nature of the union of the human soul with the body; and also about the principles of the Cartesian and Baconian philosophy. But since we then spoke about such important topics as through a lattice-window and only in a cursory way, and in the meantime all these things continue to torment me, let me now, by the right of the friendship entered upon between us, engage in a discussion with you and cordially beg you to set forth at somewhat greater length your views on the above-mentioned subjects. In particular, please be good enough to enlighten me on these two points: first, wherein you place the true distinction between Extension and Thought, and second, what defects you find in the philosophy of Descartes and Bacon, and how you consider that these can be removed and replaced by sounder views. The more frankly you write to me on these and similar subjects, the more closely you will bind me to you and place me under a strong obligation to make an equal return, if only I can.

Notes by Steven Barbone and Lee Rice (main annotators for this work) and Michael L. Morgan appear in brackets.

Here there are already in the press *Certain Physiological Essays*,[1] written by an English nobleman, a man of extraordinary learning. These treat of the nature of air and its elastic property, as proved by forty-three experiments; and also of fluidity and firmness and the like. As soon as they are printed, I shall see to it that they are delivered to you through a friend who happens to be crossing the sea. Meanwhile, farewell, and remember your friend, who is,

> Yours in all affection and devotion,
> Henry Oldenburg

London, 16/26 August 1661

LETTER 2

To the most noble and learned H. Oldenburg, from B.d.s.

[Known only from the O.P. The original is lost. No date is given, but a conjectural date is September 1661.]

Esteemed Sir,

You yourself will be able to judge what pleasure your friendship affords me, if only your modesty will allow you to consider the estimable qualities with which you are richly endowed. And although, with these qualities in mind, I feel myself not a little presumptuous in venturing upon this relationship, especially when I reflect that between friends all things, and particularly things of the spirit, should be shared, nevertheless this step is to be accredited not so much to me as to your courtesy, and also your kindness. From your great courtesy you have been pleased to belittle yourself, and from your abundant kindness so to enlarge me, that I do not hesitate to enter upon the friendship which you firmly extend to me and deign to ask of me in return, a friendship which it shall be my earnest endeavour diligently to foster.

As for my mental endowments, such as they are, I would most willingly have you make claim on them even if I knew that this would be greatly to my detriment. But lest I seem in this way to want to refuse you what you ask by right of friendship, I shall attempt to explain my views on the subjects we spoke of—although I do not think that this will be the means of binding you more closely to me unless I have your kind indulgence.

I shall begin therefore with a brief discussion of God, whom I define as a Being consisting of infinite attributes, each of which is infinite or supremely perfect

---

[1] [Robert Boyle's essays were published in 1661, with a Latin version published in London (1665) and Amsterdam (1667). The term 'physiological' is the same in sense as 'physical'—that which concerns nature. See *The Works of the Honourable Robert Boyle* (London, 1772, Vol. I, p. 359), *A physico-chymical Essay, with some Considerations touching the differing parts and redintegration of Salt-Petre.* Sections 3–11 (pp. 377seq) deal with the experiments: *The history of fluidity and firmness.* —S.B./L.R.]

in its own kind.[2] Here it should be observed that by attribute I mean every thing that is conceived in itself and through itself, so that its conception does not involve the conception of any other thing. For example, extension is conceived through itself and in itself, but not so motion; for the latter is conceived in something else, and its conception involves extension.[3]

That this is a true definition of God is evident from the fact that by God we understand a supremely perfect and absolutely infinite Being. The existence of such a Being is easily proved from this definition; but as this is not the place for such a proof,[4] I shall pass it over. The points I need to prove here in order to satisfy your first enquiry, esteemed Sir, are as follows: first, that in Nature there cannot exist two substances without their differing entirely in essence; secondly, that a substance cannot be produced, but that it is of its essence to exist; third, every substance must be infinite, or supremely perfect in its kind.[5]

With these points established, esteemed Sir, provided that at the same time you attend to the definition of God, you will readily perceive the direction of my thoughts, so that I need not be more explicit on this subject. However, in order to provide a clear and concise proof, I can think of no better expedient than to arrange them in geometrical style and to submit them to the bar of your judgment. I therefore enclose them separately herewith[6] and await your verdict on them.

Secondly, you ask me what errors I see in the philosophy of Descartes and Bacon. In this request, too, I shall try to oblige you, although it is not my custom to expose the errors of others. The first and most important error is this, that they have gone far astray from knowledge of the first cause and origin of all things. Secondly, they have failed to understand the true nature of the human mind. Thirdly, they have never grasped the true cause of error. Only those who are completely destitute of all learning and scholarship can fail to see the critical importance of true knowledge of these three points.

That they have gone far astray from true knowledge of the first cause and of the human mind can readily be gathered from the truth of the three propositions to which I have already referred; so I confine myself to point out the third error. Of Bacon I shall say little; he speaks very confusedly on this subject, and simply makes assertions while proving hardly anything. In the first place he takes for granted that the human intellect, besides the fallibility of the senses, is by its very nature liable to error, and fashions everything after the analogy of its own nature, and not after the analogy of the universe, so that it is like a mirror presenting an irregular surface to the rays it receives, mingling its own nature with the nature of reality, and so forth.[7] Secondly, he holds that the human intellect, by reason of its

---

2 [See E1Def6.]
3 [These definitions are essentially the same as given in the *Ethics*: see E1Def3 and E1Def4.]
4 [Spinoza in fact gives three proofs in E1P11.]
5 [See E1P5, E1P6, E1P8.]
6 [See *Ethics* Part 1, from the beginning to Pr. 4. (Footnote in the O.P.)]
7 [The reference is probably to *Novum Organum* I, 41, which deals with the "Idols of the Tribe."]

peculiar nature, is prone to abstractions,[8] and imagines as stable things that are in flux, and so on. Thirdly, he holds that the human intellect is in constant activity, and cannot come to a halt or rest.[9] Whatever other causes he assigns can all be readily reduced to the one Cartesian principle, that the human will is free and more extensive than the intellect, or, as Verulam more confusedly puts it, the intellect is not characterised as a dry light, but receives infusion from the will.[10] (We should here observe that Verulam often takes intellect for mind, therein differing from Descartes.) This cause, then, disregarding the others as being of little importance, I shall show to be false. Indeed, they would easily have seen this for themselves, had they but given consideration to the fact that the will differs from this or that volition in the same way as whiteness differs from this or that white object, or as humanity differs from this or that human being. So to conceive the will to be the cause of this or that volition is as impossible as to conceive humanity to be the cause of Peter and Paul.[11]

Since, then, the will is nothing more than a mental construction (*ens rationis*), it can in no way be said to be the cause of this or that volition. Particular volitions, since they need a cause to exist, cannot be said to be free; rather, they are necessarily determined to be such as they are by their own causes. Finally, according to Descartes, errors are themselves particular volitions, from which it necessarily follows that errors—that is, particular volitions—are not free, but are determined by external causes and in no way by the will. This is what I undertook to demonstrate. Etc.

LETTER 3
To the esteemed B.d.S., from Henry Oldenburg

[Known only from the O.P. The original is lost.]

Excellent Sir and dear friend,

Your very learned letter has been delivered to me and read with great pleasure. I warmly approve your geometrical style of proof, but at the same time I blame my obtuseness for not so readily grasping what you with such exactitude teach. So I beg you to allow me to present the evidence of this sluggishness of mine by putting the following questions and seeking from you their solutions.

The first is, do you understand clearly and indubitably that, solely from the definition of God which you give, it is demonstrated that such a Being exists? For my part, when I reflect that definitions contain no more than conceptions of our mind, and that our mind conceives many things that do not exist and is most prolific in

---

[8] [See *Novum Organum* I, 51.]
[9] [See *Novum Organum* I, 48.]
[10] [See Verulam's *Novum Organum*, Book 1, Aphorism 49. (Footnote in the O.P.)]
[11] [On the relation between 'humanity' and individual persons, see E1P8Schol2. Spinoza's claim that will is merely one mode of thought is developed in E1P32.]

multiplying and augmenting things once conceived, I do not yet see how I can infer the existence of God from the conception I have of him. Indeed, from a mental accumulation of all the perfections I discover in men, animals, vegetables, minerals and so on, I can conceive and form one single substance which possesses in full all those qualities; even more, my mind is capable of multiplying and augmenting them to infinity, and so of fashioning for itself a most perfect and excellent Being. Yet the existence of such a Being can by no means be inferred from this.

My second questions is, are you quite certain that Body is not limited by Thought, nor Thought by Body? For it is still a matter of controversy as to what Thought is, whether it is a corporeal motion or a spiritual activity quite distinct from what is corporeal.

My third question is, do you regard those axioms you have imparted to me as being indemonstrable principles, known by the light of Nature and standing in no need of proof? It may be that the first axiom is that of kind, but I do not see how the other three can be accounted as such. For the second axiom supposes that there exists in Nature nothing but substance and accidents, whereas many maintain that time and place are in neither category. Your third axiom, that 'things having different attributes have nothing in common' is so far from being clearly conceived by me that the entire Universe seems rather to prove the contrary. All things known to us both differ from one another in some respects and agree in other respects. Finally, your fourth axiom, namely, 'things which have nothing in common with one another cannot be the cause one of the other', is not so clear to my befogged intellect as not to require some light to be shed on it. For God has nothing formally in common with created things; yet we almost all hold him to be their cause.

Since, then, these axioms do not seem to me to be placed beyond all hazard of doubt, you may readily conjecture that your propositions based on them are bound to be shaky. And the more I consider them, the more I am overwhelmed with doubt concerning them. Against the first I hold that two men are two substances and of the same attribute, since they are both capable of reasoning; and thence I conclude that there are two substances of the same attribute. With regard to the second I consider that, since nothing can be the cause of itself, we can scarcely understand how it can be true that 'Substance cannot be produced, nor can it be produced by any other substance.' For this proposition asserts that all substances are causes of themselves, that they are each and all independent of one another, and it makes them so many Gods, in this way denying the first cause of all things.

This I willingly confess I cannot grasp, unless you do me the kindness of disclosing to me somewhat more simply and more fully your opinion regarding this high matter, explaining what is the origin and production of substances, the interdependence of things and their subordinate relationships. I entreat you, by the friendship on which we have embarked, to deal with me frankly and confidently in this, and I urge you most earnestly to be fully convinced that all these things which you see fit to impart to me will be inviolate and secure, and that I shall in no way permit any of them to become public to your detriment or injury.

In our Philosophical Society we are engaged in making experiments and observations as energetically as our abilities allow, and we are occupied in composing a History of the Mechanical Arts, being convinced that the forms and qualities of things can best be explained by the principles of mechanics, that all Nature's effects are produced by motion, figure, texture and their various combinations, and that there is no need to have recourse to inexplicable forms and occult qualities, the refuge of ignorance.

I shall send you the book I promised as soon as your Dutch ambassadors stationed here dispatch a messenger to the Hague (as they often do), or as soon as some other friend, to whom I can safely entrust it, goes your way.

Please excuse my prolixity and frankness, and I particularly urge you to take in good part, as friends do, what I have said frankly and without any disguise or courtly refinement, in replying to your letter. And believe me to be, sincerely and simply,

Your most devoted,
Henry Oldenburg

London, 27 September 1661

LETTER 4

To the noble and learned Henry Oldenburg, from B.d.S.

[Known only from the O.P. The original is lost. No date is given, but a conjectural date is October 1661.]

Most esteemed Sir,

While preparing to go to Amsterdam to spend a week or two there, I received your very welcome letter and read your objections to the three propositions which I sent you. On these alone I shall try to satisfy you, omitting the other matters for want of time.

To your first objection, then, I say that it is not from the definition of any thing whatsoever that the existence of the defined thing follows, but only (as I demonstrated in the Scholium which I attached to the three propositions) from the definition or idea of some attribute; that is (as I explained clearly in the case of the definition of God), from the definition of a thing which is conceived through itself and in itself. The ground for this distinction I have also stated in the aforementioned Scholium with sufficient clarity, I think, especially for a philosopher. A philosopher is supposed to know what is the difference between fiction and a clear and distinct conception, and also to know the truth of this axiom, to wit, that every definition, or clear and distinct idea, is true. Once these points are noted, I do not see what more is required in answer to the first question.

I therefore pass on to the solution of the second question. Here you seem to grant that, if Thought does not pertain to the nature of Extension, then Extension will not be limited by Thought; for surely it is only the example which causes you some doubt. But I beg you to note, if someone says that Extension is not limited by Extension, but by Thought, will he not also be saying that Extension is not infinite in an absolute sense, but only insofar as it is Extension? That is, does he not grant me that Extension is infinite not in an absolute sense, but only insofar as it is Extension, that is, infinite in its own kind?[12]

But, you say, perhaps Thought is a corporeal activity. Let it be so, although I do not concede it; but this one thing you will not deny, that Extension, insofar as it is Extension, is not Thought; and this suffices to explain my definition and to demonstrate the third proposition.

The third objection which you proceed to raise against what I have set down is this, that the axioms should not be accounted as 'common notions' [*notiones communes*].[13] This is not the point I am urging; but you also doubt their truth, and you even appear to seek to prove that their contrary is more probable. But please attend to my definition of substance and accident,[14] from which all these conclusions follow. For by substance I understand that which is conceived through itself and in itself, that is, that whose conception does not involve the conception of another thing; and by modification or accident I understand that which is in something else and is conceived through that in which it is. Hence it is clearly established, first, that substance is prior in nature to its accidents; for without it these can neither exist nor be conceived. Secondly, besides substance and accidents nothing exists in reality, or externally to the intellect; for whatever there is, is conceived either through itself or through something else, and its conception either does or does not involve the conception of another thing. Thirdly, things which have different attributes have nothing in common with one another;[15] for I have explained an attribute as that whose conception does not involve the conception of another thing. Fourth and last, of things which have nothing in common with one another, one cannot be the cause of another; for since in the effect there would be nothing in common with the cause, all it would have, it would have from nothing.

As for your contention that God has nothing formally in common with created things, etc., I have maintained the exact opposite in my definition. For I said that God is a Being consisting of infinite attributes, each of which is infinite, or supremely perfect, in its kind.

As to your objection to my first proposition, I beg you, my friend, to consider that men are not created, but only begotten, and that their bodies already existed,

---

12 [The distinction between the two types of infinity is given in E1Def2. The proofs of the absolute infinity of extension and of thought are given in E2P1–P2.]

13 [These are what Oldenburg had called 'indemonstrable principles' in the previous letter. Spinoza's casting of them as 'common notions' is in accordance with his discussion of them in E2P37–P40.]

14 [Spinoza rarely uses the term 'accident', which is scholastic in origin. His preferred term is 'mode', which differs significantly in sense. He links the usage to 'modification or accident' in the next sentence.]

15 [See E1P2–P3.]

but in a different form.[16] However, the conclusion is this, as I am quite willing to admit, that if one part of matter were to be annihilated, the whole of Extension would also vanish at the same time.

The second proposition does not make many gods, but one only, to wit, a God consisting of infinite attributes, etc.

LETTER 8
To the esteemed B.d.S., from Simon de Vries

[Printed in the O.P. The original is extant. There are certain omissions in the O.P. text.]

Most upright friend,

I have long wished to pay you a visit, but the weather and the hard winter have not favoured me. Sometimes I bewail my lot, in that the distance between us keeps us so far apart from one another. Fortunate, yes, most fortunate is your companion Casuarius[17] who dwells beneath the same roof, and can converse with you on the highest matters at breakfast, at dinner, and on your walks. But although we are physically so far apart, you have frequently been present in my thoughts, especially when I am immersed in your writings and hold them in my hand. But since not everything is quite clear to the members of our group (which is why we have resumed our meetings), and in order that you may not think that I have forgotten you, I have set myself to write this letter.

As for our group, our procedure is as follows. One member (each has his turn) does the reading, explains how he understands it, and goes on to a complete demonstration, following the sequence and order of your propositions. Then if it should happen that we cannot satisfy one another, we have deemed it worthwhile to make a note of it and to write to you so that, if possible, it should be made clearer to us and we may, under your guidance, uphold truth against those who are religious and Christian in a superstitious way, and may stand firm against the onslaught of the whole world.

So, when the definitions did not all seem clear to us on our first reading and explaining them, we were not in agreement as to the nature of definition. In this situation, in your absence, we consulted a certain author, a mathematician named Borelli.[18] In his discussion of the nature of definition, axiom and postulate, he

---

[16] [See E1P8Schol2.]

[17] [Johannes Caesarius, whose name is incorrectly spelled by de Vries, was probably born in Amsterdam in 1642 and is believed to have been a student of Franciscus Van den Enden through whom he may have become acquainted with Spinoza. Though the reasons as to why he may have been living with Spinoza are unclear, he is thought to have been part of a group of Collegiants who were known to frequent Rijnsburg while Spinoza resided there.]

[18] [Giovanni Alfonso Borelli (1608–1679) was a mathematician with many other interests: astronomy, physics, biology. As well as publishing an edition of Euclid (*Euclides restitutus*), he also published

also cites the opinions of others on this subject. His own opinion goes as follows: "Definitions are employed in a proof as premisses. So they must be quite clearly known; otherwise knowledge that is scientific or absolutely certain cannot be acquired from them." In another place he writes: "In the case of any subject, the principle of its structure, or its prime and best known essential feature, must be chosen not at random but with the greatest care. For if the construction and feature named is impossible, then the result will not be a scientific definition. For instance, if one were to say, 'Let two straight lines enclosing a space be called figurals', the definitions would be of non-entities, and would be impossible. Therefore from these it is ignorance, not knowledge, that would be deduced. Again, if the construction or feature named is indeed possible and true, but unknown to us or doubtful, then the definition will not be sound. For conclusions that derive from what is unknown and doubtful are also uncertain and doubtful, and therefore afford us mere conjecture or opinion, and not sure knowledge."

Tacquet[19] seems to disagree with this view; he asserts, as you know, that it is possible to proceed directly from a false proposition to a true conclusion. Clavius,[20] whose view he (Borelli) also introduces, thinks as follows: "Definitions are arbitrary terms, and there is no need to give the grounds for choosing that a thing should be defined in this way or that. It is sufficient that the thing defined should never be asserted to agree with anything unless it is first proved that the given definition agrees with that same thing." So Borelli maintains that the definition of any subject must consist of a feature or structure which is prime, essential, best known to us, and true, whereas Clavius holds that it matters not whether it be prime, or best known, or true or not, as long as it is not asserted that the definition we have given agrees with some thing unless it is first provided that the given definition agrees with that same thing. We are inclined to favour Borelli's view, but we are not sure whether you, Sir, agree with either or neither. Therefore, with such various conflicting views being advanced on the nature of definition—which is accounted as one of the principles of demonstration—and since the mind, if not freed from difficulties surrounding definition, will be in like difficulty regarding deductions made from it, we would very much like you, Sir, to write to us (if we are not giving you too much trouble and your time allows) giving your opinion on the matter, and also on the difference between axioms and definitions. Borelli admits no real distinction other than the name; you, I believe, maintain that there is another difference.

Next, the third Definition[21] is not sufficiently clear to us. I brought forward as an example what you, Sir, said to me at the Hague, to wit, that a thing can be

---

several other mathematical treatises. Like Descartes, he too finished his days under the protection of Queen Christiana of Sweden.]

19 [Andreas Tacquet published *Elements of Plane and Solid Geometry* in 1654.]

20 [Christopher Clavius (1537–1612) was another well known mathematician of the era. He helped to revise the Gregorian calendar, and in 1574 he published an edition of Euclid with commentary to which de Vries refers in this letter.]

21 [Seee E1Def3–4.]

considered in two ways: either as it is in itself, or in relation to another thing. For instance, the intellect; for it can be considered either under Thought or as consisting of ideas. But we do not quite see what difference could be here. For we consider that, if we rightly conceive Thought, we ought to comprehend it under ideas, because with the removal of all ideas we would destroy Thought. So the example not being sufficiently clear to us, the matter still remains somewhat obscure, and we stand in need of further explanation.

Finally, at the beginning of the third Scholium to Proposition 8,[22] we read: "Hence it is clear that, although two attributes may be conceived as really distinct (that is, the one without the aid of the other), it does not follow that they constitute two entities or two different substances. The reason is that it is of the nature of substance that all its attributes—each one individually—are conceived through themselves, since they have been in it simultaneously." In this way you seem, Sir, to suppose that the nature of substance is so constituted that it can have several attributes, which you have not yet proved, unless you are referring to the fifth definition[23] of absolutely infinite substance or God. Otherwise, if I were to say that each substance has only one attribute, I could rightly conclude that where there are two different attributes there are two different substances. We would ask you for a clearer explanation of this.

Next, I am most grateful for your writings which were conveyed to me by P. Balling and gave me great pleasure, particularly the Scholium to Proposition 19.[24] If I can here serve you, too, in any way which is within my power, I am yours to command. You need only let me know. I have begun a course of anatomy, and am about half way through. When it is completed, I shall begin chemistry, and thus following your advice I shall go through the whole medical course. I must stop now, and await your reply. Accept my greetings, who am,

Your very devoted,
S. J. D'Vries

1663. Given at the Hague, 24 February
   To Mr. Benedict Spinoza, at Rijnsburg

---

[22] [Probably E1P10Schol in the finished version of the *Ethics*.]

[23] [See E1Def6.]

[24] [We are not able to determine about which proposition in the final version of the *Ethics* de Vries writes.]

LETTER 9

To the learned young man Simon de Vries, from B.d.S.

*[Printed in the O.P. The original is extant. The O.P. text is an
abridged version of the original, and the last paragraph appears only
in the Dutch edition of the O.P. The letter is undated. A conjectural
date is February 1663.]*

My worthy friend,

I have received your letter, long looked for, for which, and for your cordial feelings towards me, accept my warmest thanks. Your long absence has been no less regretted by me than by you, but at any rate I am glad that my late-night studies are of use to you and our friends, for in this way I talk with you while we are apart. There is no reason for you to envy Casearius. Indeed, there is no one who is more of a trouble to me, and no one with whom I have had to be more on my guard. So I should like you and all our acquaintances not to communicate my opinions to him until he will have reached a more mature age. As yet he is too boyish, unstable, and eager for novelty rather than for truth. Still, I am hopeful that he will correct these youthful faults in a few years time. Indeed, as far as I can judge from his character, I am reasonably sure of this; and so his nature wins my affection.

As to the questions raised in your group (which is sensibly organised), I see that your difficulties result from your failure to distinguish between the kinds of definition. There is the definition that serves to explicate a thing whose essence alone is in question and the subject of doubt, and there is the definition which is put forward simply for examination. The former, since it has a determinate object, must be a true definition, while this need not be so in the latter case. For example, if someone were to ask me for a description of Solomon's temple, I ought to give him a true description, unless I propose to talk nonsense with him. But if I have in my own mind formed the design of a temple that I want to build, and from its description I conclude that I will have to purchase such-and-such a site and so many thousands of stones and other materials, will any sane person tell me that I have reached a wrong conclusion because my definition may be incorrect? Or will anyone demand that I prove my definition? Such a person would simply be telling me that I had not conceived that which in fact I had conceived, or he would be requiring me to prove that I had conceived that which I had conceived, which is utter nonsense. Therefore a definition either explicates a thing as it exists outside the intellect—and then it should be a true definition, differing from a proposition or axiom only in that the former is concerned only with the essences of things or the essences of the affections of things, whereas the latter has a wider scope, extending also to eternal truths—or it explicates a thing as it is conceived by us, or can be conceived. And in that case it also differs from an axiom and proposition in requiring merely that it be conceived, not conceived as true, as in the case of an axiom. So then a bad definition is one which is not conceived.

To make this clearer, I shall take Borelli's example of a man who says that two straight lines enclosing an area are to be called figurals. If he means by a straight line what everybody else means by a curved line, his definition is quite sound (for the figure intended by the definition would be [as shown] or some such figure), provided that he does not at a later stage mean a square or any other such figure. But if by a straight line he means what we all mean, the thing is plainly inconceivable, and so there is no definition. All these considerations are confused by Borelli, whose view you are too much inclined to embrace.

Here is another example, the one which you adduce towards the end of your letter. If I say that each substance has only one attribute, this is mere assertion unsupported by proof. But if I say that by substance I mean that which consists of only one attribute, this is a sound definition, provided that entities consisting of more than one attribute are thereafter given a name other than substance.

In saying that I do not prove that a substance (or an entity) can have more than one attribute, it may be that you have not given sufficient attention to the proofs. I advanced two proofs, the first of which is as follows: It is clear beyond all doubt that every entity is conceived by us under some attribute, and the more reality or being an entity has, the more attributes are to be attributed to it. Hence an absolutely infinite entity must be defined . . . and so on. A second proof—and this proof I take to be decisive—states that the more attributes I attribute to any entity, the more existence I am bound to attribute to it; that is, the more I conceive it as truly existent. The exact contrary would be the case if I had imagined a chimera or something of the sort.

As to your saying that you do not conceive thought otherwise than under ideas because thought vanishes with the removal of ideas, I believe that you experience this because when you, as a thinking thing, do as you say, you are banishing all your thoughts and conceptions. So it is not surprising that when you have banished all your thoughts, there is nothing left for you to think. But as to the point at issue, I think I have demonstrated with sufficient clarity and certainty that the intellect, even though infinite, belongs to *Natura naturata*, not to *Natura naturans*.[25]

Furthermore, I fail to see what this has to do with understanding the Third Definition,[26] or why this definition causes you difficulty. The definition as I gave it to you runs, if I am not mistaken, "By substance I understand that which is in itself and is conceived through itself; that is, that whose conception does not involve the conception of another thing. I understand the same by attribute, except that attribute is so called in respect to the intellect, which attributes to substance a certain specific kind of nature." This definition, I repeat, explains clearly what I mean by substance or attribute. However, you want me to explain by example—though it is not at all necessary—how one and the same thing can be signified by two names. Not to appear ungenerous, I will give you two examples. First, by 'Israel' I mean the third patriarch: by 'Jacob' I mean that same person, the latter name

---

[25] [For the distinction, see E1P29Schol.]
[26] [E1Def3–4.]

being given to him because he seized his brother's heel.[27] Secondly, by a 'plane surface' I mean one that reflects all rays of light without any change. I mean the same by 'white surface', except that it is called white in respect of a man looking at it.

With this I think that I have fully answered your questions. Meanwhile I shall wait to hear your judgment. And if there is anything else which you consider to be not well or clearly enough explained, do not hesitate to point it out to me, etc.

LETTER 10

To the learned young man Simon de Vries, from B.d.S.

[Known only from the O.P. The original is lost. Undated.
A conjectural date is March 1663.]

My worthy friend,

You ask me whether we need experience to know whether the definition of some attribute be true. To this I reply that we need experience only in the case of those things that cannot be deduced from the definition of a thing, as, for instance, the existence of modes; for this cannot be deduced from a thing's definition. We do not need experience in the case of those things whose existence is not distinguished from their essence and is therefore deduced from their definition. Indeed, no experience will ever be able to tell us this, for experience does not teach us the essences of things. The most it can do is to determine our minds to think only about the certain essences of things. So since the existence of attributes does not differ from their essence, we shall not be able to apprehend it by any experience.

As to your further question as to whether things or the affections of things are also eternal truths, I say, most certainly. If you go on to ask why I do not call them eternal truths, I reply, in order to mark a distinction, universally accepted, between these and the truths which do not explicate a thing or the affection of a thing, as, for instance, 'nothing comes from nothing'. This and similar propositions, I say, are called eternal truths in an absolute sense, by which title is meant simply that they do not have any place outside the mind, etc.

---

[27] [See Genesis 25:26 for an account of Jacob's name and 35:10 for an account of the change of this name to Israel.]

LETTER 12

To the learned and wise Lodewijk Meyer, Doctor of Medicine and Philosophy, from B.d.S.

[Printed in the O.P. The original is lost, but a copy made by Leibniz has been preserved.]

Dearest friend,

I have received two letters from you, one dated January 11 and delivered to me by our friend N.N.,[28] the other dated March 26 and sent to me by an unknown friend from Leiden. They were both very welcome, especially as I gathered from them that all is well with you and that I am often in your thoughts. My most cordial thanks are due to you for the kindness and esteem you have always seen fit to show me. At the same time I beg you to believe that I am no less your devoted friend, and this I shall endeavour to prove whenever the occasion arises, as far as my slender abilities allow. As a first offering, I shall try to answer the request made to me in your letters, in which you ask me to let you have my considered views on the question of the infinite. I am glad to oblige.

The question of the infinite has universally been found to be very difficult, indeed, insoluble, through failure to distinguish between that which must be infinite by its very nature or by virtue of its definition, and that which is unlimited not by virtue of its essence but by virtue of its cause. Then again, there is the failure to distinguish between that which is called infinite because it is unlimited, and that whose parts cannot be equated with or explicated by any number, although we may know its maximum or minimum. Lastly, there is the failure to distinguish between that which we can apprehend only by the intellect and not by the imagination, and that which can also be apprehended by the imagination. I repeat, if men had paid careful attention to these distinctions, they would never have found themselves overwhelmed by such a throng of difficulties. They would clearly have understood what kind of infinite cannot be divided into, or possess any, parts, and what kind can be so divided without contradiction. Again, they would also have understood what kind of infinite can be conceived, without illogicality, as greater than another infinite, and what kind cannot be so conceived. This will become clear from what I am about to say. However, I shall first briefly explain these four terms: Substance, Mode, Eternity, Duration.

The points to be noted about Substance are as follows. First, existence pertains to its essence; that is, solely from its essence and definition it follows that Substance exists. This point, if my memory does not deceive me, I have proved to you in an earlier conversation without the help of any other propositions. Second,

---

[28] [The friend "N.N." was quite possibly Pieter Balling, who was known to travel to and from Amsterdam and Rijnsburg and no doubt delivered letters for and from Spinoza. This letter was apparently circulated among many of Spinoza's friends, and came to be referenced as the 'Letter on the Infinite' or the 'Letter on Infinity'.]

following from the first point, Substance is not manifold; rather there exists only one Substance of the same nature. Thirdly, no Substance can be conceived as other than infinite.[29]

The affections of Substance I call Modes. The definition of Modes, insofar as it is not itself a definition of Substance, cannot involve existence. Therefore, even when they exist, we can conceive them as not existing. From this it further follows that when we have regard only to the essence of Modes and not to the order of Nature as a whole, we cannot deduce from their present existence that they will or will not exist in the future or that they did or did not exist in the past. Hence it is clear that we conceive the existence of Substance as of an entirely different kind from the existence of Modes. This is the source of the difference between Eternity and Duration. It is to the existence of Modes alone that we can apply the term Duration; the corresponding term for the existence of Substance is Eternity, that is, the infinite enjoyment of existence or—pardon the Latin—of being [*essendi*].

What I have said makes it quite clear that when we have regard only to the essence of Modes and not to Nature's order, as is most often the case, we can arbitrarily delimit the existence and duration of Modes without thereby impairing to any extent our conception of them; and we can conceive this duration as greater or less, and divisible into parts. But Eternity and Substance, being conceivable only as infinite, cannot be thus treated without annulling our conception of them. So it is nonsense, bordering on madness, to hold that extended Substance is composed of parts or bodies really distinct from one another. It is as if, by simply adding circle to circle and piling one on top of another, one were to attempt to construct a square or a triangle or any other figure of a completely different nature. Therefore the whole conglomeration of arguments whereby philosophers commonly strive to prove that extended Substance is finite collapses of its own accord. All such arguments assume that corporeal Substance is made up of parts. A parallel case is presented by those who, having convinced themselves that a line is made up of points,[30] have devised many arguments to prove that a line is not infinitely divisible.

However, if you ask why we have such a strong natural tendency to divide extended Substance, I answer that we conceive quantity in two ways: abstractly or superficially, as we have it in the imagination with the help of the senses, or as Substance, apprehended solely by means of the intellect. So if we have regard to quantity as it exists in the imagination (and this is what we most frequently and readily do), it will be found to be divisible, finite, composed of parts, and manifold. But if we have regard to it as it is in the intellect and we apprehend the thing as it is in itself (and this is very difficult), then it is found to be infinite, indivisible, and one alone, as I have already sufficiently proved.

Further, from the fact that we are able to delimit Duration and Quantity as we please, conceiving Quantity in abstraction from Substance and separating the efflux of Duration from things eternal, there arise Time and Measure: Time

---

[29] [See E1P8.]

[30] [This argument, and its relation to the divisibility of extension, receives an extended treatment by Spinoza in E1P15Schol.]

to delimit Duration and Measure to delimit Quantity in such wise as enables us to imagine them easily, as far as possible. Again, from the fact that we separate the affections of Substance from Substance itself, and arrange them in classes so that we can easily imagine them as far as possible, there arises Number, whereby we delimit them. Hence it can clearly be seen that Measure, Time and Number are nothing other than modes of thinking, or rather, modes of imagining. It is therefore not surprising that all who have attempted to understand the workings of Nature by such concepts, and furthermore without really understanding these concepts, have tied themselves into such extraordinary knots that in the end they have been unable to extricate themselves except by breaking through everything and perpetrating the grossest absurdities. For there are many things that can in no way be apprehended by the imagination but only by the intellect, such as Substance, Eternity, and other things. If anyone tries to explicate such things by notions of this kind which are nothing more than aids to the imagination, he will meet with no more success than if he were deliberately to encourage his imagination to run mad. Nor again can the Modes of Substance ever be correctly understood if they are confused with such mental constructs [*entia rationis*] or aids to the imagination. For by so doing we are separating them from Substance and from the manner of their efflux from Eternity, and in such isolation they can never be correctly understood.

To make the matter still clearer, take the following example. If someone conceives Duration in this abstracted way and, confusing it with Time, begins dividing it into parts, he can never understand how an hour, for instance, can pass by. For in order that an hour should pass by, a half-hour must first pass by, and then half of the remainder, and the half of what is left; and if you go on thus subtracting half of the remainder to infinity, you can never reach the end of the hour. Therefore many who are not used to distinguishing mental constructs from real things have ventured to assert that Duration is composed of moments, thus falling into the clutches of Scylla in their eagerness to avoid Charybdis. For to say that Duration is made up of moments is the same as to say that Number is made up simply by adding noughts together.

Further, it is obvious from the above that neither Number, Measure, nor Time, being merely aids to the imagination, can be infinite, for in that case Number would not be number, nor Measure measure, nor Time time. Hence one can easily see why many people, confusing these three concepts with reality because of their ignorance of the true nature of reality, have denied the actual existence of the infinite. But let their deplorable reasoning be judged by mathematicians who, in matters that they clearly and distinctly perceive, are not to be put off by arguments of that sort. For not only have they come upon many things inexpressible by any number (which clearly reveals the inadequacy of number to determine all things) but they also have many instances which cannot be equated with any number, and exceed any possible number. Yet they do not draw the conclusion that it is because of the multitude of parts that such things exceed all number; rather, it is because the nature of the thing is such that number is inapplicable to it without manifest contradiction.

For example, all the inequalities of the space lying between the two circles ABCD in the diagram exceed any number, as do all the variations of the speed of matter moving through that area. Now this conclusion is not reached because of the excessive magnitude of the intervening space; for however small a portion of it we take, the inequalities of this small portion will still be beyond any numerical expression. Nor again is this conclusion reached, as happens in other cases, because we do not know the maximum and minimum; in our example we know them both, the maximum being AB and the minimum CD. Our conclusion is reached because number is not applicable to the nature of the space between two non-concentric circles. Therefore if anyone sought to express all those inequalities by a definite number, he would also have to bring it about that a circle should not be a circle.

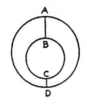

Similarly, to return to our theme, if anyone were to attempt to determine all the motions of matter that have ever been, reducing them and their duration to a definite number and time, he would surely be attempting to deprive corporeal Substance, which we cannot conceive as other than existing, of its affections, and to bring it about that Substance should not possess the nature which it does possess. I could here clearly demonstrate this and many other points touched on in this letter, did I not consider it unnecessary.

From all that I have said one can clearly see that certain things are infinite by their own nature and cannot in any way be conceived as finite, while other things are infinite by virtue of the cause in which they inhere; and when the latter are conceived in abstraction, they can be divided into parts and be regarded as finite. Finally, there are things that can be called infinite, or if you prefer, indefinite, because they cannot be accurately expressed by any number, while yet being conceivable as greater or less. For it does not follow that things which cannot be adequately expressed by any number must necessarily be equal, as is sufficiently evident from the given example and from many others.

To sum up, I have here briefly set before you the causes of the errors and confusion that have arisen regarding the question of the infinite, explaining them all, unless I am mistaken, in such a way that I do not believe there remains any question regarding the Infinite on which I have not touched, or which cannot be readily solved from what I have said. Therefore I do not think there is any point in detaining you longer on this matter.

However, in passing I should like it here to be observed that in my opinion our modern Peripatetics have quite misunderstood the demonstration whereby scholars of old sought to prove the existence of God. For, as I find it in a certain Jew named Rab Chasdai,[31] this proof runs as follows: "If there is granted an infinite

---

31 [Hasdai (or Ḥasdai, or Chasdai) Crescas was a celebrated Jewish theologian (1340?–1410). Crescas opposed the then-fashionable Aristotelian proof for the existence of God as first mover, made even more popular by Maimonides' and Thomas Aquinas' adaptations. Instead, Crescas suggested that it is not conceivable that the world should exist conditionally, and therefore it must be that there exist an uncaused cause which sustains all things.]

series of causes, all things which are, are also caused. But nothing that is caused can exist necessarily by virtue of its own nature. Therefore there is nothing in Nature to whose essence existence necessarily pertains. But this latter is absurd; therefore also the former."[32] So the force of the argument lies not in the impossibility of an actual infinite or an infinite series of causes, but only in the assumption that things which by their own nature do not necessarily exist are not determined to exist by a thing which necessarily exists by its own nature.

I would now pass on—for I am pressed for time—to your second letter, but I shall be able more conveniently to reply to the points contained therein when you will kindly pay me a visit. So do please try to come as soon as you possibly can. For the time of my moving is rapidly approaching. Enough, farewell, and keep me ever in your thoughts, who am, etc.

Rijnsburg, 20 April 1663

LETTER 32
To the most noble and learned Henry Oldenburg, from B.d.S.

[The original of this letter is extant, and held by the Royal Society, London. Spinoza retained a slightly different version of it, and it is from this that the text of the O.P. is printed. The differences are unimportant.]

Most noble Sir,

Please accept my most grateful thanks for the kind encouragement which you and the most noble Mr. Boyle have given me in the pursuit of philosophy. As far as my poor abilities will allow, I shall continue in this way, with the assurance meanwhile of your assistance and goodwill.

When you ask for my views on 'how we know the way in which each part of Nature accords with the whole, and the manner of its coherence with other parts', I presume that you are asking for the grounds of our belief that each part of Nature accords with the whole and coheres with other parts. As to knowing the actual manner of this coherence and the agreement of each part with the whole, I made it clear in my previous letter that this is beyond my knowledge. To know this it would be necessary to know the whole of Nature and all its parts. So I shall attempt to give the reasoning that compels me to this belief. But I would first ask you to note that I do not attribute to Nature beauty, ugliness, order or confusion. It is only with respect to our imagination that things can be said to be beautiful, ugly, well-ordered or confused.[33]

---

[32] [The argument to which Spinoza refers can be found in Bk. 1, Part 1, Ch. 3, and Bk. 1, Part 2, Ch. 3, of Crescas' major work, *Or Adonai*, also called *Or ha-Shem* (Ferrara: Abraham Usque, 1555).]

[33] [See E4Pref for a more expanded statement of the themes contained in this paragraph. Oldenburg refers to this letter as being 'on the unity of nature' in a letter to Boyle dated 21 November 1665.]

By coherence of parts I mean simply this, that the laws or nature of one part adapts itself to the laws or nature of another part in such wise that there is the least possible opposition between them. On the question of whole and parts, I consider things as parts of a whole to the extent that their natures adapt themselves to one another so that they are in the closest possible agreement. Insofar as they are different from one another, to that extent each one forms in our mind a separate idea and is therefore considered as a whole, not a part. For example, when the motions of particles of lymph, chyle, etc., adapt themselves to one another in accordance with size and shape so as to be fully in agreement with one another and to form all together one single fluid, to that extent only are the chyle, lymph, etc., regarded as parts of the blood. But insofar as we conceive the particles of lymph as different from the particles of chyle in respect of shape and motion, to that extent we regard them each as a whole, not a part.

Now let us imagine, if you please, a tiny worm living in the blood, capable of distinguishing by sight the particles of the blood—lymph, etc.—and of intelligently observing how each particle, on colliding with another, either rebounds or communicates some degree of its motion, and so forth. That worm would be living in the blood as we are living in our part of the universe, and it would regard each individual particle of the blood as a whole, not a part, and it could have no idea as to how all the parts are controlled by the overall nature of the blood and compelled to mutual adaptation as the overall nature of the blood requires, so as to agree with one another in a definite way. For if we imagine that there are no causes external to the blood which would communicate new motions to the blood, nor any space external to the blood, nor any other bodies to which the parts of the blood could transfer their motions, it is beyond doubt that the blood would remain indefinitely in its present state and that its particles would undergo no changes other than those which can be conceived as resulting from the existing relation between the motion of the blood and of the lymph, chyle, etc. Thus the blood would always have to be regarded as a whole, not a part. But since there are many other causes which do in a definite way modify the laws of the nature of the blood and are reciprocally modified by the blood, it follows that there occur in the blood other motions and other changes, resulting not solely from the reciprocal relation of its particles but from the relation between the motion of the blood on the one hand and external causes on the other. From this perspective the blood is accounted as a part, not as a whole. So much, then, for the question of whole and part.

Now all the bodies in Nature can and should be conceived in the same way as we have here conceived the blood; for all bodies are surrounded by others and are reciprocally determined to exist and to act in a fixed and determinate way, the same ratio of motion to rest being preserved in them taken all together, that is, in the universe as a whole. Hence it follows that every body, insofar as it exists as modified in a definite way, must be considered as a part of the whole universe, and as agreeing with the whole and cohering with the other parts. Now since the nature of the universe, unlike the nature of the blood, is not limited, but is absolutely infinite, its parts are controlled by the nature of this infinite potency in infinite ways, and are compelled to undergo infinite variations. However, I conceive that in respect to substance each individual part has a more intimate union with its whole. For, as I endeavoured to show in my first letter written some time ago when I was living at Rijnsburg, since it is of the nature of substance to be infinite, it follows that each part pertains to the nature of corporeal substance, and can neither be nor be conceived without it.

So you see in what way and why I hold that the human body is a part of Nature. As regards the human mind, I maintain that it, too, is a part of Nature; for I hold that in Nature there also exists an infinite power of thinking which, insofar as it is infinite, contains within itself the whole of Nature ideally, and whose thoughts proceed in the same manner as does Nature, which is in fact the object of its thought.

Further, I maintain that the human mind is that same power of thinking, not insofar as that power is infinite and apprehends the whole of Nature, but insofar as it is finite, apprehending the human body only. The human mind, I maintain, is in this way part of an infinite intellect.

However, to provide here an explanation and rigorous proof of all these things and of other things closely connected with this subject would take far too long, and I do not imagine that you expect this of me at this moment. Indeed, I am not sure that I have rightly understood your meaning, and my reply may not be an answer to your question. This I should like you to let me know.

As to what you say about my hinting that the Cartesian Rules of motion are nearly all wrong, if I remember correctly I said that Mr. Huygens thinks so, and I did not assert that any of the Rules were wrong except for the sixth,[34] regarding which I said I thought that Mr. Huygens too was in error. At that point I asked you to tell me about the experiment which you have conducted in your Royal Society according to this hypothesis. But I gather that you are not permitted to do so, since you have made no reply on this matter.

The said Huygens has been, and still is, fully occupied in polishing dioptrical glasses. For this purpose he has devised a machine in which he can turn plates, and a very neat affair it is. I don't yet know what success he has had with it, and, to tell the truth, I don't particularly want to know. For experience has taught me that in polishing spherical plates a free hand yields safer and better results than any machine. Of the success of his pendulums and the time of his moving to France I have no definite news as yet.

The Bishop of Munster, having made an ill-advised incursion into Frisia like Aesop's goat into the well, has met with no success.[35] Indeed, unless winter begins very early, he will not leave Frisia without great loss. There is no doubt that he embarked on this audacious venture through the persuasion of some traitor or other. But all this is too stale to be written as news, and for the last week or two

---

[34] [The sixth law states: "If a body C was at rest and exactly equal in size to a body B which moves towards it, then it must in part be pushed by B and in part cause B to rebound; so that if B approaches C with four degrees of velocity, it must transfer one degree to it and return in the direction from which it had come through the other three degrees" (*Principia* II, 50).]

[35] [The unsuccessful invasion of Holland took place on 23 September 1665. After several failed efforts, the Bishop made peace with the Dutch on 18 April 1666.]

there has been no new development worth mentioning. There appears to be no hope of peace with the English. But a rumour has recently been spread because of conjectures concerning the sending of a Dutch ambassador to France, and also because the people of Overijsel, who are making every effort to bring in the Prince of Orange—in order, as many think, to annoy the Dutch rather than to benefit themselves—have thought up a certain scheme, namely, to send the said Prince to England as mediator. But the facts are quite otherwise. The Dutch at present have no thoughts of peace, unless matters should reach such a point that they would buy peace. There is as yet some doubt as to the plans of the Swede. Many think that he is making for Metz, others for Holland. But these are simply guesses.

I wrote this letter last week, but I could not send it because the wind prevented my going to the Hague. This is the disadvantage of living in the country. Rarely do I receive a letter at the proper time, for unless an opportunity should chance to arise for sending it in good time, one or two weeks go by before I receive it. Then there is frequently a difficulty preventing me from sending a reply at the proper time. So when you see that I do not reply to you as promptly as I should, you must not think that this is because I forget you. Meanwhile, time presses me to close this letter; of the rest on another occasion. Now I can say no more than to ask you to give my warm greetings to the most noble Mr. Boyle, and to keep me in mind, who am,

In all affection yours,
B. de Spinoza

Voorburg, 20 November 1665

I should like to know whether the belief that there were two comets is held by all astronomers as a result of their motion, or in order to preserve Kepler's hypothesis.[36]

To Mr. Henry Oldenburg,
Secretary of the Royal Society,
In the Pall Mall,
in St. James' Fields,
London

---

[36] [Despite his revolutionary three laws of motion, Kepler (1571–1630) remained something of a 'closet Aristotelian' in holding that the fixed stars were parts of a solid sphere with the sun as its center. The interior of this sphere was filled with the ether. He attempted to account for the origin of comets as the condensates of the ether at random points, which were eventually destroyed by the light of the sun.]

LETTER 34

To the highly esteemed and sagacious John Hudde, from B.d.S.

[The original of this letter is extant, and held by the Royal Society, London. Spinoza retained a slightly different version of it, and it is from this that the text of the O.P. is printed. The differences are unimportant.]

Most esteemed Sir,

The proof of the unity of God on the ground that his nature involves necessary existence, which you asked for and I undertook to provide, I have hitherto been unable to send you because of other demands on my time. To engage upon it now, I shall make the following assumptions:[37]

1. The true definition of each single thing includes nothing other than the simple nature of the thing defined. Hence it follows that:

2. No definition involves or expresses a plurality, or a fixed number of individuals, since it involves and expresses only the nature of the thing as it is in itself. For example, the definition of a triangle includes nothing but the simple nature of a triangle, and not a fixed number of triangles, just as the definition of mind as a thinking thing or the definition of God as a perfect Being includes nothing other than the nature of mind and of God, and not a fixed number of minds or Gods.

3. There must necessarily be a positive cause of each thing, through which it exists.

4. This cause must either be placed in the nature and definition of the thing itself (because in effect existence belongs to its nature or is necessarily included in it) or outside the thing.

From these assumptions it follows that if in Nature there exists a fixed number of individuals, there must be one or more causes which could have produced exactly that number of individuals, no more and no less. For example, if there should exist in Nature twenty men (whom, to avoid confusion, I shall suppose to exist all at the same time and to be the first men in Nature), to account for the existence of these twenty it would not be enough to conduct an investigation into the cause of human nature in general. A reason must also be sought as to why twenty men, not more and not less, exist; for (in accordance with the third hypothesis) a reason and cause must be assigned for the existence of every man. But this cause (in accordance with the second and third hypothesis) cannot be contained in the nature of man himself, for the true definition of man does not involve the number of twenty men. So (in accordance with the fourth hypothesis) the cause of the existence of these twenty men, and consequently of each single man individually, must lie outside them. Therefore we must conclude absolutely that all things which are conceived to exist as a plurality are necessarily produced by external

---

[37] [The numbered assumptions and immediate consequences which Spinoza draws from them are further expanded in E1P8Schol2.]

causes, and not by virtue of their own nature. Now since (according to our hypothesis) necessary existence pertains to God's nature, it must be that his true definition should also include necessary existence, and therefore his necessary existence must be concluded from his true definition. But from his true definition (as I have already proved from the second and third hypothesis) the necessary existence of many Gods cannot be concluded. Therefore there follows the existence of one God only. Q.E.D.

This, esteemed Sir, seems to me at present the best way of proving the proposition. On a previous occasion[38] I have proved this same proposition in a different way, making use of the distinction between essence and existence; but having regard to the consideration which you pointed out to me, I have preferred to send you this proof. I hope it will satisfy you, and, awaiting your judgment on it, I remain meanwhile, etc.

Voorburg, 7 January 1666

LETTER 35

To the highly esteemed and sagacious John Hudde, from B.d.S.

[The original, written in Dutch, is lost. The Latin version in the O.P. was probably made by Spinoza. The Dutch edition of the O.P. prints a text that appears to be a re-translation from the Latin.]

Most esteemed Sir,

In your last letter dated 30 March[39] you have made perfectly clear what I found rather obscure in the letter you wrote me on 10 February. So since I now know what is your real line of thought, I shall frame the question in the form in which it presents itself to you, namely, whether there is only one Being which subsists through its own sufficiency or force. This I not only affirm, but undertake to prove from this basis, that its nature involves necessary existence. This may be most easily proved from God's understanding (as I did in Proposition 11 of my Geometrical Proofs of Descartes' *Principia*), or from others of God's attributes. To embark upon this task, I shall first of all briefly show what properties must be possessed by a Being that includes necessary existence. These are:

1. It is eternal. For if a determinate duration were ascribed to it, beyond the bounds of its determinate duration this Being would be conceived as not existing, or as not involving necessary existence, and this would be in contradiction with its definition.[40]

---

[38] [The proof to which Spinoza alludes is probably like that given as E1P7Dem.]
[39] [No such letter from Hudde to Spinoza is extant. It was probably destroyed by the editors of the O.P.]
[40] [See E1P19.]

2. It is simple, and not composed of parts. For in respect of their nature and our knowledge of them component parts would have to be prior to that which they compose. In the case of that which is eternal by its own nature, this cannot be so.[41]

3. It cannot be conceived as determinate, but only as infinite. For if the nature of that Being were determinate, and were also conceived as determinate, that nature would be conceived as not existing beyond those limits. This again is in contradiction with its definition.[42]

4. It is indivisible.[43] For if it were divisible, it would be divided into parts either of the same or of a different nature. In the latter case it could be destroyed, and thus not exist, which is contrary to the definition. In the former case, every part would include necessary existence through itself, and in this way one could exist, and consequently be conceived, without another. Therefore that nature could be understood as finite, which, by the foregoing, is contrary to the definition. Hence it can be seen that if we were to ascribe any imperfection to such a Being, we would at once fall into a contradiction. For whether the imperfection we would ascribe to such a nature lay in some defect, or in some limitations which such a nature would possess, or in some change which it might undergo from external causes through its lack of force, we are always reduced to saying that this nature which involves necessary existence does not exist, or does not exist necessarily.[44] Therefore I conclude that—

5. Everything that includes necessary existence can have in itself no imperfection, but must express pure perfection.[45]

6. Again, since it can only be the result of its perfection that a Being should exist by its own sufficiency and force, it follows that if we suppose that a Being which does not express all the perfections exists by its own nature, we must also suppose that a Being which comprehends in itself all the perfections exists as well. For if that which is endowed with less power exists by its own sufficiency, how much more does that exist which is endowed with greater power.[46]

To come now to the point at issue, I assert that there can only be one Being whose existence pertains to its own nature, namely, that Being which possesses in itself all perfections, and which I shall call God. For if there be posited a Being to whose nature existence pertains, that Being must contain in itself no imperfection, but must express every perfection (Note 5). And therefore the nature of that

---

[41] [See E1P15.]

[42] [See E1P20–P21.]

[43] [See E1P15.]

[44] [The account of the indivisibility of substance (and of *res extensa*) is further amplified in E1P15Schol. The existence proof is given in E1P7. The fact that Spinoza has here reversed the order indicates that he did not regard the order or status (as axioms or theorems) of the propositions in the *Ethics* to be invariant.]

[45] [This claim is expanded in E1P17 Schol.]

[46] [See E1P17Schol, and also the third of the three versions of the ontological proof which Spinoza gives in E1P11.]

Being must pertain to God (whom, by Note 6, we must also claim to exist), since he possesses in himself all perfections and no imperfections. Nor can it exist outside God; for if it were to exist outside God, one and the same nature involving necessary existence would exist in double form, and this, according to our previous demonstration, is absurd. Therefore nothing outside God, but only God alone, involves necessary existence. This is what was to be proved.

These, esteemed Sir, are at present the points I can put before you to prove what I have undertaken. I should like occasion to prove to you that I am, etc.

Voorburg, 10 April 1666

LETTER 36

To the highly esteemed and sagacious John Hudde, from B.d.S.

[The original, written in Dutch, is lost. The Latin version in the O.P. was perhaps made by Spinoza. The text of the Dutch edition of the O.P. appears to be a re-translation from the Latin.]

Most esteemed Sir,

Something has prevented me from replying any sooner to your letter dated 19 May. As I understand that for the most part you suspend judgment about the proof which I sent you (because of the obscurity, I imagine, which you find in it), I shall here endeavour to explain its meaning more clearly.

First, then, I enumerated four properties which must be possessed by a Being existing through its own sufficiency or force. These four properties and the other properties similar to them I reduced to one in the fifth note. Then, in order to deduce from a single assumption everything necessary for the proof, in the sixth note I endeavoured to prove the existence of God from the given hypothesis; and then, taking nothing more as known except the bare meaning of words, I reached the conclusion which was sought.

This in short was my intention, this my aim. I shall now clarify the meaning of each link individually, and first I shall begin with the assumed properties.

In the first you find no difficulty; it is nothing but an axiom, as is the second. For by simple I mean only that which is not composite or composed of parts that are different in nature, or of other parts that agree in nature. The proof is certainly of universal application.[47]

The meaning of the third note you have understood very well, insofar as it makes the point that, if the Being is Thought, it cannot be conceived as determined in Thought, but only as undetermined, and if the Being is Extension it

---

[47] [Individuation on the basis of parts of *different* natures is the basis of the physical account of material bodies following E2P13Schol. The social account of the origin of the civil community given beginning at E4P37Schol2 is based on parts (i.e., citizens) of *similar* natures.]

cannot be conceived as determined in Extension, but only as undetermined. And yet you deny that you understand the conclusion, which is simply based on this, that it is a contradiction to conceive under the negation of existence something whose definition includes existence, or (which is the same thing) affirms existence. And since 'determinate' denotes nothing positive, but only the privation of existence of that same nature which is conceived as determinate, it follows that that whose definition affirms existence cannot be conceived as determinate. For example, if the term 'extension' includes necessary existence, it is just as impossible to conceive extension without existence as extension without extension. If this is granted, it will also be impossible to conceive determinate extension. For if it were conceived as determinate, it would have to be determined by its own nature, that is, by extension, and this extension by which it would be determined would have to be conceived under the negation of existence. This, according to the hypothesis, is a manifest contradiction.

In the fourth note I intended only to show that such a Being cannot be divided into parts of the same nature or into parts of a different nature, whether or not those parts of a different nature involve necessary existence. For in the latter case, I said, it could be destroyed, since to destroy a thing is to resolve it into such parts that none of them express the nature of the whole, while the former case would be inconsistent with the three properties already established.

In the fifth note I have only assumed that perfection consists in being, and imperfection in the privation of being. I say 'privation'; for although Extension, for instance, denies of itself Thought, this is not an imperfection in it. But if it were deprived of extension, this would indeed argue imperfection in it, as would be the case if it were determinate. And the same would apply if it were to lack duration, position, etc.

You grant the sixth note absolutely, and yet you say that your difficulty remains quite unresolved, namely, as to why there could not be several beings existing through themselves but of different natures, just as Thought and Extension are different and perhaps can subsist through their own sufficiency. From this I cannot but believe that you understand this in a sense far different from mine. I think I can see in what sense you understand it; but in order not to waste time, I shall only make clear my own meaning. I say, then, with regard to the sixth note, that if we suppose that something which is indeterminate and perfect only in its own kind exists by its own sufficiency, then we must also grant the existence of a being which is absolutely indeterminate and perfect.[48] This Being I shall call God. For example, if we are willing to maintain that Extension or Thought (which can each be perfect in its own kind, that is, in a definite kind of being) exist by their own sufficiency, we shall also have to admit the existence of God who is absolutely perfect, that is, the existence of a being who is absolutely indeterminate.

At this point I would have you note what I recently said regarding the word 'imperfection'; namely, that it signifies that a thing lacks something which nevertheless pertains to its nature. For example, extension can be said to be imperfect only

[48] [This claim is the converse of E1P9.]

in respect of duration, position, or magnitude; that is to say, because it does not last longer, because it does not retain its position, or because it is not greater. But it will never be said to be imperfect because it does not think, for nothing like this is demanded of its nature which consists solely in extension, that is, in a definite kind of being, in which respect alone it can be said to be determinate or indeterminate, imperfect or perfect. And since God's nature does not consist in one definite kind of being, but in being which is absolutely indeterminate, his nature also demands all that which perfectly expresses being; otherwise his nature would be determinate and deficient. This being so, it follows that there can be only one Being, God, which exists by its own force. For if, let us say, we suppose that Extension involves existence, it must needs be eternal and indeterminate, and express absolutely no imperfection, but only perfection. And so Extension will pertain to God, or will be something that expresses God's nature in some way; for God is a Being which is indeterminate in essence and omnipotent absolutely, and not merely in a particular respect. And thus what is said of Extension (arbitrarily chosen) must also be affirmed of everything which we shall take to be of a similar kind. I therefore conclude, as in my former letter, that nothing outside God, but God alone, subsists by its own sufficiency. I trust that this is enough to clarify the meaning of my former letter; but you will be the better judge of that.

I might have ended here, but since I am minded to get new plates made for me for polishing glasses, I should very much like to have your advice in this matter. I cannot see what we gain by polishing convex-concave glasses. On the contrary, if I have done my calculations correctly, convex-plane glasses are bound to be more useful. For if, for convenience, we take the ratio of refraction[49] as 3 to 2, and in the accompanying diagram we insert letters according to your arrangement in your little *Dioptrics*, it will be found on setting out the equation that NI or, as it is called $z = \sqrt{(9/4)zz - xx} - \sqrt{[1 - xx]}$.[50] Hence it follows that if $x = 0$, $z = 2$, which then is also the longest. And if $x = 3/5$, z will be $43/25$, or a little more; that is, if we suppose that the ray BI does not undergo a second refraction when it is directed from the glass towards I. But let us now suppose that this ray issuing from the glass is refracted at the plane surface BF, and is directed not towards I but towards R. If therefore the lines BI and BR are in the same ratio as is the refraction—that is, as is here supposed, a ratio of 3 to 2—and if we then follow out the working of the equation, we get $NR = \sqrt{(zz - xx)} - \sqrt{(1 - xx)}$. And if again, as before, we take $x = 0$, then $NR = 1$, that is, equal to half the diameter. But if $x = 3/5$, NR will be $20/25 + 1/50$, which shows that

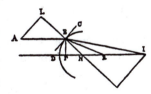

this focal length is less than the other, although the optic tube is less by a whole semi-diameter. So if we were to make a telescope as long as DI by making the

---

[49] [This ratio has the sine of the angle of incidence as numerator, and the sine of the angle of refraction as denominator.]

[50] [Spinoza uses 'xx' where we would use an exponential for squaring. The exponential notation had been introduced by Descartes, but was not widely adopted until after the seventeenth century.]

semi-diameter = $1\frac{1}{2}$ while the aperture BF remained the same, the focal length would be much less. A further reason why convex-concave glasses are less satisfactory, apart from the fact that they require twice the labour and expense, is that the rays, being not all directed to one and the same point, never fall perpendicularly on the concave surface. However, as I have no doubt that you have long since considered these points and have made more rigorous calculations about them, and have reached a decision on this question, I seek your opinion and advice regarding it, etc.

[Date probably June 1666]

LETTER 37

To the learned and experienced Johan Bouwmeester, from B.d.S.

[The original is lost, but an old copy is extant, differing in a few details from the O.P. text. The last sentence appears only in the old copy.]

Most learned Sir, and very special friend,[51]

I have been unable to reply any sooner to your last letter which reached me quite some time ago. Various concerns and troubles have kept me so occupied that it is only with difficulty that I have at last managed to extricate myself. However, since I have now obtained some degree of respite, I will not fail in my duty, but I want first of all to express my very warm thanks for your love and devotion towards me which you have abundantly shown so often by deeds, and now by letter, etc.

I pass on to your question, which is as follows: whether there is or can be a method such that thereby we can make sure and unwearied progress in the study of things of the highest importance; or whether our minds, like our bodies, are at the mercy of chance, and our thoughts are governed more by fortune than by skill. I think I shall give a satisfactory answer if I show that there must necessarily be a method whereby we can direct and interconnect our clear and distinct perceptions, and that the intellect is not, like the body, at the mercy of chance. This is established simply from the following consideration, that one clear and distinct perception, or several taken together, can be absolutely the cause of another clear and distinct perception. Indeed, all the clear and distinct perceptions that we form can arise only from other clear and distinct perceptions which are in us, and they acknowledge no other cause outside us. Hence it follows that the clear and distinct perceptions that we form depend only on our nature and its definite and fixed laws, that is, on our power itself alone, and not on chance, that is, on causes which, although acting likewise by definite and fixed laws, are yet unknown to us and foreign to our nature and power. As

---

[51] [Johan Bouwmeester (1630–1680) was a medical doctor and a member of the discussion group formed at Franciscus Van den Enden's school. — M.L.M.]

for the other perceptions, I do admit that they depend in the highest degree on chance. From this it is quite clear what a true method must be and in which it should especially consist, namely, solely in the knowledge of pure intellect and its nature and laws.[52] To acquire this, we must first of all distinguish between intellect and imagination,[53] that is, between true ideas and the others—fictitious, false, doubtful, and, in sum, all ideas which depend only on memory. To understand these things, at least as far as the method requires, there is no need to get to know the nature of mind through its first cause; it is enough to formulate a brief account of the mind or its perceptions in the manner expounded by Verulam.[54]

I think that in these few words I have explained and demonstrated the true method, and at the same time shown the way to attain it. It remains, however, for me to advise you that for all this there is needed constant meditation and a most steadfast mind and purpose, to acquire which it is most important to establish a fixed way and manner of life, and to have a definite aim in view. But enough of this for the present.

Farewell, and love him who has for you a sincere affection.

Bened. de Spinoza
Voorburg, 10 June 1666

LETTER 40

To the worthy and sagacious Jarig Jelles, from B.d.S.

[The original, written in Dutch, is lost. It may be the text reproduced in the Dutch edition of the O.P. The Latin is a translation.]

Worthy friend,

I have duly received your last letter dated the 14th of this month, but various obstacles have prevented me from replying sooner.

With regard to the Helvetius affair,[55] I have spoken about it with Mr. Vossius,[56] who (not to recount in a letter all that passed between us) laughed heartily at it, and even expressed surprise that I should question him about such a silly thing. However, disregarding this, I went to the silversmith named Brechtelt, who had tested the gold. Taking quite a different view from Vossius, he said that between

---

52 [The brief summary of his method given here is further developed in the unfinished *Tractatus de intellectus emendatione* (TIE).]

53 [See E2P40Schol, where Spinoza develops the distinction among three kinds of knowledge (imagination, reason, intuition). The term *imaginatio* in Spinoza refers most generally to sensory perception.]

54 [I.e., Francis Bacon, in the *Organon*.]

55 [Johannes Fridericus Helvetius was physician to the Prince of Orange.]

56 [Isaac Vossius (1618–1689). He wrote on the Septuagint and on poetry, and was made Canon of Windsor in 1673.]

the melting and the separation the gold had increased in weight, and had become that much heavier as was the weight of the silver he had introduced into the crucible to effect the separation. So he firmly believed that the gold which had transmuted his silver into gold contained something singular. He was not the only one of this opinion; various other persons present at the time also found that this was so. Thereupon I went to Helvetius himself, who showed me the gold and the crucible with its interior still covered with a film of gold, and told me that he had introduced into the molten lead scarcely more than a quarter of a grain of barley or of mustard-seed. He added that he would shortly publish an account of the whole affair, and went on to say that in Amsterdam a certain man (he thought it was the same man who had visited him) had performed the same operation, of which you have no doubt heard. This is all I have been able to learn about this matter.

The writer of the book you mention (in which he presumes to show that Descartes' arguments in the Third and Fourth Meditation proving the existence of God are false) is assuredly fighting his own shadow, and will do more harm to himself than to others. Descartes' axiom is, I admit somewhat obscure and confused as you have also remarked, and he might have expressed it more clearly and truthfully thus: 'The power of thought to think or to comprehend things is no greater than the power of Nature to be and to act'.[57] This is a clear and true axiom, whence the existence of God follows most clearly and forcefully from the idea of him. The argument of the said author as related by you shows quite clearly that he does not yet understand the matter. It is indeed true that we could go on to infinity if the question could thus be resolved in all its parts, but otherwise it is sheer folly. For example, if someone were to ask through what cause a certain determinate body is set in motion, we could answer that it is determined to such motion by another body, and this again by another, and so on to infinity. We could reply in this way, I say, because the question is only about motion, and by continuing to posit another body we assign a sufficient and eternal cause of this motion. But if I see a book containing excellent thoughts and beautifully written in the hands of a common man and I ask him whence he has such a book, and he replies that he has copied it from another book belonging to another common man who could also write beautifully, and so on to infinity, he does not satisfy me.[58] For I am asking him not only about the form and arrangement of the letters, with which alone his answer is concerned, but also about the thoughts and meaning expressed in their arrangement, and this he does not answer by his progression to infinity. How this can be applied to ideas can easily be understood from what I have made clear in the ninth axiom of my Geometrical Proofs of Descartes' *Principles of Philosophy*.

---

[57] [What is at issue here is Descartes' use of the notion of 'difficulty' in describing acts of comprehension (as well as divine conservation).]

[58] [The argument refers to the explanation of the representational content of a cognition or idea, which Spinoza—following Descartes—calls its 'objective reality'. The objective reality of a representation cannot be explained by an infinite series of causes, although just such a series does explain its formal reality.]

I now proceed to answer your other letter, dated 9 March, in which you ask for a further explanation of what I wrote in my previous letter concerning the figure of a circle. This you will easily be able to understand if you will please note that all the rays that are supposed to fall in parallel on the anterior glass of the telescope are not really parallel because they all come from one and the same point. But they are considered to be so because the object is so far from us that the aperture of the telescope, in comparison with its distance, can be considered as no more than a point. Moreover, it is certain that, in order to see an entire object, we need not only rays coming from a single point but also all the other cones of rays that come from all the other points. And therefore it is also necessary that, on passing through the glass, they should come together in as many other foci. And although the eye is not so exactly constructed that all the rays coming from different points of an object come together in just so many foci at the back of the eye, yet it is certain that the figures that can bring this about are to be preferred above all others. Now since a definite segment of a circle can bring it about that all the rays coming from one point are (using the language of Mechanics) brought together at another point on its diameter, it will also bring together all the other rays which come from other points of the object, at so many other points. For from any point on an object a line can be drawn passing through the centre of the circle, although for that purpose the aperture of the telescope must be made much smaller than it would otherwise be made if there were no need of more than one focus, as you may easily see.

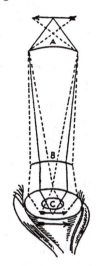

What I here say of the circle cannot be said of the ellipse or the hyperbola, and far less of other more complex figures, since from one single point of the object only one line can be drawn passing through both the foci. This is what I intended to say in my first letter regarding this matter.

From the attached diagram you will be able to see the proof that the angle formed at the surface of the eye by rays coming from different points becomes greater or less according as the difference of the foci is greater or less. So, after sending you my cordial greetings, it remains only for me to say that I am, etc.

Voorburg, 25 March 1667

LETTER 55

To the most sagacious philosopher, B.d.S., from Hugo Boxel

*[The original, written in Dutch, is lost. The O.P. gives a Latin
version, perhaps by Spinoza, and this has been re-translated into
Dutch in the Dutch edition. Conjectural date, September 1674.]*

Most sagacious Sir,

I am later than expected in replying to your letter because a slight illness has deprived me of the pleasure of study and meditation, and has prevented me from writing to you. Now, thanks be to God, I have recovered my health. In this reply I shall follow your letter step by step, passing over your outcry against those who have written about ghosts.

I say, then, that I think there are no ghosts of the female sex because I deny that they give birth. As to their shape and constitution I say nothing, because this does not concern me. A thing is said to happen fortuitously when it comes about regardless of the doer's intention. When we dig the ground to plant a vine or to make a pit or a grave, and find a treasure of which we have never had a thought, this is said to happen by chance. He who acts of his own free will in such a way that he can either act or not act can never be said to act by chance if he chooses to act; for in that case all human actions would be by chance, which would be absurd. 'Necessary' and 'free', not 'necessary' and 'fortuitous', are contrary terms. Granted that God's will is eternal, it still does not follow that the world is eternal, for God could have determined from eternity to create the world at a set time.

You go on to deny that God's will has ever been indifferent, which I dispute; nor is it as necessary as you think to pay such strict attention to this point. Neither does everyone agree that God's will is necessary, for this involves the concept of necessity. Now he who attributes will to someone means thereby that he can either act or not, according to his will; but if we ascribe necessity to him, he must act of necessity.

Finally, you say that you avoid granting any human attributes in God lest you should confuse the divine nature with human nature. Thus far I agree, for we do not apprehend in what way God acts, or in what way he wills, understands, thinks, sees, hears, etc. However, if you completely deny of God these activities and our most sublime conceptions of him, and you assert that these are not in God eminently and in a metaphysical sense, then I do not understand your God, or what you mean by the word 'God'. What we fail to apprehend ought not to be denied. Mind, which is spirit and incorporeal, can act only along with the most subtle bodies, namely, the humours. And what is the relation between body and mind? In what way does mind act along with bodies? For without these the mind is at rest, and when these are in a disordered state the mind does what it should not have done. Show me how this comes about. You cannot, and neither can I. Yet we see and sense that the mind does act, and this remains true in spite of our failure to perceive how this acting comes about. In the same way, although we do not understand how God acts and we refrain from ascribing to him human activities, yet we ought not to deny of him that, in an eminent way and beyond our comprehension, these activities are in accord with our own, such as willing, understanding, seeing and hearing with the intellect, though not with eyes or ears. Similarly, wind and air can destroy, and even overthrow, lands and mountains without the use of hands or other tools; yet this is impossible for men without the use of hands and machines. If you attribute necessity to God and deprive him of will and free choice, this raises some doubt as to whether you are not depicting and representing as a monster him who is an infinitely perfect being. To attain your purpose you will need other arguments to form a basis, for in my opinion those you have advanced have no solidity. And even if you can prove them, there are perhaps other arguments to counterbalance yours. But setting this aside, let us proceed.

To establish the existence of spirits in the world, you demand conclusive proofs. There are few of these in the world, and, apart from mathematics, none of these are as certain as we would wish. Indeed, we are satisfied with probable conjectures which are likely to be true. If the arguments by which things were proved were quite conclusive, only the foolish and the obstinate would be found to contradict them. But, my dear friend, we are not as fortunate as that. In this world we are less demanding; to some extent we rely on conjecture, and in our reasoning we accept the probable in default of demonstrative proof. This is evident from all the sciences, both human and divine, which abound in controversies and disputes whose prevalence is the reason why so many different opinions are everywhere to be found. That is why, as you know, there were once philosophers called Sceptics who doubted everything. They used to debate the case for and against so as to arrive at the merely probable in default of true reasons, and each of them believed what he thought more probable. The moon is situated directly below the sun, and therefore the sun will be obscured in some region of the earth, and if the sun is not obscured in daytime, then the moon is not situated directly below it. This is conclusive proof, reasoning from cause to effect and from effect to cause. There are some proofs of this sort, but very few, which cannot be contradicted by anyone if only he grasps them.

With regard to beauty, there are some things whose parts are in proportion with one another, and are better composed than others. God has bestowed on man's understanding and judgment a sense of agreeableness and harmony with that which is well-proportioned, and not with that which lacks proportion. This is the case with harmonious and discordant sounds, where our hearing can well distinguish between harmony and discord because the former brings pleasure and the latter annoyance. A thing's perfection is also beautiful, insofar as it lacks nothing. Of this there are many examples, which I omit to avoid prolixity. Let us only consider the world, to which we apply the term Whole or Universe. If this is true, as indeed is the case, the existence of incorporeal things does not spoil it or degrade it. Your remarks as to Centaurs, Hydras, Harpies, etc., are quite misplaced, for we are speaking of the most universal genera, of the prime grades of things, which comprehend under them various and innumerable species: we are speaking of the eternal and the temporal, cause and effect, finite and infinite, animate and inanimate, substance and accident or mode, the corporeal and the spiritual, and so on.

I say that spirits are like God because he also is spirit. You demand as clear an idea of spirits as of a triangle, which is impossible. Tell me, I beg you, what idea you have of God, and whether it is as clear to your intellect as is the idea of a triangle. I know that you have none such, and I have said that we are not so fortunate as to be able to apprehend things by means of conclusive proofs, and that, for the most part, the probable holds sway in this world. Nevertheless, I affirm that just as body can exist without memory, etc., so can memory, etc., exist without body, and that just as a circle can exist without a sphere, so too can a sphere exist without a circle. But this is to descend from the most universal genera to particular species, which are not the object of this discussion.

I say that the Sun is the centre of the world, that the fixed stars are more distant from the earth than is Saturn, and Saturn than Jupiter, and Jupiter than Mars. So in the limitless air some bodies are more distant from us and some nearer to us, and these we term higher and lower.

It is not the upholders of the existence of spirits who discredit philosophers, but those who deny it; for all philosophers, both of ancient and modern times, think themselves convinced of the existence of spirits. Plutarch bears witness to this in his treatises on the opinions of philosophers and on the daemon of Socrates, and so do all the Stoics, Pythagoreans, Platonists, Peripatetics, Empedocles, Maximus Tyrius, Apuleius and others. Of modern philosophers not one denies spectres. Reject, then, the testimony of so many wise men who had eyes and ears, reject the narratives of so many philosophers, so many historians. Assert that they are all foolish and crazy like the common herd—and yet your answers are unconvincing, even absurd, and generally irrelevant to the main point at issue, and you fail to produce any proof to confirm your view. Caesar, along with Cicero and Cato, does not laugh at spectres, but at omens and presentiments. And yet, if he had not mocked at Spurina on the day he was to die, he would not have suffered all those stab-wounds from his enemies. But let this suffice for the time, etc.

LETTER 56

To the highly esteemed and judicious Hugo Boxel, from B.d.S.

[The original, written in Dutch, is lost. The O.P. gives a Latin version, perhaps by Spinoza, and this has been re-translated into Dutch in the Dutch edition. Conjectural date, September 1674.]

Most esteemed Sir,

I hasten to reply to your letter received yesterday, for if I delay any further I shall have to postpone my reply longer than I could wish. I should have been anxious about your health, had I not learned that you are better. I hope that you are by now completely recovered. When two people follow different first principles, the difficulty they experience in coming together and reaching agreement in a matter involving many other questions might be shown simply from this discussion of ours, even if it were not confirmed by rational considerations. Tell me, pray, whether you have seen or read any philosophers who have maintained that the world was made by chance, taking chance in the sense you give it, that God had a set aim in creating the world and yet departed from his resolve. I am unaware that any such idea has ever entered the thoughts of any man. I am similarly at a loss to understand the reasoning whereby you try to convince me that chance and necessity are not contraries. As soon as I perceive that the three angles of a triangle are necessarily equal to two right angles, I also deny that this comes about by chance; likewise, as soon as I perceive that heat is the necessary effect of fire, I also deny that this happens by chance. That 'necessary' and 'free' are contraries seems no less absurd and opposed to reason. Nobody can deny that God freely knows himself and all other things, and yet all are unanimous in granting that God knows himself necessarily. Thus you fail, I think, to make any distinction between constraint [*coactio*] or force, and necessity.[59] That a man wills to live, to love, etc., does not proceed from constraint, but is nevertheless necessary, and far more so is God's will to be, to know and to act. If, in addition to these points, you reflect that a state of indifference is nothing but ignorance or a condition of doubt, and that a will that is always constant and determined in all things is a virtue and a necessary property of the intellect, you will see that my view is in complete accord with the truth. If we maintain that God was able not to will what he willed, but that he was not able not to understand what he willed, we are attributing to God two different kinds of freedom, the freedom of necessity, and the freedom of indifference. Consequently, we shall conceive God's will as different from his essence and his intellect, and in this way we shall fall into one absurdity after another.

The attention which I requested in my former letter you have not deemed necessary, and if is for this reason that you have failed to direct your thoughts to the main point at issue, and have disregarded what was most relevant.

Further, when you say that you do not see what sort of God I have if I deny in him the actions of seeing, hearing, attending, willing, etc., and that he possesses those faculties in an eminent degree, I suspect that you believe there is no greater perfection than can be explicated by the afore-mentioned attributes. I am not surprised, for I believe that a triangle, if it could speak, would likewise say that God is eminently triangular, and a circle that God's nature is eminently circular. In this way each would ascribe to God its own attributes, assuming itself to be like God and regarding all else as ill-formed.

The briefness of a letter and the pressure of time do not permit me to deal with my view of the divine nature and with the questions you have propounded; anyway, to bring up difficulties is not to advance rational arguments. It is true that in this world we often act from conjecture, but it is not true that philosophical thinking proceeds from conjecture. In the common round of life we have to follow

---

[59] [Spinoza constantly inveighs against the confusion between external coercion and internal necessity. The libertarian notion of a freedom of indifference makes freedom into random activity or caprice.]

what is probable, but in speculative thought we have to follow what is true. A man would perish of hunger and thirst if he refused to eat and drink until he had obtained perfect proof that food and drink would be good for him, but this does not hold in the field of contemplation. On the contrary, we should take care not to admit as true anything that is merely probable. When one false proposition is allowed entry, innumerable others follow.

Again, because the sciences of things divine and human abound with quarrels and controversies, it cannot be concluded therefrom that the whole of the subject-matter with which they deal is uncertain. There have been many whose zeal for controversy was such that they even scoffed at geometrical proof. Sextus Empiricus and other Sceptics whom you quote say that it is false that the whole is greater than its part, and they pass similar judgment on other axioms.

However, leaving aside and granting the fact that in default of proof we must be content with the probable, I say that a probable proof must be such that, although open to doubt, it cannot be contradicted; for that which can be contradicted is akin, not to truth, but to falsehood. If, for example, I say that Peter is alive because I saw him yesterday in good health, this is indeed probable insofar as nobody is able to contradict me. But if somebody else says that yesterday he saw Peter unconscious, and that he believes that since then Peter has died, he makes my statement seem false. That your conjecture regarding spectres and ghosts seems false and has not even a show of truth, I have demonstrated so clearly that I find nothing in your reply worthy of consideration.

To your question as to whether I have as clear an idea of God as of a triangle, I reply in the affirmative. But if you ask me whether I have as clear a mental image of God as of a triangle, I reply in the negative. We cannot imagine God, but we can apprehend him by the intellect.[60] Here it should also be observed that I do not claim to have complete knowledge of God, but that I do understand some of his attributes—not indeed all of them, or the greater part—and it is certain that my ignorance of very many attributes does not prevent me from having knowledge of some of them. When I was studying Euclid's Elements, I understood early on that the three angles of a triangle are equal to two right angles, and I clearly perceived this property of a triangle although I was ignorant of many others.

As regards spectres or ghosts, I have not as yet heard of any intelligible property of theirs; I have heard only of fantasies beyond anyone's understanding. In saying that spectres or ghosts here below (I follow your usage of words, though I do not know why matter here below should be inferior to matter above) are made of very tenuous, rarefied and subtle substance, you seem to be speaking of spiders' webs, air or mist. To say that they are invisible is, in my view, tantamount to saying not what they are, but what they are not. But perhaps you wish to indicate that they render themselves visible or invisible as and when they please, and that our imagination will find no more difficulty in this than in other impossibilities.

---

[60] [See E2P47: "The human mind has an adequate knowledge of the eternal and infinite essence of God."]

The authority of Plato, Aristotle and Socrates[61] carries little weight with me. I should have been surprised if you had produced Epicurus, Democritus, Lucretius or one of the Atomists or defenders of the atoms.[62] It is not surprising that those who have thought up occult qualities, intentional species, substantial forms and a thousand more bits of nonsense[63] should have devised spectres and ghosts, and given credence to old wives' tales with view to disparaging the authority of Democritus, whose high reputation they so envied that they burned all the books which he had published amidst so much acclaim.[64] If you are minded to put your trust in such people, what reason have you to deny the miracles of the Holy Virgin and all the saints? These have been reported by so many renowned philosophers, theologians and historians that I could produce a hundred of these latter to scarcely one of the former.

In conclusions, most esteemed Sir, I find that I have gone further than I intended, and I will trouble you no longer with matters which I know you will not concede, your first principles being far different from my own, etc.

LETTER 57

To the most distinguished and acute philosopher, B.d.S., from Ehrenfried Walther von Tschirnhaus

[Known only from the O.P. The original is lost. The letter was addressed to Schuller, who transmitted to Spinoza the part that concerned him.]

Distinguished Sir,

It surprises me, to say the least, that when philosophers demonstrate that something is false, at the same time they are showing its truth. For Descartes, at the beginning of his Method,[65] thinks that the certainty of the intellect is equal for all, and in the *Meditations* he proves it. The same line is taken by those who think that they can prove something to be certain on the grounds that it is accepted by separate individuals as being beyond doubt.

---

61 [The inventory of Spinoza's library contains a Latin translation of the complete works of Aristotle, but nothing whatever by Plato.]

62 [Epicurus (341–271 B.C.), Democritus (460–370 B.C.) and Lucretius (99–55 B.C.) all supported the atomic theory, and were accordingly held in favor by seventeenth-century scientists.]

63 [The terms 'intentional species' and 'substantial forms' are mediaeval. They were widely criticized in the seventeenth century as involving an appeal to unknown and unknowable ('occult') qualities of things which explain nothing. This is the same accusation which the Cartesians (and Leibniz) were to make against Newton's theory of gravitation as a *vis insita*.]

64 [The story comes from Diogenes Laertius, *Lives of the Philosophers*.]

65 [The Dutch version has 'in the same paragraph' instead of 'at the beginning of his Method'. The opening paragraphs of this letter have been obviously omitted, and probably referred to specific passages in Descartes. The Dutch editors probably made the change in the light of the omission.]

But setting this aside, I appeal to experience, and I humbly request you to give careful consideration to the following. For thus it will be found that if of two men one affirms something and the other denies it, and they are fully conscious of what it is they are saying, although they appear verbally to contradict each other, yet when we consider what is in their minds they are both speaking the truth, each according to his own thinking. I bring up this point because it is of immeasurable value in our common dealings, and if this single fact were taken into account, innumerable controversies and the ensuing disputes would be averted, even though this truth in conception is not always true in an absolute sense, but is taken as true only on the basis of what is assumed to be in a man's understanding. This rule is of such general application that it holds good in the case of all men, even those who are mad or are asleep. For whatever they say they see (although it may not appear so to us) or have seen, it is quite certain that this is really so.

This is also seen very clearly in the case under consideration, that of Free Will. For both he who argues for and he who argues against seem to me to speak the truth, according to how one conceives freedom. Descartes says that that is free which is not compelled by any cause, whereas you say that it is that which is not determined to something by any cause. I agree with you that in all things we are determined to something by a definite cause, and that thus we have no free will. But on the other hand I also agree with Descartes that in certain matters (as I shall soon make clear) we are not in any way compelled, and so have free will. The present question will furnish me with an example.

The problem is of a threefold nature. First, do we have in an absolute sense a power over things which are external to us? This is denied. For example, that I am at this moment writing a letter is not something that is absolutely within my power, since I would certainly have written sooner had I not been prevented either by my being away or by the company of friends. Secondly, do we have in an absolute sense power over the movements of our bodies which follow when the will determines them thereto? I reply affirmatively with this reservation—if we are in good health; for if I am well, I can always set myself to write, or not. Thirdly, when I am in a position to exercise my reason, can I do so quite freely, that is, absolutely? I reply in the affirmative. For who would tell me, without gainsaying his own consciousness, that I can not in my thoughts think that I want to write or not to write? And with regard to the act of writing, too, since external causes permit (and this concerns the second question) that I should possess the capacity both to write and not to write, I agree with you that there are causes which determine me to write just now—that you wrote to me in the first place and in that letter requested me to reply as soon as I could, and, with the present opportunity arising, I would not willingly let it pass. I also agree with Descartes, on the testimony of my consciousness, that things of that kind do not on that account constrain me, and that I can still (as seems impossible to deny) really refrain from writing, in spite of those considerations. And, again, if we were under the compulsion of external circumstances, who could possibly acquire the habit of virtue? Indeed, if this point were granted, all wickedness would be excusable. But does it not frequently come about that, being determined to something by external things, we still resist this with a firm and steady mind?

To give a clearer explanation of the above rule, you are both telling the truth according to your own conception, but if we look to absolute truth, this belongs only to Descartes' view. For in your mind you are assuming as certain that the essence of freedom consists in our not being determined by any thing. On this assumption both sides are in the right. However, the essence of any thing consists in that without which it cannot even be conceived, and freedom can surely be clearly conceived, even though in our actions we are determined to something by external causes, or even though there are always causes which incite us to act in a certain way, but without being completely dominant. But freedom cannot be conceived at all on the assumption that we are under compulsion. See, in addition, Descartes, Volume 1, letters 8 and 9, and also Volume 2, page 4. But let this suffice. I beg you to reply to the difficulties here raised, and you will find me not only grateful, but also, health permitting,[66]

Your most devoted,
N.N.

8 October 1674

LETTER 58

To the most learned and wise G. H. Schuller, from B.d.S.

[Known only from the O.P. The original is lost.]

Most wise Sir,

Our friend J.R.[67] has sent me the letter which you were kind enough to write to me, together with your friend's judgment of the views expressed by Descartes and myself on the question of free will, for which I am most grateful. Although I am at present fully occupied with other matters and my health is also causing me some concern, I feel impelled both by your exceptional courtesy and by your devotion to truth, which I particularly value, to satisfy your wish as far as my slender abilities allow. Indeed, I do not know what your friend means in the section preceding his appeal to experience and his request for careful attention. As to what he goes on to say, 'if one of two men affirms something of a thing and the other denies it' etc., this is true if he means that the two men, while using the same words, nevertheless have different things in mind. I once sent some examples of this to our friend J.R., and I am now writing to him to let you have them.

So I now pass on to that definition of freedom which he ascribes to me, but I do not know whence he has taken it, I say that that thing is free which exists and acts

---

[66] [The last phrase, beginning 'and you will find me . . .', is found only in the Dutch edition.]

[67] [Most likely this is Jan Rieuwertsz of Amsterdam, who was a bookseller and a publisher. His bookstore was a center for liberal thinkers, and he published all Spinoza's works (though in secret except for the PPC).]

solely from the necessity of its own nature,[68] and I say that that thing is constrained (*coactus*) which is determined by something else to exist and to act in a fixed and determinate way. For example, although God exists necessarily, he nevertheless exists freely because he exists solely from the necessity of his own nature. Similarly, too, God freely understands himself and all things absolutely, because it follows solely from the necessity of his own nature that he should understand all things. So you see that I place freedom, not in free decision, but in free necessity.

However, let us move down to created things, which are all determined by external causes to exist and to act in a fixed and determinate way. To understand this clearly, let us take a very simple example. A stone receives from the impulsion of an external cause a fixed quantity of motion whereby it will necessarily continue to move when the impulsion of the external cause has ceased. The stone's continuance in motion is constrained, not because it is necessary, but because it must be defined by the impulsion received from the external cause. What here applies to the stone must be understood of every individual thing, however complex its structure and various its functions. For every single thing is necessarily determined by an external cause to exist and to act in a fixed and determinate way.[69]

Furthermore, conceive, if you please, that while continuing in motion the stone thinks, and knows that it is endeavouring, as far as in it lies, to continue in motion. Now this stone, since it is conscious only of its endeavour[70] and is not at all indifferent, will surely think it is completely free, and that it continues in motion for no other reason than that it so wishes. This, then, is that human freedom which all men boast of possessing, and which consists solely in this, that men are conscious of their desire and unaware of the causes by which they are determined. In the same way a baby thinks that it freely desires milk, an angry child revenge, and a coward flight. Again, a drunken man believes that it is from his free decision that he says what he later, when sober, would wish to be left unsaid. So, too, the delirious, the loquacious, and many others of this kind believe that they act from their free decision, and not that they are carried away by impulse. Since this preconception is innate in all men, they cannot so easily be rid of it. For although experience teaches us again and again that nothing is less within men's power than to control their appetites, and that frequently, when subject to conflicting emotions, they see the better course and pursue the worse,[71] they nevertheless believe themselves to be free, a belief that stems from the fact that in some cases our desire has no great force and can easily be checked by the recurrence to mind of some other thing which is frequently in our thoughts.

---

[68] [The definition of 'freedom' is given in E1Def7, and E1P17 states that "God acts solely from the laws of his own nature, constrained by none."]

[69] [See E1P28, which asserts that the chain of causes is infinite.]

[70] [Here 'endeavour' is *conatus*, which is introduced beginning at E3P6 and plays a major role not just in Spinoza's psychology but also in the account of virtue central to his moral philosophy.]

[71] [Viz., "*meliora videant et deteriora sequantur.*" Spinoza uses this expression elsewhere; see E3P2Schol. It is original to Spinoza in this form, but is found in Ovid (*Metamorphoses*, VII, 20), in another form: "*Video meliora proboque, deteriora sequor*" (I see and approve the better, but I follow the worse). Cf. Paul's Epistle to the Romans, 7:15–19.]

I have now, if I am not mistaken, sufficiently set forth my views on free and constrained necessity and on imaginary human freedom, and with this your friend's objections are readily answered. For when he says, along with Descartes,[72] that the free man is he who is not constrained by any external cause, if by constrained he means acting against one's will, I agree that in some cases we are in no way constrained and that in this sense we have free will. But if by constrained he means acting necessarily, though not against one's will, I deny that in any instance we are free, as I have explained above.

But your friend, on the contrary asserts that 'we can employ our rational faculty in complete freedom, that is, absolutely', in which assertion he is somewhat overconfident. 'For who', he says, 'would deny, without gainsaying his own consciousness, that with my thoughts I can think that I want to write, or do not want to write?' I should very much like to know what consciousness he is talking about, apart from that which I illustrated above with the example of the stone. For my part, not to gainsay my own consciousness—that is, reason and experience—and not to cherish prejudice and ignorance, I deny that, by any absolute power of thought, I can think that I want, or do not want, to write. But I appeal to the consciousness of the man himself, who has doubtless experienced in dreams that he has not the power to think that he wants, or does not want, to write, and that, when he dreams that he wants to write, he does not have the power not to dream that he wants to write. I think that he must likewise have experienced that the mind is not at all times equally fitted to thinking of the same object, but that just as the body is more fitted to have the image of this or that object aroused in it, so the mind is more apt to regard this or that object.

When he further adds that the causes of his resolving to write have indeed urged him to write, but have not constrained him, if you will weigh the matter impartially he means no more than this, that his mind was at the time in such a state that causes which might not have swayed him at other times—as when he is assailed by some strong emotion—were at this time easily able to sway him. That is, causes which might not have constrained him at other times did in fact constrain him then, not to write against his will, but necessarily to want to write.

When he goes on to say that 'if we were constrained by external causes, nobody could acquire the habit of virtue', I do not know who has told him that we cannot be of strong and constant mind from the necessity of fate, but only from free will.

As to his final remark, that 'on this basis all wickedness would be excusable', what of it? Wicked men are no less to be feared and no less dangerous when they are necessarily wicked. But on this point please see my Appendix to Books 1 and 2 of *Principia Cartesiana* demonstrated in geometric form, Part II, Chapter 8.[73]

Lastly, I should like your friend who raises these objections to tell me how he reconciles the human virtue that springs from free decision with God's preordainment. If he admits with Descartes that he does not know how to effect this

---

72 [A more extended critique of Descartes' account of freedom is given in E1P33Schol2.]
73 [The appendix to the PPC is entitled *Cogitata Metaphysica* (CM). CM2.8 is entitled, "Of the Will of God."]

reconciliation, then he is trying to hurl against me the weapon by which he himself is already transfixed. But to no purpose. If you will examine my view attentively, you will see that it is quite consistent.

The Hague
[October 1674]

LETTER 59

To the most distinguished and acute philosopher, B.d.S., from Ehrenfried Walther von Tschirnhaus

[Known only from the O.P. The original is lost.]

Most distinguished Sir,

When shall we have your Method of rightly directing the reason in acquiring knowledge of unknown truths, and also your General Treatise on Physics? I know that you have but recently made great advances in these subjects. I have already been made aware of the former, and the latter is known to me from the lemmata attached to the second part of your *Ethics*,[74] which provide a ready solution to many problems in physics. If time and opportunity permit, I humbly beg you to let me have the true definition of motion, together with its explanation. And since extension when conceived through itself is indivisible, immutable, etc., how can we deduce a priori the many and various forms that it can assume, and consequently the existence of figure in the particles of a body, which yet are various in any body and are different from the figures of the parts which constitute the form of another body?

    In our conversation you pointed out to me the method you adopt in seeking out truths as yet unknown. I find this method to be of surpassing excellence, and yet quite simple, as far as I understand it; and I can say that by following this single procedure I have made considerable advances in mathematics. I would therefore like to have from you the true definition of an adequate, a true, a false, a fictitious and a doubtful idea. I have sought the difference between a true and an adequate idea, but as yet I have not been able to discover anything but this: on investigating a thing and a definite concept or idea, then (in order further to discover whether this true idea was also the adequate idea of some thing) I asked myself what was the cause of this idea or concept. On discovering this, I again asked what was the cause of this further concept, and thus I continued enquiring into the causes of the causes of ideas until I could come upon a cause for which I could not again see any other cause than this, that out of all possible ideas which I had at my command, this one alone also positively existed. If, for example, we ask

---

[74] [These are the axioms, lemmata and definitions following E2P13, which deal with the principle of individuation as Spinoza conceives it and also offer a basic outline of Spinoza's physics.]

wherein consists the true source of our errors, Descartes will reply that it consists in our giving assent to things not yet clearly perceived. But although this be a true idea of the matter in question, I shall still be unable to determine all that it is necessary to know on this subject unless I also possess an adequate idea of this matter. To acquire this I again ask what is the cause of this concept—that is, why we give assent to things not clearly understood, and I reply that this comes about through our lack of knowledge. But at this point we cannot raise the further question as to what is the cause of our not knowing some things, and therefore I realise that I have discovered the adequate idea of our errors.

Here, incidentally, let me put this question to you. Since it is established that many things expressed in an infinite number of ways have an adequate idea of themselves, and that from any adequate idea all that can possibly be known of the thing can be inferred, though they can be more easily elicited from one idea than from another, is there any means of knowing which idea should be utilised in preference to another? For example, an adequate idea of a circle consists in the quality of its radii, but it also consists in the equality with one another of an infinite number of rectangles constructed from the segments of intersecting chords. One could go on and say that the adequate idea of a circle can be expressed in an infinite number of ways, each of which explicates the adequate nature of a circle. And although from each of these everything else knowable about a circle can be deduced, this comes about more easily from one idea than from another. So, too, one who considers the applicates of curves[75] will make many inferences concerning the measurements of curves, but this will be done more effectively if we consider tangents, etc.

In this way I have tried to give some indication of the progress I have made in this study. I await its completion, or if I am anywhere in error, its correction, and also the definition I have asked for. Farewell.

5 January 1675

LETTER 60

To the noble and learned Ehrenfried Walther von Tschirnhaus, from B.d.S.

[Known only from the O.P. The original is lost.]

Most noble Sir,

Between a true and an adequate idea I recognise no difference but this, that the word 'true' has regard only to the agreement of the idea with its object [*ideatum*],

---

[75] [The method of exhaustion was the oldest method for measuring the area under a curve by evaluating the perimeter of polygons tangential to the curve as their sides increased until a limit was reached. The method of applicates (or ordinates) involved drawing lines at right angles across the curves so as to be bisected by their diameters. The method of exhaustion led to the integral calculus (developed by Leibniz and Newton), whereas that of applicates developed into co-ordinate geometry.]

whereas the word 'adequate' has regard to the nature of the idea in itself.[76] Thus there is no real difference between a true and an adequate idea except for this extrinsic relation.

Next, in order that I may know which out of many ideas of a thing will enable all the properties of the object to be deduced, I follow this one rule, that the idea or definition of the thing should express its efficient cause.[77] For example, in order to investigate the properties of a circle, I ask whether from the following idea of a circle, namely, that it consists in an infinite number of rectangles, I can deduce all its properties; that is to say, I ask whether this idea involves the efficient cause of a circle. Since this is not so, I look for another cause, namely, that a circle is the space described by a line of which one point is fixed and the other moveable. Since this definition now expresses the efficient cause, I know that I can deduce from it all the properties of a circle, etc. So, too, when I define God as a supremely perfect Being,[78] since this definition does not express the efficient cause (for I take it that an efficient cause can be internal as well as external), I shall not be able to extract therefrom all the properties of God, as I can do when I define God as a Being, etc. (see *Ethics*, Part 1, Definition 6).[79]

As for your other questions, namely, concerning motion, and those which concern method, since my views on these are not yet written out in due order, I reserve them for another occasion.

As to your remarks that he who considers the applicates of curves will make many deductions regarding the measurement of curves, but will find this easier by considering tangents, etc., I think, on the contrary, that the consideration of tangents will make it more difficult to deduce the many other properties than the consideration of a succession of applicates; and I assert absolutely that from certain properties of a thing (whatever be the given idea) some things can be discovered more easily and others with greater difficulty—though they all concern the nature of that thing. But this one point I consider should be kept in mind, that one must seek such an idea that everything can be elicited therefrom, as I have said above. For if one is to deduce from some thing all that is possible, it necessarily follows that the last will prove more difficult than the earlier, etc.

The Hague
[January 1675]

---

[76] [See E2Def4.]

[77] [From an axiomatic perspective, this claim amounts to the requirement that all definitions be constructive. Spinoza's understanding of geometrical construction follows closely that of Thomas Hobbes.]

[78] [Spinoza here gives his own reasons for rejecting this definition, used by Descartes (see the third Meditation). For Spinoza, the definition of a thing is that from which all the properties of that thing can be deduced. Cf. E1P8Schol2.]

[79] [E1Def6: "By God I mean an absolutely infinite being; that is, substance consisting of infinite attributes, each of which expresses eternal and infinite essence."]

LETTER 63

To the distinguished and acute philosopher B.d.S., from G. H. Schuller

[The original is extant. The O.P. text is somewhat abridged. The translation is taken from the original.]

Most noble and distinguished Sir,

I should blush for my long spell of silence which has exposed me to the charge of ingratitude for the favour which, of your kindness, you have extended to my undeserving self, if I did not reflect that your generous courtesy inclines to excuse rather than accuse, and if I did not know that, for the common good of your friends, you are engaged in important studies such that it would be culpable and wrong to disturb without good cause. For this reason I have kept silent, being content meanwhile to learn from friends of your good health. But the purpose of this letter is to inform you that our noble friend Mr. von Tschirnhausen,[80] who is in England and still, like us, enjoying good health, has three times in his letters to me bidden me to convey to you, Sir, his dutiful regards and respectful greetings. He repeatedly asks me to put before you the following difficulties, and at the same time to ask for the reply he seeks from you.

Would you, Sir, please convince him by a positive proof,[81] and not by *reductio ad absurdum*, that we can not know any more attributes of God than thought and extension? Further, does it follow from this that creatures constituted by other attributes can not on their side have any idea of extension? If so, it would seem that there must be constituted as many worlds as there are attributes of God.[82] For example, our world of extension, to call it so, is of a certain size; there would exist worlds of that same size constituted by different attributes. And just as we perceive, apart from thought, only extension, so the creatures of those worlds must perceive nothing but their own world's attribute, and thought.

Secondly, since God's intellect differs from our intellect both in essence and existence, it will therefore have nothing in common with our intellect, and therefore (Book 1, Proposition 3)[83] God's intellect cannot be the cause of our intellect.

---

[80] [Ehrenfried Walther von Tschirnhaus (1651–1708) was a German count and a brilliant thinker. —M.L.M.]

[81] [Note printed in the O.P.: "I earnestly beg you please to solve the problems here raised, and to send me your reply."]

[82] [A common misinterpretation of Spinoza is to see each attribute as constituting a distinct world or substance, and this view has its historic roots in these remarks by Tschirnhaus. Part of the difficulty, however, lies in the incompleteness of Spinoza's own explanation of the nature of the attributes, and perhaps more has been written on this aspect of his metaphysics than on any other. It is common to distinguish a 'subjective' from an 'objective' interpretation of the attributes.]

[83] [In its final form E1P3 says only that two substances having different attributes have nothing in common. E1P17Schol deals with the predication of 'intellect' to both finite modes and to God.]

Thirdly, in the Scholium to Proposition 10[84] you say that nothing in Nature is clearer than that each entity must be conceived under some attribute (which I understand very well), and that the more reality or being it has, the more attributes appertain to it. It would seem to follow from this that there are entities which have three, four, or more attributes, whereas from what has been demonstrated it could be inferred that each entity consists of only two attributes, namely, a certain attribute of God and the idea of that attribute.

Fourthly, I should like to have examples of those things immediately produced by God, and of those things produced by the mediation of some infinite modification. It seems to me that thought and extension are of the first kind, and of the latter kind, intellect in thought and motion in extension, etc.[85]

These are the questions, distinguished Sir, which our afore-mentioned Tschirnhausen joins with me in asking you to elucidate, if it should be that you have time to spare. He further relates that Mr. Boyle and Oldenburg had formed a very strange idea of your character. He has not only dispelled this, but has furthermore given them reasons that have induced them to return to a most worthy and favourable opinion of you, and also to hold in high esteem the *Tractatus Theologico-Politicus*. In view of your directions,[86] I did not venture to inform you of this.

Be assured that I am in all things at your service, and that I am, most noble Sir,

Your most devoted servant,
G. H. Schuller

Amsterdam, 25 July 1675

Mr. A. Gent[87] and J. Rieuw[88] send their dutiful greetings.

LETTER 64
To the learned and experienced G. H. Schuller, from B.d.S.

[Known only from the O.P. The original is lost.]

Most experienced Sir,

I am glad that you have at last found opportunity to favour me with one of your letters, always most welcome to me. I earnestly beg you to do so regularly. . . , etc.

---

[84] [E1P10Schol. The proposition asserts that each attribute must be conceived through itself.]

[85] [Note printed in the O.P.: "The face of the whole of Nature, which, although varying in infinite ways, always remains the same. See Part 2, Proposition 13, Scholium."]

[86] [Had Spinoza requested that Schuller and Tschirnhaus not speak about him or his works? This is also suggested in Ep70 and Ep72.]

[87] [We are unable to identify this man.]

[88] [Jan Rieuwertsz.]

And now to the questions you raise. To the first I say that the human mind can acquire knowledge only of those things which the idea of an actually existing body involves, or what can be inferred from this idea. For the power of any thing is defined solely by its essence (Pr. 7, Part III, *Ethics*),[89] and the essence of mind consists (Pr. 13, II)[90] solely in its being the idea of an actually existing body. Therefore the mind's power of understanding extends only as far as that which this idea of the body contains within itself, or which follows therefrom. Now this idea of the body involves and expresses no other attributes of God than extension and thought. For its ideate (*ideatum*), to wit, the body (Pr. 6, II) has God for its cause insofar as he is considered under the attribute of extension, and not under any other attribute. So (Ax. 6, I)[91] this idea of the body involves knowledge of God only insofar as he is considered under the attribute of extension. Again, this idea, insofar as it is a mode of thinking, also has God for its cause (same Pr.) insofar as he is a thinking thing, and not insofar as he is considered under any other attribute. Therefore (same Axiom) the idea of this idea involves knowledge of God insofar as he is considered under the attribute of thought, and not under any other attribute. It is thus clear that the human mind—i.e., the idea of the human body— involves and expresses no other attributes of God except these two. Now (by Pr. 10, II),[92] no other attribute[93] of God can be inferred or conceived from these two attributes, or from their affections. So I conclude that the human mind can attain knowledge of no other attribute of God than these two, which was the point at issue. With regard to your further question as to whether there must therefore be constituted as many worlds as there are attributes, I refer you to the Scholium on Pr. 7, II of the *Ethics*.[94]

Moreover, this proposition could be more easily demonstrated by *reductio ad absurdum*, a style of proof I usually prefer to the other in the case of a negative proposition, as being more appropriate to the character of such propositions. But you ask for a positive proof only, and so I pass on to the second question, which asks whether, when both their essence and existence are different, one thing can be produced from another, seeing that things that differ thus from one another appear to have nothing in common. I reply that since all particular things, except those that are produced by like things, differ from their causes both in essence and

---

89 [E3P7: "The conatus with which each thing endeavours to persist in its own being is nothing but the actual essence of the thing itself."]

90 [E2P13: "The object of the idea constituting the human mind is the body—i.e., a definite mode of extension actually existing, and nothing else."]

91 [E1Ax6: "A true idea must agree with its ideate."]

92 [E2P10: "The being of substance does not pertain to the essence of man; i.e., substance does not constitute the form of man."]

93 [Spinoza speaks in the opening definitions and propositions of E1 of an "infinity of infinite attributes." Though he cannot speak of the *number* of attributes as infinite, this is because his concept of number is finitary. E1P9 clearly requires that the attributes be infinite in number in the modern (transfinite) sense of this term.]

94 [E2P7 is the famous proposition expressing the parallelism: "The order and connection of ideas is the same as the order and connection of things."]

existence, I see no difficulty here. As to the sense in which I understand God to be the efficient cause of both the essence and existence of things, I think I have made this quite clear in the Scholium and Corollary to Pr. 25, I of the *Ethics*.[95]

The axiom in the Scholium to Pr. 10, I, as I have indicated towards the end of the said Scholium, derives from the idea we have of an absolutely infinite Entity, and not from the fact that there are, or may be, entities having three, four, or more attributes.[96]

Lastly, the examples you ask for of the first kind are: in the case of thought, absolutely infinite intellect; in the case of extension, motion and rest. An example of the second kind is the face of the whole universe, which, although varying in infinite ways, yet remains always the same. See Scholium to Lemma 7 preceding Pr. 14, II.[97]

Thus, most excellent Sir, I think I have answered your objections and those of our friend. If you think there still remains any difficulty, I hope you will not hesitate to tell me, so that I may remove it if I can. Farewell, etc.

The Hague, 29 July 1675

LETTER 65

To the acute and learned philosopher B.d.S., from Ehrenfried Walther von Tschirnhaus

[Known only from the O.P. The original is lost.]

Most esteemed Sir,

Will you please let me have a proof of your assertion that the soul can not perceive any more attributes of God than extension and thought. Although I can understand this quite clearly, yet I think that the contrary can be deduced from the Scholium to Pr. 7, Part II of the *Ethics*, perhaps only because I do not sufficiently perceive the correct meaning of this Scholium. I have therefore resolved to explain how I come to this conclusion, earnestly begging you, esteemed Sir, to come to my aid with your customary courtesy wherever I do not rightly follow your meaning.

---

[95] [E1P25 states that God is efficient cause both of the existence and the essence of things.]

[96] [E1P10Schol in fact denies Tschirnhaus' interpretation of an infinity of attributes as constitutive of an infinity of entities.]

[97] [E2P13Schol, Spinoza does not use the expression, 'face of the entire universe', but speaks of conceiving the whole of nature as one infinite individual whose parts vary in infinite ways without any change in nature itself. Motion-and-rest and infinite intellect are called immediate infinite modes (of extension and thought respectively), but it is curious that Spinoza gives an example only for extension of an infinite mediate mode.]

My position is as follows. Although I do indeed gather from your text that the world is one, it is also no less clear therefrom that the world is expressed in infinite modes, and that therefore each single thing is expressed in infinite modes. Hence it seems to follow that, although the particular modification which constitutes my mind and the particular modification which expresses my body are one and the same modification, this is expressed in infinite modes—in one mode through thought, in another through extension, in a third through some attribute of God unknown to me, and so on to infinity. For there are infinite attributes of God, and the order and connection of their modifications seems to be the same in all cases. Hence there now arises the question as to why the mind, which represents a particular modification—which same modification is expressed not only by extension but by infinite other modes—why, I ask, does the mind perceive only the particular modification expressed through extension, that is, the human body, and not any other expression through other attributes?

But time does not permit me to pursue this subject any further. Perhaps these difficulties will all be removed by continued reflection.

London, 12 August 1675

LETTER 66

To the noble and learned Ehrenfried Walther von Tschirnhaus, from B.d.S.

[Known only from the O.P. The original is lost.]

Most noble Sir,

... However, in reply to your objection, I say that although each thing is expressed in infinite modes in the infinite intellect of God, the infinite ideas in which it is expressed cannot constitute one and the same mind of a particular thing, but an infinity of minds. For each of these infinite ideas has no connection with the others, as I have explained in that same Scholium to Proposition 7, Part II of the *Ethics*,[98] and as is evident from Pr. 10, Part I.[99] If you will give a little attention to these, you will see that no difficulty remains, etc.

The Hague, 18 August 1675

---

[98] [The brevity of Spinoza's answer to Tschirnhaus ignores the fact that Spinoza himself writes, at the end of E2P7Schol, "For the present, I cannot give a clearer explanation."]

[99] [E1P10: "Each attribute of substance must be conceived through itself."]

LETTER 70

To the most illustrious and acute philosopher, B.d.S., from G. H. Schuller, Doctor of Medicine

[Not in the O.P. The original is extant, and was first published by Van Vloten in 1860.]

Most learned and illustrious Sir, my most venerable patron,

I hope that you have duly received my last letter, together with the *Processus* of an anonymous writer,[100] and that you still enjoy good health, as I do.

I had had no letter for three months from our friend Tschirnhaus, whence I had entertained the gloomy conjecture that he had met with misfortune in journeying from England to France. But now, having received a letter, I am overjoyed and, in obedience to his request, it is my duty to convey its contents to you, and to let you know, with his most dutiful greetings, that he has arrived safely in Paris, that he has there met Mr. Huygens as we had advised him to do, and has therefore made every effort to win his favour, so that he is highly regarded by him. He mentioned that you, Sir, had recommended him to seek an introduction to Huygens, for whom you have the highest regard. This pleased him very much, so that he replied that he likewise had a high regard for you, and had lately received from you the *Tractatus Theologico-Politicus*, which is esteemed by many there, and there are eager inquiries as where any more writings of the same author are published. To this Mr. Tschirnhaus has replied that he knows of none except for the 'Proofs of the First and Second Parts of Descartes' Principia'. Otherwise he said nothing about you except for the above, and hopes that this will not displease you.

Huygens has recently sent for our Tschirnhaus and informed him that Mr. Colbert[101] is looking for someone to instruct his son in mathematics, and if a situation of this kind was acceptable to him, he would arrange it. To this our friend replied by asking for some time to think it over, and eventually declared himself willing to accept. So Huygens came back with the answer that Mr. Colbert was very happy with this proposal, especially as his ignorance of the French language would compel him to speak to his son in Latin.

As to the objection he recently advanced, he replies that the few words I wrote at your instruction have given him a deeper understanding of your meaning, and that he has already entertained the same thoughts (since they particularly admit of explanation in these two ways), but that he had taken the line set out in his objection for the following two reasons. First, because otherwise Propositions 5 and 7

---

[100] [This was the *Processus anonymi*, which judging from Spinoza's response in Ep72, was not written so anonymously, but by a relative of Schuller. Also judging from Spinoza's remarks, it seems that it was a book on alchemy, a discipline for which Spinoza had little interest.]

[101] [Jean Baptiste Colbert (1619–1683) was the Chancellor of the Exchequer under the reign of Louis XIV. He attempted to draw several of the day's leading scientists and scholars to Paris.]

of Book II would seem to be in contradiction.[102] 'In the first of these it is maintained that ideata are the efficient cause of ideas, whereas in the proof of the latter this seems to be refuted by reason of the citing of Axiom 4, Part I.[103] Or else, as I am inclined to think, I am not correctly applying the axiom in accordance with the author's intention, and this I would very much like to learn from him, if his leisure permits. The second cause which has prevented me from following his explanation as set out is this, that in this way the attribute of Thought is given a much wider scope than the other attributes.[104] Now since each of the attributes constitutes the essence of God, I fail to see how the one thing does not contradict the other. I will add only this, that if I may judge other minds by my own, there will be considerable difficulty in understanding Propositions 7 and 8 of Book II,[105] and this simply because the author has been pleased (doubtless because they seemed so plain to him) to explain the demonstrations attached to them so briefly and sparingly.'

He further relates that in Paris he has met a man named Leibniz[106] of remarkable learning, most skilled in the various sciences and free from the common theological prejudices. He has established a close friendship with him, based on the fact that like him he is working at the problem of the perfecting of the intellect, and indeed he considers there is nothing better or more important than this. In Ethics, he says, Leibniz is most practised, and speaks solely from the dictates of reason uninfluenced by emotion. He adds that in physics and especially in metaphysical studies of God and the Soul he is most skilled, and he finally concludes that he is a person most worthy of having your writings communicated to him, if consent is first given; for he thinks that the Author will derive considerable advantage therefrom, as he undertakes to show at some length, if this should please you. But if not, have no doubt that he will honourably keep them secret in accordance with his promise, just as in fact he has made not the slightest mention

---

[102] [As Spinoza notes in his reply (Ep72), Tschirnhaus is apparently confused. E2P5 states: "The formal being of ideas recognises God as its cause only insofar as he is considered as a thinking thing, and not insofar as he is explicated by any other attribute; that is, the ideas both of God's attributes and of individual things recognise as their efficient cause not the things of which they are ideas— that is, the things perceived—but God himself insofar as he is a thinking thing." E2P7 is the celebrated statement of parallelism: "The order and connection of ideas is the same as the order and connection of things."]

[103] [E1Ax4: "The knowledge of the effect depends on, and involves, the knowledge of the cause."]

[104] [Tschirnhaus' claim that, in allowing both ideas of things (bodies) and ideas of ideas, Spinoza had violated the parallelism by making thought more extensive than extension, has been echoed by many commentators to the present day.]

[105] [For E2P7 see above. E2P8: "The ideas of non-existing individual things must be comprehended in the infinite idea of God in the same way as the formal essences of individual things or modes are contained in the attributes of God." In his reply (Ep72), Spinoza ignores this question; but, in the scholium to E2P8, he notes, "Should anyone want an example for a clearer understanding of this matter, I can think of none at all that would adequately explicate the point with which I am here dealing." Perhaps this scholium resulted from Tschirnhaus' puzzlement.]

[106] [Leibniz stayed in Paris from 1672 until 1676 trying to persuade Louis XIV to direct his attentions to Egypt and to leave Europe in peace.]

of them. This same Leibniz thinks highly of the *Tractatus Theologico-Politicus*,[107] on which subject he once wrote you a letter, if you remember. I would therefore ask you out of your gracious kindliness, unless there is strong reason against it, not to refuse your permission, but if you can, to let me know your decision as soon as possible. For when I have received your reply, I can send our Tschirnhaus an answer, which I am anxious to do Tuesday evening, unless you are delayed by more important business.

Mr. Bresser[108] has returned from Cleves, and has sent here a considerable quantity of the native beer. I have asked him to send you half a tun, which he has promised to do with his most friendly greetings.

Finally, I beg you to excuse the clumsiness of my style and the haste of my pen, and to command me in any service, so that I may have a real occasion of proving that I am,

> Most illustrious Sir,
> Your most ready servant,
> G. H. Schuller

LETTER 72
To the most learned and experienced G. H. Schuller, from B.d.S.

[Not in the O.P. The original, in private hands, was first published in 1860 by Van Vloten.]

Most experienced Sir, and honoured friend,

I am very pleased to learn from your letter, received today, that you are well and that our friend Tschirnhaus has happily accomplished his journey to France. In his conversations with Mr. Huygens he has, in my opinion, conducted himself with discretion, and furthermore I am very glad that he found so convenient an opportunity for that which he had intended.

I do not see what he finds in Axiom 4, Part I to contradict Proposition 5, Part 2. For in this proposition it is asserted that the essence of any idea has God for its cause insofar as he is considered as a thinking thing, while that axiom says that the knowledge or idea of an effect depends on the knowledge or idea of the cause. But to tell the truth, I do not quite follow the meaning of your letter in this matter, and I believe that either in your letter or in his copy there is a slip of the pen. For you write that in Proposition 5 it is asserted that *ideata* are the efficient cause of ideas, whereas

---

[107] [As a diplomat, Leibniz acquired the habit of professing whatever views were most likely to please his audience. In his own writings he described the TTP as "intolerably impudent" and "monstrous."]

[108] [Possibly Jan Bresser who is incorrectly believed by some to have written the poem which precedes the PPC. Whether he is originally from the Cleves district or was simply visiting there is also not known, but it is coincidental that Schuller is from that area while Tschirnhaus served time in the army there.]

this very point is expressly denied in that same proposition. I now think that the whole confusion arises from this, and so at present it would be pointless for me to try to write at greater length on this matter. I must wait until you explain his meaning to me more clearly, and until I know whether he has a sufficiently correct copy.[109]

I believe I know Leibniz, of whom he writes, through correspondence, but I do not understand why he, a councillor of Frankfurt, has gone to France. As far as I can judge from his letter, he seemed to me a person of liberal mind and well versed in every science. Still, I think it imprudent to entrust my writings to him so hastily. I should first like to know what he is doing in France, and to hear our friend Tschirnhaus' opinion of him after a longer acquaintance and a closer knowledge of his character. However, greet that friend of ours in my name with all my duty, and if I can serve him in any way, let him command what he will, and he will find me most ready to comply in all things.

I congratulate our most worthy friend Mr. Bresser on his arrival or his return. I thank him very much for the beer that is promised, and shall repay him in whatever way I can. Finally, I have not yet made trial of the *Process* of your kinsman, nor do I think that I can turn my mind to essay it. For the more I think about it, the more I am convinced that you have not made gold, but have insufficiently separated out what was hidden in the antimony. But more of this on another occasion; at the moment I am pressed for time. Meanwhile, if I can be of service to you in any matter, here I am, whom you will always find,

Most distinguished Sir,
Your very good friend and ready servant,
B. de Spinoza

The Hague, 18 November 1675
Mr. G. H. Schuller, Doctor of Medicine,
de Kortsteegh in de gestofeerde hoet, Amsterdam

LETTER 81
To the most noble and learned Mr. Ehrenfried Walther von Tschirnhaus, from B.d.S.

[Known only from the O.P. The original is lost.]

Most noble Sir,

My statement in my letter concerning the Infinite,[110] that it is not from the multitude of parts that an infinity of parts is inferred, is clear from this consideration:

---

[109] [These propositions are printed as notes to Ep70. Spinoza's assumption that Tschirnhaus may have received a corrupted text of them is plausible in the light of Tschirnhaus' strange reading in Ep70.]

[110] [Ep12.]

if it were inferred from the multitude of parts, we would not be able to conceive a greater multitude of parts, but their multitude would have to be greater than any given number. This is not true, because in the entire space between the two non-concentric circles we conceive there to be twice the number of parts as in half that space, and yet the number of parts both in the half as well as the whole of this space is greater than any assignable number.[111]

Further, from Extension as conceived by Descartes, to wit, an inert mass, it is not only difficult, as you say, but quite impossible to demonstrate the existence of bodies. For matter at rest, as far as in it lies, will continue to be at rest, and will not be set in motion except by a more powerful external cause.[112] For this reason I have not hesitated on a previous occasion to affirm that Descartes' principles of natural things are of no service, not to say quite wrong.

The Hague, 5 May 1676

LETTER 82
To the acute and learned philosopher B.d.S., from Ehrenfried Walther von Tschirnhaus

[Known only from the O.P. The original is lost.]

Most learned Sir,

I should like you to do me the kindness of showing how, from Extension as conceived in your philosophy, the variety of things can be demonstrated a priori. For you mention Descartes' view, by which he maintains that he cannot deduce this variety from Extension in any other way than by supposing that this was an effect produced in Extension by motion started by God. Therefore, in my opinion, it is not from inert matter that he deduces the existence of bodies, unless you discount the supposition of God as mover. For you have not shown how this must necessarily follow a priori from the essence of God, a point whose demonstration Descartes believed to surpass human understanding. Therefore, knowing well that you entertain a different view, I seek from you an answer to this question, unless there is some weighty reason why you have hitherto refrained from making this public. If there had been no need for this—which I do not doubt—you would

---

[111] [This is another indication of Spinoza's reserving the term 'number' for finite magnitudes: he will speak of 'infinity' but not of an 'infinite number'. The false assumption that multiplying an infinite number by a finite number (here, two) produces an infinity with 'twice the number of parts' was common to seventeenth-century thinkers, and appears also in Newton.]

[112] [Spinoza's conception of extension or matter is, unlike that of Descartes, essentially dynamic. Motion must be imposed on the material universe in Descartes' view by divine 'thrust'. This is because there is no concept of force within Cartesian physics and it must be imported by God. This feature figures heavily in Descartes' explanation of divine concurrence.]

have given some kind of indication of your meaning. But be quite assured that, whether you speak to me frankly or with reserve, my regard for you will remain unchanged.

However, my particular reasons for making this request are as follows. In mathematics I have always observed that from any thing considered in itself—that is, from the definition of any thing—we are able to deduce at least one property; but if we wish to deduce more properties, we have to relate the thing defined to other things. It is only then, from the combination of the definitions of these things, that new properties emerge. For example, if I consider the circumference of a circle in isolation, I can infer nothing other than that it is everywhere alike or uniform, in respect of which property it differs essentially from all other curves; nor shall I ever be able to deduce any other properties. But if I relate it to other things, such as the radii drawn from the centre, or two intersecting chords, or many other things, I shall in some way be able to deduce more properties. This seems to be at variance to some extent with Proposition 16 of the *Ethics*,[113] almost the most important proposition of the first book of your Treatise. In this proposition it is taken for granted that several properties can be deduced from the given definition of any thing, which seems to me impossible if we do not relate the thing defined to other things. In consequence, I fail to see how from an Attribute considered only by itself, for example, Extension, an infinite variety of bodies can arise. Or if you think that, while this cannot be inferred from a single Attribute considered by itself, it can so be from all taken together, I should like you to instruct me on this point, and how this should be conceived. Farewell, etc.

Paris, 23 June 1676

LETTER 83
To the most noble and learned Mr. Ehrenfried Walther von Tschirnhaus, from B.d.S.

[Known only from the O.P. The original is lost. The signature appears only in the Dutch edition of the O.P.]

Most noble Sir,

With regard to your question as to whether the variety of things can be demonstrated a priori solely from the conception of Extension, I think I have already made it quite clear that this is impossible. That is why Descartes is wrong in defining matter through Extension; it must necessarily be explicated through an attribute which expresses eternal and infinite essence. But perhaps, if I live long

---

[113] [E1P16: "From the necessity of the divine nature there must follow infinite things in infinite ways, that is, everything that can come within the scope of infinite intellect."]

enough,[114] I shall some time discuss this with you more clearly; for as yet I have not had the opportunity to arrange in due order anything on this subject.

As to what you add, that from the definition of any thing, considered in itself, we can deduce only one property, this may hold good in the case of the most simple things, or in the case of mental constructs [*entia rationis*], in which I include figures, but not in the case of real things.[115] Simply from the fact that I define God as an Entity to whose essence existence belongs, I infer several properties of him, such as that he necessarily exists, that he is one alone, immutable, infinite, etc. I could adduce several examples of this kind, which I omit for the present.

Finally, I beg you to enquire whether Mr. Huet's Treatise (the one against the *Tractatus Theologico-Politicus*), of which you previously wrote, has yet been published, and whether you will be able to send me a copy. Also, do you yet know what are the recent discoveries about refraction?[116]

And so farewell, most noble Sir, and continue to hold in your affection,

Yours,
B.d.S.

The Hague, 15 July 1676

---

[114] [Spinoza died only seven months after writing this letter.]

[115] [Spinoza was partly indebted to Hobbes in his account of constructive definition.]

[116] [This could refer to Newton's discovery in 1670 that a prism refracts white light into colored beams which have various capacities for further refraction; this was communicated in 1672 and discussed for several more years. It could also refer to Erasmus Bartholinus' 1669 publication *Experimenta crystalli islandici disdiaclastici*, which reported on the double refraction achieved by passing light through a piece of Iceland spar.]

LIST OF PROPOSITIONS
FROM THE *ETHICS*

Part I: Concerning God

Definitions (3)
Axioms (4)

P1   *Substance is by nature prior to its affections.* (4)

P2   *Two substances having different attributes have nothing in common.* (4)

P3   *When things have nothing in common, one cannot be the cause of the other.* (5)

P4   *Two or more distinct things are distinguished from one another either by the difference of the attributes of the substances or by the difference of the affections of the substances.* (5)

P5   *In the universe there cannot be two or more substances of the same nature or attribute.* (5)

P6   *One substance cannot be produced by another substance.* (5)

P7   *Existence belongs to the nature of substance.* (6)

P8   *Every substance is necessarily infinite.* (6)

P9   *The more reality or being a thing has, the more attributes it has.* (7)

P10 *Each attribute of one substance must be conceived through itself.* (7)

P11 *God, or substance consisting of infinite attributes, each of which expresses eternal and infinite essence, necessarily exists.* (8)

P12 *No attribute or substance can be truly conceived from which it would follow that substance can be divided.* (10)

P13 *Absolutely infinite substance is indivisible.* (10)

P14 *There can be, or be conceived, no other substance but God.* (10)

P15 *Whatever is, is in God, and nothing can be or be conceived without God.* (10)

P16 *From the necessity of the divine nature there must follow infinite things in infinite ways [modis] (that is, everything that can come withing the scope of infinite intellect).* (13)

P17 *God acts solely from the laws of his own nature, constrained by none.* (14)

P18 *God is the immanent, not the transitive, cause of all things.* (15)

P19 *God [is eternal], that is, all the attributes of God are eternal.* (16)

P20 *God's existence and his essence are one and the same.* (16)

P21 *All things that follow from the absolute nature of any attribute of God must have existed always, and as infinite; that is, through the said attribute they are eternal and infinite.* (16)

P22 *Whatever follows from some attribute of God, insofar as the attribute is modified by a modification that exists necessarily and as infinite through that same attribute, must also exist both necessarily and as infinite.* (17)

P23 *Every mode which exists necessarily and as infinite must have necessarily followed either from the absolute nature of some attribute of God or from some attribute modified by a modification which exists necessarily and as infinite.* (17)

P24 *The essence of things produced by God does not involve existence.* (18)

P25 *God is the efficient cause not only of the existence of things but also of their essence.* (18)

P26 *A thing which has been determined to act in a particular way has necessarily been so determined by God; and a thing which has not been determined by God cannot determine itself to act.* (18)

P27 *A thing which has been determined by God to act in a particular way cannot render itself undetermined.* (18)

P28 *Every individual thing, i.e., anything whatever which is finite and has a determinate existence, cannot exist or be determined to act unless it be determined to exist and to act by another cause which is also finite and has a determinate existence, and this cause again cannot exist or be determined to act unless it be determined to exist and to act by another cause which is also finite and has a determinate existence, and so ad infinitum.* (18)

P29 *Nothing in nature is contingent, but all things are from the necessity of the divine nature determined to exist and to act in a definite way.* (19)

P30 *The finite intellect in act or the infinite intellect in act must comprehend the attributes of God and the affections of God, and nothing else.* (20)

P31 *The intellect in act, whether it be finite or infinite, as also will, desire, love, etc., must be related to* Natura naturata, *not to* Natura naturans. (20)

P32 *Will cannot be called a free cause, but only a necessary cause.* (21)

P33 *Things could not have been produced by God in any other way or in any other order than is the case.* (21)

P34 *God's power is his very essence.* (24)

P35 *Whatever we conceive to be within God's power necessarily exists.* (24)

P36 *Nothing exists from whose nature an effect does not follow.* (24)
Appendix (24)

Part II: Of the Nature and Origin of the Mind

Definitions (29)
Axioms (30)
P1 *Thought is an attribute of God; i.e., God is a thinking thing.* (30)
P2 *Extension is an attribute of God; i.e., God is an extended thing.* (30)
P3 *In God there is necessarily the idea both of his essence and of everything that necessarily follows from his essence.* (30)
P4 *The idea of God, from which infinite things follow in infinite ways, must be one, and one only.* (31)
P5 *The formal being of ideas recognizes God as its cause only insofar as he is considered as a thinking thing, and not insofar as he is explicated by any other attribute; that is, the ideas both of God's attributes and of individual things recognize as their efficient cause not the things of which they are ideas, that is, the things perceived, but God himself insofar as he is a thinking thing.* (31)
P6 *The modes of any attribute have God for their cause only insofar as he is considered under that attribute, and not insofar as he is considered under any other attribute.* (32)
P7 *The order and connection of ideas is the same as the order and connection of things.* (32)
P8 *The ideas of nonexisting individual things or modes must be comprehended in the infinite idea of God in the same way as the formal essences of individual things or modes are contained in the attributes of God.* (33)
P9 *The idea of an individual thing existing in actuality has God for its cause not insofar as he is infinite but insofar as he is considered as affected by another idea of a thing existing in actuality, of which God is the cause insofar as he is affected by a third idea, and so ad infinitum.* (33)
P10 *The being of substance does not pertain to the essence of man; i.e., substance does not constitute the form [forma] of man.* (34)
P11 *That which constitutes the actual being of the human mind is basically nothing else but the idea of an individual actually existing thing.* (35)
P12 *Whatever happens in the object of the idea constituting the human mind is bound to be perceived by the human mind; i.e., the idea of that thing will necessarily be in the human mind. That is to say, if the object of the idea constituting the human mind is a body, nothing can happen in that body without its being perceived by the mind.* (36)
P13 *The object of the idea constituting the human mind is the body— i.e., a definite mode of extension actually existing, and nothing else.* (36)

P14   *The human mind is capable of perceiving a great many things, and this capacity will vary in proportion to the variety of states which its body can assume.* (40)

P15   *The idea which constitutes the formal being of the human mind is not simple, but composed of very many ideas.* (40)

P16   *The idea of any mode wherein the human body is affected by external bodies must involve the nature of the human body together with the nature of the external body.* (40)

P17   *If the human body is affected in a way [modo] that involves the nature of some external body, the human mind will regard that same external body as actually existing, or as present to itself, until the human body undergoes a further modification which excludes the existence or presence of the said body.* (41)

P18   *If the human body has once been affected by two or more bodies at the same time, when the mind afterward imagines one of them, it will straightway remember the others too.* (42)

P19   *The human mind has no knowledge of the body, nor does it know it to exist, except through ideas of the affections by which the body is affected.* (43)

P20   *There is also in God the idea or knowledge of the human mind, and this follows in God and is related to God in the same way as the idea or knowledge of the human body.* (43)

P21   *This idea of the mind is united to the mind in the same way as the mind is united to the body.* (43)

P22   *The human mind perceives not only the affections of the body but also the ideas of these affections.* (44)

P23   *The mind does not know itself except insofar as it perceives ideas of affections of the body.* (44)

P24   *The human mind does not involve an adequate knowledge of the component parts of the human body.* (44)

P25   *The idea of any affection of the human body does not involve an adequate knowledge of an external body.* (45)

P26   *The human mind does not perceive any external body as actually existing except through the ideas of affections of its own body.* (45)

P27   *The idea of any affection of the human body does not involve adequate knowledge of the human body.* (46)

P28   *The ideas of the affections of the human body, insofar as they are related only to the human mind, are not clear and distinct, but confused.* (46)

P29   *The idea of the idea of any affection of the human body does not involve adequate knowledge of the human mind.* (46)

P30   *We can have only a very inadequate knowledge of the duration of our body.* (47)

P31   *We can have only a very inadequate knowledge of the duration of particular things external to us.* (47)

Part III: Concerning the Origin and Nature of the Emotions

Postulates (62)

P1   *Our mind is in some instances active and in other instances passive. Insofar as it has adequate ideas, it is necessarily active; and insofar as it has inadequate ideas, it is necessarily passive.* (62)

P2   *The body cannot determine the mind to think, nor can the mind determine the body to motion or rest, or to anything else (if there is anything else).* (63)

P3   *The active states* [actiones] *of the mind arise only from adequate ideas; its passive states depend solely on inadequate ideas.* (65)

P4   *No thing can be destroyed except by an external cause.* (66)

P5   *Things are of a contrary nature, that is, unable to subsist in the same subject, to the extent that one can destroy the other.* (66)

P6   *Each thing, insofar as it is in itself, endeavors to persist in its own being.* (66)

P7   *The conatus with which each thing endeavors to persist in its own being is nothing but the actual essence of the thing itself.* (66)

P8   *The conatus with which each single thing endeavors to persist in its own being does not involve finite time, but indefinite time.* (67)

P9   *The mind, both insofar as it has clear and distinct ideas and insofar as it has confused ideas, endeavors to persist in its own being over an indefinite period of time, and is conscious of this conatus.* (67)

P10   *An idea that excludes the existence of our body cannot be in our mind, but is contrary to it.* (67)

P11   *Whatsoever increases or diminishes, assists or checks, the power of activity of our body, the idea of the said thing increases or diminishes, assists or checks the power of thought of our mind.* (68)

P12   *The mind, as far as it can, endeavors to think of those things that increase or assist the body's power of activity.* (69)

P13   *When the mind thinks of those things that diminish or check the body's power of activity, it endeavors, as far as it can, to call to mind those things that exclude the existence of the former.* (69)

P14   *If the mind has once been affected by two emotions at the same time, when it is later affected by the one it will also be affected by the other.* (69)

P15   *Anything can indirectly* [per accidens] *be the cause of Pleasure, Pain, or Desire.* (70)

P16   *From the mere fact that we imagine a thing to have something similar to an object that is wont to affect the mind with pleasure or pain, we shall love it or hate it, although the point of similarity is not the efficient cause of these emotions.* (70)

P17   *If we imagine that a thing which is wont to affect us with an emotion of pain has something similar to another thing which is wont to affect us with an equally great emotion of pleasure, we shall hate it and love it at the same time.* (70)

P18   *From the image of things past or future man is affected by the*
      same emotion of pleasure or pain as from the image of a thing
      present. (71)

P19   *He who imagines that what he loves is being destroyed will feel*
      pain. If, however, he imagines that it is being preserved, he will
      feel pleasure. (72)

P20   *He who imagines that a thing that he hates is being destroyed will*
      feel pleasure. (72)

P21   *He who imagines that what he loves is affected with pleasure or*
      pain will likewise be affected with pleasure or pain, the intensity
      of which will vary with the intensity of the emotion in the object
      loved. (72)

P22   *If we imagine that someone is affecting with pleasure the object of*
      our love, we shall be affected with love toward him. If on the other
      hand we think that he is affecting with pain the object of our love,
      we shall likewise be affected with hatred toward him. (73)

P23   *He who imagines that what he hates is affected with pain will feel*
      pleasure; if, on the other hand, he thinks of it as affected with
      pleasure, he will feel pain. Both of these emotions will vary in
      intensity inversely with the variation of the contrary emotion in
      that which he hates. (73)

P24   *If we imagine someone to be affecting with pleasure a thing that*
      we hate, we shall be affected with hate toward him too. If on the
      other hand we think of him as affecting with pain the said thing,
      we shall be affected with love toward him. (74)

P25   *We endeavor to affirm of ourselves and of an object loved whatever*
      we imagine affects us or the loved object with pleasure, and, on
      the other hand, to negate whatever we imagine affects us or the
      loved object with pain. (74)

P26   *We endeavor to affirm of that which we hate whatever we imagine*
      affects it with pain, and on the other hand to deny what we
      imagine affects it with pleasure. (74)

P27   *From the fact that we imagine a thing like ourselves, toward which*
      we have felt no emotion, to be affected by an emotion, we are
      thereby affected by a similar emotion. (75)

P28   *We endeavor to bring about whatever we imagine to be conducive*
      to pleasure; but we endeavor to remove or destroy whatever we
      imagine to be opposed to pleasure and conducive to pain. (76)

P29   *We also endeavor to do whatever we imagine men to regard with*
      pleasure, and on the other hand we shun doing whatever we
      imagine men to regard with aversion. (76)

P30   *If anyone has done something which he imagines affects others*
      with pleasure, he will be affected with pleasure accompanied by
      the idea of himself as cause; that is, he will regard himself with
      pleasure. If, on the other hand, he imagines he has done

something which affects others with pain, he will regard himself with pain. (76)

P31   *If we think that someone loves, desires, or hates something that we love, desire, or hate, that very fact will cause us to love, desire, or hate the thing more steadfastly. But if we think he dislikes what we love, or vice versa, then our feelings will fluctuate.* (77)

P32   *If we think that someone enjoys something that only one person can possess, we shall endeavor to bring it about that he should not possess that thing.* (77)

P33   *If we love something similar to ourselves, we endeavor, as far as we can, to bring it about that it should love us in return.* (78)

P34   *The greater the emotion with which we imagine the object of our love is affected toward us, the greater will be our vanity.* (78)

P35   *If anyone thinks that there is between the object of his love and another person the same or a more intimate bond of friendship than there was between them when he alone used to possess the object loved, he will be affected with hatred toward the object loved and will envy his rival.* (78)

P36   *He who recalls a thing which once afforded him pleasure desires to possess the same thing in the same circumstances as when he first took pleasure therein.* (79)

P37   *The desire arising from pain or pleasure, hatred or love, is proportionately greater as the emotion is greater.* (80)

P38   *If anyone has begun to hate the object of his love to the extent that his love is completely extinguished, he will, other things being equal, bear greater hatred toward it than if he had never loved it, and his hatred will be proportionate to the strength of his former love.* (80)

P39   *He who hates someone will endeavor to injure him unless he fears that he will suffer a greater injury in return. On the other hand, he who loves someone will by that same law endeavor to benefit him.* (81)

P40   *He who imagines he is hated by someone to whom he believes he has given no cause for hatred will hate him in return.* (81)

P41   *If anyone thinks that he is loved by someone and believes that he has given no cause for this (which is possible through Cor. Pr. 15 and Pr. 16, III), he will love him in return.* (82)

P42   *He who, moved by love or hope of honor, has conferred a benefit on someone, will feel pain if he sees that the benefit is ungratefully received.* (83)

P43   *Hatred is increased by reciprocal hatred, and may on the other hand be destroyed by love.* (83)

P44   *Hatred that is fully overcome by love passes into love, and the love will therefore be greater than if it had not been preceded by hatred.* (83)

P45   *If anyone imagines that someone similar to himself is affected with hatred toward a thing similar to himself, which he loves, he will hate him.* (84)

P46   *If anyone is affected with pleasure or pain by someone of a class or nation different from his own and the pleasure or pain is accompanied by the idea of that person as its cause, under the general category of that class or nation, he will love or hate not only him but all of that same class or nation.* (84)

P47   *The pleasure that arises from our imagining that the object of our hatred is being destroyed or is suffering some other harm is not devoid of some feeling of pain.* (84)

P48   *Love and hatred toward, say, Peter are destroyed if the pain involved in the latter and the pleasure involved in the former are associated with the idea of a different cause; and both emotions are diminished to the extent that we think Peter not to have been the only cause of either emotion.* (85)

P49   *Love and hatred toward a thing that we think of as free must both be greater, other conditions being equal, than toward a thing subject to necessity.* (85)

P50   *Anything can be the indirect cause of hope or fear.* (85)

P51   *Different men can be affected in different ways by one and the same object, and one and the same man can be affected by one and the same object in different ways at different times.* (86)

P52   *To an object that we have previously seen in conjunction with others or that we imagine to have nothing but what is common to many other objects, we shall not give as much regard as to that which we imagine to have something singular.* (87)

P53   *When the mind regards its own self and its power of activity, it feels pleasure, and the more so the more distinctly it imagines itself and its power of activity.* (88)

P54   *The mind endeavors to think only of the things that affirm its power of activity.* (88)

P55   *When the mind thinks of its own impotence, by that very fact it feels pain.* (88)

P56   *There are as many kinds of pleasure, pain, desire and consequently of every emotion that is compounded of these (such as vacillation) or of every emotion that is derived from these (love, hatred, hope, fear, etc.), as there are kinds of objects by which we are affected.* (89)

P57   *Any emotion of one individual differs from the emotion of another to the extent that the essence of the one individual differs from the essence of the other.* (90)

P58   *Besides the pleasure and desire that are passive emotions, there are other emotions of pleasure and desire that are related to us insofar as we are active.* (91)

P59   *Among all the emotions that are related to the mind insofar as it is
active, there are none that are not related to pleasure or desire.* (92)
Definitions of the Emotions (93)
General Definition of Emotions (101)

Part IV: Of Human Bondage, or the Strength of the Emotions

Preface (102)
Definitions (104)
Axiom (105)

P1   *Nothing positive contained in a false idea can be annulled by the
presence of what is true, insofar as it is true.* (105)

P2   *We are passive insofar as we are a part of Nature which cannot be
conceived independently of other parts.* (106)

P3   *The force [vis] whereby a man persists in existing is limited, and
infinitely surpassed by the power of external causes.* (106)

P4   *It is impossible for a man not to be part of Nature and not to
undergo changes other than those which can be understood solely
through his own nature and of which he is the adequate cause.* (106)

P5   *The force and increase of any passive emotion and its persistence
in existing is defined not by the power whereby we ourselves
endeavor to persist in existing, but by the power of external causes
compared with our own power.* (107)

P6   *The force of any passive emotion can surpass the rest of man's
activities or power so that the emotion stays firmly fixed in him.* (107)

P7   *An emotion cannot be checked or destroyed except by a contrary
emotion which is stronger than the emotion which is to be
checked.* (107)

P8   *Knowledge of good and evil is nothing other than the emotion of
pleasure or pain insofar as we are conscious of it.* (108)

P9   *An emotion whose cause we think to be with us in the present is
stronger than it would be if we did not think the said cause to be
with us.* (108)

P10   *We are affected toward a future thing which we imagine to be
imminent more intensely than if we were to imagine its time of
existence to be farther away from the present. We are also affected
by remembrance of a thing we imagine to belong to the near past
more intensely than if we were to imagine it to belong to the
distant past.* (109)

P11   *An emotion toward a thing which we think of as inevitable
[necessarius] is more intense, other things being equal, than
emotion toward a thing possible, or contingent, that is, not
inevitable.* (109)

P12   *Emotion toward a thing which we know not to exist in the present,
and which we imagine to be possible, is, other things being equal,
more intense than emotion toward a contingent thing.* (109)

P13   *Emotion toward a contingent thing which we know not to exist in the present is, other things being equal, feebler than emotion toward a thing past.* (110)

P14   *No emotion can be checked by the true knowledge of good and evil insofar as it is true, but only insofar as it is considered as an emotion.* (110)

P15   *Desire that arises from the true knowledge of good and evil can be extinguished or checked by many other desires that arise from the emotions by which we are assailed.* (110)

P16   *The desire that arises from a knowledge of good and evil insofar as this knowledge has regard to the future can be the more easily checked or extinguished by desire of things that are attractive in the present.* (111)

P17   *Desire that arises from the true knowledge of good and evil insofar as this knowledge is concerned with contingent things can be even more easily checked by desire for things which are present.* (111)

P18   *Desire arising from pleasure is, other things being equal, stronger than desire arising from pain.* (111)

P19   *Every man, from the laws of his own nature, necessarily seeks or avoids what he judges to be good or evil.* (113)

P20   *The more every man endeavors and is able to seek his own advantage, that is, to preserve his own being, the more he is endowed with virtue. On the other hand, insofar as he neglects to preserve what is to his advantage, that is, his own being, to that extent he is weak.* (113)

P21   *Nobody can desire to be happy, to do well and to live well without at the same time desiring to be, to do, and to live; that is, actually to exist.* (114)

P22   *No virtue can be conceived as prior to this one, namely, the conatus to preserve oneself.* (114)

P23   *Insofar as a man is determined to some action from the fact that he has inadequate ideas, he cannot be said, without qualification, to be acting from virtue; he can be said to do so only insofar as he is determined from the fact that he understands.* (114)

P24   *To act in absolute conformity with virtue is nothing else in us but to act, to live, to preserve one's own being (these three mean the same) under the guidance of reason, on the basis of seeking one's own advantage.* (114)

P25   *Nobody endeavors to preserve his being for the sake of some other thing.* (115)

P26   *Whatever we endeavor according to reason is nothing else but to understand; and the mind, insofar as it exercises reason, judges nothing else to be to its advantage except what conduces to understanding.* (115)

P27   *We know nothing to be certainly good or evil except what is really conducive to understanding or what can hinder understanding.* (115)

P28   *The mind's highest good is the knowledge of God, and the mind's highest virtue is to know God.* (115)

P29   *No individual thing whose nature is quite different from ours can either assist or check our power to act, and nothing whatsoever can be either good or evil for us unless it has something in common with us.* (116)

P30   *No thing can be evil for us through what it possesses in common with our nature, but insofar as it is evil for us, it is contrary to us.* (116)

P31   *Insofar as a thing is in agreement with our nature, to that extent it is necessarily good.* (116)

P32   *Insofar as men are subject to passive emotions, to that extent they cannot be said to agree in nature.* (117)

P33   *Men can differ in nature insofar as they are assailed by emotions that are passive, and to that extent one and the same man, too, is variable and inconstant.* (117)

P34   *Insofar as men are assailed by emotions that are passive, they can be contrary to one another.* (118)

P35   *Insofar as men live under the guidance of reason, to that extent only do they always necessarily agree in nature.* (118)

P36   *The highest good of those who pursue virtue is common to all, and all can equally enjoy it.* (119)

P37   *The good which every man who pursues virtue aims at for himself he will also desire for the rest of mankind, and all the more as he acquires a greater knowledge of God.* (120)

P38   *That which so disposes the human body that it can be affected in more ways, or which renders it capable of affecting external bodies in more ways, is advantageous to man, and proportionately more advantageous as the body is thereby rendered more capable of being affected in more ways and of affecting other bodies in more ways. On the other hand, that which renders the body less capable in these respects is harmful.* (122)

P39   *Whatever is conducive to the preservation of the proportion of motion-and-rest, which the parts of the human body maintain toward one another, is good; and those things that effect a change in the proportion of motion-and-rest of the parts of the human body to one another are bad.* (123)

P40   *Whatever is conducive to man's social organization, or causes men to live in harmony, is advantageous, while those things that introduce discord into the state are bad.* (123)

P41   *Pleasure is not in itself bad, but good. On the other hand, pain is in itself bad.* (124)

P42   *Cheerfulness [hilaritas] cannot be excessive; it is always good. On the other hand, melancholy is always bad.* (124)

P43   *Titillation [titillatio] can be excessive and bad. But anguish [dolor] can be good to the extent that titillation or pleasure is bad.* (124)

P44 Love and desire can be excessive. (124)

P45 Hatred can never be good. (125)

P46 He who lives by the guidance of reason endeavors as far as he can
to repay with love or nobility another's hatred, anger, contempt,
etc. toward himself. (126)

P47 The emotions of hope and fear cannot be good in themselves. (126)

P48 The emotions of over-esteem [existimatio] and disparagement
[despectus] are always bad. (127)

P49 Over-esteem is apt to render its recipient proud. (127)

P50 In the man who lives by the guidance of reason, pity is in itself
bad and disadvantageous. (127)

P51 Approbation [favor] is not opposed to reason; it can agree with
reason and arise from it. (127)

P52 Self-contentment [acquiescentia in se ipso] can arise from reason,
and only that self-contentment which arises from reason is the
highest there can be. (128)

P53 Humility is not a virtue; that is, it does not arise from reason. (128)

P54 Repentance is not a virtue, i.e., it does not arise from reason; he
who repents of his action is doubly unhappy or weak. (129)

P55 Extreme pride, or self-abasement, is extreme ignorance of oneself. (129)

P56 Extreme pride, or self-abasement, indicates extreme weakness of
spirit. (129)

P57 The proud man loves the company of parasites or flatterers, and
hates the company of those of noble spirit. (130)

P58 Honor is not opposed to reason, but can arise from it. (131)

P59 In the case of all actions to which we are determined by a passive
emotion, we can be determined thereto by reason without that
emotion. (131)

P60 Desire that arises from the pleasure or pain that is related to one
or more, but not to all, parts of the body takes no account of the
advantage of the whole man. (132)

P61 Desire that arises from reason cannot be excessive. (133)

P62 Insofar as the mind conceives things in accordance with the
dictates of reason, it is equally affected whether the idea be of the
future, in the past, or the present. (133)

P63 He who is guided by fear, and does good so as to avoid evil, is not
guided by reason. (133)

P64 Knowledge of evil is inadequate knowledge. (134)

P65 By the guidance of reason we pursue the greater of two goods and
the lesser of two evils. (134)

P66 Under the guidance of reason we seek a future greater good in
preference to a lesser present good, and a lesser present evil in
preference to a greater future evil. (135)

P67 A free man thinks of death least of all things, and his wisdom is a
meditation of life, not of death. (135)

P68   *If men were born free, they would form no conception of good and evil so long as they were free.* (135)

P69   *The virtue of a free man is seen to be as great in avoiding dangers as in overcoming them.* (136)

P70   *The free man who lives among ignorant people tries as far as he can to avoid receiving favors from them.* (136)

P71   *Only free men are truly grateful to one another.* (137)

P72   *The free man never acts deceitfully, but always with good faith.* (137)

P73   *The man who is guided by reason is more free in a state where he lives under a system of law than in solitude where [he] obeys only himself.* (137)

Appendix (138)

Part V: Of the Power of the Intellect, or of Human Freedom

Preface (143)

Axioms (145)

P1   *The affections of the body, that is, the images of things, are arranged and connected in the body in exactly the same way as thoughts and the ideas of things are arranged and connected in the mind.* (145)

P2   *If we remove an agitation of the mind, or emotion, from the thought of its external cause, and join it to other thoughts, then love or hatred toward the external cause, and also vacillations, that arise from these emotions will be destroyed.* (145)

P3   *A passive emotion ceases to be a passive emotion as soon as we form a clear and distinct idea of it.* (145)

P4   *There is no affection of the body of which we cannot form a clear and distinct conception.* (146)

P5   *An emotion toward a thing which we imagine merely in itself, and not as necessary, possible, or contingent, is the greatest of all emotions, other things being equal.* (146)

P6   *Insofar as the mind understands all things as governed by necessity, to that extent it has greater power over emotions, i.e., it is less passive in respect of them.* (147)

P7   *Emotions which arise or originate from reason are, if we take account of time, more powerful than those that are related to particular things which we regard as absent.* (147)

P8   *The greater the number of causes that simultaneously concur in arousing an emotion, the greater the emotion.* (148)

P9   *An emotion that is related to several different causes, which the mind regards together with the emotion itself, is less harmful, and we suffer less from it and are less affected toward each individual cause, than if we were affected by another equally great emotion which is related to only one or to a few causes.* (148)

P10   As long as we are not assailed by emotions that are contrary to our nature, we have the power to arrange and associate affections of the body according to the order of the intellect. (148)

P11   In proportion as a mental image is related to more things, the more frequently does it occur—i.e., the more often it springs to life—and the more it engages the mind. (150)

P12   Images are more readily associated with those images that are related to things which we clearly and distinctly understand than they are to others. (150)

P13   The greater the number of other images with which an image is associated, the more often it springs to life. (150)

P14   The mind can bring it about that all the affections of the body— i.e., images of things—be related to the idea of God. (150)

P15   He who clearly and distinctly understands himself and his emotions loves God, and the more so the more he understands himself and his emotions. (150)

P16   This love toward God is bound to hold chief place in the mind. (151)

P17   God is without passive emotions, and he is not affected with any emotion of pleasure or pain. (151)

P18   Nobody can hate God. (151)

P19   He who loves God cannot endeavor that God should love him in return. (151)

P20   This love toward God cannot be tainted with emotions of envy or jealousy, but is the more fostered as we think more men to be joined to God by this same bond of love. (151)

P21   The mind can exercise neither imagination nor memory save while the body endures. (153)

P22   Nevertheless, there is necessarily in God an idea which expresses the essence of this or that human body under a form of eternity [sub specie aeternitatis]. (153)

P23   The human mind cannot be absolutely destroyed along with body, but something of it remains, which is eternal. (153)

P24   The more we understand particular things, the more we understand God. (154)

P25   The highest conatus of the mind and its highest virtue is to understand things by the third kind of knowledge. (154)

P26   The more capable the mind is of understanding things by the third kind of knowledge, the more it desires to understand things by this same kind of knowledge. (154)

P27   From this third kind of knowledge there arises the highest possible contentment of mind. (154)

P28   The conatus, or desire, to know things by the third kind of knowledge cannot arise from the first kind of knowledge, but from the second. (155)

P29   *Whatever the mind understands under a form of eternity it does not understand from the fact that it conceives the present actual existence of the body, but from the fact that it conceives the essence of the body under a form of eternity.* (155)

P30   *Our mind, insofar as it knows both itself and the body under a form of eternity, necessarily has a knowledge of God, and knows that it is in God and is conceived through God.* (155)

P31   *The third kind of knowledge depends on the mind as its formal cause insofar as the mind is eternal.* (156)

P32   *We take pleasure in whatever we understand by the third kind of knowledge, and this is accompanied by the idea of God as cause.* (156)

P33   *The intellectual love of God which arises from the third kind of knowledge is eternal.* (156)

P34   *It is only while the body endures that the mind is subject to passive emotions.* (157)

P35   *God loves himself with an infinite intellectual love.* (157)

P36   *The mind's intellectual love toward God is the love of God wherewith God loves himself not insofar as he is infinite, but insofar as he can be explicated through the essence of the human mind considered under a form of eternity. That is, the mind's intellectual love toward God is part of the infinite love wherewith God loves himself.* (157)

P37   *There is nothing in Nature which is contrary to this intellectual love, or which can destroy it.* (158)

P38   *The greater the number of things the mind understands by the second and third kinds of knowledge, the less subject it is to emotions that are bad, and the less it fears death.* (158)

P39   *He whose body is capable of the greatest amount of activity has a mind whose greatest part is eternal.* (159)

P40   *The more perfection a thing has, the more active and the less passive it is. Conversely, the more active it is, the more perfect it is.* (160)

P41   *Even if we did not know that our mind is eternal, we should still regard as being of prime importance piety and religion and, to sum up completely, everything which in Part IV we showed to be related to courage and nobility.* (160)

P42   *Blessedness is not the reward of virtue, but virtue itself. We do not enjoy blessedness because we keep our lusts in check. On the contrary, it is because we enjoy blessedness that we are able to keep our lusts in check.* (161)

ETHICS: CITATIONS IN PROOFS

This appendix provides a list of all the propositions, corollaries, and scholia in the *Ethics*, together with all the definitions, axioms, propositions, corollaries, and scholia to which Spinoza refers in the proofs of propositions and corollaries and in the scholia. The significance of a given item and its meaning are determined, to a large degree, by the roles that the item plays in the *Ethics*. The following list should be helpful to those who want to consult, for a given item, all the places that Spinoza recalls and uses it in the work. The citations in the right-hand column agree in both order and number with their appearance in each proposition. That is, their order reflects the order in which Spinoza refers to them in the text. Spinoza sometimes refers to the same proposition multiple times in the text, and each reference is recorded. We hope that this list will be a valuable aid to the study of the *Ethics*.

Abbreviations are as follows: P=Proposition; A=Axiom; D=Definition; C=Corollary; S=Scholium; L=Lemma; Post=Postulate; Def Em=Definitions of Emotions (at the end of Part III); Gen Def Em=General Definition of Emotions (at the end of Part III). Items in the right-hand column should be read, for example, IIIP17C=Part III, Proposition 17, Corollary.

Part I: Concerning God

P1	ID3, ID5
P2	ID3
P3	IA5, IA4
P4	IA1, ID3, ID5, ID4
P5	IP4, IP1, ID3, IA6, IP4
P6	IP5, IP2, IP3
P6C	IA1, ID3, ID5, IP6
P7	IP6C, ID1
P8	IP5, IP7, ID2, IP7, IP5
P8S1	IP7
P8S2	IP7
P9	ID4
P10	ID4, ID3
P10S	ID6
P11	IA7, IP7
P11S	IP6
P12	IP8, IP7, IP5, IP6, IP2, ID4, IP10, IP7

A searchable version of this appendix is available from the title support page for this volume at www.hackettpublishing.com.

P13	IP5, IP12, IP11
P13C	
P13S	IP8
P14	ID6, IP11, IP5
P14C1	ID6, IP10S
P14C2	IA1
P15	IP14, ID3, ID5, IA1
P15S	IP6C, IP8S2, IP12, IP13C, IP12, IP8, IP5, IP12, IP14
P16	ID6
P16C1	
P16C2	
P16C3	
P17	IP16, P15
P17C1	
P17C2	IP11, IP14C1, IP17, ID7
P17S	IP16, IP16C1
P18	IP15, IP16C1, IP14, ID3
P19	ID6, IP11, IP7, ID8, ID4, IP7
P19S	IP11
P20	IP19, ID8, ID4
P20C1	
P20C2	IP20
P21	IP11, ID2, IP11, IP11, IP20C2
P22	
P23	ID5, IP15, ID8, ID6, IP19, IP21, IP22
P24	ID1
P24C	IP14C1
P25	IA4, IP15
P25S	IP16
P25C	IP15, ID5
P26	IP25, IP16
P27	IA3
P28	IP26, IP24C, IP21, IA1, ID3, ID5, IP25C, IP22
P28S	IP15, IP24C
P29	IP15, IP11, IP16, IP21, IP28, IP24C, IP26, IP26, IP27
P29S	IP14C1, IP17C2
P30	IA6, IP14C1, IP15, IP15
P31	ID5, IP15, ID6, IP29S
P31S	
P32	IP28, IP23, ID7
P32C1	
P32C2	IP29
P33	IP16, IP29, IP11, IP14C1
P33S1	
P33S2	ID7, IP17S

P34	IP11, IP16, IP16C
P35	IP34
P36	IP25C, IP34, IP16

Part II: Of the Nature and Origin of the Mind

P1	IP25C, ID5, ID6
P2	[same as IIP1]
P2S	IID4, ID6
P3	II P1, IP16, IP35, IP15
P3S	I32C1, I32C2, IP16, IP34, IP16
P4	IP30, IP14C1
P5	IIP3, IP25C, IP10, IA4
P6	IP10, IA4
P6C	
P7	IA4
P7C	
P7S	
P8	[P7 and P7S]
P8C	
P8S	
P9	IIP8C, IIP8S, IIP6, IP28, IIP7
P9C	IIP3, IIP9, IIP7
P10	IP7, IID2, IIA1
P10S	IP5
P10C	IIP10, IP15, IP25C
P10SC	
P11	IIP10C, IIA2, IIA3, IIP8C, IP21, IP22, A1
P11C	
P11S	
P12	IIP9C, IIP11, IIP11C
P12S	IIP7S
P13	IIP9C, IIP11C, IIA4, IIP11, IIIP36, IIP12, IIA5
P13C	
P13S	
P13SL1	IP5, IP8, IP15S
P13SL2	IID1
P13SL3	IID1, IIP13SL1, IP28, IIP6, IIP13SA1
P13SL3C	
P13SL4	IIP13SL1
P13SL5	
P13SL6	
P13SL7	IIP13SL4
P13SL7S	
P14	IIPost3, IIPost6, IIP12

P15	IIP13, IIPost1, IIP8C, IIP7
P16	IIP13SL3CA1, IA4
P16C1	
P16C2	
P17	IIP12, IIP16, IIP16C1
P17C	IIPost5, IIP13SL3CA2, IIP12, IIP17
P17S	IIP13C, IIP17C, IIP16C, ID7
P18	IIP17C
P18S	IIP16
P19	IIP13, IIP9, IIPost4, IIP7, IIP11C, IIP12, IIP16, IIP17
P20	IIP1, IIP3, IIP11, IIP9, IIP7
P21	IIP12, IIP13
P21S	IIP7S, IIP13
P22	IIP20, IIP12, IIP11C, IIP21
P23	IIP20, IIP19, IIP11C, IIP16, IIP13, IIP22
P24	IIP13SL3C, IIPost1, IIP13SL4, IIP13SL3CA1, IIP13SL3, IIP3, IIP9, IIP7, IIP13, IIP11C
P25	IIP16, IIP9, IIP7
P26	IIP7, IIP13, IIP16, IIP16C1
P26C	IIP17S, IIP26, IIP25
P27	IIP16, IIP25D
P28	IIP16, IIPost3, IIP24, IIP25
P28S	
P29	IIP27, IIP13, IA6
P29C	IIP23, IIP19, IIP26, IIP29, IIP27, IIP25, IIP28, IIP28S
P29S	
P30	IIA1, IP21, IP28, IIP9C, IIP11C
P31	IP28, IIP30
P31C	IIP31, IP33S1, IP29
P32	IIP7C, IA6
P33	IIP32, IP15
P34	IIP11C, IIP32
P35	IIP33
P35S	IIP17S
P36	IP15, IIP32, IIP7C, IIP24, IIP28, IIP6C
P37	IID2
P38	IIIP7C, IIP16, IIP25, IIP27, IIP12, IIP13, IIP11C
P38C	IIP13SL2, IIP38
P39	IIP7C, IIP16, IIP7C, IIP13, IIP11C
P39C	
P40	IIP11C
P40S1	IIP17S, IIP17C, IIP18
P40S2	IIP29C, IIP18S, IIP38C, IIP39, IIP39C, IIP40
P41	IIP35, IIP34
P42	IIP40S2

Part III: Concerning the Origin and Nature of the Emotions

P17	IIIP13S, IIIP16
P17S	IIP44S, IIPost1, IIP13SL3CA1
P18	IIP17, IIIP17C, IIP44S, IIP16C2
P18S1	IIP17, IIP44S
P18S2	
P19	IIIP12, IIIP13S, IIP17, IIIP11S, IIIP11S
P20	IIIP13, IIIP13S, IIIP11S
P21	IIIP19, IIIP11S, IIIP11S, IIIP11S, IIIP19
P22	IIIP21, IIIP13S
P22S	IIIP21
P23	IIIP11S, IIIP20, IIIP11S, IIIP13, IIIP11S
P23S	IIIP27
P24	[same as IIIP22]
P24S	
P25	IIIP21, IIIP12, IIP17, IIP17C, IIIP13
P26	IIIP23 [just as IIIP25 follows from IIIP21]
P26S	
P27	IIP17S, IIP16, IIIP23
P27S	IIIP22S
P27C1	IIIP27 [just as IIIP22 follows from IIIP21]
P27C2	IIIP23
P27C3	IIIP27, IIIP13, IIIP9S
P27C3S	IIIP22S
P28	IIIP12, IIP17, IIP7C, IIIP11C, IIIP9S, IIIP13S, IIIP20, IIIP13
P29	IIIP27, IIIP13S, IIIP28
P29S	
P30	IIIP27, IIP19, IIIP23
P30S	IIIP13S, IIP17C, IIIP25
P31	IIIP27, IIIP17S
P31C	IIIP28
P31S	IIIP29S
P32	IIIP27, IIIP27C1, IIIP28
P32S	
P33	IIIP12, IIIP29, IIIP13S
P34	IIIP33, IIIP13S, IIIP11, IIIP11S, IIIP30, IIIP30S
P35	IIIP34, IIIP30S, IIIP28, IIIP31, IIIP11S, IIIP13S, IIIP15C, IIIP23
P35S	IIIP24, IIIP15C
P36	IIIP15, IIIP28
P36C	IIIP36
P36CS	
P37	IIIP11S, IIIP7, IIIP5, IIIP9S, IIIP11S
P38	IIIP13S, IIIP28, IIIP21, IIIP37, IIIP33, IIIP13C, IIIP23, IIIP11S, IIIP13S
P39	IIIP13S, IIIP28, IIIP28, IIIP37
P39S	IIIP9S, IIIP28

P40	IIIP27, IIIP13S
P40S	
P40C1	IIIP40
P40C2	IIIP40, IIIP26, IIIP39
P40C2S	IIIP30, IIIP30S, IIIP25, IIIP39
P41	[same as IIIP40]
P41S	[same as IIIP40C2S]
P41C	[same as IIIP40C1]
P41CS	
P42	IIIP33, IIIP34, IIIP30S, IIIP12, IIIP19
P43	IIIP40, IIIP30, IIIP29, IIIP41, IIIP37, IIIP26
P44	[same as IIIP38]; IIIP13S, IIIP37
P44S	IIIP6
P45	IIIP40, IIIP13S, IIIP21, IIIP13S
P46	IIIP16
P47	IIIP27
P47S	IIP17C
P48	IIIP13S
P49	ID7, IIIP13S, IIIP48, ID7, IIIP48
P49S	IIIP27, IIIP34, IIIP40, IIIP43
P50	[same as IIIP15]; see also IIIP18S2
P50S	IIIP18S2, IIIP15C, IIIP28, IIIP25
P51	IIPost3, IIP13SL3CA1
P51S	IIIP39S, IIIP28, IIIP49
P52	IIP18, IIP18S
P52S	IIIP12, IIIP15, IIIP27C
P53	IIP19, IIP23, IIIP11S
P53C	IIIP29S, IIIP27
P54	IIIP7
P55	IIIP54, IIIP11S
P55C	[same as IIIP53C]
P55S	IIIP24S, IIIP32S, IIIP53, IIP40S1, IIIP28
P55SC	IIIP24S, IIIP13S, IIIP11S, IIIP9S, IIIP11S
P55SCS	IIIP52S
P56	IIIP11S, IIIP1, IIIP3, IIP40S, IIP17, IIP17S, P9S
P56S	
P57	IIP13SL3A1, IIIP9S, IIIP11, IIIP11S, IIIP9S
P57S	
P58	IIIP53, IIP43, IIP40S2, IIIP1, IIIP9, IIIP9S, IIIP1
P59	IIIP11, IIIP11S, IIIP1, IIIP58
P59S	

Part IV: Of Human Bondage, or the Strength of the Emotions

P1	IIP35, IIP33, IIP32, IIIP4
P1S	IIP16C2, IIP35S, IIP17

P2	IIID2, IIID1
P3	IVA1
P4	IP24C, IIIP7, IP34, IIIP4, IIIP6, IVP3, IP16, IP21
P4C	
P5	IIID1, IIID2, IIIP7, IIP16
P6	IVP5, IVP3
P7	IVP5, IIP6, IIIP5, IVA1, IIP12
P7C	IVP7
P8	IVD1, IVD2, IIIP7, IIIP11S, IIP22, IIP21, IIP21S
P9	IIP17S, IIP16C2, IIP17
P9S	IIIP18
P9SC	
P10	IVP9
P10S	IVD6
P11	IP33S1, P9
P12	IVD3, IVD4, IIIP18
P12C	IVP9C, IVP10, IVP12
P13	IVD3, IIP18, IIP18S, IIP17C, IVP9
P14	IVP1, IVP8, IVP7
P15	IVP8, Def Em I, IIIP37, IIIP3, IIID2, IIIP7, IVP5, IVP3, IVP7
P16	IVP9C, IVP15
P17	[same as IVP16, from IVP12C]
P17S	
P18	Def Em I, IIIP7, IIIP11S
P18S	IIIP4, IVD8, IIIP7
P19	IVP8, IIIP28, IIIP9S, Def Em I
P20	IVD8, IIIP7, IIIP4, IIIP6
P20S	IIIP10
P21	Def Em I, IIIP7
P22	IIIP7, IVD8
P22C	IVP22, IVP21
P23	IIIP1, IIID1, IIID2, D8, IIIP1, IIID2, D8
P24	IVD8, IIIP3, IVP22C
P25	IIIP7, IIIP6, IVP22C
P26	IIIP7, IIIP6, IIIP9S, IIP40S2, IIP40, IVP22C, IVP25, IVD1
P27	IVP26, IIP41, IIP43, IIP43S, IIP40S
P28	ID6, IP15, IVP26, IVP27, IVD1, IIIP1, IIIP3, IVP23
P29	IIP10C, IP28, IIP6, IVP8, IIIP11S
P30	IVP8, IIIP11S, IIIP4, IIIP5
P31	IVP30, IVA3, IIIP6
P31C	IVP29, IVP31
P32	IIIP7, IIIP3S
P32S	
P33	IIID1, IIID2, IIIP7, IIIP56, IIIP51

P34	IIIP16, IIIP32, IIIP32S, IIIP55S, Def Em VII, IIIP40, IIIP40S, IIIP39, P30, IIIP59
P34S	IVP30, IVP31, IIIP31, Def Em 6
P35	IVP33, P34, IIIP3, IIID2, IVP19, IIP41, IVP31C
P35C1	IVP31C, IIID2, IVP35
P35C2	IVP20, IVD8, IIIP3, IVP35, IVP35C1
P35C2S	
P36	IVP24, IVP26, IVP28, IIP47, IIP47S
P36S	IVP34, IVP35, IIP47
P37	IVP35C1, IVP19, IVP24, IVP26, Def Em I, IIP11, IIP47, IP15, IIIP31, IIIP31C, IVP36, IIIP37
P37S1	IVP18S, IIIP57S
P37S2	IIIP29S, IVP19, IVP20, IIIP40C2, IIIP28, IVP35C1, IVP4C1, IVP6, IVP33, IVP34, IVP35S, IVP4C, IVP33, IVP7, IIIP39, IVP17S
P38	IIP14, IVP26, IVP27, IIP14, IVP26, IVP27
P39	IIPost4, IIPost3, IIPost6, IVP38
P39S	
P40	IVP35, IVP26, IVP27
P41	IIIP11, IIIP11S, IVP38
P42	IIIP11S, IIIP11, IVP39, IIIP11S, IVP38
P43	IIIP11S, IVP6, IVP38, IVP41, IVP5, IVP3
P44	Def Em VI, IIIP11S, IVP43, IIIP37, IVP6, IVP43
P44S	
P45	IIIP39, IVP37
P45S	
P45C1	IVP37, IIIP39
P45C2	IIIP39, IVP37S
P45C1S	IVP41
P46	IVP45C1, IVP19, IVP37, IIIP43, IIIP44, IIIP59S
P46S	
P47	Def Em XIII, IVP41, IVP43
P47S	
P48	Def Em XXI, Def Em XXII, IVP26, IVP27
P49	IIIP41S, Def Em XXX, IIIP25, Def Em XXVIII
P50	Def Em XVIII, IVP41, IIIP27C3, IVP37, IVP27
P50C	
P50S	IIIP27
P51	Def Em XIX, IIIP59, IIIP3, IVP37, IIIP11S, Def Em XIX
P51S	Def Em 20, IVP45
P52	Def Em XXV, IIIP3, IIP40, IIP43, IIID2, IIIP3
P52S	IVP25, IIIP53C, IIIP55C
P53	Def Em XXVI, IIIP7, IIIP55, IVP26
P54	[same as IVP53] and Def Em XXVII
P54S	

P55	Def Em XXVIII, Def Em XXIX
P56	IVP22C, IVP24, IVP24, IIP43, IVD8, IVP55
P56C	
P56S	
P57	Def Em XXVIII, Def Em VI, IIIP13S
P57S	IIIP55S, IIIP41S
P58	Def Em XXX, IVP37S1
P58S	IVP52S, IVP44S
P59	IIIP3, IIID2, P41, P41, P43, Def Em I, P45C1, IVP19
P59S	
P60	IVP6, IIIP6, IIIP7, IIIP12
P60S	IVP44S, IVP9C
P61	Def Em I, IIIP3, IIID2
P62	IIP44C2, IIP43, IIP43S, IIP41, IID4
P62S	IIP31, IIP44S, IVP16
P63	IIIP3, IIIP59, Def Em XIII
P63S	
P63C	IIIP59, IVP61, IVP8
P63CS	
P64	IVP8, Def Em III, IIIP6, IIIP7, IIID2, IIIP3, IIP29
P64C	
P65	IVP63C
P65C	IVP63C
P66	IVP62, IVP65
P66C	IVP66C to IVP66 as IVP65C to IVP65
P66S	IVP1 to IVP18
P67	IVP63, IVP63C, IVP24
P68	IVP64C
P68S	IVP4, IIIP27, IVP37
P69	IVP7, IVP3, IVP5, IIIP59S, Def Em XL, Def Em XLI
P69C	
P69S	IIIP59S
P70	IIIP39, IIIP42, IVP37
P70S	
P71	IVP35, IVP35C1, IVP37, Def Em XXXIV
P71S	
P72	IVP24, IVP31C
P72S	
P73	IVP63, IVP66S, IVP37, IVP37S2
P73S	IIIP59, IVP37, IVP46, IVP50S

Part V: Of the Power of the Intellect, or of Human Freedom

P1	IIP7, IIPC2, IIP7, IIP18, IIIP2
P2	Def Em VI, Def Em VII

P3	Gen Def Em, IIP21, IIP21S, IIIP3
P3C	
P4	IIP38, IIP12, IIP13L2
P4C	Gen Def Em, VP4
P4S	IP36, IIP40, VP2, IVP61, IIIP31C, IVP37S1, IVP59, IIIP3
P5	IIIP49, IVP11, IIP35S
P6	IP29, IP28, VP5, IIIP48
P6S	
P7	IIP17, IVP6, IVP9, IIP40S2, IIP38, VA1
P8	IIIP7, IVP5
P8S	VA2
P9	IVP26, IVP27, IIIP7, IIP11, IIIP48
P10	IVP30, IVP27, IVP26, IIP40S2, IIP47S, VP1
P10S	VP7, IVP46, IVP46S, IIP18, IVP52, VP6, VP7, VP8, IVP63C, IIIP59
P11	VP8
P12	IIP40S2, VP11, IIP18
P13	IIP18
P14	VP4, IP15
P15	IIIP53, VP14, Def Em VI
P16	VP14, VP15, VP11
P17	IIP32, IID4, Gen Def Em, IP20C2, Def Em II, Def Em III
P17C	VP17, Def Em VI, Def Em VII
P18	IIP46, IIP47, IIIP3, IIIP59, Def Em VII
P18C	
P18S	VP3, IIIP59
P19	VP17C, IIIP19, IIIP28
P20	IVP28, IVP36, IVP37, Def Em XXIII, VP18, IIIP35S, IIIP31
P20S	VP4S, VP2 with VP4S, VP7, VP9, VP11, VP10S, VP12, VP13, VP14, IVP5, IIP47S, VP3, VP4S, VP14, VP15, IIP45, VP15, VP16, IIIP1, IIIP3
P21	IIP8C, IIP26, IIIP17S, IIIP18S
P22	IP25, IA4, IP16, IIP3
P23	VP22, IIP13, IIP8C, VP22
P23S	
P24	IP25C
P25	IIP40S2, VP24, IVP28, IVD8, IIIP7
P26	Def Em I
P27	IVP28, P25, P24, Def Em II, IIP43, Def Em XXV
P28	IIP40S2, IIP40S2, IIP40S2, Def Em I
P29	VP21, IIP26, ID8, IIP44C2, VP23, IIP13
P29S	IIP45, IIP45S
P30	ID8
P31	VP29, VP21, VP23, VP30, IIP46, IIP40, IIP40S2, IIID1
P31S	

P32	VP27, Def Em XXV, VP30
P32C	VP32, Def Em VI, VP29
P33	VP31, IA3
P33S	VP32C
P34	IIP17S, IIP16C2, Gen Def Em, VP21
P34C	
P34S	
P35	ID6, IID6, IIP3, IP11, ID1, VP32C
P36	VP32C, IIP3, VP32, VP32C, IP25C, IIP11C, VP25
P36C	
P36S	Def Em 25, Def Em 30, VP35, VP27, IP15, IIP47S
P37	VP33, VP29
P37S	IVA
P38	IIP11, VP23, VP29, VP37, IVP30
P38S	IVP38S, VP27, VP21
P39	IVP38, IVP30, VP10, VP14, VP15, VP16, VP33
P39S	
P40	IID6, IIIP3, IIIP3S
P40C	VP23, VP29, IIIP3, VP21, IIIP3, Gen Def Em, VP40
P40S	IP21
P41	IVP22C, IVP24
P41S	
P42	VP36, VP36S, VP32C, IIIP59, IIIP3, IVD8, VP32, VP3C

SELECTED BIBLIOGRAPHY

Allison, Henry E. *Benedict de Spinoza: An Introduction*. New Haven, CT: Yale University Press, 1987.

Bennett, Jonathan. *A Study of Spinoza's Ethics*. Cambridge, MA: Hackett, 1984.

Cover, J. A., and Mark Kulstad (eds.). *Central Themes in Early Modern Philosophy*. Cambridge, MA: Hackett, 1990.

Curley, Edwin. *Behind the Geometrical Method*. Princeton, NJ: Princeton University Press, 1988.

Curley, Edwin. *Spinoza's Metaphysics: An Essay in Interpretation*. Cambridge, MA: Harvard University Press, 1969.

Curley, Edwin M., and Moreau, P.-F. (eds.). *Spinoza: Issues and Directions*. Leiden: Brill, 1990.

Delahunty, R. J. *Spinoza*. London: Routledge and Kegan Paul, 1985.

Della Rocca, Michael. *Representation and the Mind-Body Problem in Spinoza*. New York: Oxford University Press, 1996.

Donagan, Alan. *Spinoza*. Chicago: University of Chicago Press, 1988.

Freeman, Eugene, and Maurice Mandelbaum (eds.). *Spinoza: Essays in Interpretation*. LaSalle, IL: Open Court, 1975.

Garrett, Don. *The Cambridge Companion to Spinoza*. Cambridge: Cambridge University Press, 1996.

Grene, Marjorie (ed.). *Spinoza: A Collection of Critical Essays*. Garden City, NY: Doubleday Anchor, 1973.

Hampshire, Stuart. *Spinoza and Spinozism*. Oxford: Oxford University Press, 2005.

Hampshire, Stuart. *Spinoza*. Harmondsworth, Middlesex, England: Penguin, 1951.

Israel, Jonathan. *Radical Enlightenment*. Oxford: Oxford University Press, 2001.

Kashap, S. Paul. *Spinoza and Moral Freedom*. Albany: State University of New York Press, 1987.

Kashap, S. Paul (ed.). *Studies in Spinoza: Critical and Interpretive Essays*. Berkeley: University of California Press, 1972.

Kennington, Richard (ed.). *The Philosophy of Baruch Spinoza*. Washington, DC: Catholic University of America, 1980.

Lloyd, Genevieve. *Spinoza and the Ethics*. London: Routledge, 1996.

Lloyd, Genevieve. *Part of Nature: Self-Knowledge in Spinoza's Ethics*. Ithaca, NY: Cornell University Press, 1994.

Mason, Richard. *The God of Spinoza: A Philosophical Study*. Cambridge: Cambridge University Press, 1997.

Nadler, Steven M. *Spinoza's Heresy: Immortality and the Jewish Mind*. Oxford: Oxford University Press, 2001.

Parkinson, G.H.R. *Spinoza's Theory of Knowledge*. Oxford: Clarendon Press, 1954.

Shahan, Robert W., and John Biro (eds.). *Spinoza: New Perspectives*. Norman: University of Oklahoma Press, 1978.

Smith, Steven B. *Spinoza's Book of Life: Freedom and Redemption in the* Ethics. New Haven, CT: Yale University Press, 2003.

Strauss, Leo. *Spinoza's Critique of Religion.* New York: Schocken, 1965.

Wolfson, Harry Austryn. *The Philosophy of Spinoza.* 2 vols. Cambridge, MA: Harvard University Press, 1934.

Woolhouse, R. S. *Descartes, Spinoza, Leibniz: The Concept of Substance in Seventeenth-Century Metaphysics.* New York: Routledge, 1993.

Yovel, Y. (ed.). *Spinoza on Knowledge and the Human Mind.* Leiden: Brill, 1994.

Yovel, Y. (ed.). *God and Nature: Spinoza's Metaphysics.* Leiden: Brill, 1991.